PEARSON CUSTOM
Education

Teaching Math and Writing for Students
with Mild/Moderate Disabilities

PEARSON

Please visit our website at *www.pearsonlearningsolutions.com.*

Attention bookstores: For permission to return any unsold stock, contact us at *pe-uscustomreturns@pearson.com.*

Pearson Learning Solutions, 501 Boylston Street, Suite 900, Boston, MA 02116
A Pearson Education Company
www.pearsoned.com

Printed in the United States of America.
30 16

ISBN 10: 1-256-20084-0
ISBN 13: 978-1-256-20084-0

Table of Contents

Chapter 1

Introduction

After reading this chapter, you will be able to:

1. Discuss the setting demands found in most public school classrooms and suggest implications for students with exceptional needs

2. Discuss the instructional demands found in most public school classrooms and suggest implications for students with exceptional needs

3. Elaborate on the reasoning for using the teaching strategies and methods suggested in this book

4. Identify the primary legislation that determines service delivery to children and youth with identified disabilities and other learning needs

5. Explain how each of the four major legislative acts (IDEIA-04, Section 504, ADA, and NCLB) contributes to meeting the needs of a majority of students with disabilities and exceptional needs

6. Discuss the educational implications of the legislative acts protecting students who are English speakers of other languages, highly mobile, or homeless

7. Explain how students with disabilities can benefit from opportunities offered in the legislation for occupational and career programs

Children in the United States are required to attend school until they reach a state-mandated minimum age, usually 16 years of age. Federal and state laws, legislative acts of Congress, and Supreme Court decisions mandate that all students receive instruction that provides equal opportunity to learn and subsequently meet state curriculum standards and pass standardized assessments to demonstrate that learning. The emphasis on all students, including students with disabilities and other special needs, meeting state curriculum standards by attending general education classes has increased in recent years; however, at the same time, support services and instructional programs offered outside the general classroom have decreased. As a result of this increased emphasis on inclusion, all teachers must be prepared to work with a variety of students with unique individual needs.

In the past, educators could generally expect that most students in their classrooms would look, learn, and behave pretty much as they themselves did. In today's classrooms, though, growing diversity in terms of students' daily lives, belief systems, and values often presents a totally different picture (McEwan, 2000). Further, teachers should expect to find students achieving on three to five different grade levels in most classrooms. This means that even without students who have stated disabilities, teachers cannot use a one-size-fits-all curriculum to meet the unique needs of every child.

WHO ARE THE STUDENTS WE SERVE?

In Chapter 2, we will describe in detail the characteristics of students who have specific disabilities that meet guidelines for special education services as well as other exceptionalities, such as students who are culturally and linguistically diverse, at risk for school failure, and gifted and talented. Most likely, some students in your classroom may fit into more than one of the categories, such as a student who has a specific learning disability in addition to being gifted or talented or culturally and linguistically diverse. The typical public school classroom, whether a general or special education setting, will have students who:

1. Are racially diverse: In 2006, 55.9 percent of students were Caucasian, 16.9 percent were Black, 20.5 percent were Hispanic, 4.5 percent were Asian/Pacific Islander, and 1.2 percent were American Indian/Alaska Native (School Data Direct, 2008).

2. Live in poverty: 40.9 percent of the nation's K–12 students received free or reduced-price lunch in 2006 (Center for Public Education, 2007).

3. Speak a language other than Standard English: Students who are ELL constituted 8.5 percent of the nation's K–12 students in 2006 (U.S. Census Bureau, 2008).

4. Live in diverse family groups: In 2003, 68 percent of elementary and high school students lived in two-parent families, 23 percent lived with a mother only, and 5 percent lived with a father only (U.S. Census Bureau, 2008).

5. Have a disability: In 2006, 13 percent of all students had a diagnosed disability (School Data Direct, 2008).

6. Will be gifted: While no specific data is collected on the number of gifted students in public schools, the National Association for Gifted Children estimates that approximately 6 percent of students are gifted (National Association for Gifted Children, 2008).

7. May have difficulty with basic reading skills: While national reading scores have risen when assessed at both the fourth and eighth grades, students who are eligible for free or reduced-price lunch continue to score lower than their peers who are not eligible for subsidized lunch (National Center for Education Statistics, 2007b). Further, the gaps in reading achievement between Caucasian–Black and Caucasian–Hispanic students have not significantly decreased since 1992 (National Center for Education Statistics, 2007b).

8. May have difficulty with basic mathematics skills: As with reading, national mathematic scores have risen as assessed in both fourth and eighth grades. Further, students who are eligible for free or reduced-price lunch continue to score lower than their peers who are not eligible for subsidized lunch (National Center for Education Statistics, 2007a). Further, the gaps in mathematic achievement between Caucasian–Black and Caucasian–Hispanic students have not significantly decreased since 1992 (National Center for Education Statistics, 2007a).

9. Will be students with other exceptional needs: At any point in time you may have students who have special needs due to a change in family conditions—for example, temporary illness, divorce, death of a family member, or homelessness may cause a change in a student's academic performance or behavior.

These conditions will affect how students feel about themselves and their abilities to achieve in academic tasks.

Take a moment to recall the class you liked best as a student and where you felt most competent; then recall the class you remember as a struggle because you felt incompetent or unable to meet expectations. Chances are three factors affected your perceptions in both classes: the setting (environment) and instructional (curriculum and teaching methods used) demands of the classroom, as well as knowledge of your own strengths and weaknesses as a student. In the next section, we will examine the setting and instructional demands found in most public school classrooms.

SETTING DEMANDS

While we all have been students, we may not have recognized or been aware of the setting demands we were required to meet. As teachers, however, we must be keenly aware of these demands and how they will affect the students we teach. If we take the time to examine what happens in most elementary classrooms, for example, we will see a very busy place, and to the untrained eye the classroom might even look chaotic. Weinstein and Mignano (2003) offered the following vivid description of the complex environment found in the elementary classroom. Teachers and students are placed in *contradictory* roles. Students are asked to be cooperative by sharing and working harmoniously with peers, but within minutes they may be placed in a competitive situation of working against peers for special privileges or prizes from the treasure chest. Teachers ask students not to talk during seatwork or independent practice but often arrange desks so that students are seated directly next to or across from one another to be ready for times when they want students to work in groups.

Students and teachers work together in a *multidimensional* situation as well, where a broad range of events take place (Weinstein & Mignano, 2003). Teachers would like to be viewed as helping and caring by giving each student individual attention, but they also are called upon to maintain a schedule of teaching tasks, evaluate student performance, and manage student behavior, such as attending to students' collective and individual educational needs in addition to taking attendance, completing required paperwork, collecting money for field trips or lunch, settling disagreements among students, offering counsel to students with problems, and communicating with parents.

Further, these various activities may be taking place *simultaneously* (Weinstein & Mignano, 2003). That is, at any given moment, some students may be participating in reading groups with the teacher, while others are working at computers, in cooperative learning groups, or alone at their desks. The teacher must attend simultaneously to the reading group and all the other activities taking place around the room. At the same time, the teacher must be ready to respond *immediately* (Weinstein & Mignano, 2003) to any problems that arise in the other groups, inappropriate behavior of students at the computers, or straying attention of students in any of the activities. Despite the teacher's careful planning on any given day, the *unpredictable* may happen—student disputes, visits from the principal or other school officials, fire drills, sudden storms that send students back from recess early, or even serious events that send students home early.

As teachers and students work within these classrooms, both groups exist in the public eye and suffer from a *lack of privacy* (Weinstein & Mignano, 2003), since all behavior can be observed by others around them. Students spend the entire day watching the teacher's movements, body language, and reactions to students' responses and behaviors. As a result, teachers must try to keep their feelings private by avoiding movements or facial expressions that might betray their inner feelings or be misinterpreted by students. Students also lack privacy. Even if the teacher misses off-task behaviors or decides to let a mistaken answer go by, there is always a peer who notices. Students cannot hide even the smallest event; it is very difficult to have a private conversation with the teacher, ask for additional assistance, avoid sharing a poor grade on an assignment, or conceal a mistake.

Finally, every class builds a collective *history* (Weinstein & Mignano, 2003) of past events. This history lives in the memory of each student and the history of who has been disciplined, won the most prizes, had a fight, earned both good and poor grades, or whose parent has been called. This history may follow students from grade to grade and sometimes on to middle and high school. This gives the teacher yet another task of helping to build a positive history for this group of students.

Secondary classrooms share the same characteristics of being contradictory, multidimensional, unpredictable, simultaneous, public, immediate, and remembered (Weinstein, 2003), but there are some differences (Bender, 2004). For example, by the time students reach secondary school, they are expected to be independent and responsible but are also expected to follow, without question, the teacher's rules and directions. Due to differences in the organization of the day, students must remember when and where classes meet, and during short passing periods breaks students must remember which books and materials to retrieve from their lockers for the next class or even several classes (Bender, 2004). Other differences include the time constraints of semesters rather than a year, time limitations of individual class periods, and larger numbers of students (often 90+ compared to the 25 or fewer for early childhood and elementary classes) across a number of classes. These differences found in secondary schools can make it more difficult for teachers to know their students well. Problems experienced by beginning teachers may be attributed to their lack of understanding of the complexity in their classrooms (Weinstein & Mignano, 2003). In addition, students with exceptional learning needs (ELN) and other diverse characteristics may experience difficulty with setting demands without support and specific instructions regarding how to meet teacher, school, and peer expectations for behavior.

It is important to remember that these setting demands construct the environment where teaching and learning must take place and may be overlooked. Therefore, understanding that (a) teacher and student roles are contradictory, (b) many classroom tasks are multidimensional, (c) numerous events are unpredictable, (d) happen simultaneously in a (e) public space (f) requiring the teacher's immediate attention, and (g) are part of a collective history is essential for managing and teaching in today's diverse and complex classroom. Finally, it is important to note that delivering and receiving instruction within classrooms such as those described above imposes another set of demands, described in the following section.

INSTRUCTIONAL DEMANDS

At the elementary level, teachers generally structure their lessons around small-group, whole-class, and individual-instructional activities using a variety of methods, which include lectures, demonstrations, class discussions, role-plays, and field trips (Bender, 2004). Student placement in groups varies depending on the activity to be completed, so students may work in several types of groups each day. For example, reading groups will most likely be homogenous, containing students with similar skill levels, whereas a group assigned to complete a social studies project may contain students with varying skill levels. Teachers use a variety of instructional materials, such as commercial children's literature, grade-level texts for academic content with accompanying workbooks, and teacher-made and technology-based materials.

In contrast, secondary-level teachers use a narrower range of instructional methods, generally lecturing to the whole class using a textbook as the basis for class discussions and assignments. While teachers may be willing to offer assistance to students who are having difficulty, generally students are required to seek out the teacher and independently request help (Bender, 2004). Specific content areas, such as occupational skills courses or the performing arts, offer more hands-on activities and may provide for more individual student–teacher interaction during class time. However, secondary teachers are mindful of the need to teach the content so that students can meet graduation requirements and pass standardized content exams such as the national Advanced Placement and state mandated End-of-Course (EOC) and exit exams. They feel pressured to keep up the pace of instruction to cover content within the allotted time of a semester or year. Teachers expect students to have independent study skills and the prerequisite content knowledge required to attain new skills and knowledge. In addition, they expect students to organize course materials, listen to lectures and demonstrations, take notes, participate in class activities and discussions, complete assignments, and study independently for exams (Mastropieri & Scruggs, 2001).

As students progress through elementary and middle school they must master the academic skills and strategies required to achieve success in rigorous content-area classes and meet those realities noted in Table 1.1. Deshler and Schumaker note that a performance gap exists for most secondary students with high incidence disabilities and that as this gap increases over time students become disengaged and discouraged as the student realizes she can not meet the requirements for graduation (Deshler & Schumaker, 2006) which can lead to unsatisfactory ends such as dropping out. To change this trend, teachers at all levels must use research-based interventions and teaching materials to prepare students to meet the ultimate demands of secondary education and adult life after school.

In this book we will discuss models of instruction designed to increase access to the curriculum using research-based methods known to be effective for students with diverse and exceptional needs by supporting the academic achievement of all learners.

MODELS OF INSTRUCTION

In this section we will highlight five instructional methods that have been shown to be effective in inclusive classrooms and should be the foundation for meeting the needs of students in a diverse classroom. These are teaching metacognitive and cognitive skills, using Universal Design for Learning (UDL) in planning lessons, providing authentic Project-Based Learning (PBL) experiences, integrating technology into teaching and learning, and using collaboration and co-teaching when planning and delivering instruction.

Metacognitive and Cognitive Skills and Knowledge

Schools, districts, and state education agencies that are working to implement the requirements of No Child Left Behind (NCLB) as well as state accountability systems are seeking ways to help and support students who struggle to learn the standard curriculum given the setting and instructional demands found in most classrooms. Metacognitive and cognitive strategy instruction offers an effective method for helping students become self-directed learners.

The Metacognitive Framework for Learning presented in Chapter 6 provides teachers and students a common language and framework from which to both access and deliver academic content and social skills instruction. The instructional methods and cognitive theory upon which this model is based promote the acquisition, maintenance, and generalization of both content knowledge and metacognitive and cognitive strategy knowledge and skills (Borkowski, 1992; Flavell, Miller, & Miller, 2002; Hartman & Sternberg, 1993; Spencer & Logan, 2005). Last, empirical evidence suggests that metacognitive knowledge instruction can not only increase student achievement as required by NCLB standards, but it can foster the development of traits described as desirable by teachers, business leaders, and educational administrators (Anderman, 2004; Bouffard, & Couture, 2003; Harlen & Crick, 2003; Ngeow & Kong, 2001; Nichols, Jones, & Hancock, 2003; Palmer & Wehmeyer, 2003). The metacognitive model presented in this book is designed to help P–12 students develop and apply metacognitive knowledge. Teachers need to provide students with explicit instruction in metacognitive and cognitive knowledge and strategies because students with exceptional learning needs (ELN) often lack this type of knowledge. This metacognitive model provides P–12 students and their teachers with an effective way of learning content material.

TABLE 1.1 Realities of Secondary Schools

Realities	Description
1. Pressure to cover large amounts of content	• Because secondary teachers see themselves as "content experts" whose role is to disseminate information to meet standards and assessment and to prepare students for postsecondary settings, they believe that lecture is the most efficient way to accomplish their goals. • An information explosion in content areas causes stress and a sense of urgency in teachers to cover more in less time.
2. Complexity of content-area textbooks	• Texts are written under the assumption that students know how to access information from the written word. • Many texts are written beyond the grade level where they are used, are poorly organized, and not user-friendly. • Texts are often characterized as "encyclopedic" and lacking depth. • Texts are densely packed with facts, names, and details that may obscure meaning.
3. Significant academic diversity	• Classrooms have become more diverse in recent years, but content teachers do not believe it is their responsibility to teach students how to learn the content. • Teachers lack time and knowledge to consider student differences when planning.
4. Limited opportunities for academic interactions	• Teachers see students for limited periods of time and primarily only in classroom setting. • It is difficult for teachers to become familiar with individual students' strengths and needs. • Within the context of the secondary class period there is less time available for monitoring learning and adjusting lesson plans.
5. Instruction geared to achieving students	• The focus of content classes is generally on the achieving students, thus the lower-level students are often left behind and feel disconnected.
6. Limited time for planning and teaching	• The demands of grading, conferences, and other teacher duties mean that teachers must plan on their own time.
7. Limited opportunities for collegial study, planning, or teaching	• Teachers have little common time that would allow opportunities for collaboration, conversation about teaching, or sharing of resources. • Teachers may not have sufficient support or problem-solving sessions for implementation of new methods presented at in-service workshops.

Sources: Bender (2004); Deshler, Ellis, & Lenz (1996); Thousand, Rosenberg, Bishop, & Villa (1997).

Universal Design for Learning (UDL)

When teachers adopt UDL they make fundamental shifts in their thinking, planning, and teaching in four ways. First, they understand that students with ELN fall along a continuum of learner differences just as all students do. Second, they understand that teachers should be adjusting for learner differences among all students, not just those with exceptional needs. Third, they understand that instructional materials used to teach any curriculum should be varied and diverse rather than centering on a single textbook. Finally, they understand that instead of remediating students or asking them to change, the curriculum should be made flexible to accommodate learner differences found in all students.

The goal of UDL and the teachers who use it is to provide alternatives to make the curriculum accessible and appropriate for individuals with different backgrounds, abilities, and disabilities, but these teachers also understand that *universal* in *Universal Design* does not mean that there is one solution for everyone. Rather, teachers who use UDL know the unique nature of each learner and the need to accommodate differences, create learning experiences that suit the learner, and maximize his or her ability to progress (Rose & Meyer, 2002).

All educators must know how to enhance curriculum features that are not already in place to meet the needs of any student in their classroom, whether an exceptionality is present or not. When teachers do not use general education curriculum materials and standards because the curriculum as it is presented in texts and commercial teaching materials does not match some students' exceptional needs, they may be doing students a disservice by alternating or changing curricula so that it is not sufficiently challenging and thereby inadvertently undermining a student's ability to successfully meet general education standards (Ellis, 1997; King-Sears, 2001; Pugach & Warger, 2001; Thousand, Rosenberg, Bishop, & Villa, 1997).

UDL presents the opportunity for curriculum-centered dialogue between general and special educators that allows them to discuss the appropriateness and quality of the curriculum for all students. Curriculum-centered dialogues have the potential both to increase the degree to which teaching methods and instructional materials meet the needs of students from various racial, ethnic, cultural, linguistic, and socioeconomic backgrounds and to support students with exceptional needs (Pugach & Warger, 2001). Technology and digital materials offer one path to an accessible curriculum (Rose & Meyer, 2002). UDL teaching methods incorporate any technology that will support student learning based on the belief that all students can benefit from technology that is integrated into classroom activities.

Integrating Technology to Provide Access to the Curriculum

When writing about using technology to provide equal access to learning experiences for all students, French (2002) stated that "providing equal access to educational opportunities is simply the right thing to do" (p. 1). The presence of technology in public school classrooms is seen as the equalizer of the 21st century (Flippo, Inge, & Barcus, 1995; cited in Cavanaugh, 2002). Parsad and Jones (2005) noted that by the fall of 2003 nearly 100% of the schools in the United States had access to the Internet, and 93% of classrooms were connected to the Internet. Through the use of technology already present in many U.S. public classrooms, students with ELN can decrease their isolation and increase their success in the general classroom (Cavanaugh, 2002).

No doubt a large number of the readers of this text belong to a group of students known as the Millennial Generation (Millennials)—persons born after 1982 and have grown up so exposed to and comfortable with technologies of all types that it is seemingly transparent to them (Peterson-Karlan & Parette, 2005). As a result, students with disabilities who also are Millennials may expect to use technology as part of their educational experience. Unfortunately, Millennial students report being dissatisfied with the level of comfort with technology demonstrated by their teachers versus their own preferences to use technology (Peterson-Karlan & Parette, 2005). Furthermore, data collected for the U.S. Department of Education (Parsad & Jones, 2005) note growing discrepancies in student preferences for and skills in technology use and what schools are providing. This is an issue teachers must address if they want to provide equal access for all students in their classrooms. Therefore, being familiar with and being able to integrate technologies, including assistive technology, into their planning and delivery of accessible learning experiences for all is vital.

Project-Based Learning

With this teaching method, learning is made relevant and useful to students by establishing connections to life outside the classroom, addressing real-world concerns, and developing skills needed in adult living situations. Learning of content takes place in authentic moments of the process, rather than in isolation. PBL focuses on student investigations, either in groups or individually, guided by state curriculum standards and teacher expertise. When students participate in PBL they become active learners, rather than passive learners of the teacher's understanding of a topic. When PBL is used, students are engaged in learning activities that are long term, interdisciplinary, student centered, and integrated with real-world issues. Teachers are engaged as the coach, facilitator, and co-learner. Students' projects can be shared with an authentic audience who has a mutual interest in the information presented, such as peers, teachers, parents, mentors, and the community at large. The powerful instructional principles of differentiating and scaffolding instruction and facilitating socially constructed knowledge (Ellis, 2000) will be discussed in Chapter 9.

Collaborative Teaching

Tutoring, basic skills instruction, and homework completion are often the primary activities occurring in special education resource rooms and inclusion classes, particularly at the secondary level. Despite its widespread use, the use of tutoring interventions in inclusive secondary classes has shown mixed results. Co-teaching, on the other hand, has been associated with positive outcomes for students with disabilities (Mastropieri & Scruggs, 2001). In addition, data reveal a high level of teacher satisfaction with this collaborative effort (Mastropieri & Scruggs, 2001).

Henley, Ramsey, and Algozzine (2002) noted that general education teachers often refer students with unique needs to be evaluated for a disability in hopes that special education services will help students meet general education requirements. However, the very act of referral can have a negative effect on students and their families, who may feel they are being rejected, as well as on the relationship between the general and special educators. For example, when the student is not eligible for special education services, the general education teacher can feel helpless and without support for the problems a difficult student might present. If a true co-teaching relationship exists, however, the special educator can support all students within a classroom who need help and provide the general educator with the support needed to implement strategies and teaching methods that will improve academic achievement. We advocate the use of collaboration and co-teaching as effective practices that support implementation of cognitive and metacognitive strategy use, development of problem-solving skills, and curriculum design and modification using UDL and assistive technology.

LAWS AND REGULATIONS THAT MANDATE PROGRAMS AND SERVICES FOR STUDENTS WITH DIVERSE NEEDS

This section provides a review for readers who have prior knowledge while offering an overview to readers who have little or no prior knowledge of the laws and legislative acts that inform teaching of students with ELN in the United States, including students who are not served by special education programs. Specifically, we will cover legislation that provides protections, educational services, accommodations, and specific programs for children and youth who are in special education programs. Several legislative acts and laws are also described that offer protection to students who have exceptional needs but who are not eligible for special education services, including students with needs due to cultural and linguistic differences or environmental circumstances. Finally, we will address legislation that supports occupational education for students with ELN.

We will begin with the No Child Left Behind Act (NCLB Act), because this act, which encompasses all P–12 public education, has a number of important provisions that directly affect the educational experience of students with disabilities and their teachers. We will explain each of those provisions and discuss possible implications for children with disabilities and other exceptional needs.

No Child Left Behind Act (NCLB)

When passed by Congress in 2001, the NCLB Act (U.S. Department of Education, n.d.) replaced the Elementary and Secondary Education Act (ESEA). This landmark act requires that schools bring all students to proficiency in reading and math by the 2013–2014 school year. Indeed, the stated purpose of NCLB is to "ensure that all children have a fair, equal, and significant opportunity to obtain a high-quality education. . . ." (20 U.S.C. §6301). In fact, accountability has been referred to as the foundation of NCLB (Simpson, LaCava, & Graner, 2004). Thus, five provisions of NCLB address school accountability. The first provision, accountability through adequate yearly progress (AYP), requires schools to assess students annually to demonstrate progress. Schools are allowed to report scores of diverse students in subgroups such as ethnicity, income level, disability, and English language speakers of other languages; however, each group must make adequate yearly progress toward proficiency. Failure to demonstrate AYP for any subgroup has consequences for a school that will then be deemed a *failed school*.

What does NCLB mean for students with special needs and their teachers? The Council for Exceptional Children (CEC; 2004a) stated that the "enactment of NCLB has significant implications for special education policy and practice mainly in the areas of school accountability and personnel certification/licensure issues" (p. 6). The implications of these two issues are explained in the following paragraphs.

ACCOUNTABILITY The requirements for demonstrating that all students make AYP toward meeting standards and goals are likely to have two significant implications for students with disabilities, their teachers, and their schools. First, schools are required to show AYP toward meeting the goal of 100% proficiency in reading and math for all students, in Grades 3 through 8, within 12 years. Since *all children* now includes children with disabilities, their scores will help determine a school's compliance with the NCLB accountability clause. While it is still unclear exactly what this means, CEC (2004b) suggests that most likely local schools will feel pressured to ensure that students with disabilities are exposed to the general curriculum in order to meet content standards. According to CEC (2004b), this will have the direct effect of increasing the linkage of IEP goals to content standards.

A second implication for accountability relates to the use of accommodations during test taking. According to NCLB, students with disabilities may take the tests in any one of four ways that meet their individual needs (National Association of Protection and Advocacy Systems, 2004):

Option 1: Students with ELN are assessed in the same manner as other students.

Option 2: Students with ELN are assessed with approved accommodations or modifications.

Option 3: Students with ELN are given an alternate assessment that is based on the same achievement standards as the regular assessment.

Option 4: Students with ELN are given an alternate assessment based on different achievement standards—for example, basing the assessment on a life skills curriculum rather than an academic one.

However, a student may be counted as participating in a state assessment *only* if his or her test score is counted in the statewide accountability system. One reason that a student's score might be eliminated or determined to be invalid is that accommodations used during assessment were not allowable. For this reason you must be aware of regulations within your state regarding accommodations considered reliable and valid; that is, listed on the state's approved accommodations list.

The second provision, accountability through highly qualified teachers, requires that all teachers of core academic subjects are appropriately certified to teach the subject(s). This provision includes paraprofessionals who are required to meet minimum qualification standards. This provision is based on the educational research that links the achievement of students to the quality of their teachers (Simpson et al., 2004).

PERSONNEL CERTIFICATION/LICENSURE Originally, NCLB required states to develop a plan for ensuring that all teachers be highly qualified by the end of the 2005–2006 school year, but this date was recently extended until 2007 by the secretary of education (Simpson et al., 2004). The term *highly qualified* is defined as requiring that all teachers:

1. Have obtained full state certification as a teacher or passed the state teacher licensing examination and hold a license to teach in the state and do not have certification or licensure requirements waived on an emergency, temporary, or provisional basis.
2. Hold a minimum of a bachelor's degree.
3. Have demonstrated subject area competence in each of the academic subjects in which the teacher teaches, in a manner determined by the state.

All public school teachers who teach a core academic subject, whether new hires or veteran teachers with advance degrees, must meet these standards. At this time, this regulation is being interpreted to mean that *all teachers* includes special education teachers. This means that special education teachers must hold dual certification in special education and the core subject area(s) they teach. The *core academic subjects* include English, reading or language arts, mathematics, science, foreign languages, civics and government, economics, arts, history, and geography.

The third provision, use of scientifically researched practices (SRP), promotes the use of effective teaching methods based on scientific research. To be considered as SRP, these teaching methods must meet rigorous standards, have been shown to lead to positive results, and have been subject to rigorous peer review. Simpson and colleagues (2004) described the controversy surrounding the choice of randomized experimental group design as the preferred standard of scientific evidence. In general, however, the idea that teachers should use well-documented effective teaching practices is viewed as a positive step toward improving the academic success of all students, including those with ELN.

The fourth provision, expanded options for parents, encourages parents to become more involved with their child's education. For example, expanded parental rights to their student's assessment data and school or school district report cards are included in NCLB. Report cards describe school's overall effectiveness and progress toward meeting AYP. If parents, based on such information, determine that their child is attending a school deemed as a failing school, they have the option of moving their child to another school and requesting supplemental services.

The fifth provision, increased school district control and flexibility, allows schools that are meeting NCLB standards to use federal dollars for a variety of programs, such as increased technology resources, professional development for teachers and support staff, and drug-free, bully-free school programs. Thus, schools are able to provide increased educational opportunities to their students based on local interests, unique needs, and other considerations.

While there remains some uncertainty and controversy about NCLB, there is little doubt that it has the potential for having a significant impact on student learning and achievement. As you begin or continue your teaching career, you may wish to examine how the NCLB programs, procedures, and results in your state and school district will affect your teaching and career options. This information is available from your state's board of education and local school report cards.

Individuals with Disabilities Education Improvement Act-04

On December 3, 2004, President George W. Bush signed the reauthorized Individuals with Disabilities Education Improvement Act (IDEIA) of 2004 to become IDEA-04. See Table 1.2 for details regarding new provisions and changes to IDEA-97 that have direct implications for teachers and support staff in public schools. These topics include definitions of highly qualified special educators and other school personnel based on requirements of NCLB, changes to the evaluation process, and allocation of funds to support low achieving students who do not have disabilities.

These provisions of IDEA-04 will have a direct impact on teacher certification requirements, evaluation for determination of and continuing eligibility of students,

TABLE 1.2 Changes and New Provisions for IDEA-04

Teacher qualifications	• Highly qualified teachers should be fully licensed in special education and competent in the curriculum of the subject areas in which they teach. (See discussion under NCLB Act.) • All educators and related services providers, such as paraprofessionals, should meet state standards for highly qualified personnel.
Early intervention services	• Allows IDEA funds to be used for services to help students who have not been identified with disabilities; including additional academic and behavior supports to help the students succeed in the general education setting.
Evaluation	• Establishes a timeline of 60 days from parental consent to completion of the evaluation process. • Schools cannot ask for dispute resolution to override parents' refusal to consent for special education/related services. • When parental consent is refused, schools are not responsible to provide free, appropriate public education (FAPE) or develop an IEP [Individualized Education Program]. • Revaluations may not occur more than once a year unless agreed to by all parties, but must occur at least once every three years unless all parties agree that it is unnecessary. • Removes the native language requirements but states that evaluations should be offered in the language and format most likely to yield accurate information on what the child knows and the academic, developmental and functional levels. • Provides new provisions for summaries of academic achievement, functional performance, and recommendations for assisting the individual in meeting their postsecondary goals.
Learning disabilities	• Removes the requirement to use a discrepancy model when identifying a suspected learning disability. • Allows evaluation team to use "response-to-treatment" (response to a scientific, research-based intervention) as a part of the evaluation process for LD.
IEP	• Removes the requirement for benchmarks and short-term objectives. • Revises the requirements for parental reporting. Now requires descriptions in the IEP of how the student's progress towards meeting the annual goals will be measured and when reports on progress will be provided. • Removes the specific age requirements for including transition goals in IEPs. New provision requires a statement of measurable postsecondary goals based on age-appropriate transition assessment related to training, education, employment, and, if appropriate, independent living skills.

IEP: Team attendance	• New provisions state that when parents and local education agency (LEA) agree
	  ○ A team member may be excused if his or her related service or content area is not being modified or discussed.
	  ○ A team member may be excused, even if his or her related service or content area is being discussed, if written input for the development of the IEP has been provided prior to the meeting.

(continued)

TABLE 1.2 Changes and New Provisions for IDEA-04 (*continued*)

Students transferring into new settings	• As students move from special education early childhood programs, schools must consider recommendations in the family service plan. • When a student enters from another LEA, either from within the state or from another state, the previous IEP and related services provided must be honored while the receiving LEA evaluates the student and develops a new IEP.
Change in the IEP	• Parties may agree not to hold a meeting to make changes, but to develop a written document to amend or modify the current IEP.

Discipline	• This new provision to give schools the right to consider special circumstances for each case when deciding to change a placement because the student with a disability has violated the code of conduct.
	• This changes the wording related to the length of time a student may be removed to an alternative setting without a hearing from 45 days to 45 school days.
	• Schools may remove a student to an interim setting who has inflicted serious bodily injury to another person without a hearing.
	• New criteria for determining whether a behavior was a manifestation of a student's disability now state
	  o "if the conduct in question was caused by, or had a direct and substantial relationship to, the child's disability; or
	  o if the conduct in question was the direct result of the LEA's failure to implement the IEP" [CEC, 2004b, p. 19–20].
	• Protections for students who are not yet eligible under IDEA require that the parents must put their concerns regarding child's need for special education services in writing so that LEA has knowledge of the child's need.
	• If parent refuses special education services or if the evaluation team determines no disability exists, then the school is not required to consider any disability during proceedings to change placement.
	• The definition of "substantial evidence" was deleted from the new bill.

Procedural safeguards	• Complaints must be submitted no more than two years from persons should have or did know about the issues being disputed. • The complaining party must submit a due process complaint notice before filing a complaint. • Allows for mediation process to be requested prior to filing a complaint. • Creates a new dispute resolution process called "resolution session" which must convene prior to a due process hearing unless all parties agree otherwise. • Resolutions sessions must be conducted within 15 days of the request for a hearing and the compliant must be resolved within 30 days of the request OR a due process hearing may occur. • A decision made by a hearing officer must be based on substantive grounds as to whether or not the child received FAPE [Free Appropriate Public Education]. This includes, if procedural errors impeded the student's right to FAPE, significantly impeded the parent's opportunity to participate, sor caused deprivation of educational benefits. • Parties have 90 days from the hearing officer's decision to bring civil action.

Note: This table contains the changes and new provisions viewed as important to or of interest to public school teachers, both special and general educators.

Source: From Council for Exceptional Children (2004b).

development of Individualized Education Programs (IEP), methods used to determine a learning disability, discipline of students with ELN, and procedural safeguards.

The Rehabilitation Act Amendments of 1973 (Section 504)

When students do not qualify for special education services under IDEA-04, they may be protected by Section 504 of the Rehabilitation Act Amendments of 1973. These are students who do not require support for their learning needs but need other types of accommodations, such as a student with attention-deficit hyperactivity disorder (ADHD) or one who uses a wheelchair. Public schools are included in legislation that prohibits agencies receiving federal funds from discriminating against persons who have physical and mental impairments. Provisions of this legislation require schools to follow procedures similar to IDEA to identify and provide accommodations for students with special needs but not special education.

The Rehabilitation Act Amendments were among the civil rights legislation in the United States. For many years this legislation was underutilized by schools because they assumed that they had only to comply with the special education laws (i.e., Pub. L. No. 94-142 and later IDEA-97). More recently, Section 504 has provided protection and services to a variety of students that are not served under IDEA. To receive protection or service under Section 504, a person must be otherwise qualified to take a class, belong to a school club, or participate in any other school activity but is hampered by or denied participation because of a disability (Rosenfeld, 1999; Smith, 2002). For example, if a student who is a wheelchair user is able to sing well enough to belong to the mixed chorus, he or she may not be denied participation because accommodations for a wheelchair are necessary. Here the disability does not automatically make the student eligible for special education services but allows for protection from discrimination and eligibility for accommodations under Section 504. See Figure 1.1 for definitions and criteria for determining eligibility under Section 504.

Since students with Section 504 plans should not need and rarely receive the extensive services given students with IEPs, general education teachers are the primary provider of instruction and accommodations for these students. In some cases special educators may be involved in developing the 504 plan based on their expertise with students who have ELN. In addition, a school nurse, social worker, and psychologist may collaborate with the general educator. How students are selected, what format is used for the 504 plan, and who does the monitoring for compliance are all local decisions. Thus, each district must establish its own procedures for referral, evaluation, determination of eligibility, accommodations, reevaluation, and monitoring compliance. One drawback to this freedom is a lack of uniformity that may affect families that are mobile. As they move and change school districts, the services provided for a child change depending on how a school district implements IDEA, Section 504, or the level of support may be different (see Figure 1.2 for more information).

Americans with Disabilities Act of 1990 (ADA)

The Americans with Disabilities Act (ADA) prohibits discrimination on the basis of disability in employment, state and local government, public accommodations, commercial facilities, transportation, and telecommunications. Protection from discrimination

---

Definitions found in Section 504 Amendments

The three sections of the Amendments that define the term disability, who is eligible for services, and what services should be provided are important to all teachers. First, Section 504, 29 U.S.C. §794, states that:

> "No otherwise qualified individual with a disability in the United States, as defined in section 7(20), shall, solely by reason of her or his disability, be excluded from the participation in, be denied the benefits of, or be subjected to discrimination under any program or activity receiving Federal financial assistance. . . ."

Further, Section 504, 29 U.S.C. §705(B), states that a person is considered to have a physical or mental impairment if the person:

> "(a) has a physical or mental impairment which substantially limits one or more of such person's major life activities, (b) has a record of such an impairment, or (c) is regarded as having such an impairment."

Finally, Section 504, 34 C.F.R. §104.33(b)(1), states that a free, appropriate public education is defined as:

> "the provision of regular or special education and related aids and services that . . . are designed to meet individual educational needs of persons with disabilities as adequately as the needs of persons without disabilities are met and . . . are based upon adherence to specified procedures."

Eligible Criteria

Students who may be eligible for accommodations under Section 504 include

- Students who have attention deficit–hyperactive disorder
- Students who are addicted to substances such as drugs and alcohol but are no longer using illegal substances
- Students who have temporary medical conditions that may require homebound services or hospitalization
- Students with long-lasting or serious medical conditions such as cancer, organ transplants, or communicable diseases such as AIDS
- Students with health problems such as allergies, asthma, cardiac conditions, or epilepsy• Students with orthopedic or other physical conditions but who are not eligible for special education services
- Students with learning disabilities, attention deficit–hyperactive disorder, or low IQ scores who do not meet eligibility requirements for special education

---

FIGURE 1.1 Section 504

Sources: Office of Education and Civil Rights. (n.d.); Wright & Wright (2004).

under ADA is provided if a person has a disability or has a relationship or association with an individual with a disability. Section 12132 of ADA uses the same definition of disability as Section 504: a person who has a physical or mental impairment that substantially limits one or more major life activities, a person who has a history or record of such impairment, or a person who is perceived by others as having such impairment (U.S. Department of Justice, 2002). And just as Section 504 does not specifically name all the impairments that are covered, neither does ADA. The decision about what impairments may be eligible for accommodations is left to employers, which may

1. Section 504 requires removal of barriers to participation in educational programs. IDEA requires provision of remedial programs and other services.
2. Section 504 has a broad definition of a disability as a condition that limits major life activities. IDEA requires that students fall under a specific category of disability that limits ability to benefit from educational programs and requires special education to achieve benefits from educational programs.
3. Section 504 assumes that general education teachers are the educators responsible for providing instruction and recommended accommodations for students. IDEA assumes that a team of service providers will collaborate to meet the needs of students with IEPs.
4. Section 504 requires schools to undertake additional expenditures but provides no additional funding. IDEA does provide LEAs with additional funds.
5. Section 504 has no age restrictions so that persons are protected from birth to death. IDEA services and protections are restricted by age eligibility to attend a public school until age 21.

FIGURE 1.2 Distinctions Between Section 504 and IDEA
Sources: Rosenfeld (1999); Smith (2002).

mean that some employees will not be given appropriate accommodations or make it necessary to take issues to the legal system.

The provisions governing public schools are found in Title II of ADA, which covers responsibilities of state and local governments regardless of size or acceptance of federal funding. Therefore, state and local governments, which include public schools, are required to give persons with disabilities equal opportunities to benefit from their programs, services, and activities (e.g., public education, employment, transportation, recreation, and health care). Based on these requirements, public schools must provide fully accessible buildings and classrooms, not only for students who need such accommodations but for all persons who have business in the building, such as family members of enrolled students (U.S. Department of Justice, 2002). If a building cannot be altered to meet the ADA requirements, programs must be relocated. An additional requirement is that schools must communicate effectively with people who have hearing, vision, or speech disabilities. This may mean translating written communications into Braille for guardians who have visual impairments or providing a sign language interpreter for parents with hearing impairments. Schools are not required to assume undue financial and administrative burdens, but they are required to make reasonable modifications to policies, practices, and procedures to avoid discrimination.

The Americans with Disabilities Act and Section 504 are seen as virtually identical by the Office of Civil Rights, which is responsible for compliance oversight. The primary difference between these two acts is that Section 504 is limited to agencies and organizations who receive federal funds, whereas the ADA applies to the much broader arena of public places and spaces.

Assistive Technology Act of 2004 (H.R. 4278)

On October 25, 2004, President Bush signed the Assistive Technology Act of 2004 (ATA), which provides federal funding to 50 states and six territories. The first ATA, passed in 1988, provided funds for 10 years, so that states could establish infrastructures for administering assistive technology resources. Each state has established a statewide AT project that makes resources available to persons with disabilities, their caregivers, and the professionals who work with them. (To find the AT project in your state, see the list of resources in the Appendix.)

The reauthorized act changed the priority to increasing access to needed devices for individuals with disabilities. States are now required to spend the bulk of their grants on services to directly help individuals. Grant funds must be spent in one of two ways:

    a. Use 60 percent of assistive technology fund on direct aid programs, including reutilization, demonstration programs, alternative financing, and device loan programs,

    b. OR use 70 percent of grant funds on direct aid programs, but states are given full discretion on how to allocate funds for at least two, but up to four of the programs listed in option A. (Boehner, 2004, p. 2)

In addition, the act requires states to submit applications for funding with detailed descriptions of planned programs and measurable goals. Further, states must evaluate the effectiveness of their activities and provide an annual report to Congress. As an educator, you should be familiar with your state's AT project and with how it can support students' access to and use of AT to improve their learning in your classroom.

The legislation outlined above determines how children are educated in the United States, provides specific educational benefits and access to educational materials and facilities, defines how teachers and other educational professionals are qualified, and protects these rights for all children. In addition, there is legislation to provide for and protect the educational rights of other students with special needs, such as students who are gifted or talented, homeless or highly mobile, and English speakers of other languages.

LEGISLATIVE SUPPORTS FOR STUDENTS WITH OTHER SPECIAL NEEDS

Legislative acts that include entitlement provisions for students who are gifted or talented, homeless or highly mobile, and English speakers of other languages are important to educators, and particularly for special educators. Entitlement provisions within laws give a person rights to benefits specified especially by that law. For example, students with disabilities may qualify for additional protections and services because they are English speakers of other languages (ESOL). Further special circumstances surrounding these students, such as homelessness, may occur after students are placed in special education programs and therefore have implications on the delivery of special education services.

Gifted and Talented

Students who are gifted and talented can be found in all cultural and socioeconomic groups. Therefore, Congress has passed and recently reauthorized an act that provides funds for research and demonstration projects. Target populations are those who are gifted and talented *and* who are economically disadvantaged, have limited English proficiency, or have disabilities. The Jacob K. Javits Gifted and Talented Students Education Act of 1989 provided federal grant funding for scientifically based research, demonstration projects, innovative strategies, and similar activities designed to build and enhance the ability of elementary and secondary schools to meet the special educational needs of gifted and talented students. The major emphasis of the program was on serving students traditionally underrepresented in gifted and talented programs and to reduce the achievement gap of those students. Underrepresented students include students from minority groups determined by factors such as race, low socioeconomic status, or disabilities.

Congress reauthorized the Jacob K. Javits Gifted and Talented Students Education Act as Title V, Part D, Subpart 6, of the No Child Left Behind Act of 2001 to support education of gifted and talented students. This portion of NCLB reauthorizes the U.S. Department of Education to continue funding grants, providing leadership, and sponsoring a national research center on the education of gifted and talented students.

One program established with Javits funds is the National Research Center on the Gifted and Talented, located at the University of Connecticut, in collaboration with the University of Virginia, Yale University, and Columbia University. The center serves as a resource for teachers and schools looking for effective ways to identify and help gifted and talented students from populations traditionally underserved and underrepresented in gifted and talented programs (see the resource list in the Appendix).

English Speakers of Other Languages (ESOL)

No Child Left Behind, in the 2001 reauthorization of the ESEA, authorized programs for students who are limited English proficient (LEP) or are immigrants under Title III, known as the English Language Acquisition, Language Enhancement, and Academic Achievement Act.

The purposes of this part of NCLB are to help ensure that students who are LEP, including immigrant children and youth, attain English proficiency, develop high levels of academic attainment in English, and meet the same standards as *all* students are expected to meet in the core academic subjects. Further, school districts are required to develop and sustain high-quality language instruction educational programs and use research-based methods when teaching students who are LEP or immigrants. Further, states are required to promote parental and community participation in language instruction programs for the parents and communities of limited English proficient children. The NCLB regulations hold state educational agencies, local educational agencies, and schools accountable for demonstrated improvements in the English proficiency of students who are LEP each school year.

Several questions remain about the impact of NCLB's accountability requirements of annual yearly progress as it relates to students who are ESOL. The act currently requires that students be tested in English after they have been in school for 3 years. Ortiz (cited in Chamberlain, 2004) noted that some of these students, particularly from low-incidence language groups, are at considerable disadvantage if the assessments are available only in English. That is, if assessments are provided only in English, a student's ability to succeed is directly related to his or her ability to function in English, not academic competency for the task. This is especially true if teachers are not allowed to explain directions or unfamiliar terminology. In addition, Ortiz (in Chamberlain, 2004) noted that accommodations and modifications known to be effective in assessment

Homeless children and youths are those who

- lack a fixed, regular, and adequate nighttime residence, including children and youths who share housing with other persons due to loss of housing, economic hardship, or a similar reason;
- are living in motels, hotels, trailer parks, or camping grounds due to the lack of alternative adequate accommodations;
- are living in emergency or transitional shelters;
- are abandoned in hospitals;
- are awaiting foster care splacement;
- have a primary nighttime residence that is a public or private place not designed for or ordinarily used as a regular sleeping accommodation for human beings; for example, persons who are living in cars, parks, public spaces, abandoned buildings, substandard housing, bus or train stations, or similar settings; or
- are migratory children who qualify as homeless

FIGURE 1.3 Definition of Homelessness
Source: National Coalition for the Homeless (n.d.).

situations with students who are ESOL and also have a disability have not been determined. Therefore, since we do not have effective accommodations or appropriate language modifications, students' assessment results may not accurately record student's actual academic achievements. As a teacher you should seek out and be familiar with procedures used in your school district for assessment of students with ESOL.

Children Who Are Homeless or Highly Mobile

The Stewart B. McKinney Homeless Assistance Act (Pub. L. No. 100-77), now known as the McKinney-Vento Act, was signed into law by President Ronald Reagan on July 22, 1987. This act is the first and only major federal legislative response to homelessness. The McKinney Act originally consisted of 15 programs providing a range of services to homeless people, including emergency shelter, transitional housing, job training, primary health care, education, and some permanent housing. Title VII of the McKinney Act has implications for schools and teachers by authorizing education and job training programs, including the Education of Homeless Children and Youth Program.

The primary purpose of the educational provisions is to ensure that children who are homeless can continue their education. Figure 1.3 provides the definition used to determine homelessness for children of school age. Prior to this bill, when students did not have a legal residence within a particular school district, they could be dropped from the district's attendance rolls. According to McKinney, schools must either continue students' education in the school of origin or enroll them in a public school where non-homeless students who live in the district attend (Sec. 722). This means students are allowed to continue attending the school where they were when they became homeless. Students who become homeless in between academic years are able to return to their school of origin for the following academic year (Sec. 722).

In 2001, the act was reauthorized and renamed as McKinney-Vento Act. New requirements include provisions that allow students to remain in the school of origin for the duration of their homelessness, and if students become permanently housed during the academic year, they are entitled to stay in the school of origin for the remainder of the academic year (Sec. 722). Additional provisions require written notifications to parents and rights to appeal school district decisions.

This section has outlined the major points of legislation (IDEA-04, Section 504, NCLB, and ADA) that protects and serves students with disabilities as well as legislation that ensures protection for students with other exceptional needs, such as giftedness, homelessness, and language differences. In addition to these regulations, Congress has provided special legislation to cover occupational and career education. While occupational and career programs in public schools are open to all students, several of these acts have provisions for specific special populations. We will look at these provisions in the next section of this chapter.

LEGISLATION THAT SUPPORTS OCCUPATIONAL EDUCATION FOR STUDENTS WITH EXCEPTIONAL LEARNING NEEDS

The Perkins Vocational and Applied Technology Education Act of 1990

This act, which amended previous Perkins Acts, reflects efforts to improve the quality of vocational programs in general and to provide services to special populations. The educational focus shifts from teaching job-specific skills to integration of vocational and academic skills, leading to the reform known as the Tech-Prep.

The last reauthorization of the Perkins Vocational and Applied Technology Education Act in 1998 contains two major changes from the 1990 act. First, set-aside funding for students with special needs is gone, and local school districts must set and meet performance standards for these programs, but Tech-Prep remained intact, if not stronger, because separate funding was incorporated into the reauthorization.

Originally, implementation of Tech-Prep required an extensive reorganization of vocational programs to meet the requirement that programs deliver academic and job-related information to students in curricula that are clearly related to the workplace (Green & Weaver, 1994).

The Tech-Prep curriculum is competency based, stressing assessment of the competencies needed by workers in realistic settings, including (a) basic skills (e.g., reading, writing, arithmetic, listening, speaking), (b) thinking skills (e.g., creativity, decision making, problem solving, reasoning, the ability to visualize abstract information), and (c) personal qualities (e.g., responsibility, self-esteem, sociability, self-management, integrity). Another requirement of Tech-Prep programs is that the number of years students are enrolled in secondary and postsecondary vocational or technical programs must be combined (e.g., 2 + 2 = 2 years of secondary and 2 years of postsecondary training; 4 + 2 = 4 years of secondary and 2 years of postsecondary training) to provide a smooth transition with continuity of curricula between secondary and technical or community colleges. For example, a secondary student who took either 2 or 4 years of Transportation Technology would be transitioned into a 2-year automotive program at a community college.

Tech-Prep programs present positive opportunities for students with disabilities if the curriculum consistently offered to *all* students contains (a) a common core of math, communication, and science; (b) an emphasis on transition from school to postsecondary settings; (c) opportunities for career planning; and (d) connections between school years and the future. At the same time, however, these programs may present problems for students with disabilities. Target students suggested for Tech-Prep classes are the middle quartiles of the typical high school student body, and target occupations are midrange jobs that require education and training beyond high school (Schell & Babich, 1993). There is a possibility that Tech-Prep classes may become so academically oriented that students with exceptional learning needs are likely to encounter failure. However, the educational and job-training benefits have been shown to benefit students with disabilities (Hughes, Bailey, & Karp, 2002), and school personnel should seek placements in Tech-Prep classes for students with exceptional needs when appropriate.

The School-to-Work Opportunities Act (STWOA)

This act, signed into law on May 4, 1994, and sunsetted (the act's authority ended) in October 2002, was not written solely for students with special needs but also to increase students' awareness of career opportunities. The act offered states initial seed money to plan, implement, and establish STOWA programs for all students in public schools. When the act was discontinued, the intent was that states would continue the programs under their own budgets.

STWOA was intended to serve all students and was an effort to increase opportunities for youth to prepare for careers that were not traditional for their race, gender, or disability. Therefore, *all students* refers to male and female students from a variety of backgrounds and circumstances, including disadvantaged youth; persons with diverse racial, ethnic, or cultural backgrounds (e.g., American Indian, Alaskan Natives, and Native Hawaiians); students with disabilities; and others with special needs, such as English language learners, children of migrant workers, youth at risk of dropping out, and academically gifted or talented students (Evers, 2009).

One purpose of the act was to establish school-to-work transition systems that enabled all youth to identify potential careers and move into the workplace (Council for Exceptional Children, 1994). Funding was provided to programs such as Tech-Prep, career academies, school-to-apprenticeship programs, cooperative education, youth apprenticeship, and business–education partnerships. These programs were required to include school-based and work-based learning components as well as guidance and counseling, workplace mentoring, technical assistance for employers, and coordination with employers.

The Workforce Investment Act (WIA; Pub. L. No. 105-220)

Enacted in 1998 (American Federation of State, County, and Municipal Employees, n.d.), WIA requires that state programs—including employment services, unemployment insurance, vocational rehabilitation, adult education, welfare-to-work, and postsecondary vocational education—be coordinated. Further, the Rehabilitation Act Amendments of 1998 are included in the WIA to integrate all federal, state, and local programs into a comprehensive training act.

A primary purpose was to create a customer-friendly training system. This one-stop delivery system provides all employment-related and training services at one physical site, supplemented by additional sites and technological networks as necessary. Services include (a) job training, (b) adult education, (c) amendments to Wagner-Peyser and related acts, (d) amendments to the Vocational Rehabilitation Act, and (e) general provisions. Note that WIA does not include vocational education available in public schools that is covered by other legislation. All youth between the ages of 14 and 21 who meet one or more of the six barriers to successful workforce entry are eligible for services. The barriers include (a) school dropout; (b) basic literacy skills deficiency; (c) homeless, runaway, or foster child; (d) pregnant or a parent; (e) an offender; or (f) need help completing an educational program or securing and holding a job (American Federation of State, County, and Municipal Employees, n.d.). Further, specific sections of the act note individuals with disabilities as members of the target populations. With this in mind, school personnel who work with students to implement transition plans should be familiar with their local WIA youth programs and how to access services in order to inform students and families of the postsecondary services available to them, especially for those students who exit school without graduating.

Summary

The diverse classrooms found in most public schools today create many challenges for teachers who must meet a variety of unique individual needs. In addition, the growing emphasis on standards-based curriculum and accountability for student learning has further increased pressures for teachers. Finally, the instructional and setting demands found in today's classrooms may be quite different from the ones most teachers experienced as children. Given these realities, using effective teaching practices becomes vitally important for the success of both teachers and students. Educators need planning and teaching practices that are also cost and time efficient, or they may resort to low-level or no accommodations for differences among students. Students indicate that they want to be challenged with engaging classroom activities that are related to their perceived educational goals and have purpose for their lives; offering metacognitive strategies and project-based learning experiences in a UDL classroom employing co-teaching methods can offer challenges while supporting individual needs.

Students with exceptional learning needs have protections and assurances provided by a variety of legislative acts. In fact, acts such as No Child Left Behind, Section 504, IDEA-04, ADA, and Perkins mandate that students with all types of exceptional needs have full access to educational settings and resources. These rights include having highly qualified teachers, participating in the assessment process, and receiving remedial or special education services to enhance and support their learning experiences. When students are in elementary school, teachers and parents have program and placement choices; however, at the secondary level those choices increase and often determine postsecondary transition paths. Finally, the graduation outcomes for students with exceptional needs continue to be of concern to families, educators, and administrators. The increasing standards for high school graduation and exit exams can be barriers to obtaining a high school diploma or to even finishing high school.

As you think about what you have read in the chapter, consider that while we have laws to mandate what we *must* do, only families, students, and educators can determine what we *should* do. The purpose of this book is to provide information about planning and instructional practices that will allow teachers to provide effective and efficient instruction to a diverse population of students. The practices explained and illustrated in this book will provide teachers with methods that can be implemented in any classroom, curriculum, and content area.

References

American Federation of State, County, and Municipal Employees, AFL-CIO (n.d.). *The workforce investment act*. Retrieved on January 3, 2003, from http://www.afscme.org/pol-leg/wiahome.htm: Author.

Anderman, L. H. (2004). Student motivation across subject-area domains. *Journal of Educational Research, 97*(6), 283–285.

Bender, W. (2004). *Learning disabilities: Characteristics, identification, and teaching strategies* (4th ed.). Boston: Allyn & Bacon.

Boehner, J. (2004). *Bill summary: Assistive technology act of 2004*. Washington, DC: House Education & the Workforce Committee. Retrieved on December 12, 2004, from http://edworkforce.house.gov/issues/108th/education/at/billsummary.htm

Borkowski, J. G. (1992). Metacognitive theory: A framework for teaching literacy, writing, and math skills. *Journal of Learning Disabilities, 25,* 253–257.

Bouffard, T., & Couture, N. (2003). Motivational profile and academic achievement among students enrolled in different school tracks. *Educational Studies, 29*(1), 19–38.

Cavanaugh, T. (2002). The need for assistive technology in educational technology. *Educational Technology Review, 10*(1). Retrieved February 3, 2005, from http://aace.org/pubs/etr/issue2/cavanaugh.cfm

Center for Public Education (2007). *The United States of education: A guide to our changing demographics and their implications for public schools*. Retrieved December 28, 2008, from http://www.centerforpubliceducation.org/site/c.kjJXJ5MPIwE/b.3567939/k.E55/The_United_States_of_education_A_guide_to_our_changing_demographics_and_their_implications_for_public_schools.htm#race

Chamberlain, S. (2004). An interview with Asa G. Hilliard, III, and Aba A Ortiz: The effects of No Child Left Behind on diverse learners. *Intervention in School and Clinic, 40*(2), 96–105.

Council for Exceptional Children. (1994). *Summary of the School-to-Work Opportunities Act*. Reston, VA: Author.

Council for Exceptional Children. (2004a). *No Child Left Behind Act of 2001: Reauthorization of the Elementary and Secondary Education Act: A technical assistance resource*. Retrieved on December 29, 2004, from http://www.cec.sped.org/pp/OverviewNCLB.pdf

Council for Exceptional Children. (2004b). *The new IDEA: CEC's summary of significant issues*. Arlington, VA: Author. Retrieved January 6, 2009, from http://www.cec.sped.org/Content/NavigationMenu/PolicyAdvocacy/IDEAResources/CEC_Summary_of_Selected_IDEA_Reauthorization_Issues.pdf

Deshler, D. D., Ellis, E. S., & Lenz, B. K. (1996) *Teaching adolescents with learning disabilities: Strategies and methods* (2nd ed.). Denver, CO: Love

Deshler, D., & Schumaker, J. B. (2006). *Teaching adolescents with disabilities: Accessing the general education curriculum*. Thousand Oaks, CA: Corwin Press.

Ellis, E. (1997). Watering up the curriculum for adolescents with learning disabilities: Goals of knowledge dimension. *Remedial and Special Education, 18*(6), 326–346.

Ellis, E. (2000). *Project-based learning strategies for differentiating instruction*. Tuscaloosa, AL: Masterminds.

Evers, R. B. (2009). Developing career and occupational skills in students with learning disabilities. In G. Blalock, J. R. Patton, P. Kolar, & D. Bassett (Eds.), *Transition and students with learning disabilities: Facilitating the movement from school to adult life* (2nd ed.) Austin, TX: Don Hammill Institute.

Flavell, J. H., Miller, P. H., & Miller, S. A. (2002). *Cognitive development* (4th ed.) Upper Saddle River, NJ: Prentice Hall.

French, D. (2002). Editorial on accessibility: An integral part of online learning. *Educational Technology Review, 10*(1). Retrieved February 3, 2005, from http://aace.org/pubs/etr/issue2/french-ed.cfm

Green, J. E., & Weaver, R. A. (1994). *Tech Prep: A strategy for school reform*. Bloomington, IN: Phi Delta Kappa Educational Foundation.

Harlen, W., & Crick, R. D. (2003). Testing and motivation for learning. *Assessment in Education, 10*(2), 169–207.

Hartman, H. J., & Sternberg, R. J. (1993). A broad BACEIS for improving thinking. *Instructional Science, 21*(5), 400–425.

Henley, M., Ramsey, R., & Algozzine, R. (2002). *Characteristics of and strategies for teaching students with mild disabilities*. Boston: Allyn & Bacon.

Hughes, K. L., Bailey, T. R., & Karp, M. M. (2002). School-to-work: Making a difference in education. *Phi Delta Kappan, 84*(4), 272–279.

King-Sears, M. E. (2001). Three steps for gaining access to the general education curriculum for learner with disabilities. *Intervention in School and Clinic, 37*(2), 87–76.

Mastropieri, M. A., & Scruggs, T. E., (2001). Promoting inclusion in secondary classrooms. *Learning Disability Quarterly, 24*, 265–274.

McEwan, B. (2000). *The art of classroom management: Effective practices for building equitable learning communities*. Upper Saddle River, NJ: Merrill/Pearson Education.

National Association for Gifted Children. (2008). *Frequently asked questions*. Retrieved December 28, 2008, from http://www.nagc.org/index2.aspx?id=548

National Association of Protection and Advocacy Systems. (2004). *Children with disabilities under No Child Left Behind: Myths and realities*. Retrieved December 5, 2004, from http://www.wrightslaw.com/nclb/info/myths.realities.napas.htm

National Center for Education Statistics. (2007a). *Nation's Report Card: Mathematics 2007*. Retrieved on December 5, 2008, from http://nces.ed.gov/pubsearch/pubsinfo.asp?pubid = 2007494

National Center for Education Statistics. (2007b). *Nation's Report Card: Reading 2007*. Retrieved on December 5, 2008, from http:// nces.ed.gov/pubsearch/pubsinfo.asp?pubid = 2007496

Ngeow, K., & Kong, Y. (2001). *Learning to learn: Preparing teachers and students for problem-based learning*. Bloomington, IN: ERIC Clearinghouse on Reading, English, and Communication. (ERIC Document Reproduction Service No. ED457524)

Nichols, W. D., Jones, J. P., & Hancock, D. R. (2003). Teachers' influence on goal orientation: Exploring the relationship between eighth graders' goal orientation, their emotional development, their perceptions of learning, and their teachers' instructional strategies. *Reading Psychology, 24*(1), 57–85.

Office of Education and Civil Rights. (n.d.). *Protecting children with disabilities: Frequently asked questions about Section 504 and the education of children with disabilities*. Retrieved December 28, 2004, from http://www.ed.gov/about/offices/list/ocr/504faq.html

Palmer, S. B., & Wehmeyer, M. L. (2003). Promoting self-determination in early elementary school: Teaching self-regulated problem-solving and goal-setting skills. *Remedial and Special Education, 24*(2), 115–126.

Parsad, B., & Jones, J. (2005). *Internet access in U.S. public schools and classrooms: 1994–2003* (NCES 2005–015). Washington, DC: U.S. Department of Education. National Center for Education Statistics.

Peterson-Karlan, G. R., & Parette, P. (2005). Millennial students with mild disabilities and emerging assistive technology trends. *Journal of Special Education Technology, 20*(4), 27–38.

Pugach, M. C., & Warger, C. L. (2001). Curriculum matters: Raising expectations for students with disabilities. *Remedial and Special Education, 22*(4), 194–196, 213.

Rose, D. H., & Meyer, A. (2002). *Teaching every student in the digital age: Universal design for learning*. Alexandria, VA: Association for Supervision and Curriculum Development.

Rosenfeld, S. J. (1999). Section 504 and IDEA: Basic similarities and differences. Washington, DC: LDOnLine. Retrieved December 28, 2004, from http://www.ldonline.org/ld_indepth/legal_legislative/edlaw504.html

Schell, J. W., & Babich, A. M. (1993). Tech-Prep and the development of higher-order thinking skills among learners with special needs. *Journal for Vocational and Special Needs Education, 16*(1), 6–13.

School Data Direct (2008). *School Environment*. Retrieved on December 28, 2008, from http://www.schooldatadirect.org/app/data/q/stid=1036196/llid=162/stllid=676/locid=1036195/catid=1015/secid=4570/compid=859/stype=

Simpson, R., LaCava, P. G., & Graner, P. S. (2004). The No Child Left Behind Act: Challenges and implications for educators. *Intervention in School and Clinic, 40*(2), 67–75.

Smith, T. E. C. (2002). Section 504: What teachers need to know. *Intervention in School and Clinic, 37*(5), 259–266.

Spencer, S. S., & Logan, K. R. (2005). Improving students with learning disabilities ability to acquire and generalize a vocabulary learning strategy. *Learning Disabilities: A Multidisciplinary Journal, 13*, 87–94.

Thousand, J., Rosenberg, R. L., Bishop, K., & Villa, R. (1997). The evolution of secondary inclusion. *Remedial and Special Education, 18*(5), 270–284.

U.S. Census Bureau. (2008). *School enrollment—Social and economic characteristics of students: October 2003.* Retrieved December 28, 2008, from http://www.census.gov/prod/2008pubs/p20-559.pdf

U. S. Department of Education (n.d.). *No Child Left Behind Act.* Retrieved on August 28, 2009, from http://www.ed.gov/nclb/landing.jhtml

U.S. Department of Justice. (2002). *A guide to disability rights laws.* Washington, DC: Author.

Weinstein, C. S. (2003). *Secondary classroom management: Lessons from research and practice* (2nd ed.). Boston: McGraw-Hill.

Weinstein, C. S., & Mignano, A. J. (2003). *Elementary classroom management: Lessons from research and practice* (3rd ed.). Boston: McGraw-Hill.

Wright, P., & Wright, P. (2004). The Rehabilitation Act of 1973 (29 U.S.C., Chapter 16) *Wrightslaw: Special education law.* Hartfield, VA: Harbor House Law Press.

Chapter 4

Using Assessment Data to Plan and Teach

After reading this chapter, you will be able to:

1. Define the purpose of assessment
2. Correlate the types of assessments with the purposes of assessment
3. Use the principles of Universal Design for Learning (UDL) to remove barriers that affect assessment
4. Select appropriate accommodations for assessment situations
5. Select appropriate learning strategies to support students during assessments
6. Select appropriate test-taking skills to support students during assessments

Prior to the 1990s, the primary purposes of assessment were to assign grades to individual students for administrative purposes, such as grade promotion, or to predict a person's ability to compete in college classes, as the SAT or ACT exams did, but in the 1990s, Goals 2000 introduced a new dimension to assessment: accountability. A decade later, the passage of No Child Left Behind (NCLB) added state accountability for student achievement to ensure that all students were participating and achieving—but most important, that students were making progress toward higher achievement rates. Under the mandates of NCLB, schools are held accountable for the educational success of every child, including those with exceptional learning needs. During the 2003–2004 school year, over 95% of students with disabilities in 41 states participated in statewide reading assessment (U.S. Government Accountability Office [USGAO], 2005). As there are over 6 million students with disabilities (13% of all students) enrolled in our public schools (USGAO, 2005), teachers should expect to have students with disabilities in their classes and to be held accountable for the educational progress of all students within their classrooms. To provide effective instruction to meet the learning needs of all students, including those with exceptional learning needs, teachers must engage in a continual cycle of assessment, planning, and instruction. This chapter will discuss the purposes and types of assessments, how to use the principles of Universal Design for Learning when constructing classroom assessments, selection of appropriate accommodations for both teacher-made and mandated state assessments, and preparing students for assessments by incorporating test-taking skills into instruction.

PURPOSES OF ASSESSMENT

We are all familiar with testing and assessment. Every reader of this text has been through years of education that included hundreds of tests and other types of assessment, but I have never met a student who honestly liked to take tests. In fact, every time I have elected to cancel a test in one of my college courses, the class has risen in a deafening cheer. This dislike of tests on the part of students who become teachers can lead to teachers who do not like to give tests. Teachers like to teach, teachers want to teach, and many of us cannot think of any other occupation that would suit us, but most of us do not like to test. Yet, as Popham (2005) reminded us, we must assess if we want to be better teachers. This is the primary reason to assess: to know what students learned and, just as important, what they did not learn; to know if the methods and materials we used or provided were helpful; and finally, to know what to do next. Assessments give us the data we need to be reflective about our teaching and the learning experiences of our students.

Certainly, that is the most important reason to assess students, but over the years organizations and agencies outside the field of education have become interested in what is happening in schools. They are particularly interested in the progress of students who are achieving at substantially lower levels, such as groups of students who are minorities, disadvantaged, or disabled (Hogan, 2007). This rise in interest for minority groups began during the civil rights movement of the 1960s and has had an impact on education. The major impact can be seen in the passage of laws that have implications for assessment of students in these minority groups. The following section is a brief overview of the laws as they relate specifically to the rise of accountability for the learning of all students. Other purposes of these laws were discussed in Chapter 1.

Laws That Related to Assessment

Each of the laws described here have increased the accountability of schools for the education of all children, including students with exceptional learning needs (ELN) (see Chapter 1 for details). The first of these laws was the Elementary and Secondary Education Act (ESEA) of 1965. Hogan (2007) noted that provisions of this act led to development of educational programs to specifically address the disparity in the education of students in minority groups. This resulted in the need to evaluate new programs to demonstrate that the needs of minority students were being met. Hogan further stated that this led to the emerging accountability movement. Other laws enacted as a result of the civil rights movement, such as the Rehabilitation Act of 1973 and the Americans with Disabilities Act of 1990, further delineated the responsibilities of the educational institutions toward minority groups and specifically those with disabilities. The No Child Left Behind Act of 2001 (NCLB) requires that all students, including those with disabilities, are assessed for their ability to meet state educational standards. In 1972, Congress passed the Education of All Handicapped Children Act (EAHC), the first legislation that specifically addressed the rights of students with disability to a free and appropriate education in public schools. The latest reauthorization of this legislation is the Individuals with Disabilities Educational Improvement Act of 2004 (IDEIA-04), which contains regulations to ensure that students with disabilities are assessed without bias in a nondiscriminatory manner. Further, within the reauthorized IDEIA-04, Section 614 (b)(6)(B) states, "In determining whether a child has a specific learning disability, a local educational agency may use a process that determines if the child responds to scientific, research-based intervention as a part of the evaluation procedures." From this statute has come a new term and concept (Kame'enui, 2007) known as Response to Intervention (RTI; defined below). Another statute of IDEIA-04 notes that if using RTI to evaluate students for learning disabilities, local educational agencies are not required to find a severe discrepancy between achievement and intellectual ability to determine the existence of a learning disability and eligibility for special education services. Since its inception, RTI has been "conspicuously and actively invoked in the current discourse of the special education and, possibly, general education communities" (Kame'enui, 2007, p. 7). In the next section, we will explain the major components of RTI and its implementation in classrooms.

RTI is designed as a multitiered process to identify and support students with learning and behavior problems (National Center for Learning Disabilities, n.d.-b). The process begins with research-based, high-quality instruction and universal screening of all students in general education classrooms. Students who struggle with any aspect of instruction are then provided with interventions at increasing levels of intensity. Progress is monitored to note student learning rates and levels of performance. Throughout this process decisions are made based on individual student responses to instructional interventions. The National Center on Learning Disabilities (n.d.-b) notes the essential components for effective implementation of RTI are (a) high-quality, scientifically based classroom instruction, (b) ongoing student assessment, (c) tiered instruction, and (d) parent involvement. Figure 4.1 provides details that illustrate how these components are infused into the RTI multitiered process.

In addition to providing a process that focuses on high-quality instruction and differentiated instruction with frequent monitoring of progress, RTI offers an opportunity

Tier 1: Primary prevention with universal interventions	• Targets all students • Is preventive and proactive • Is expected to be effective for 80% to 90% of students	• Completed in the general education classroom • Includes the universal core instructional program • Provides curriculum-based screening of all students • Includes short-term progress monitoring of "at-risk" students
Tier 2: Secondary prevention with targeted group interventions	• Targets the 5% to 10% of students who are "at-risk" • Provides a rapid response to learning needs	• Uses small-group tutoring in reading and math • Duration from 8 to 20 weeks • Provides for dual discrepancy evaluation to determine responsiveness
Tier 3: Tertiary prevention with intensive individual interventions	• Targets the 1% to 5% of students who have not responded to Tier 2 interventions • Is assessment-based • Provides high-intensity interventions	• Individualized programming and progress monitoring • Provides for a multidisciplinary evaluation • Identifies specific disability • Determines placement

FIGURE 4.1 The Three Tiers of the Response to Intervention Process

Sources: Information from Fuchs & Fuchs (2007); National Center on Learning Disabilities (n.d.-b); Sugai (n.d.).

Note: At any time during this process, a parent or guardian may request a formal evaluation. The RTI process does not negate the parental right to a timely formal evaluation.

for educators to address the disproportionate representation in special education programs of students with cultural and linguistic differences. According to Hosp and Reschly (2003) (n.d.), RTI may be able to address this disproportionality in the following ways. First, since the goal of RTI is to improve learning outcomes of all students and seeks to meet the individual learning needs of all students, the expected outcome should be met by all students, including those who are culturally or linguistically different. Second, with a focus on individual student needs, the tiered delivery will allow for more efficient delivery of instruction to like students. For example, students who are "at risk" may not arrive at the schoolhouse door with the vocabulary needed to be successful readers. Their lack of vocabulary is similar to the vocabulary needs of students who are learning English as a second language. Thus, both groups of students' learning may be addressed with similar instruction and interventions. Third, the use of reliable measures for universal screening can be used to make decisions, thus both identifying the need and bypassing any teacher bias that may exist.

In addition to the legal requirements for inclusive assessment practices, Airasian (2005) noted that there are ethical and moral issues of fairness during assessments for teachers to consider. Foremost of these is collecting and interpreting valid and reliable data for decision making. Beyond that, teachers should be careful to inform students of their expectations, teach the content to be assessed, avoid making quick judgments about student ability or stereotyping them with labels, refrain from using language that might be offensive or harmful to students from diverse backgrounds, and remove bias toward persons who are English language learners (ELL) or are culturally different. While all of these might seem like obvious civilities, if we are not aware and vigilant, classroom assessments can be skewed and will not reflect students' actual knowledge or skill levels. Furthermore, in the course of working with students, particularly students with exceptional needs, teachers have access to assessment data as well as personal data collected during assessment activities. Another of our ethical duties is to safeguard the privacy of that information and never use it to harm or bully a student. And just as important, we should recognize the limitations of the data when making critical decisions. Any assessment data are snapshots of student knowledge and skills on a given day in a given place.

ADDITIONAL PURPOSES OF ASSESSMENT   Accountability has become a major influence on how teachers view assessment and the primary purpose of assessment, but it is important that teachers understand that there are other purposes for assessment that can be useful on a daily basis and lead to increased rates of success on state accountability assessments. In the section below, we will discuss six purposes for assessing students in classrooms (Airasian, 2005; Hogan, 2007; Popham, 2005). As this list of purposes for assessment clearly demonstrates, assessment is "not just a closing activity" (Gagnon & Collay, 2001, p. 113), for a lesson or unit of instruction but is ongoing activity that should happen continuously before, during, and after instruction.

ESTABLISHING CLASSROOM EQUILIBRIUM (AIRASIAN, 2005)   Teachers make many decisions on a daily basis that are assessments used to keep order and civility in their classrooms. These decisions may include selecting rules, routines, and classroom procedures; seating students to ensure quiet work settings; sending a student who needs a break on an errand; and dealing with students who are disruptive. These decisions help to ensure that classrooms run smoothly for effective teaching and learning.

PLANNING AND CONDUCTING INSTRUCTION AND DETERMINING INSTRUCTIONAL EFFECTIVENESS (AIRASIAN, 2005; POPHAM, 2005)   As noted at the beginning of the chapter, this is one primary reason for assessment. Teachers make decisions about what content to teach and how to teach that content based not only on state standards but also on personal observations of students as they work and answer questions during class and how well students complete quizzes, in-class and homework assignments, and classroom tests. All of this information helps the teacher determine what needs to be retaught as well as what should be taught next. In addition, teachers use this information to determine the most effective teaching methods and strategies to support student learning.

DIAGNOSING STUDENT'S STRENGTHS AND WEAKNESSES AND PLACING PUPILS (AIRASIAN, 2005; POPHAM, 2005)   By diagnosing students' strengths and weaknesses, teachers can plan for placing students in appropriate reading or math groups, selecting peer partners, and assigning students for project-based learning groups. Further, after diagnosing weakness, teachers can plan for remediation in areas where students need to learn knowledge or skills for moving forward in the content and avoiding future failures. The diagnosis of student strengths will identify students who have prior knowledge and skills and allow teachers to plan enrichment activities to challenge and keep these learners engaged. Teachers often use preassessment quizzes or assignments to gather information about the entire class, but checklists and observation are also methods used for diagnosing.

PROVIDING FEEDBACK AND MOTIVATIONAL INCENTIVES (AIRASIAN, 2005; HOGAN, 2007) Formative assessment allows teachers to check student progress during the teaching and learning process rather than waiting until the end of a lesson or unit of lessons to determine student's achievement. It can be asked during a lecture to check student's understanding at that moment, a teacher–student conference, or a homework assignment that checks students' abilities to use and apply new knowledge. Providing students with positive formative feedback can be an incentive for them to keep working on a difficult skill or long-term project. Offering opportunities for receiving formative feedback also helps students feel safe to take risks as they learn rather than feeling that all work must be done perfectly the first time. Providing formative assessment feedback to parents and guardians provides valuable information they can use to help students with homework and studying for tests and helps to avoid unpleasant surprises when grades are given.

DIAGNOSING PUPIL PROBLEMS AND DISABILITIES (AIRASIAN, 2005; HOGAN, 2007) When teachers diagnosis student strengths and weakness, they may recognize that individual students need more remediation or enrichment than can be provided in the general education classroom. At this point, a teacher may refer the student for additional diagnosis or for placement in special education, gifted/talented, or English as Second Language (ESL) programs. Smith, Dowdy, Polloway, and Blalock (1997) noted there are five purposes for assessing students with disabilities: (1) conducting initial identification and screening, (2) determining and evaluating teaching programs and strategies, (3) determining current performance level and educational needs, (4) deciding about classification and program placement, and (5) developing the individual education program (IEP). Purposes 1–4 are also useful for determining eligibility for gifted and talented or ESL programs.

JUDGING AND GRADING ACADEMIC LEARNING AND PROGRESS (AIRASIAN, 2005; HOGAN, 2007; POPHAM, 2005) Judging and grading student work is the most common use of classroom assignments and tests and is the primary purpose of state and district standardized assessments. When teachers assess at the end of unit or semester, they are using *summative* assessment, which provides a summation of knowledge and skills students have learned during instruction. Summative assessments can include tests, project and research reports, and portfolios of work that require students to demonstrate that they have met learning objectives and/or state standards. Typically teachers will use a combination of formative and summative assessment data to judge student achievement and assign a grade.

Regardless of their precise reasons for assessing at any given moment, teachers must continue to make judgments about student learning in a variety of ways. Meanwhile, under NCLB, teachers will be asked to prepare students for high-stakes assessments that will determine student movement to the next grade or graduation, if individual schools make the "grade," and, in some cases, if teachers and principals will keep their jobs. Both NCLB and IDEIA-04 regulations require that students with disabilities must be included in these high-stakes assessments, but can students with disabilities succeed on these tests?

Across the country, educators, administrators, and caregivers are working to help students with disabilities succeed in this new task. In the next section we will discuss some of the problem areas in assessment, explore how using UDL when constructing the initial assessment can diminish or exclude the overall effect of barriers, and describe how to construct an accessible assessment. As we have noted elsewhere in this text, even with UDL-designed teaching materials and assessment, some students remain who need additional accommodations, therefore we will explore the accommodations that are being used to support assessment experiences. On an additional note, it is not our intent in this chapter to teach you how to construct assessments that are reliable and valid or that assess higher-order thinking and learning or how to write specific test items, as those topics are far too complex for one chapter; we leave that to other texts that are devoted solely to assessment. Our intent is to provide you with information to supplement and extend what you already know or will learn, so that you can plan and design assessments that eliminate barriers for the most participants possible.

IMPEDIMENTS TO STUDENT SUCCESS ON HIGH-STAKES AND CLASSROOM ASSESSMENTS

Recently the term *high-stakes assessments* has come into use in the educational literature and around the teacher's lounge. High-stakes occur with tests that have exceptionally important consequences for individuals (Hogan, 2007). With the implementation of NCLB, tests given at the end of courses or to measure yearly progress have been termed high-stakes. This is because the results of the tests can have far-reaching implications for states, school districts, schools, teachers, and even individual students. Generally these tests fall into one of two categories, individual and large-scale tests.

- Individual high-stakes tests include exit exams that determine graduation status. Twenty-five states expected to have such requirements in place by 2009 (Cortiella, 2004). Also, at least 17 states have tests that determine eligibility for promotion to the next grade or movement to the next level of a content area (e.g., Algebra II or French III). Both of these assessments hold individual students accountable rather than the school, district, or state. Critics of exit exams cite evidence that failure may lead to dropping out of school.
- Large-scale tests include the NCLB-mandated examinations of student progress toward meeting state standards, where students are expected to show annual yearly progress (AYP). Consequences for students with ELN who fail or score poorly on AYP tests include increased likelihood that they (a) are likely to be held back in a class, (b) will drop out of school before graduation, (c) will be tracked into low-level courses that do not lead to a standard high school diploma, and (d) will not earn a high school diploma (Cortiella, 2004).

According to Cortiella (2004), five barriers generally impede success of students with disabilities on high-stakes assessments: These are encountering inadequate opportunities to learn, being placed in more restrictive settings, failing to provide reasonable accommodations, not offering remediation or offering in an ineffective manner, and relying too heavily on data from one test score (see Figure 4.2 for additional information).

In addition to the external barriers described by Cortiella (2004), students may experience barriers caused by their disability or exceptional need. These barriers inhibit the student's ability to participate successfully in the assessment. Most often these barriers limit the student's ability to demonstrate accurately his or her level of achievement in content knowledge and skills, and occasionally the barriers inhibit participation

Barrier	Reasons
1. There is an inadequate opportunity to learn because students are not exposed to subject matter included on tests.	• Few states require that IEPs address state standards. • No systematic assurance exists that IEPs align curriculum standards with instruction in special education classes. • Special educators are not familiar with their state standards.
2. More restrictive placements are used by states with high school graduation exit exams.	• States with exit exams tend to place students with exceptional learning needs (ELN) in more restrictive environments • In more restrictive settings, students have less exposure to standards-based curriculum.
3. Lack of reasonable accommodations exists, in part, because there is considerable disagreement about what accommodations are and whether their use changes the validity of the text given.	• State may limit the number and types of accommodations to a predetermined list. • Increased number of states are restricting calculator use and oral administration of tests.
4. Inadequate access to remediation may be due to high costs of providing such resources.	• Few states offer or mandate remediation for students who are ELN and fail exit or promotion exams.
5. Over-reliance on a single test score can mean that students with disabilities are negatively affected.	• States frequently make decisions based on a single assessment event, such as the exit exam.

FIGURE 4.2 External Barriers That Impede Success on High-Stakes Assessments
Source: Information from Cortiella (2004).

altogether. If teachers and other school personnel are aware of these barriers, however, assessments and assessment settings can be designed to allow all students equal opportunity to demonstrate their learning. In Figure 4.3, those barriers are linked to characteristics of specific disabilities and exceptionalities.

USING UNIVERSAL DESIGN TO CONSTRUCT ASSESSABLE ASSESSMENT FOR ALL STUDENTS

In Chapter 7 you will learn about using Universal Design for Learning to design lesson plans and classroom activities with your specific students in mind can eliminate barriers to learning. The principles of UDL can be used to design and implement effective assessment in your classroom. Further states and districts are beginning to develop large-scale assessments using the principles of UDL. In this section we will illustrate how states and districts are using ULD and how teachers can follow their leads when designing assessments for their classroom students.

Johnstone, Altman, and Thurlow (2006) stated that "the goal of universally designed assessments is to provide the most valid assessment possible for the greatest number of students, including students with disabilities" (p. 2). To create accessible

Characteristic	Disability or Exceptionality	Barriers
Physical limitations	Students with sensory disabilities, traumatic brain injury, cerebral palsy, spinal cord injury, and other similar disabilities Students with other health impairments	1. Students may not be able to hold a writing instrument, see the test, hear directions or questions presented orally, or have either the physical or mental stamina required during long testing sessions.
Poor comprehension	Perception and processing difficulties (such as found in students with learning disabilities or sensory disabilities) Underdeveloped language skills (students who are deaf, English language learners, or who are at risk due to limited exposure to language)	2. Student may not clearly understand directions or questions that are presented orally and therefore may not follow directions correctly or adequately interpret questions. 3. Written directions and questions may be too lengthy or complicated and contain unfamiliar words and phrases. 4. Reading level may be above student's ability level. 5. Questions requiring inferences, evaluation, or deductive reasoning may not be understood.
Auditory perceptual	Students with LD involving auditory perception Students with ADHD: distractible type	1. Teachers may speak too quickly and may not clearly enunciate words and syllables. 2. Students must process the spoken words and translate to written answers, a task that can be impossible for some to accomplish. 3. Even reasonable background noise, both in and outside the classroom, can be a major hurdle for these students. 4. Some students may be unable to discriminate which sounds are from the teacher and which are irrelevant to the assessment task.
Visual perception	Students with LD involving visual perception	1. If assessment information is presented on chalkboards, smart boards, or overhead transparencies to be copied, some students may not be able to accurately copy. They may transpose numbers, letters, and even words and lose their place when moving from board to paper. 2. Noting answers on a separate answer sheet can be difficult and result in correct answers being placed in the wrong answer slot.

FIGURE 4.3 Barriers Related to Specific Characteristics of a Disability or Exceptionality That Students May Encounter During Assessments

Characteristic	Disability or Exceptionality	Barriers
		3. Visual distractions on the board or near the screen may clutter their field of vision and cause confusion.
		4. Illegible or unclear copies of test materials present a deciphering difficulty to these students.
		5. Formatting that is not consistent across all multiple choice questions or presents long lists of matching items may confuse and cause students to spend too much time trying to figure out the question rather than answering it.
		6. Lengthy tests of 2–3 pages can discourage students who read slowly or need time to process questions.
		7. Some students may experience difficulty interpreting symbols and abbreviations, such as found in advanced mathematics.
		8. Visual distractions, both in and outside the classroom, can interrupt the student's concentration, such as teacher movement around the room, a classmate going to the pencil sharpener, or movement in the hallway.
Time constraints	Any or all of the disabilities and exceptionalities noted above	These students will have difficulty completing assessment at the same rate as their general education peers.
Anxiety	Any or all of the disabilities and exceptionalities noted above	Based on their previous school experiences, these students may associate test taking with failure. As a result, they may be unable to function in a traditional test setting.

FIGURE 4.3 *(Continued)*

Source: Information from Rose & Dolan (2006); Salend (2001); Wood (2006).

assessments, all students must be taken into account at the beginning stages of construction. This is the same procedure used when designing universal lesson plans, bearing in mind the full range of student abilities, interests, and cultural differences from the beginning. The overall design principles suggested by the National Center on Educational Outcomes (NCEO) researchers (Johnstone, Altman, Thurlow, & Moore, 2006) are that universally designed assessments (UDA):

1. Do not change the standard of performance. They do not change the constructs of the assessment, water down the tasks, or make them easier for some students or groups of students.

2. Are not meant to replace accommodations. Users of UDA should assume that common accommodations will be needed by some students with disabilities, such as extended time, changes in formats that provide large print or Braille, scheduling differences that provide for breaks during testing, or alterative responses that allow the use of scribes or word processors. The general education test should be designed to allow for these common accommodations to fit into the plan (Johnstone, Altman, & Thurlow, 2006).

3. May benefit all students, including English language learners. This is especially important as teachers find themselves facing classrooms with increasing numbers of students who are second language learners. Salend (2001) noted that simply translating assessments into the student's native language does not remove the cultural bias that may exist and ultimately may create new problems associated with differences in language syntax and word meanings.

Additional research conducted at NCEO by Thompson and Thurlow (2002) revealed seven elements of universally designed assessments that should be present when assessments are initially constructed. In the section below, we will discuss how the elements can be used by teachers to construct universally designed classroom assessments and tests. As you read this section, consider how these elements meet the overall design principles mentioned above.

The Seven Elements

Thompson and Thurlow (2002) asserted that very few students need alternatives to standardized state and district assessments, but they believe there is "a much larger group of students who do need changes in the regular assessment" (p. 1). Thompson and Thurlow also assert that the need for accommodations can be reduced by using UDL, which includes the seven elements of design offered in Table 4.1. A more thorough discussion of these is offered below.

ACCESSIBLE, NONBIASED ITEMS   When teachers respect the diversity of their classrooms, they want to reduce bias to a minimum as they construct tests (Johnstone, Altman, & Thurlow, 2006; Johnstone, Altman, Thurlow, & Moore, 2006). As a first step, teachers should be aware of the characteristics of the learners in their classroom—aware of exceptional learning needs, cultural differences, or other subgroups so that they can recognize the bias of potential barriers within their assessments. See Figure 4.4 for an example of a chart for collecting important demographic information during the first few days of class. In addition, teachers can give students interest inventories, write autobiographies of learning needs, and, of course, assess perquisite skills and knowledge needed for specific content areas.

INCLUSIVE ASSESSMENT POPULATION   Assessments should be given to every student in the classroom—the full range, from the gifted to those with exceptional learning needs, especially if these students are expected to participate in the state and national assessments. Each assessment activity should be developed from the start with options to remove barriers to learning for the largest number of students, and all options should be available to all students. For example: Students with dyslexia, who are ELL, and

TABLE 4.1 Seven Elements of Universally Designed Assessments

Element	Explanation
Inclusive assessment population	Tests designed for state, district, or school accountability must include every student except those in the alternate assessment, and this is reflected in assessment design and field testing procedures.
Precisely defined constructs	The specific constructs tested must be clearly defined so that all construct irrelevant cognitive, sensory, emotional, and physical barriers can be removed.
Accessible, nonbiased items	Accessibility is built into items from the beginning, and bias-review procedures ensure that quality is retained in all items.
Amenable to accommodations	The test design facilitates the use of needed accommodations (e.g., all items can be Brailled).
Simple, clear, and intuitive instructions and procedures	All instructions and procedures are simple, clear, and presented in understandable language.
Maximum readability and comprehensibility	A variety of readability and plain-language guidelines are followed (e.g., sentence length and number of difficult words are kept to a minimum) to produce readable and comprehensible text.
Maximum legibility	Characteristics that ensure easy decipherability are applied to text and to tables, figures, illustrations, and response formats.

Source: Thompson & Thurlow (2002). Reprinted with permission.

those with below-grade-level reading levels will benefit from many of the same options, such as having an audio copy of the assessment and more time.

PRECISELY DEFINED CONSTRUCTS   Well-constructed tests measure exactly what they are intended to measure (Hogan, 2007; Popham, 2005); for example, math tests should measure ability to use math facts, theorems, formulas, problem-solving ability, and so forth but should not be assessments of reading ability. "A construct is the trait or characteristic" (Hogan 2007, p. 68) we wish to measure—that is, the knowledge and skills of the students we teach. We will discuss how teachers can assure their content constructs later in this chapter, but there are also "non-construct-oriented barriers, including cognitive, sensory, emotional, and physical barriers" (Thompson & Thurlow, 2002, p. 4). In fact, Johnstone (2003) cited research that demonstrated students' performance on math tests was as limited as their ability to read well. A universally designed test should remove these barriers. For example, a read-aloud or audio copy option might be offered for the math word problems. Johnstone (2003) reported that research studies conducted from 1993 through 2000 repeatedly found that students with poor reading skills scored higher on math tests when the questions were read to them. This would eliminate the non-construct barrier of reading skills from the assessment of math skills. In another situation, on a science test with fill-in-the-blank questions, teachers could offer difficult to spell vocabulary in a word bank to all students. This would eliminate the non-construct barrier of spelling ability from the construct of science knowledge.

ID#	Identifier	Gender	Race	Parent Status	SES/ Lunch Status	Reading Level	Math Level	Language, Exceptionality or Special Need	Other

FIGURE 4.4 Form for Student Demographic Information

There are two cautionary notes when considering how to accommodate for both teacher tests and standardized tests. First, accommodations that change the construct being assessed are considered as non-standard accommodations and are therefore controversial and are generally to be avoided by teachers and school districts (National Center for Learning Disabilities [NCLD], 2007). Use of nonstandard accommodations may cause the data to be disregarded in state and school reports of AYP. Second, while generally speaking all states note the importance of using accommodations in the classroom prior to using in an assessment situation, very few states mandate a specific time period; for example, Colorado and Wyoming mandate that accommodations must be used in the classroom for at least 90 days prior to use in the assessment setting (NCLD, 2007). Regardless of what your state mandates, remember that the student should be familiar and comfortable with any accommodations used during state and district tests. Thus teachers should know which accommodations are allowed by their states and districts and use those in their classroom assessments.

AMENABLE TO ACCOMMODATIONS Tests should be constructed so that additional accommodations can be added if they are needed by specific students. Even the best universally designed test cannot meet the needs of all students, and occasionally specific accommodations will be needed (Thompson & Thurlow, 2002). For example, a student who uses Braille to read and write will need options that include a Braille copy and a means to respond in Braille. This means that the need for this accommodation should be considered during the initial construction of the test—if there is a need to use a graphic, such as a map, chart, or photo, how will these be presented to the student who is not able to see them? The teacher might consider how the question could be asked without the map, chart, or photo or if the content could be assessed in a different way for a specific student. Additional suggestions include avoiding the use of vertical or diagonal text and removing items that distract, such as clip art, icons, and other decorative items (Johnstone, 2003). These are the ways that tests can be amenable to specific, individual accommodations.

SIMPLE, CLEAR, AND INTUITIVE INSTRUCTIONS AND PROCEDURES Clearly every assignment, including tests, should have directions, and these directions should be understandable by the persons who are taking the test. Seems a bit simplistic, but it is not. When teachers write tests, they know precisely what they want students to do, and much of that seems obvious to them. Ah, but the teacher's intentions are not always obvious to the student, especially to students with ELN. Have you ever participated in the popular class activity of writing out the directions to a peanut butter and jelly sandwich? Did you remember to start with getting the ingredients out of their storage places? Did you remember to say "open the jar of peanut butter"? In this author's experience, those are the two most frequently forgotten directions, but without doing both of those first steps, the task is not possible. Teachers can also forget the obvious direction. Therefore, check the directions before giving the test. Teachers can conduct a test run for instructions and procedures by giving a short sample test a day or two before the real test. Then ask students to tell you about any unclear directions, procedures, or questions. This can serve as both a test run for teachers and a review for the students. A possible side effect would be the relief of some test anxiety as students will see a sample of likely questions. One part of writing

TABLE 4.2 Plain-Language Editing Strategies

Strategy	Description
Reduce excessive length.	Reduce wordiness and remove irrelevant material.
Use common words.	Eliminate unusual or low-frequency words and replace with common words (e.g., replace *utilize* with *use*).
Avoid ambiguous words.	For example, *crane* should be avoided because it could be a bird or a piece of heavy machinery.
Avoid irregularly spelled words.	Examples of irregularly spelled words are *trough* and *feign*.
Avoid proper names.	Replace proper names with simple common names such as first names.
Avoid inconsistent naming and graphic conventions.	Avoid multiple names for the same concept. Be consistent in the use of typeface.
Avoid unclear signals about how to direct attention.	Well-designed heading and graphic arrangement can convey information about the relative importance of information and order in which it should be considered.
Mark all questions.	Give an obvious graphic signal (e.g., bullet, letter, number) to indicate separate questions.

Source: Thompson & Thurlow (2002). Reprinted with permission.

simple and clear directions can be accomplished if you are aware of maximum readability issues noted below.

MAXIMUM READABILITY AND COMPREHENSIBILITY   Table 4.2 provides an overview of plain-language editing strategies that will increase the readability and comprehensibility of tests. In addition to the strategies for making tests readable and comprehensible, Johnstone (2003) added five ways that teachers can improve their tests: (1) break compound complex sentences into several shorter sentences, placing the most important facts first; (2) sequence steps in directions in exact order of events; (3) introduce one idea, fact, or process at a time; (4) if some information is important to the statement, place that at the beginning of the sentence, (e.g., time and setting); and (5) make all noun–pronoun relationships very clear. Finally, teachers should use shorter sentences, fewer words per line, and sparingly use multisyllabic words to increase readability of their classroom assessments (Johnstone, 2003).

MAXIMUM LEGIBILITY   The physical appearance of text and the shapes of letters and numbers enable people to read text easily. That is legibility, and the most legible text can be read quickly with ease and understanding (Johnstone, 2003; Thompson & Thurlow, 2002). Table 4.3 provides an overview of the characteristics of legible text. If teachers can eliminate physical features that interfere with students focus or understanding of test questions or tasks, they can lower bias (Thompson & Thurlow, 2002).

Using the principles of Universal Design to construct tests is relatively new, since UDL has been discussed and used for less than 10 years. Early research in test development, however, resulted in guidelines that remove barriers that interfered with accurately measuring the content being tested, and while using these guidelines may not

TABLE 4.3 Characteristics of Legible Text

Dimension	Characteristics of Legible Text
Contrast (degree of separation of tones in print from the background paper)	• White or glossy paper should be avoided to reduce glare. Blue paper should not be used. • Black type on matte pastel or off-white paper is most favorable for both contrast and eye strain • Avoid gray scale and shading, particularly where pertinent information is provided.
Type Size (standard measuring unit for type size is the point)	• The point sizes most often used are 10 and 12 point for documents to be read by people with excellent vision reading in good light • Fourteen-point type increases readability and can increase test scores for both students with and without disabilities, compared to 12-point type. Large print for students with vision impairments is at least 18 point. • Type size for captions, footnotes, keys, and legends need to be at least 12 point also. • Larger type sizes are most effective for young students who are learning to read and for students with visual difficulties. Large print is beneficial for reducing eye fatigue. • The relationship between readability and point size is also dependent on the typeface used.
Spacing (the amount of space between each character)	• Letters that are too close together are difficult for partially sighted readers. Spacing needs to be wide between both letters and words. • Fixed-space fonts seem to be more legible for some readers than proportional-spaced fonts.
Leading (the amount of vertical space between lines of type)	• Insufficient leading makes type blurry and gives the text a muddy look. • Increased leading, or white space between lines of type, makes a document more readable for people with low vision. • Leading should be 25–30 percent of the point (font) size for maximum readability. • Leading alone does not make a difference in readability as much as the interaction between point size, leading and line length. • Suggestions for leading in relationship to type size: • 12-point type needs between 2 and 4 points of leading. • 14-point type needs between 3 and 6 points of leading. • 16-point type needs between 4 and 6 points of leading. • 18-point type needs between 5 and 6 points of leading.

increase student achievement, we have been able to determine that their use will give teachers a more accurate picture of student learning (Haladyna, 1999; McMillan, 2000; Popham, 2005). These guidelines can help teachers make more precise measurements of student learning by removing non-construct barriers, unclear or confusing language, and bias based on physical appearance.

However, even with the use of UDL, some students will need additional accommodations to succeed on both teacher-made tests and high-stakes assessments. We will discuss accommodations that can be built into tests and additional accommodations that can be offered to students with specific needs in the next section.

TABLE 4.3 (*Continued*)

Dimension	Characteristics of Legible Text
Typeface (characters, punctuation, and symbols that share a common design)	• Standard typeface, using upper and lower case, is more readable than italic, slanted, small caps, or all caps. • Avoid font styles that are decorative or cursive. Standard serif or sans serif fonts with easily recognizable characters are recommended. • Text printed completely in capital letters is less legible than text printed completely in lowercase, or normal mixed-case text. • Italic is far less legible and is read considerably more slowly than regular lower case. • Boldface is more visible than lowercase if a change from the norm is needed.
Justification (text is either flush with left or right margins—justified—or staggered/ ragged—unjustified)	• Staggered right margins are easier to see and scan than uniform or block-style right-justified margins. • Justified text is more difficult to read than unjustified text—especially for poor readers. • Justified text is also more disruptive for good readers. • A flush left/ragged right margin is the most effective format for text memory. • Unjustified text may be easier for poorer readers to understand because the uneven eye movements created in justified text can interrupt reading. • Justified lines require the distances between words to be varied. In very narrow columns, not only are there extra wide spaces between words, but also between letters within the words.
Line Length (length of the line of text; the distance between the left and right margin)	• Longer lines, in general, require larger type and more leadin. • Optimal length is 24 picas—about 4 inches. • Lines that are too long make readers weary and may also cause difficulty in locating the beginning of the next line, causing readers to lose their place. • Lines of text should be about 40–70 characters, or roughly eight to twelve words per line.
Blank Space (Space on a page that is not occupied by text or graphics)	• Use the term "blank space" rather than "white space" because the background is not always white. • Blank space anchors text on the paper. • Blank space around paragraphs and between columns of type helps increase legibility. • A general rule is to allow text to occupy only about half of a page. Too many test items per page can make items difficult to read.

Source: Thompson, Johnstone, & Thurlow (2002). Reprinted with permission.

SELECTING APPROPRIATE ACCOMMODATIONS FOR STUDENTS WHO NEED ADDITIONAL SUPPORT

When selecting accommodations for students to use in classroom activities and assessments, teachers should consider what students will be allowed to use on the state and national assessments as well. In some cases the accommodations allowed by school districts and local public schools may not match those allowed during the state and national assessments. It is imperative that teachers and school personnel be familiar with both types of accommodations and how to prepare students for all types of assessment situations.

Classroom Assessments

When administering either formative or summative classroom assessments, teachers may wish to allow the student whatever accommodations were permitted during the learning experience. This will provide a link between the learning and assessment and is especially important if the accommodation can be used on the state and national assessment. By allowing use during instruction, students with disabilities are able to practice and become proficient in using the accommodation (Thurlow, Elliott, & Ysseldyke, 2003) well before the assessment situation occurs. This eliminates the possibility that the accommodation can become a variable in the testing situation.

Upon occasion, local schools may allow assessment accommodations in classroom settings that would not ever be allowed during state and national assessments, such as retaking the test, reducing the number of answer choices, simplifying the language, providing prompts, and giving feedback. This can be problematic, as students and their families may come to expect these accommodations as the norm in other educational settings, such as higher education or during end of course and national assessments. If accommodations that are not allowed elsewhere are allowed during classroom assessments, students and their families must be informed in a clear, direct manner that such accommodations will not be allowed in all assessment situations. Table 4.4 provides a worksheet that teachers can use to interview students who need accommodations for both classroom and state assessments. Table 4.5 provides typical accommodations that can be provided for specific assessment needs.

Providing appropriate accommodations that remove barriers for students with expectation needs during any assessment situation is vital to their ability to demonstrate what they have learned. Equally important is that these students are not only prepared with academic knowledge and skills and have been given accommodations but also that they have the test-taking skills that will allow them to benefit from the accommodations and demonstrate what they have learned. In the next section we will discuss the ethics of teaching test-taking skills and the more appropriate ways to prepare students for the demands of the assessment instrument.

Teaching Strategies for Assessment

As the emphasis on accountability has risen, so has anxiety risen about student preparation for these high-stakes tests in teachers, students, parents, and school administrators. Popham (2005) noted that this anxiety has led to cheating on high-stakes tests, with unhappy results for all concerned. In this section we will discuss ways to prepare students for the testing situation.

Two guidelines provided by Popham (2005) will direct our discussion of teaching test-taking skills. The first is that "No test-preparation practice should violate the ethical norms of the educational profession" (Popham, 2005, p. 305). The second is that "No test-preparation should increase students' test scores without simultaneously increasing students' mastery of the assessment domain tested" (Popham, 2005, p. 307). Just as Popham suggested, we suggest that teachers provide students with generalized test-taking skills and practice in taking tests with varied formats. In addition, we stress that teaching students cognitive strategies for test-taking situations will provide much needed support for remembering content, formulating correct answers, and understanding the test formats. In the remainder of this section we will discuss those three test preparation methods.

TABLE 4.4 Worksheet for Selecting Appropriate Accommodations

Presentation Accommodations

Useful for students who:	Ask the student . . .	Accommodations to provide
Have print disabilities because they are not able to use standard print for learning	• Can you read and understand print directions? • Do you need directions repeated frequently? • Have you been identified as have a reading disability?	

Response Accommodations

Useful for students who:	Ask the student . . .	Accommodations to provide
Have physical, sensory or learning disabilities and have difficulty with memory, sequencings, directionality, alignment, and organization	• Can you use a pencil or other writing instrument? • Do you have a disability that affects your ability to spell? • Do you have trouble with tracking from one page to another and maintaining your place?	

Timing or Scheduling Accommodations

Useful for students who:	Ask the student . . .	Accommodations to provide
• Need more time • Cannot concentrate for extended periods • Have health-related disabilities • Fatigue easily • Need a special diet • Have other medical needs	• Can you work continuously during the entire time allocated for test administration? • Do you tire easily because of health impairments? • Do you need shorter working periods and frequent breaks?	

Setting accommodations

Useful for students who:	Ask the student . . .	Accommodations to provide
Are easily distracted in large group settings, or who concentrate best in small groups	• Are you easily distracted by others? • Do you have difficulty staying on task? • Do you have behaviors that would disrupt others?	

Source: Information from National Center for Learning Disabilities (n.d.-a).

Generalized test-taking skills are the skills necessary to prepare and study for tests. These include reading, understanding, and following written and oral directions; understanding the requirements of specific types of questions (e.g., multiple choices, matching, essay); marking answer sheets correctly; proofreading and correcting answers; managing time during the test; and controlling test anxiety. Each of these skills

TABLE 4.5 Accommodations for Specific Needs

Accommodation	Reasons	Examples
Change in assessment setting	Student may 1. Have difficulty in focusing 2. Need to use special equipment 3. Be unable to attend school 4. Need an assistant, scribe, or sign language interpreter	• Separate room • Study carrel • Special lighting • Adaptive furniture • Hospital or home setting • Computer equipment • Needs read-aloud of assessments directions and questions • Individual or small group administration
Changes in duration or organization of time	Student may 1. Need extra time due to special equipment 2. Lack stamina for long testing sessions 3. Have perceptual difficulties 4. Read slowly 5. Have difficulty in writing	• Extended time • Unlimited time • Take frequent breaks
Changes in scheduling	Student may 1. Take medication or need medical attention 2. Need to coordinate with side effects of medication 3. Lack stamina for long testing sessions 4. Be anxious or easily frustrated	• Take subtests in different order • Take over multiple days • Take test at a specific time of day
Changes in presentation	Student may 1. Have a physical or sensory disability 2. Have perceptual difficulties 3. Need assistive devices 4. Have difficulties with directions 5. Have underdeveloped language skills (e.g., deaf, ELL)	• Have directions repeated • Modified answer sheet with larger bubbles • Use large print, Braille, or read-aloud • Audio/video cassettes or CDs • Use a magnification device • Use a non-English language interpreter • Use a sign language interpreter
Changes in response mode	Student may 1. Have a physical or sensory disability 2. Have perceptual difficulties 3. Need assistive devices 4. Have difficulties with directions 5. Have underdeveloped language skills (e.g., deaf, ELL)	• May mark in test booklet • Use a scribe • Use a word processor • Use reference materials (e.g., dictionary or spell checker)

Sources: Information from Salend (2001); Thurlow (2002); Wood (2006).

can be taught within the general curriculum that is taught daily in any classroom, as illustrated in detail below.

General study skills are one of the most important skills we can teach, but we often do not teach them. As will be discussed in Chapter 6, on metacognitive strategies, teachers often make assumptions about what study skills and strategies students have learned in previous years or courses and do not realize that some of those skills are not generalized across years and courses without prompting. Listed below are ways to encourage students to use appropriate study skills.

- At the beginning of the school year, provide partially completed note-taking guides for textbook reading and lectures. As the year progresses, fade out the amount of support you give in each note-taking guide until you feel the students are ready to take notes on their own.
- Teach students how to use prompts found in their textbooks that point to important information. This would include organizational items such as headings, bold or italicized and *cue* words, charts, tables, and illustrations, and chapter summaries. Encourage students to read end-of-chapter questions prior to reading the chapter content. Prompt them to use those questions as note-taking guides.
- Support the use of graphic organizers or concept maps by providing those, when appropriate, for note-taking, answering essay questions, and organizing content to be learned. As the year progresses, fade out the provision of these devices, but require students to create their own.
- Help students organize study groups or peer partners and support those groups with class time to meet. As with other strategies mentioned above, gradually fade out your support and class time given to these groups, but continue to prompt students to meet outside of class prior to assessments.
- Teach metacognitive strategies, such as problem-solving strategies and mnemonic devices for learning and organizing information. Memory devices such as chunking and visual or keyword pictures are helpful for remembering information. Specific test-taking strategies will be discussed later in this section and in Chapter 6, where metacognitive strategies are discussed in detail. Prompt students to use those when appropriate, teach them to prompt each other in their study groups, and review or add strategies as the need arises.
- Provide as much constructive feedback about their use of the above strategies as possible. Make a point to giving credit to their use of these items when they do well on assessments. As the year progresses, ask the students to explain what helped them do well on assignments and assessments. Hopefully they will begin to attribute their success to proper use of the study skills you have taught them. If not, prompt them to do so until they are doing that independently.

General test-taking strategies that would apply to all types of questions can be taught or reviewed each time you give an assessment in class. One issue that often affects all students, but especially those with exceptional needs, is time. During the course of the school year, give timed tests so that students can become accustomed to managing their time. When you give timed tests, teach, prompt, and review these strategies.

- Teach students to note how many questions are on the test and how much time they can allot to each question. For example, if you give a test that has 30 multiple choice questions and two short answer essays and it must be completed in 45 minutes, help the students determine how much time to give to the multiple choice and how much to the essays.

- Prompt them to skip questions that are too difficult or are consuming too much time and then return to those after they have completed all questions in the section.
- Prompt them to use any cognitive strategies that they have learned; this is especially important for those students who have a strategy to calm test anxiety. These will be discussed later in this section.

Mastering test directions can be taught and then reviewed any time an assessment is given in the classroom. First, teach the vocabulary to students prior to the first assessment given in your classroom. For example, tell the students what is expected when terms such as *discuss, explain, describe, compare and contrast*, and *justify* appear in test directions. Use these words throughout the school year on your teacher-made assessments and homework assignments. Provide specific feedback with examples if students are not meeting those expectations.

Mastering test formats can be tricky for students who are not able to adjust to change quickly, but it is not ethically responsible to offer all classroom and practice tests in the same format as the high-stakes tests; rather, make sure that your students are familiar with all possible formats that they may encounter on assessments.

- During the school year offer questions in a variety of formats—multiple choice, matching, true/false, sentence completion, and essay—on each assessment given in your classroom.
- Offer these questions in a variety of page formats—single column and double column, but be sure to offer more than the one used by the high-stakes assessment. After all, the goal is to help students learn to generalize, not to teach them to be successful on a single assessment.
- Teach students how to answer these questions by giving homework or in-class work that uses a variety of questioning formats.

Taking multiple choice tests can be particularly difficult for some students. Salend (2001) suggested these strategies be taught to students:

- Demonstrate and prompt students to read the question and think of the correct answer before reading the choices.
- Explain that if choices contradict each other, most likely one of them is correct. If choices are very similar, they are most likely incorrect answers. Choices that seem absurd, contain irrelevant information, or are obviously false are incorrect.
- Teach them to look for clues in the stem, such as subject, verb, tense, and modifiers such as *a* or *an*. Check for any other clues in the stem to help select the correct answer.
- Give them practice with multiple choice questions by including some on each of your class assessments.

Using separate answer sheets can pose difficulties for all students because the possibility of getting off track if the student skips a question exists for all, but especially for students who have visual acuity and visual processing problems.

- Show students how to use a ruler or sheet of scrap paper to keep their place on the answer sheet.

- Use Scantron answer sheets or teacher-made bubble sheets regularly during your classroom tests so that students have practice with them prior to the high-stakes assessment.

Cognitive strategies that are research-based and developed specifically for test-taking situations are helpful to all students, but again offer the support during testing situations needed by many students with exceptional and diverse needs. Cognitive strategies can be useful both for remembering the content being assessed and taking specific types of tests, such as objective versus essay questions (see Table 4.6 for examples). Learning and using strategies for test taking should not be substituted for studying and learning the content, but teaching students strategies that help them remember what they have learned is particularly helpful to students with long- and short-term memory deficits.

TABLE 4.6 Examples of Test-Taking Strategies

Study	Memory	Test-Taking
Develop a study plan and schedule study sessions. There are a number of planners to print on the Learning Toolbox.	**Key Word:** designed to increase recall of vocabulary words. Selecting the key words in reading and lectures will help you by helping you remember the big ideas in your reading.	**BRAVE:** to overcome test anxiety. **B**reathe deeply. **R**elax. **A**ttitude is everything. **V**isualize yourself in your favorite place. **E**nd is in sight.
CON-AIR is designed to help students study from texts and other printed materials. **C**opy chapter headings and subheadings. **O**rganize note cards. **N**umber the cards under categories. **A**rrange the note cards in columns. **I**dentify each card's correct place. **R**eview the note cards.	**BREAK:** to help memory of information **B**reak memorizing into short periods. **R**ecite information aloud. **E**stablish mnemonics. **A**lways try to picture information in your mind. **K**ey words help.	**CRAM** and/or **PIRARTES** can help pick the right answer on objective questions. **C**over the answers. **R**ead the question carefully. **A**nswer the question without looking at the answers. **M**atch your answer to one of the given choices.
WORRY: to organize information from books and notes **W**ork with note cards from both reading and lecture notes. **O**utline main ideas covered in both reading and lecture. **R**ead note cards from reading for facts. **R**ead lecture notes for facts. **Y**es, you're ready after one more reading of your outline.	**Pegword:** useful for remembering lists of information in a specific order	**FLEAS** is useful for staying on task and getting done in the allotted time. **F**irst read the directions. **L**ook over the test. **E**asiest questions answered first. **A**nswer the questions that are worth more. **S**kip a question.

Sources: Information from Deshler, Ellis, & Lenz (1996); Minskoff, Allsopp, Minskoff, & Kyger (n.d.).

Summary

In this chapter, we have discussed why students with disabilities are included by law in high-stakes assessments. We have outlined the six additional purposes of assessment and how data from these can help teachers in their daily work of teaching. However, many students with exceptional needs face barriers to successful completion of both high-stakes and classroom assessments. Therefore, we discussed the use of UDL to construct assessable assessments for all students and thereby reduce the need for accommodations. Nevertheless, some students may still need accommodations, and we offered methods for determining and selecting appropriate accommodations. Finally, we suggested ways to support students by teaching them test-taking skills.

References

Airasian, P. W. (2005). *Classroom assessment: Concepts and applications* (5th ed.). New York: McGraw-Hill.

Cortiella, C. (2004). *Implications of high-stakes testing for students with learning disabilities.* Retrieved September 8, 2009, from http://www.greatschools.net/LD/school-learning/high-stakes-testing-learning-disabilities.gs?content = 886

Deshler, D. D., Ellis, E. S., & Lenz, B. K. (1996). *Teaching adolescents with learning disabilities: Strategies and methods.* Denver: Love Publishing.

Fuchs, L. S., & Fuchs, D. (2007). A model for implementing responsiveness to intervention. *Teaching Exceptional Children, 39*(5), 14–20.

Gagnon, G. W., & Collay, M. (2001). *Designing for learning: Six elements in constructivist classroom.* Thousand Oaks, CA: Corwin Press.

Haladyna, T. M. (1999). *Developing and validating multiple-choice test items* (2nd ed.). Mahwah, NJ: Lawrence Erlbaum Associates.

Hogan, T. P. (2007). *Educational assessment: A practical introduction.* Hoboken, NJ: Wiley and Jossey-Bass.

Hosp. J. L., & Reschly, D. J. (2003). Referral rates for intervention or assessment: A meta-analysis of racial differences. *The Journal of Special Education, 37,* 67–80.

Johnstone, C., Altman, J., Thurlow, M., & Moore, M. (2006). *Universal Design online manual.* Minneapolis: University of Minnesota, National Center on Educational Outcomes.

Johnstone, C. J. (2003). *Improving validity of large-scale tests: Universal Design and student performance* (Technical Report 37). Minneapolis: University of Minnesota, National Center on Educational Outcomes. Retrieved June 30, 2007, from http://education.umn.edu/NCEO/OnlinePubs/Technical37.htm

Johnstone, C. J., Altman, J., & Thurlow, M. (2006). *A state guide to the development of universally designed assessments.* Minneapolis: University of Minnesota, National Center on Educational Outcomes.

Kame'enui, E. J. (2007). A new paradigm: Response to Interventions. *Teaching Exceptional Children, 39*(5), 6–7.

McMillan, J. H. (2000). *Essential assessment concepts for teachers and administrators.* Thousand Oaks, CA: Corwin Press.

Minskoff, E., Allsopp, D., Minskoff, J., & Kyger, M. (n.d.). *The learning toolbox.* Web site hosted by James Madison University. Retrieved on April 21, 2008, from http://coe.jmu.edu/learningToolbox/index.html

National Center for Learning Disabilities. (n.d.-a). *No Child Left Behind: Determining appropriate assessment accommodations for students with disabilities: A parent advocacy brief from National Center for Learning Disabilities.* New York: Author. Retrieved on August 10, 2007, from http://www.ncld.org/images/stories/downloads/advocacy/accommodations.pdf

National Center for Learning Disabilities. (n.d.-b). *What is RTI?* New York: Author. Retrieved on December 26, 2008, from http://www.rtinetwork.org/Learn/What/ar/WhatIsRTIhttp://www.rtinetwork.org/Learn/What/ar/WhatIsRTI

National Center for Learning Disabilities. (2007). *State testing accommodations: A look at their value and validity.* New York: Author.

Popham, W. J. (2005). *Classroom assessment: What teachers really need to know* (4th ed.). Boston: Allyn & Bacon.

Rose, D. H., & Dolan, R. P. (2006). *Implications of Universal Design for classroom assessment*. In D. H. Rose & A. Meyer (Eds.), *A practical reader in Universal Design for Learning*. Cambridge, MA: Harvard Educational Press.

Salend, S. J. (2001). *Creating inclusive classrooms: Effective and reflective practices* (4th ed.). Upper Saddle River, NJ: Merrill/Pearson Education.

Smith, T. E. C., Dowdy, C. A., Polloway, E. A., & Blalock, G. E. (1997). *Children and adults with learning disabilities*. Boston: Allyn & Bacon.

Sugai, G. (n.d.). *School-wide positive behavior support and Response to Intervention*. New York: National Center on Learning Disabilities. Retrieved on December 15, 2008, from http://www.rtinetwork.org/Learn/Behavior/ar/Schoolwide Behavior

Thompson, S., & Thurlow, M. (2002). *Universally designed assessments: Better tests for everyone!* (Policy Directions No. 14). Minneapolis: University of Minnesota, National Center on Educational Outcomes. Retrieved June 7, 2007, from http://education.umn.edu/NCEO/OnlinePubs/Policy14.htm

Thompson, S. J., Johnstone, C. J., & Thurlow, M. L. (2002). *Universal Design applied to large scale assessments* (Synthesis Report 44). Minneapolis: University of Minnesota, National Center on Educational Outcomes. Retrieved June 26, 2007, from http://education.umn.edu/NCEO/OnlinePubs/Synthesis44.html

Thurlow, M. (2002). *Issue brief: Accommodations for student with disabilities in high school*. National Center on Secondary Education and Transition, *1*(1). Retrieved on July 14, 2007, from http://www.ncset.org/publications/viewdesc.asp?id=247

Thurlow, M. L., Elliott, J. L., & Ysseldyke, J. E. (2003). *Testing students with disabilities: Practical strategies for complying with district and state requirements* (2nd ed.). Thousand Oaks, CA: Corwin Press.

U.S. Government Accountability Office. (2005). *Most students with disabilities participated in statewide assessments, but inclusion options could be improved*. Report to the ranking minority member, Committee on Health, Education, Labor, and Pension, U.S. Senate. Washington, DC: Author. Retrieved on June 7, 2007, from http://www.gao.gov/new.items/d05618.pdf

Wood, J. W. (2006). *Teaching students in inclusive settings: Adapting and accommodating instruction* (5th ed.). Upper Saddle River, NJ: Merrill/Pearson Education.

Chapter 7

Designing Instruction to Meet the Needs of All Learners: Universal Design for Learning

After reading this chapter, you will be able to:

1. Define Universal Design for Learning (UDL)
2. Discuss the reasoning behind using UDL to provide equal access to instruction
3. Explain the principles of UDL
4. Detect barriers to student learning with the LEARNS strategy
5. Apply the principles of UDL to remove barriers to learning through the use of the LEARNS strategy

INTRODUCTION

"Individuals with disabilities now have the right to a free appropriate public school education, and can expect to find educational buildings that are physically accessible to them. It remains a tragedy, however, that the curricula—the materials and methods for learning inside those building—are frequently NOT available or accessible to children with disabilities." (Rose, 2001a)

The regulations found in laws and acts of Congress (IDEIA-04, NCLB, ADA, and Assistive Technology Act; see Table 7.1) compel educators and school personnel to provide students with disabilities access to the general education curriculum whenever appropriate. To meet the requirements of the new regulations found in IDEIA-04 and NCLB, general educators and related service personnel need to employ practices that will support all students, support all students' efforts to meet state standards, and help all students pass grade-level assessments and exit exams. However, with fixed, uniform learning materials, teachers are left with the burden of individualizing instruction by providing supplementary adaptations or accommodations for student with special learning needs. Unfortunately, few teachers have either the time or expertise to adequately adapt the curriculum materials to meet the diverse needs of their students (Pisha & Stahl, 2003). Because teachers do not have time, expertise, or resources, students are not receiving the appropriate educational experience they deserves and are entitled to by law. For example, McGuire, Scott, and Shaw (2006) cited a number of studies and reports that decry the fate of many students with disabilities in our public schools. Comments quoted in their article include concerns that (a) special education is broken; (b) there is a need to prevent and forestall educational problems; (c) large numbers of students experience low academic performance, high dropout rates, and poor postschool outcomes; and (d) many general educators do not have the proper attitudes, accommodations, and adaptations in place to educate students with disabilities (p. 166).

To meet the goals of IDEIA-04 and NCLB, the general curriculum must be accessible to all students, and educators must use research-based practices that will achieve results for students who have disabilities. An accessible curriculum can be developed using the principles of Universal Design for Learning (UDL) from the onset. As teachers, we should be aware of UDL as an idea that is gaining acceptance in the educational community. The principles of a UDL curriculum were developed to meet the needs of the full range of students who are actually in our schools, students with a wide range of sensory, motor, cognitive, linguistic, and affective abilities and disabilities rather than a narrow range of students in the middle (Hitchcock & Stahl, 2003). Other groups with exceptional needs that are found in typical classrooms are students who are English language learners (ELL), at risk for school failure, and gifted or talented. In addition, special education classrooms are just as diverse as general education classrooms, and as special education teachers we are compelled to meet the needs of our students who have exceptional needs that are related to their diversity as well as the needs brought about by their disability. Universal Design in education allows educator to prepare, in advance, for these very different needs and, to the extent feasible, design and deliver instruction so as to meet those needs. The information in this chapter offers a way to plan and teach that will accomplish those goals.

As you begin this chapter about UDL, an example from architecture may be helpful in anticipation of the information to follow. Buildings built before the Americans

TABLE 7.1 Review the Laws: IDEA-04, NCLB, ADA, & AT ACT

Access to the General Education Curriculum

The Law	Law's Regulations	Reference Within the Law	Implications
IDEA-04	Adds that students with IEPs should have • Teachers who have high expectations • Ensured access to general education curriculum in the regular classroom	20 U.S.C. § 1400(c)(5)(A)	• General and special educators must take equal responsibility for supporting student's work within the general education curriculum and general education classrooms.
	• Established the National Instructional Materials Accessibility Standard (NIMAS)	20 U.S.C. § 1474(e)(2)	• Increases the ability for educators & students to access digital materials
	• Established a standard for preparing electronic files	*Id.* at § 1474(e)(3)(B)	• Preparation and distribution of digitized materials is standardized, making access possible regardless of the software or computer (PC vs. Mac) selected by a school.
	• Established a process for preparation, delivery, and purchase of digitized instruction materials	*Id.* at §§ 1412(a)(23), 1413(a)(6)	
	• Universal design—The term "Universal Design" has the meaning given the term in section 3 of the Assistive Technology Act of 1998 (29 U.S.C. 3002).	§ 602(35)	• Schools should consider the use of UDL and technology as a means to provide access to the general education curriculum.
	• To support the use of technology, including technology with Universal Design principles and assistive technology devices, to maximize accessibility to the general education curriculum for children with disabilities.	§ 611 (e)(2)(C)(v)	
	• Universal Design—The state educational agency (or, in the case of a districtwide assessment, the local educational agency) shall, to the extent feasible, use Universal Design principles in developing and administering any assessments under this paragraph.	§ 612(a)(16)(E)	

(Continued)

TABLE 7.1 Review the Laws: IDEA-04, NCLB, ADA, & AT ACT (*Continued*)

Access to the General Education Curriculum

The Law	Law's Regulations	Reference Within the Law	Implications
NCLB	• Purpose of the act is to ensure that all children have access to high quality and accessible curriculum and reach proficiency on challenging state standards.		• Schools must include students with disabilities as part of the ALL in NCLB. • Both NCLB and IDEIA-04 share requirements for raising expectations for students with disabilities.
ADA-1990	• Public schools must provide fully accessible buildings and classrooms.	Title II	• Schools must provide all students (and visitors, such as parents) equal access to classrooms within a school. • Classrooms should be built or retrofitted to allow students with disabilities full participation in that classroom.
ATA-2004	• Option A: Use 60 percent of assistive technology funds on direct aid programs, including AT reutilization, demonstration programs, alternative financing, and device loan programs. • Option B: Use 70 percent of grant funds on direct aid programs, but states are given full discretion on how to allocate funds for at least two, but up to four, of the programs listed in option A.		• Educators and students have access to Assistive Technology Projects in all 50 states. • Educators and related services providers can attend conferences and professional development opportunities provided by their state's AT project. • Students and their teachers/caregivers can borrow AT for evaluation purposes prior to purchase. • Schools in some states may be eligible for grant funds to purchase AT.

Involvement in the General Education Curriculum

The Law	Law's Regulations	Reference Within the Law	Implications
IDEA-04	IEP must contain a statement of • How the student's disability affects the child's involvement and progress in the general education curriculum	20 U.S.C. § 1414(d)(1)(A)(i)(I), (II), (IV)	• The first provision: Understanding the effects of a student's disability is a first step to designing an appropriate educational program and general education

TABLE 7.1 *(Continued)*

Involvement in the General Education Curriculum

The Law	Law's Regulations	Reference Within the Law	Implications
	• Measurable annual goals that enable the student to be involved in and make progress in the general education curriculum • The program modifications or support for school personnel that will be provided for the student to be involved in and make progress in the general education curriculum		classrooms. Also includes a statement about functional performance that acknowledges that functional performance is a critical element to be measured (Karger, 2005). • The second provision: Student progress must be a part of the discussion, which implies that the student should be making progress. Again, functional goals are extended into the general education classroom, recognizing their importance for some students with disabilities (Karger, 2005). • The third provision: stresses that access must include appropriate supports and can guide teachers to consider how they can adapt instruction to enable student participation in the general education curriculum (Karger, 2005).
	The IEP team must include • The extent to which a student will not participate with nondisabled peers in the regular class	20 U.S.C. § 141(d)(1)(A)(i)(V)	• These three provisions, while not requiring that all students with IEPs be placed in the general education classroom, increased the obligation for schools to consider such placement and must *justify* not selecting that placement (emphasis added).
	• At least one regular education teacher of the student and one special education teacher of the student	*Id.* § 141(d)(1)(B)(ii)–(iii)	
	In addition, a student cannot be removed from the general education class simply because modification(s) to the general education curriculum is required.	34 C.F.R. § 300.552(e)	• Further, the second provision clearly indicates that the teacher must be the student's regular education teacher.

(Continued)

TABLE 7.1 Review the Laws: IDEA-04, NCLB, ADA, & AT ACT (*Continued*)

Progress in the General Education Curriculum

The Law	Law's Regulations	Reference Within the Law	Implications
IDEA-04	The IEP must • Include descriptions of how student's progress in meeting annual goals will be measured & when periodic reports will be given	20 U.S.C. § 1414(d)(1)(A)(i)(III)	• IEP teams will need to agree on assessment methods to use, how often goals should be assessed, and how often to report results. • IEP teams will need to be accepting of change and flexible in choices of teaching methods, accommodations, or modification if student progress is not evident. • This provision requires that students receive effective instruction in the content and held to high expectations for successful learning. • Appropriate assessments are most effective when used during instruction.
	• Be review periodically, but at least once annually; during the review, revisions must be made to address lack of expected progress, when appropriate All students with disabilities must be	*Id.* § 1414(d)(4)(A)(i), (i)(I)	
	• Included in all state & district assessment programs, including NCLB assessments	20 U.S.C. § 1412(a)(16)(A)	
	• Given appropriate accommodations & alternative assessments, as necessary & prescribed in IEPs		
	If the student does not participate in above described assessment, the IEP must contain an explanation of why the student cannot participate & why the alternative assessment is more appropriate	*Id.* § 141(d)(1)(A)(i)(VI)	

Sources: Individuals with Disabilities Education Improvement Act of 2004. Retrieved on August 8, 2006, from (2005); Simpson, LaCava, & Graner (2004).

with Disabilities Act (ADA) had to be retrofitted to meet this law that requires all public buildings be accessible for persons with limited mobility and other physical limitations. The universal designs used to make spaces accessible included adding curb cuts for sidewalks and ramps for wheelchair users, elevators in buildings built before elevators existed, doors that can be opened by persons with limited physical stamina, and Braille labels on doors and elevators. However, many of these retrofits are architecturally unattractive and may not be fully useful to users. For example, historical and other older buildings often cannot be retrofitted to allow users to enter via the front door, and instead users might be required to enter through an alleyway or at the rear of the building. This hardly provides a warm or welcoming entrance. Other buildings have had to build ramps that interrupt the beautiful facades of the buildings and sometimes are not easily navigated due to steep slopes. Compare these retrofits to the accommodations made in buildings constructed since ADA, where access is considered in the original design of the building and needs of persons with limited mobility and strength are built into and blend with the design. After ADA was passed, architects struggled with the retrofits because they were costly in both expense and construction time—for example, finding space to add the accessible stall within the confines of an already constructed public restroom. On the other hand, architects had few problems making those accommodations in new construction. In fact, they are so seamless that most of us rarely even notice them. When was the last time you actually paid attention to the fact that a door opened automatically for you, or that you could Rollerblade down a curb cut to cross the street, or that you took advantage of the extra room in an airport restroom's accessible stall because you were pulling a carry-on bag. Thinking about UDL in construction of buildings leads us to draw two conclusions, which are presented in the UDL literature.

First, designing instructions that include accommodations is easier than retrofitting them into existing lesson plans and less costly in teacher time and effort. Second, many, if not most, accommodations benefit all students just as curb cuts benefit all walkers, moms with baby strollers, bicycle riders, and so on. To that end, we will explore the principles of UDL, benefits of using this thinking when designing learning experiences, and a strategy for applying UDL principles when planning instruction. In the next section we will define UDL, outline its history, and explain the principles of UDL established by CAST.

DEFINITION OF UDL

To begin, think about these two statements by Bowe, who is deaf, that define what he considers a disability to be:

> "Disability is something you experience, not something you are." (Bowe, 2000, p. 10)
> "Disability is an interaction between a person and an environment." (Bowe, 2000)

As you read the following two definitions of UDL, reflect about how the use of UDL would enhance the experience and interactions of persons with disabilities.

> In terms of learning, universal design means the design of instructional materials and activities that *make the learning goals achievable by individuals with wide differences in their abilities to see, hear, speak, move, read, write, understand English, attend, organize, engage, and remember.* Universal design for learning is achieved by means of *flexible curricular materials and activities* that provide alternatives for students with differing abilities. These *alternatives are built into the instructional design and operating systems of educational materials; they are not added on after-the-fact.* (emphasis added: Council for Exceptional Children, 1999)

Here is the second definition: UDL is "the design of products and environments to be usable by all people, to the greatest extent possible, without the need for adaptation or specialized design" (Mace,1997).

AN OVERVIEW AND BRIEF HISTORY OF UDL

Rose and Meyer founded the Center for Applied Special Technology (CAST) in the early 1990s. They began to apply the concepts they knew from the architectural concepts of Universal Design and coined the term Universal Design for Learning (UDL). The CAST researchers developed electronic books and templates for eBooks with built-in features to make the books accessible to young readers with disabilities. These first efforts at creating books were published by Don Johnston Developmental Equipment (e.g., Gateway Stories and Gateway Authoring System). Eventually those prototypes evolved into the Wiggleworks literacy program, which was published in collaboration with Scholastic. This early intervention literacy program has been marketed successfully for all young children, but it contains many built features that make the program accessible to students with sensory, physical, and learning disabilities. As teachers used these early UDL materials, they noted that students without disabilities enjoyed using the electronic texts (Rose & Meyer, 2000). As the CAST researchers continued their work they saw similarities between Universal Design for access to physical spaces and their work on making instructional materials more accessible for learners. Thus they began further development of the ideas behind Universal Design for Learning.

While UDL is grounded in the principles of Universal Design in architecture, it is also supported by recent research that has allowed researchers to detect activity in human brains (Hitchcock, Meyer, Rose, & Jackson, 2002). A key idea that formed the foundation of UDL (Rose & Meyer, 2002) is that human learning is distributed across three interconnected networks in the brain: recognition, strategic, and affective networks.

Using fMRI/PET (functional magnetic resonance imaging/positron-emission tomography) scans, scientists are able to view patterns of glucose burning as these patterns light up during activities of reading such as looking at words, listening to others read, or reading aloud. During these scans, researchers found that the brain has separate parts or modules that can be rearranged, replaced, or interchanged easily as the brain processes information. Rose described the specialized processors as operating "like a well functioning ad-hoc committee" (Hitchcock, Rose, & Danielson, 2000, p. 1). During these glucose burns, activity patterns are seen distributed throughout the brain as tasks vary. Activity occurs in both hemispheres as well as the front, middle, and rear sections of the brain. Researchers noted that after a number of trials with a new task the level of the glucose burn is reduced, and if a familiar task is repeated with new information, there are lower levels of glucose burn than seen when executing a new task. Researchers discovered differences in the glucose within each subject. Hitchcock and colleagues (2000) concluded that when teachers teach isolated facts and figures they may be making learning more difficult or even compromising learning because within individual brains the functioning can vary significantly. This may explain why teachers find variances in how students with similar achievement levels learn, or why some students may do well on one learning task but not in another. Finally and perhaps most important, researchers also noticed that these glucose burns appeared to be a series of networks that attended to different tasks. Each of these networks—recognition, strategic, and affective—performs its task parallel to the others, and while they are interconnected, each is a specialized network.

The recognition networks "are specialized to sense and assign meaning to patterns we see; they enable us to identify and understand information, ideas and concepts"

(Rose & Meyer, 2002, p. 12). Recognition networks help students recognize the information to be learned. The strategic networks "are specialized to generate and oversee mental and motor patterns" thus enabling students "to plan, execute and monitor actions and skills" (Rose & Meyer, 2002, p. 12). Strategic networks allow students to apply strategies to process information. The affective networks "are specialized to evaluate patterns and assign them emotions significance; they enable us to engage with tasks and learning and with the world around us" (Rose & Meyer, 2002, p. 13). Affective networks allow students to fully engage with the learning task.

During the glucose burns discussed above, parallel processing is occurring as the brain attempts to recognize an image. As Hitchcock and colleagues (2000) explained, the brain is looking for context and content. To accomplish that, the back of our brains attempts to *recognize* the images while the front brain is determining a *strategy* for investigating. At the same time, our *affective* system is determining if this image is important to us.

Taking what they learned from their brain research one step further, Rose and Meyer determined that these three networks parallel Vygotsky's three prerequisites of learning. Vygotsky's (1978) theory states that there are three prerequisites for learning to take place. Students must be able to recognize the information to be learned, apply strategies to process information, and engage fully with the task presented. Data from the brain research reported by CAST suggest that the networks allow students to accomplish Vygotsky's prerequisites as the recognition network recognizes the information to be learned, the strategic network processes the information, and the affective network engages the students interest in the task. In the next section, we will explore how the brain research translates to using UDL in our teaching practices.

Assumptions Must Shift

UDL shifts our assumptions about teaching and learning in four fundamental ways:

1. Students with disabilities are not a separate category of learners; instead they are one of a continuum of learners, all with differences. We should not focus *only* on categorical differences, such as disabilities/nondisabled, ELL/English speakers, or at risk/gifted. When we have a limited focus we may miss many differences between learners within the categories and likewise miss similarities across categories of learners (Rose & Meyer, 2000).

2. The student is not seen as the one who must change, but rather the focus shifts from remediation or fixing students to creating a flexible curriculum with options embedded within the curriculum that accommodates learner differences. Originally our curriculum was designed to assimilate and acculturate a variety of immigrants who came to the United States into one culture with little regard for those who were not Anglo-Saxon Christians (e.g., slaves from Africa and China or Native Americans), but as our population has changed and we have invited many cultures and religions into our communities and schools, we have not changed the way we teach. We still use the printed and spoken word as the primary ways of delivering instruction and assessing learning. UDL asks us to reconsider this approach to take into account the variety of learners we teach. The UDL approach is similar to but not quite the same as a teaching approach known as *differentiating instruction*, because that approach is centered

mostly on a learning style philosophy and does not generally take learners with disabilities or the entire learning environment into account (Hitchcock & Stahl, 2003).

3. Curriculum materials should be varied and diverse, including digital and online resources, rather than centering on a single textbook or solely on print materials. We should consider the wide variety of options available to us, such as audio books, including online talking dictionaries, podcasts, video, interactive Internet sites, and so forth.

4. Teacher adjustments for learner differences should occur for all students, not just those with disabilities. Just as you and I take advantage of automated doors, curb cuts, and moving walkways, all students should be offered options for how they take in and express learning experiences.

The *central practical premise* of UDL is that a curriculum should include alternatives to make it accessible and appropriate for individuals with different backgrounds, learning preferences, abilities, and disabilities in widely varied learning contexts (see Figure 7.1). However, the *universal* in Universal Design does *not* imply *one* optimal solution for everyone, but rather it reflects an awareness of the unique nature of each learner and the need to accommodate differences, creating learning experiences that suit the learner and maximize his or her ability to progress (Rose & Meyer, 2000). Further, UDL does not imply that there is one medium for instruction but that *universal* implies multiple teaching methods and types of media (Rose & Meyer, 2000). UDL curriculums are not available for purchase because UDL is not a single method or program (see Figure 7.2) but is a way of thinking and acting when teachers plan and implement instruction (Hitchcock & Stahl, 2003).

As we discussed in Chapter 1, some teachers in both general and special education have had a deficit view of students with exceptional needs: They have seen what is "wrong" with the student or that the students with exceptional needs are the problem and then attempt to fix the "wrong" part of the student. Certainly it is important for educators to be able to recognize that a student has a disability or any other specific need—without that knowledge we would not understand what to do to eliminate the barriers found in the interaction of the student with the curriculum. Too often in the past, though, teachers have used accommodations and modifications that we have come to understand lower standards and water down the curriculum that every student should learn. Ellis (1997) suggested that accommodations and modifications that require less work (such as fewer spelling words), basing grades on effort rather than actual achievement, providing high-interest/low-vocabulary materials, or providing special content classes outside the general education classroom may seem like logical practices, but they actually limit achievement of students with disabilities. Rather than looking at the students as having the problem, teachers who use UDL look for the barriers to learning that exist in classrooms, teaching materials, and teaching methods. When these barriers are removed, learning becomes possible for a wider audience of students and lessens the need for many of the individual accommodations generally provided (Rose & Meyer, 2002). Furthermore, principles of UDL provide a framework for general and special educators as they collaborate to plan and teach in order to meet the growing diversity found in public school classrooms (see Figure 7.3).

Bowe (2000) suggested that educators can design learning experiences based on the seven principles of Universal Design used in designing accessible buildings and products.

1. **Equitable Use:** Design or find curricular materials that are accessible to all learners.
   a. Provide the same means of use for all learners; identical whenever possible; equivalent when not.
   b. Avoid segregating or stigmatizing any learners.
   c. Make provisions for privacy, security, and safety equally available to all learners.
   d. Make the design appealing to all learners.
2. **Flexibility in Use:** Design or find curricular materials that meet the widest variety of preferences.
   a. Provide a variety of ways to use the learning materials.
   b. Accommodate for right- or left-handed access and use.
   c. Provide adaptability to the user's pace.
3. **Simple & Intuitive Use:** Design or find curricular materials that avoid unnecessary complexity and are easy to use and understand.
   a. Eliminate unnecessary complexity.
   b. Be consistent with user expectations and intuition.
   c. Accommodate a wide range of literacy and language skills.
   d. Arrange information in order of its importance.
   e. Provide effective prompting and feedback during and after task completion.
4. **Perceptible Information:** Design or find curricular materials that provide information effectively to the user, regardless of conditions or the user's sensory abilities and are effective in all kinds of settings
   a. Use different modes (pictorial, verbal, tactile) for redundant presentation of essential information.
   b. Maximize legibility of essential information.
   c. Differentiate elements in ways that can be described (i.e., make it easy to give instructions or directions).
   d. Provide compatibility with a variety of techniques or devices used by people with sensory limitations.
5. **Tolerance for Errors:** Design or find curricular materials that accommodate errors by minimizing hazards and the adverse consequences of accidental or unintended actions.
   a. Arrange elements to minimize hazards and errors: Most-used elements should be the most accessible; hazardous elements should be eliminated, isolated, or shielded.
   b. Provide warnings of hazards and errors (e.g., tell students about the errors most frequently made by students in the past).
   c. Provide failsafe features (e.g., allow students to use computer with spell and grammar check; use calculators for advanced math problems).
   d. Discourage unconscious action in tasks that require vigilance.
6. **Low Physical Effort:** Design or find curricular materials that require minimal effort to use so that the device or instruction can be used efficiently, comfortably, and with a minimum of fatigue.
   a. Allow user to maintain a neutral body position.
   b. Use reasonable operating forces (e.g., automatic door openers minimize operating force; specific keyboards for persons who must type with one hand, or who need something other than QWERTY keys, do the same for students who need them).
   c. Minimize sustained physical effort.
7. **Size & Space for Approach and Use:** Design or find curricular materials that accommodate variations, and provide appropriate size and space for approach, reach, manipulation, and use regardless of user's body size, posture, or mobility.
   a. Provide a clear line of sight to important elements for any seated or standing user.
   b. Make reach to all components comfortable for any seated or standing user.

FIGURE 7.1 The Principles of Universal Design

Sources: Information from Bowe (2000); McGuire, Scott, & Shaw (2006).

c. Accommodate variations in hand and grip size.

d. Provide adequate space for the use of assistive devices or personal assistance.

McGuire, Scott, and Shaw (2006, p. 170) suggested two additional principles that would make the original principles more applicable to education.

8. **A Community of Learners:**
   a. The instructional environment promotes interaction and communication among students and between students and faculty.

9. **Instructional Climate:**
   a. Instruction is designed to be welcoming and inclusive.
   b. Teachers hold high expectations for all students.

Providing Physical Access

- Assures that classrooms, labs, and fieldwork are accessible to individuals with a wide range of physical abilities and disabilities.
- Assures that equipment and activities
  - Minimize sustained physical effort
  - Provide options for operation
  - Accommodate right- and left-handed students,
  - Accommodate those with limited physical abilities
- Assures the safety of all students

Varying Delivery Methods

- Uses multiple modes to deliver content. Alternate delivery methods, including:
  - Lecture and demonstrations by students as well as the teacher
  - Discussion, including whole and small groups as well as peer partners
  - Hands-on activities as well as project-based learning
  - Internet-based activities, such as Web Quests and using online dictionaries, podcasts, electronic textbooks
  - Fieldwork, including homework assignments in the community as well as school-sponsored field trips and outdoor activities around the school and in the community
- Assures that content is accessible to students with a wide range of abilities, disabilities, interests, and previous experiences
  - Provide printed materials that vary the degree of support. For example, teacher-made worksheet with examples completed, digital materials that can be read by text-to-speech software, and hyperlinked electronic books.
  - Provide written summaries of content delivered orally.
  - Provide printed materials early to allow the student to prepare ahead of time.

Web Pages

Should be accessible by

- Providing printed materials digitally
- Providing text descriptions of graphics presented on Web pages
- Creating printed and Web-based materials in simple, intuitive, and consistent formats that support, enrich, or assess student knowledge
- Arranging content in order of importance

FIGURE 7.2 Translating the Seven Principles Into Classroom Teaching Practices

Interaction

Encourages a variety of ways for students to interact with each other and with you. These methods may include

- In-class questions answered with raised paddle, thumbs-up, or hand on nose
- Peer groups
- Collaborative discussions
- Heterogeneous group work
- Internet-based communications (discussion boards/chat rooms)

Feedback

- Provide effective prompting during an activity and feedback after the assignment is complete.
- Prompting can be verbal or physical or visual.
- Feedback can be brief or extensive, such as in a task analysis.

Demonstration of Knowledge

Provide multiple ways for students to demonstrate knowledge. For example, as an alternative to traditional tests and papers, provide options for demonstrating knowledge.

- Project-based learning reports
- Group work reports
- Demonstrations
- Portfolios
- Dynamic assessments
- Presentations
- Experiments
- Role-plays

FIGURE 7.2 (*Continued*)

Employing Universal Design principles to fully include one group of students can generate unanticipated benefits to others. Consider this list of students who might benefit from closed captioning in videos shown in your classroom.

- Students for whom English is a second language. Often their reading skills are better than their spoken English skills.
- Students who are deaf. By reading what they cannot hear, captioning provides access to deaf students.
- Students with visual impairments. Captioning is generally not useful for students with visual impairments, but there is one exception. Students who are deaf and have low vision (i.e., they can see large print) can benefit from captioning if the captions are large enough for them to see.
- Students watching the video in a noisy environment. By reading what they cannot hear, students watching the tape in a noisy environment will benefit from captioning.
- Students who have learning disabilities. Some may comprehend material better when they both see text and hear it spoken aloud.

FIGURE 7.3 Who Benefits from UDL?

As mentioned above, three networks found in the brain inform the foundations of the UDL framework (Orkwis & McLane, 1998; Rose, 2001b):

1. Because individuals have diverse *recognition* networks, teachers should provide multiple, flexible methods of presentation. Alternative modes of presentation reduce perceptual and learning barriers. For example, important teacher demonstrations could be recorded on digital video, saved to a classroom computer, and enhanced with captions of the teacher's explanation. These videos are then made available to any student who wishes to review the demonstration for clarification or review.

2. Because individuals have diverse *strategic* networks, teachers should provide multiple, flexible methods of expression and apprenticeship. Students can respond with preferred means to accommodate for strategic and motor system barriers. For example,

   a. Paper/pencil assignments may present barriers to those who have physical or written expression difficulties; for those students, responding using a computer or voice recorder may eliminate that barrier.

   b. Oral presentation can present barriers for some students with speech, expressive language, or anxiety disorders; for these students, using a multimedia presentation format or creating a video may eliminate those barriers.

   c. Artwork can be fun for most students, but for some it is very difficult or impossible. Offering students opportunities to use digital programs such as KidPics, or PaintShop or digital libraries of clip art may eliminate this barrier.

   d. Organization of reports, essays, and notes from reading can present barriers to students with difficulty in attending and organizing; for these students, using a graphic organizer or concept map, such as Inspiration, may eliminate that barrier.

3. Because individuals have diverse *affective* networks, teachers should provide multiple, flexible options for engagement. Students' interests in learning are matched with ways of presenting and responding, which can increase motivation to meet cognitive challenges of learning.

   a. Finding the right balance of support and challenge to give a student is the key to engagement in learning activities, especially as every child has a different need for being supported or challenged. Therefore, providing varying levels of support with scaffolds and setting varying levels of challenge will allow the curriculum to be flexible enough to remove barriers for those who need them but will not be too easy for the high achievers. For example, offering *optional* bare-bones note-taking guides or graphic organizers for lectures, demonstrations, or videos will support those who have difficulty writing, attending, or organizing but will not take away autonomy from those who prefer to take notes in their own way.

   b. Generally children and youth enjoy a degree of novelty in learning experiences, but some may be more comfortable with familiar tasks and higher degrees of repetition when learning. Providing multiple levels of novelty and familiarity will support most learners. For example, when researching a topic for a report/ research paper, allow students to use standard print and library resources as well as Internet searches, WebQuests, or interviews of experts (in person or via an Internet site).

c. While students in the same grade or class may be close in chronological age, they have not developed at the same rate, either physically or cognitively, and they may have cultural differences that affect learning. As a result, individuals will be attracted to different content and formats of presentation. Providing important concepts and big ideas in a variety of formats and contents will help remove barriers of development and culture. For example, provide students the choice to use graphic organizers or concept maps rather than note cards; rather than writing a book report, allow them to make a video or PowerPoint presentation or allow them to choose to discuss either the book or the life of the author and events that caused the author to write the book; or give students opportunities to chose to work in small-group work or with a single partner or to complete individual work for some activities.

d. Students may be more fully engaged in learning if they contribute to the learning process. A curriculum that allows students to contribute is often referred to as being "half full" (Orkwis & McLane, 1998, p.19). This does not mean that planning is unfinished or incomplete but that the curriculum is flexible enough to allow direct student input. For example, activities that allow for student contributions to the curriculum include project-based learning experiences, WebQuests, book clubs, and class blogs.

It is important to note, just as UDL is not one size fits all, we should not make the mistake of thinking that access to information is the same as access to learning (Rose & Meyer, 2000). UDL is more than just making the information accessible, which can be counterproductive. For example, text-to-speech readers can read to students, which is wonderful if the task is to read for content; but if the task is to learn how to decode new words, then text-to-speech software is counterproductive (Rose & Meyer, 2000). Therefore, it is important to understand the learning task goals before assuming that technology is the answer to gaining access to learning. Just as Ellis (1997) noted that some accommodations used with students who have disabilities water down the curriculum and do not actually facilitate true learning, teachers cannot assume that merely giving students access to information equals student learning. Teachers must clearly understand what goal is to be accomplished, determine what students can and cannot do, and decide what barriers exist before they can decide how to change the task to support learner differences (Rose & Meyer, 2000). The strategy presented in the next section is meant to support teachers as they consider the demographics of their students, determine what barriers to learning may be present, and plan instruction.

USING THE LEARNS STRATEGY TO PLAN UDL LESSONS

All teachers, regardless of grade or content taught, are now teaching students with diverse learning needs in their classrooms. In the previous chapters, you have read about those students and the laws, IDEIA and NCLB, that have placed an increased emphasis on inclusion of these students in general education classrooms and on teacher accountability for the learning gains of all students. The LEARNS strategy (see Figure 7.4) provides a framework for applying the principles of UDL by helping you plan instruction and use materials that support all students, while increasing student engagement and integrating the appropriate use of technology in your lessons.

	Learning Goal(s) matched to appropriate state standard	
STEP 1: Learning goal Determine the learning goals based on state standards.		
	Teaching activity	**Skills necessary to complete task or activity**
STEP 2: Note teacher **Expectations.** What must students be able to do to complete learning tasks successfully or to achieve mastery of content taught?		
STEP 3: Areas of strength and need for each student are noted.	**Note academic and/or social strengths and weaknesses with name of student(s)**	**Note general academic and social implications or ways that these problems are evident in the classroom**
STEP 4: Review Compare and contrast Step 2 and Step 3, and note major areas where any students will encounter barriers to learning if you do not make any accommodations.	**Skills necessary to complete task or activity**	**Note barriers to learning with name of student(s)**
STEP 5: Note accommodations. Determine methods, strategies, and materials that will meet most students' needs.	**Area of need with name of student(s)**	**Universal Design features that will eliminate barriers to learning**
STEP 6: Specify individual accommodations needed by students whose special needs are not met by UDL provisions.	**Unmet need with name of student(s)**	**Accommodations for individual needs**

FIGURE 7.4 The LEARNS Strategy Worksheet for Designing UDL Lesson Plans

The LEARNS strategy for planning UDL lessons uses the following six steps (see Figure 7.4):

Step 1: **L**earning goal: Determine what content will be taught.

Step 2: Note teacher **E**xpectations for lesson objective.

Step 3: **A**reas of strength and need for each student are noted.

Step 4: **R**eview and determine barriers.

Step 5: **N**ote accommodations needed.

Step 6: **S**pecify individual accommodations needed for specific students.

The LEARNS strategy is based on three assumptions. First, all instructional environments present barriers to learning. These barriers may be in the physical environment or in the instructional methods and materials used for instruction. Barriers may include the inability to *see or hear* the teacher due to seating arrangements; the inability to *use* the printed materials due to visual impairment, language difference, or reading disability; and the inability to *communicate* learning because of language difference, language disability, speech impairment, or inability to physically use instructional materials or a cognitive processing disability. These are just some of the possible barriers to learning commonly found in classrooms.

The second assumption of LEARNS is that with analysis of student needs and strengths, the tasks required to acquire knowledge and skills, and the barriers within the instructional setting and tasks, teachers can plan instruction that meets the needs of diverse students in their classroom. Once the analysis is completed, teachers can select instructional methods, materials, and accommodations that can remove barriers for more than one student and maximize students' learning opportunities. Selecting accommodations for groups of students in their classrooms will minimize the amount of time required to differentiate instruction. For example, an audio text might be used by students who are ELL as well students who are visually impaired or have a reading disability.

The third assumption of LEARNS is that by planning ahead to meet those diverse needs, teachers can reduce the amount of time required to add on accommodations. Think back to the beginning of this chapter and the discussion of adding Universal Design accommodations to existing buildings versus building the accommodations into the design of the building. The same is true for teachers who must retrofit lessons with accommodations. LEARNS can help teachers design their lessons with accommodations already in mind. This ensures building the most effective accommodations into the lesson, allowing all students opportunities to select or reject the accommodations they need, and providing equitable access to the curriculum for all students.

The LEARNS strategy was mainly designed to use the principles of UDL, but it also includes elements of differentiated instruction. These two approaches are quite similar and use many of the same principles for designing instruction. When differentiating instruction, teachers first must recognize that students have differing background knowledge, readiness, language, preferences in learning, and interests. Then, teachers plan their instruction with the intent of maximizing each student's growth and individual success by meeting each student where he or she is and assisting in the learning process (Hall, 2002). These are the same ideals held by teachers who use UDL to plan instruction, with the primary difference being that UDL users recognize that instructional environments present barriers and that these barriers must be removed.

Using the LEARNS strategy does not eliminate the continuing need for special education services; in fact, Step 6 in the strategy provides for inclusion of special education services and specialized accommodations for individual students who require them. Further, UDL is not intended to eliminate or replace special education and its related services, because even if teachers design curricula, assessments, and teaching methods that are accessible to a wide variety of students, some students with specific disabilities will continue to need the services and educational setting found in individualized special education programs (McGuire, Scott, & Shaw, 2006). There will always be the need for some specific accommodations, such as sign language interpreters for students who are deaf, speech and language services, orientation and mobility and Braille instruction, and individual instruction in basic skills, but applying the LEARNS strategy with Universal Design concepts in course planning will ensure full access to the content for most students.

Using the Steps

STEP 1: LEARNING GOAL: DETERMINE WHAT CONTENT WILL BE TAUGHT Teachers may use several methods to determine what to teach. They may begin with a scope and sequence of a long-term instructional plan for their grade or content, use the curriculum guide provided by a textbook publisher, or have a specific skill set that needs to be taught to prepare students for other content work. Whatever the method used to determine content to be taught, the first step of LEARNS requires that content be linked to state standards, as most assessments required by NCLB are based on state standards, and therefore actual content taught should be based on the same standards.

Once the standard has been selected the teacher should determine the final learning goal(s) that will be assessed and develop each goal's learning objectives for the lesson. The final task for Step 1 is to determine the level of Bloom's Taxonomy. Determining the Bloom's level will assure that a portion of the learning experiences presented to the students is above the knowledge level so that some experiences include application and synthesis of knowledge.

STEP 2: NOTE TEACHER EXPECTATIONS FOR LESSON OBJECTIVE In this step teachers will determine the tasks required to complete each of the lesson objectives. Complete a task analysis for each of the tasks. For example, let's assume that students are to read a book for a book report. Tasks may include reading print, taking notes, finding additional information (research skills), following a plot and understanding plot development, distinguishing characters and remembering their actions, and understanding allegories and other literary devices while reading. Then, for the writing portion of the assignment, students will need to be able to organize their thoughts about the book/author, be able to compose the report, and complete basic writing tasks such as spelling, sentence structure, and punctuation. Each of these tasks may present a barrier to any of the students in your classroom, depending on their special needs and abilities.

STEP 3: AREAS OF STRENGTH AND NEED FOR EACH STUDENT ARE NOTED To determine the areas of strength and need for each student, we suggest completing a demographic worksheet for your class (see Chart 7.1; an example will also be provided in the instructor's manual). Information you might collect includes gender; age; race/ethnicity;

CHART 7.1 Class Demographics

ID#	Student Name	Gender	Native Language	Race	Parent Status	SES/ Lunch Status	Reading Level	Math Level	Language, Exceptionality, or Other Special Need	Other
1										
2										
3										
4										
5										
6										
7										
8										
9										
10										
11										
12										
13										
14										
15										
16										
17										
18										
19										
20										
21										
22										
23										
24										
25										
26										
27										
28										
29										
30										

socioeconomic status; reading and math competency levels; special needs, such as disability, ELL status, gifted/talented; and any other information that might be pertinent for your content area. For example, secondary teachers may want to know how students preformed in prerequisite courses (i.e., how well did the student do in Algebra I, if enrolled in an Algebra II class now?). Once these data are collected, teachers are able to see areas of concern that should be addressed, such as students who are not reading on grade level or have a disability that requires accommodations. Once this task is done, the demographics information can be used again for other planning sessions and need only be reviewed periodically to update or add new students.

STEP 4: REVIEW AND DETERMINE BARRIERS   Now the teacher is ready to compare the required tasks (Step 2) with possible areas of need (Step 3) and determine the barriers that may exist in the instructional environment. The first task here would be to look for barriers that affect more than one student. For example, one of the tasks noted in Step 2 is reading the text and teacher-made print materials. Imagine that one student has a reading disability, several other students do not read on grade level, and two students are ELL; then the teacher may assume that reading print materials presented during the lesson will present a barrier for all of these students (see Figure 7.5). In addition, if one or more students are reading above grade level or are considered gifted/talented, some of the print materials may present a barrier to higher-order thinking and advancement of their learning, so then the teacher will need to extend the learning and provide appropriate print materials for their learning abilities.

Each task in Step 2 should be reviewed so that barriers and students affected by the barrier can be determined. To facilitate the process required for Step 4, completing a Common Barriers Inventory prior to beginning Step 4 may be helpful (see Figure 7.5). In addition, this inventory will help teachers think about their classroom organization and most often used instructional groupings, materials, methods, student tasks, and student methods of response. Knowing and understanding what conditions and learning experiences exist in any classroom is essential to understanding what barriers may face students and obstruct their learning. Teachers may be unintentionally creating a barrier to learning in seating or placement of student desks near a noisy window area, in grouping of students, or in assigning a task that is difficult for students to complete. Once the teacher has determined the present conditions, possible barriers, and which students may be adversely affected by one or more barriers, the teacher is ready to note accommodations that would eliminate each of the barriers.

While this task may seem time-consuming, in most cases many tasks used in any one lesson will be repeated in lessons throughout the year. Once a teacher determines that a barrier exists for a particular task, that would be true for this task across all lessons, and similar accommodations for eliminating the barriers could be repeated across lessons and content areas. For example, if a student has difficulty writing legibly due to a specific disability, this student may have difficulty producing work that requires handwriting or drawing. Therefore, barriers could exist in language arts, social studies, math, science, art, and so forth. In many tasks found in all of these content areas, students might benefit from using a word processor to complete required tasks.

STEP 5: NOTE ACCOMMODATIONS NEEDED   At this point the teacher is ready to make decisions about ways and means to eliminate barriers found in Step 4. Let's continue

(The first item has been completed to illustrate the purpose of each column.)			
	Present Situation	**Possible Barriers**	**Students Who May Experience a Barrier Are Those Who**
Classroom organization	**Physical space** • Room designed for 20 students but 25 enrolled • West wall of windows facing the playground • Room next to a restroom • Whiteboard across the room from windows	• Size of the room and spacing of the seating • Placement of board, materials, and student seats • Teacher's voice volume • Windows, doorways, and hallway traffic	• Use wheelchairs • Have sensory impairments • Have attention impairments
	Routines		
	Climate		
	Rules		
	Other		
Instructional groupings	**Whole class**		
	Small groups		
	Individual		
	Peer mediated		
Instructional materials	**Textbooks**		
	Workbooks/worksheets		
	Trade books		
	Teacher-made handouts		

FIGURE 7.5 Common Barriers Found in Classrooms, Materials, and Curricula

Sources: Bowe (2000); Center for Applied Special Technology (CAST, 2006); Friend & Bursuck (2006); Rose & Meyer (2002).

	Present Situation	Possible Barriers	Students Who May Experience a Barrier Are Those Who
	Posters		
	Journals, newspapers, or newspapers		
	Computer		
Instructional methods used by teacher	Lecture to whole group		
	One to one		
	Group work		
	Project-based learning (group or independent)		
	Activity based		
Instructional presentation methods used by teacher	Demonstration		
	Videos		
	Audio materials (tape/ CD, includes music)		
	PowerPoint presentations		
	Chalkboard or white-board		
	Note-taking guides or handouts		

FIGURE 7.5 (*Continued*)

	Present Situation	Possible Barriers	Students Who May Experience a Barrier Are Those Who
	Images (photographs, maps, drawings, time-lines, graphs, charts, tables, etc.)		
Student tasks during instruction	Whole-class discussions		
	Small-group discussions		
	Independent reading		
	Use manipulatives		
	Independent practice of tasks		
	Homework		
Student tasks for response	Oral responses to questions		
	Oral reading		
	Handwritten work (paper/pencil tasks)		
	Drawings/diagrams/ graphic organizers		
	Essays and papers (research or term)		
	Project results (reports or three-dimensional items)		

FIGURE 7.5 (*Continued*)

	Present Situation	Possible Barriers	Students Who May Experience a Barrier Are Those Who
	Project results (oral presentation)		
Student tasks outside instructional setting	Library research		
	Online research		
	Data collection		
	Interviews		

FIGURE 7.5 Common Barriers Found in Classrooms, Materials, and Curricula

with the example of print materials for the book report. Assume that you have selected a state standard that requires students read and write about a book they have read. One way to eliminate barriers presented by print is to allow students to select a book at their reading level, another is to allow students to use an audio book or a digital copy with a screen reader such as Kurzweil or allow students to read a graphic novel, and still another is to allow students to form a book club and read a book together. Suppose, however, that your students must all read the same book as might be required in middle and high school classes; then, providing audio and digital copies of the book might be most helpful. Reviewing the chapters on technology and methods for teaching specific content will provide more examples of ways to eliminate barriers to learning.

STEP 6: SPECIFY INDIVIDUAL ACCOMMODATIONS NEEDED FOR SPECIFIC STUDENTS As previously noted, the first five steps of LEARNS do not eliminate *every* barrier for *every* student. Students with disabilities may have very specific accommodations or modifications that need to be in place. For example, students with hearing impairments may need voice amplification or a sign language interpreter, while students with physical disabilities may need a special desk, preferential seating, a personal assistant, or specialized assistive technology. These special accommodations would be found on the student's Individual Education Program or related to a teacher by the special educator and would be routine for most lessons and class activities. As a teacher becomes more familiar and comfortable with UDL principles, some of these specialized accommodations also may be eliminated though use of UDL; however, teachers should not expect that all individual accommodations will or can be eliminated.

Summary

The classroom environment and learning tasks required can affect the learning of all students, but especially those with who are diverse learners with exceptional needs and, in particular, students with disabilities. Schools and teachers are guided by the laws (IDEIA-04, NCLB, ADA, and AT Act) that support inclusion of students with disabilities and assess for all students to a high-quality, accessible curriculum based on challenging state standards. Further, classrooms have become more diverse and contain students with exceptional needs, such as ELL and G/T, as well as students with disabilities. Teachers are faced with designing classrooms and instruction to meet the needs of this diverse population and helping these students meet state standards. This can seem like a daunting task, but using UDL when planning classroom design, instruction, and assessments can ease the teachers' task as they plan for instruction. While UDL is not intended to create a one-size-fits-all curriculum, understanding how students recognize information, generate and oversee mental and motor patterns, and engage with the learning task will help teachers find the barriers to learning that are present in their classroom and learning tasks. Finally, the LEARNS strategy provides a method for identifying demands of learning tasks, needs of individual and groups of students, barriers within learning tasks that will affect student learning, and accommodations. When teachers use LEARNS to plan, they avoid the need to retrofit their lessons and are able to meet the needs of most students.

This chapter began with a quote from Rose's testimony before the U.S. Senate's Appropriations Committee. Rose (2001a) made a final recommendation to the committee, which is a clarion call to all educators:

"The over-arching recommendation I make to you is that we extend the same kinds of protections now afforded to physical spaces and to information in the workplace to a new area, the most important space for our future—the learning space. Our future as a culture depends on us to make the learning spaces, those most precious spaces in the lives of our children, accessible and supportive of every single child. I believe that if we make the learning spaces of our schools accessible to all of our children, we will save both the short-term costs of mis-educating our children in the present and the long-term costs of NOT educating them in the future." (p. 67)

References

Bowe, R. G. (2000). *Universal Design in education: Teaching nontraditional students*. Westport, CT: Bergin & Garvey.

Center for Applied Special Technology (CAST). (2006). *Teaching every child*. Available at http://www.cast.org/teachingeverystudent/

Council for Exceptional Children. (1999). *Research connections (No. 5)*. Arlington, VA: Author.

Ellis, E. (1997). Watering up the curriculum for adolescents with learning disabilities: Goals for the knowledge dimension. *Remedial and Special Education, 18*(6), 326–346.

Friend, M., & Bursuck, W. D. (20090. *Including students with special needs: A practical guide for classroom teachers*. Upper Saddle River, NJ: Pearson.

Hall, T. (2002). *Differentiated instruction*. Wakefield, MA: National Center on Accessing the General Curriculum. Retrieved August 8, 2006, from http://www.cast.org/publications/ncac/ncac_diffinstruc.html

Hitchcock, C., Rose, D., & Danielson, L. (2000). *Assessing the general curriculum: Promoting a Universal Design for Learning*. Presentation at American Youth Policy Forum on Capitol Hill, Washington, DC. Retrieved on January 1, 2006, from http://www.aypf.org/fournbriefs/2000/fb110300.html

Hitchcock, C., & Stahl, S. (2003) Assistive technology, Universal Design, Universal Design for Learning: Improved learning opportunities. *Journal for Special Education Technology, 18*(4). Retrieved on June 26, 2006, from http://jset.unlv.edu/18.4/hitchcock/first.html

Hitchcock, S., Meyer, A., Rose, D., & Jackson, R. (2002). Providing new access to the general curriculum: Universal Design for Learning. *Teaching Exceptional Children, 35*(2), 8–17.

Individuals with Disabilities Education Improvement Act of 2004. Retrieved on August 8, 2006, from http://www.ed.gov/about/offices/list/osers/osep/index.html

Karger, J. (2005). What IDEA & NCLB suggest about curriculum access for students with disabilities. In D. Rose, A. Meyer, & S. Hitchcock (Eds.), *The universally designed classroom: Accessible curriculum and digital technologies*. Cambridge, MA: Harvard Press.

Mace, R. (1997). *The principles of universal design, version 2.0*. Raleigh, NC: Center for Universal Design.

McGuire, J. M., Scott, S. S., & Shaw, S. F. (2006). Universal Design and it applications in educational environments. *Remedial and Special Education, 27*(3), 166–175.

Orkwis, R., & McLane, K. (1998). A curriculum every student can use: Design principles for student access. Eric/OSEP Topic Brief. Retrieved on June 26, 2006, from http://www.eric.ed.gov/ERICWebPortal/Home.portal?_nfpb=true#x0026;ERICExtSearch_SearchValue_0=Orkwis+and+McLane&ERICExtSearch_SearchType_0=au#x0026;_pageLabel=RecordDetails#x0026;objectId=0900000b8009404d#x0026;accno=ED423654

Pisha, B., & Stahl, S. (2003). The promise of new learning environments for students with disabilities. *Intervention in School & Clinic, 41*(2), 67–75.

Rose, D. (2001a). Text of testimony before the Senate Appropriations Committee. *Journal for Special Education Technology, 16*(4). Retrieved on June 26, 2006, from http://jset.unlv.edu/16.4/asseds/rose.html

Rose, D. (2001b). Universal Design for Learning: Deriving guiding principles from networks that learn. *Journal for Special Education Technology, 16*(1). Retrieved on June 26, 2006, from http://jset.unlv.edu/16.1/asseds/rose.html

Rose, D., & Meyer, A. (2000). The concept of Universal Design. *Journal for Special Education Technology, 15*(1). Retrieved on June 26, 2006, from http://jset.unlv.edu/15.1/asseds/rose.html

Rose, D., & Meyer, A. (2002). *Teaching every student in the digital age: Universal Design for Learning*. Alexandria, VA: Association for Supervision and Curriculum Development.

Simpson, R. L., LaCava, P. G., & Graner, P. S. (2004). The No Child Left Behind Act: Challenges and implications for educators. *Intervention in School and Clinic, 40*(2), 67–75.

Vygotsky, L. S. (1978). *Mind and society: The development of higher mental processes*. Cambridge, MA: Harvard University Press.

Teaching Students with Autism Spectrum Disorders/Pervasive Developmental Disorders

From Chapter 9 of *Teaching Students Who Are Exceptional, Diverse, and At Risk in the General Education Classroom*, 5/e. Sharon Vaughn. Candace S. Bos. Jeanne Shay Schumm. Copyright © 2011 by Pearson Education. All rights reserved.

Teaching Students with Autism Spectrum Disorders/Pervasive Developmental Disorders

Laura Bolesta/Merrill

FOCUS QUESTIONS

1. What are autism spectrum disorders (ASD) and what disabilities are included in this category?

2. What are the most prevalent characteristics of children with autism spectrum disorders?

3. What types of assessments are done to identify students with autism spectrum disorders?

4. What general instructional accommodations would you consider for students with an autism spectrum disorder?

5. What might you do to assess a student with an autism spectrum disorder who engages in severe challenging behavior such as self-injury or aggression?

CONTRIBUTORS TO THIS CHAPTER:

Mark F. O'Reilly, The University of Texas at Austin

Jeff Sigafoos, Victoria University, New Zealand

Giulio Lancioni, The University of Bari, Italy

Russell Lang, The University of California at Santa Barbara

INTERVIEW
KELLY PAGE

Kelly Page is a public elementary school special education teacher in the Southwest. Her job involves supporting teachers and students within inclusive general education settings. She is responsible for 10 students with a variety of disabilities. Several of these students are diagnosed with an autism spectrum disorder (ASD).

One of my students is Carl. Carl is 11 years old and is diagnosed with Asperger syndrome. He has excellent language skills and can carry on a conversation. In fact, Carl has the ability to engage in conversations using words and constructs far above his age level. However, he only wants to talk about insects and spiders. He seems to know everything there is to know about bugs. For hundreds of different insects and spiders, he can tell you their Latin names, what they eat, and where they live. No matter what else you try to talk to him about he always seems to find a way to tie it back to this topic. When I started to work with him initially he had no classroom friends, struggled completing his schoolwork, and often got very upset. When plans changed at the last minute or when he did not want to complete his schoolwork, he would cry, scream, and occasionally try to leave the classroom without permission. On the playground he would catch bugs and take them to show to people. The other children made fun of him and would not include him in their games. Carl attended general education classes and did excellent in Science, but he struggled in English. One of the more common tasks in English class was creative writing and Carl absolutely refused to participate. His English teacher saw no reason why such an intelligent student would not complete his work and would throw such a fit. She often wanted to punish Carl with bad grades and send him out of the classroom to go to the office. My initial goals for Carl included improving social skills, eliminating his

tantrums, and improving his performance in English. The first priority was explaining Asperger syndrome to his English teacher and modifying the creative writing assignment to be on Carl's level. Just because Carl excels in some areas does not mean he excels everywhere. In fact the abstract thinking and imagination required in the creative writing assignments is exactly the type of thing individuals with Asperger's may struggle with.

Another of my students is Erin. Erin also has an ASD, but she and Carl are very different. Erin is a 5-year-old kindergartener with a diagnosis of severe mental retardation and autism. Erin currently spends half of her day in a typical kindergarten class and the other half of her day working one-on-one with me. Erin does not have any functional language and often intentionally hits her head on solid objects when she gets upset. We try and block her from doing this, but she frequently gets in a hard hit. She has had a red bruise on her face and forehead for most of the year. I spend a lot of time worrying about her safety. Erin also waves her hands in front of her face pretty constantly and seems unaware or disinterested in other people. Eye contact with Erin is rare and she will almost always turn her head or close her eyes if I try to make her look at me. Goals for Erin include simple self-help skills (toileting), requesting items with sign language, and reducing her self-injury. I noticed that head hitting seems to increase after she has worked on something for a few minutes. Specifically, if we work on sign language for too long she gets really upset. I think head hitting may be Erin's way of asking for a break from work. I have decided to plan Erin's instruction so that she only works for brief periods of time and practices requesting only items she really likes, and when she starts to look like she may be about to get upset, I prompt her to sign for a break from work.

Introduction

Both Carl and Erin have been diagnosed with autism spectrum disorders (ASD). Students with ASD have difficulty communicating or interacting socially with other people. Some of these students may have mental retardation. A lot of these students also engage in challenging behavior such as aggression, tantrums, and self-injury. They also tend to be rigid in terms of what they want to talk about and things they like to do. These students can get very upset when anyone interferes with their interests and activities, as seen in the examples of Kelly's students. In this chapter, we first describe the characteristics of ASD and then outline the best ways to organize the curriculum to teach students with ASD.

Definitions of Autism Spectrum Disorders/Asperger Syndrome and Pervasive Developmental Disorders

You will note that the chapter title mentions two conditions: autism spectrum disorders (ASD) and pervasive developmental disorders (PDD). The term **pervasive developmental disorder (PDD)** is a diagnostic category used by the American Psychiatric Association to describe five related disabilities, namely, autistic disorder or autism, Rett syndrome, childhood disintegrative disorder, Asperger syndrome, and pervasive developmental disorder–not otherwise specified (PDD–NOS) (American Psychiatric Association, 2000; National Research Council, 2001). **Autism spectrum disorders (ASD)** has recently become a popular term to describe a subgroup of PDD, namely, autism and Asperger syndrome.

The number of individuals diagnosed with ASD has risen dramatically in the last 10 years (Centers for Disease Control and Prevention, 2009). In 2006, approximately 211,610 students who were classified with autism received special education services in our schools. This is nine times more than the number of students receiving school services in 1994. Data from several studies using the current diagnostic criteria place the numbers of students with this disorder somewhere between 2 and 6 per 1,000 individuals. The most commonly cited statistic at the time of writing this chapter was 1 in 150 children age 8 have an ASD (Centers for Disease Control and Prevention, 2009. It is unclear why there is such a rise in students diagnosed with ASD. The rise may be due to changes in diagnostic practices (Rutter, 2005) and the inclusion of autism as a special education category in the early 1990s. Nevertheless, some true rise in the rate of ASD cannot be firmly discounted. However, research findings on the influence of environmental factors, such as the measles-mumps-rubella vaccine, have not shown a relationship between these vaccines and the increases in ASD (Honda, Shimizu, & Rutter, 2005).

One of the main reasons for using the term *ASD* to describe autism and Asperger syndrome is that these disabilities incorporate many of the same symptoms and differ primarily in the severity of expression of those symptoms. The other categories of PDD are extremely rare (i.e., Rett syndrome, childhood disintegrative disorder) or may not be very clear (PDD–NOS). In this section, each of the five PDD categories is described. However, the remainder of the chapter focuses on teaching students with ASD. There are quantitative and qualitative differences in the learning and behavioral characteristics exhibited by individuals who have each disability. Table 9.1 displays each disorder as well as the characteristics that set the disorders apart. Delays are usually noted in early childhood and may co-occur with mental retardation. At this time, there is no identified cause for many of these disabilities. Given the lack of knowledge about cause, there are no empirically validated strategies for prevention or cure at this time.

Autism

Autism is a developmental disability that typically appears during the first 3 years of life. Although people diagnosed with autism are considered to have a severe disability, the range in ability level within this group is varied (National Research Council, 2001). Some individuals with autism may function independently or almost independently.

To be diagnosed with autism, a child must have documented features in three areas:

1. *Six or more of any combination of the following*:
   - Impairments in social interactions (e.g., poor eye contact, lack of responsiveness, inability to establish relationships)
   - Impairments in communication (e.g., no formal spoken language, robotic sounding speech with little tone inflection, use of made-up gibberish words, and repeating exactly what has been heard)
2. *Stereotypical behavior* (e.g., body rocking, hand flapping, or fascination with objects or specific parts of objects)

TABLE 9.1 Comparison of Disabilities Across Developmental Areas

	SOCIAL INTERACTION	COMMUNICATION	STEREOTYPES	COGNITION
Autism	Little or no eye contact Autistic leading Unawareness of social situations	Little to no verbal communication Repetitive, echolalic, or robotic speech	Inflexible routines Motor repetitions (finger flapping, body rocking)	May have mental retardation May have savant characteristics
Rett Syndrome	Loss of social skills within the first few years Loss of interest in social environment	Severely impaired expressive and receptive language	Develops hand movements such as hand-wringing or hand-washing between ages 5 and 30 months	Often associated with severe or profound mental retardation
Childhood Disintegrative Disorder	Loss of interest in environment but not until 2–10 years of age Lack of social or emotional reciprocity	Loss of language skills around 2–10 years of age Repetitive use of language Lack of make-believe play	Develops repetitive motor movements such as hand-flapping and finger waving Restricted interests and activities	Usually associated with mental retardation as the loss of skills in all areas is progressive
Asperger Syndrome	Lack of ability to read social cues Awkward eye contact Interest in social environment	No clinically significant delay in language Use of language (pragmatics) may be delayed (e.g., loudness or socially appropriate use)	Restricted areas of interest (e.g., preoccupation with a topic) Inflexible adherence to certain routines Repetitive motor movements	No clinically significant delay in cognition

3. *Onset before age 3* (note, this is not necessarily as a loss of skills but rather as an emergence of delay in skill development). The child must not meet criteria for Rett syndrome or childhood disintegrative disorder, in which loss of skills is reported before age 5.

The physical features of people with autism might not suggest a disability. Rather, the disability is generally manifested in their language and their personal and social behavior. The Individuals with Disabilities Education Improvement Act (2004) defines *autism* as follows:

> A developmental disability significantly affecting verbal and nonverbal communication and social interaction, generally evident before age 3, that adversely affects a child's performance. Other characteristics often associated with autism are engagement in repetitive activities and stereotyped movements, resistance to environmental change or change in daily routines, and unusual responses to sensory experiences. The term does not apply if a child's educational performance is adversely affected primarily because the child has a serious emotional disturbance.

After having Terry, a student with autism, in his seventh-grade language block for several months, Thomas Salome expressed these thoughts:

> I was worried about how it would work with the other students; if it would take away time and attention from them. I was concerned that Terry would be a distraction to the students. But now that Terry has been part of our class for several months, I feel that the more he is in the classroom, the less the children even notice the noise or occasional outbursts. The students have learned that Terry does things that are not okay for them to do.

Tips for Teachers 9.1 presents Thomas's advice for working with students like Terry in the classroom.

Asperger Syndrome

Asperger syndrome is the next most common PDD. Despite serious impairments in social skills, abstract thinking, and the ability to relate to and identify emotions, these students are often in the normal IQ range and may have extensive verbal abilities. As a result many people

Go to **www.autism-society.org**, the website of The Autism Society of America, to learn more about autism. This site serves the needs of students with autism and their families.

WORKING WITH STUDENTS WITH AUTISM

- *Don't let the behavior overwhelm you.* Develop a behavior-management plan and implement small steps. Decide what you will put up with and what behaviors must stop, and target those.

- *Talk to the student's parents and other teachers.* Find out what works and what does not work with this student. For example, does the child like to be offered choices during the day (e.g., what to do next) or would the child prefer a more set schedule with a routine?

- *Systematically expect more and more of the student.* At first, it might be enough that the student sits with the class during circle time. However, over time you may require increased participation (e.g., answering questions).

- *Develop a picture and word schedule for daily activities.* Picture schedules may have photographs or drawings that represent activities that will occur during the day. Referencing this schedule may help the child understand what is coming next and transition between activities and environments more smoothly. This type of schedule will help you introduce changes in routine slowly, and let the student know in advance that these changes are going to occur.

- *Use peers to help redirect the student's behavior.* Classmates can be a source of support for a student with ASD. They can help prompt appropriate behavior and even praise a student for his or her accomplishments.

- *Take ownership of the student.* Every child in your class is your responsibility and you have been entrusted with their education and well-being. Children with ASD can be challenging, but you will feel a deep sense of accomplishment when they make progress.

do not immediately recognize the child with Asperger syndrome in the classroom. Asperger syndrome is diagnosed by documenting behaviors in six different areas:

1. Qualitative impairment in social interaction (e.g., eye contact, failure to develop peer relationships) and lack of social or emotional reciprocity
2. Stereotypical behavior such as abnormal preoccupation with one or more areas of interest in either intensity or focus (e.g., Carl's interest in insects from the beginning of the chapter), inflexible adherence to routines or rituals, and stereotyped motor mannerisms (e.g., finger flapping)
3. Presence of an impairment in a social, occupational, or vocational area (e.g., inability to get a job or make friends)
4. No clinically significant delay in language; in other words, in terms of vocabulary and semantics, language ability is comparable to a same-age peer without a disability, but speech may sound robotic or monotone
5. No clinically significant delays in cognition, self-help, adaptive skills, (e.g. eating, dressing, toileting), or curiosity about the environment
6. Must not meet the criteria for schizophrenia, because schizophrenia would likely better explain the majority of the symptoms shared with Asperger syndrome

Because Asperger syndrome is not immediately obvious, this disability can create unique challenges for school systems and teachers (Portway & Johnson, 2005). If students with Asperger syndrome are overlooked and considered just to be quirky or immature, they are not likely to receive the supports and services they need. Without support, many of these students will experience social isolation, anxiety, and depression (Rayner, 2005). Parents of children with Asperger syndrome state that once school personnel understand the characteristics of Asperger syndrome they do a better job of making accommodations and providing support (e.g., teaching social skills and modifying class assignments). In turn, these supports have a positive effect on these students' quality of life (Brewin, Renwick, & Schormans, 2008).

Consider the example of Rusty. Rusty is a 15-year-old boy who just started high school. In middle school his teacher (Mrs. Page) was well aware of his Asperger diagnosis and made the minor accommodations necessary for him to make progress and feel successful at school. Among other things, Mrs. Page would reexplain complex directions for some assignments in very concrete terms, which Rusty was better able to understand. She would also offer Rusty slightly modified assignments to scaffold his learning experiences to better meet his current

Go to **www.udel.edu/bkirby/ asperger** for information and support for individuals with Asperger syndrome.

abilities and educational goals. However, now in high school, Rusty changes classes and has many teachers. Many of his new teachers are unaware of his diagnosis and think of Rusty as just a peculiar kid who fails to complete work or participate in class because of laziness. In his history class Rusty is asked to work in a team of three students to prepare a presentation for the class. The topic of the presentation is how different people in different countries interpreted certain events during World War II. Rusty struggles to understand the topic and to recognize the frustration of the other members in his group. Ultimately, he is embarrassed and earns a poor grade. With slight modifications (e.g., allowing independent work and better explanation of the assignment), Rusty may have succeeded. However, because the teacher did not recognize the disability or understand its implications, Rusty experienced unnecessary failure.

Rett Syndrome

To be diagnosed with Rett syndrome, a child must have normal prenatal and perinatal development, normal psychomotor development for the first 5 months, and normal head circumference at birth. The child also exhibits normal development in the following areas until a loss of skills occurs between 5 and 48 months. These deficits include the following:

- Deceleration of head growth
- Loss of hand skills with subsequent development of stereotyped hand movements (e.g., hand washing or hand wringing)
- Loss of social engagement
- Poor gait or trunk movements
- Severely impaired receptive and expressive communication (Sigafoos et al., 2009)

This syndrome is extremely rare, occurring in approximately 1 in 15,000 live births, and occurs only in females (National Institutes of Health, 2001). A genetic cause for Rett syndrome has been isolated. As these girls begin to regress developmentally, they exhibit symptoms that are superficially similar to autism (e.g., loss of communication skills). These children eventually suffer from multiple disabilities.

Childhood Disintegrative Disorder

To be diagnosed with childhood disintegrative disorder, a child must have a normal pattern of development through age 2. Between the ages of 2 and 10, the child must demonstrate a regression of skills in two of the following: language, social skills, adaptive skills, bowel or bladder control, play skills, and motor skills. The child must also exhibit delays in social interaction, communication, and stereotypical behaviors. Last, the child must not meet the criteria for any other PDD or schizophrenia. This is an extremely rare condition, occurring in approximately 1 in 50,000 live births (Frombonne, 2002).

Robin Sachs/PhotoEdit Inc.

What physical behaviors do children with autism exhibit? What other impairments may occur in people diagnosed with autism?

Pervasive Developmental Disorder—Not Otherwise Specified

A child is diagnosed with pervasive developmental disorder–not otherwise specified (PDD–NOS) when delays are exhibited in social interaction or communication or if stereotypical behaviors develop and the child does not meet the criteria for another PDD. Essentially, the diagnosis is used when no other diagnosis seems appropriate but there are obvious delays for no apparent reason, such as traumatic birth or neurological development.

Characteristics of Students with Autism Spectrum Disorders/Asperger Syndrome

Go to **www.autism.org** where you can find a variety of links on several autism-related issues and interventions for individuals with autism.

Autism spectrum disorders cover a wide range of abilities and difficulties as described earlier in the chapter. Three core deficits are common to ASD: in social skills, in communication skills, and in repetitive behaviors and routines. Each student with ASD will possess these deficits to some degree. Being aware of these core areas of functioning can help you tailor your curriculum and instruction to the needs of a specific student.

Social Skills

Students with ASD do not interact with other people in a typical fashion (National Research Council, 2001). In fact, they may not wish to interact with people at all. They can have difficulty interpreting the social cues of other people. For example, they may be unable to discriminate the different intentions of a wink versus a frown. They may appear not to notice other people at all and can give the impression that they are deaf. Other students with ASD may be interested in people but lack core social skills to initiate, respond to, and maintain social interactions.

Additionally, students with ASD have difficulty seeing the world from the perspective of another person. They are unable to "get in the head" of another person and recognize that other people have goals and feelings. This means that they are unable to comprehend the behavior of other people. The social world may therefore be an unpredictable place for students with ASD.

A related problem is that many students with ASD have difficulty regulating their emotions. They may engage in what appears to be spontaneous outbursts of aggression (hitting other students), self-injury (banging their heads), or sadness (weeping). This pattern can also impede social integration.

Communication Skills

Many children with autism do not talk at all and others only develop extremely limited verbal language, which they use to make one-word requests (Charman, Drew, Baird, & Baird, 2003). Some of these children seem to pass the early milestones of language acquisition (e.g., babbling), but then they stop. Others may develop some language later, at age 9 or 10, for example.

Those who develop language use it in unusual ways. Many use single words or phrases but do not combine these words and phrases into meaningful sentences. They may repeat what they hear verbatim, a condition called echolalia. For example, when you ask, "Would you like a cookie?" they might repeat, "Would you like a cookie?" instead of answering the question. Other students may have mild delays in language development or may, in fact, possess large or even precocious vocabularies, yet they have difficulty sustaining conversations with others. This last difficulty is typical of students with high-functioning autism and Asperger syndrome. A student with Asperger syndrome may be more than able to carry on a detailed monologue about a favorite topic (e.g., Carl and his insects described before) but will not give any other students an opportunity to engage in a conversation about the topic. They appear to talk *at* people and seem oblivious to any attempts at initiation by others. These students may also have difficulty interpreting the body language, tone of voice, and turn of phrase of other students.

Body language, including facial expressions, posture, orientation, and gestures, rarely matches what these students are saying. Tone of voice is often monotone, high-pitched, or robotic. Students with Asperger syndrome will often speak like adults and will not use the vocal nuances of their peer group. A child with Asperger syndrome may be expressing genuine interest in a topic or an individual but fail to accurately communicate this interest. For example, after hearing a joke they enjoyed instead of saying, "That was cool joke, can you tell another?" they may instead say "I require a second amusing anecdote now." When making this sincere, yet peculiar and precocious request they might also fail to make eye contact and their voice and expression may make them appear bored or disinterested.

With such deficits in communication skills, these students can have difficulty expressing their wants and needs. They may therefore communicate their intent by other means such as grabbing, pulling, screaming, hitting, and self-injury. Young adults with high-functioning autism (i.e., those students with autism who may not have a diagnosis of mental retardation or who may have mild levels of mental retardation) or Asperger syndrome may become aware of these difficulties. This awareness that they are different can in some instances cause frustration, embarrassment, and social isolation, which may ultimately result in secondary psychiatric issues such as anxiety and depression.

Repetitive Behaviors and Routines

Many students with ASD engage in repetitive motor behaviors (National Research Council, 2001). These can be subtle (repeated head turning when they appear to be alone) or blatant (continuous and vigorous body rocking). Other typical types of repetitive motor behaviors include hand flapping, finger flicking, and toe walking.

Children with ASD tend to insist on sameness or consistency in the environment. For example, they will engage with certain toys but not play with them in a typical fashion. Instead of pretend play with toy cars, they may endlessly line them up in rows. Any change in daily routines such as time, venue, and menu for meals; route to school; personal hygiene; and bedtime routines can result in challenging behavior. These children may also be intensely preoccupied with very specific interests such as train schedules, dinosaurs, or specific TV shows.

It appears that such behaviors and routines may underpin consistency and predictability in the child's world. As a result, any attempt to interfere with the repetitive behaviors and routines can result in extreme upset and challenging behavior.

Identification and Assessment of Students with Autism Spectrum Disorders

Children with severe ASD will most likely have a diagnosis before arriving in your classroom. However, it is also possible you may be involved in initial evaluations or screenings for ASD. If this is needed, you may be asked to document student performance in the areas of language, social, academic, or adaptive behaviors. You may even be asked to complete rating scales describing student behavior in your class. These rating scales are often simple and require little, if any, specialized knowledge to complete.

If you are not involved in the identification evaluation, you will certainly be involved in ongoing assessment and reevaluation. As a classroom teacher, you may be expected to monitor progress in areas in which delays are commonly reported. For example, you might have to monitor how a child with Asperger syndrome uses language in conversations and interacts with his or her peers. Keeping some sort of record or data concerning progress is paramount. For example, consider Carl's case described in the beginning of this chapter. Carl struggles with peer relationships. You might want to keep track of how often Carl interacts with his classmates without discussing insects. By simply making a note in a special folder at the end of the day detailing any interaction you witnessed, over time you may be able to gauge some progress. If his appropriate interactions increase, then you have some evidence that he may be making improvements in both controlling his perseverations and social skills.

The assessment of contextual variables is also important for this population of students. A contextual variable is something that is unique to a particular situation, for example, the environmental differences between the classroom and the lunchroom and even the differences between one teacher and another. Students with ASD may learn something in one context but then fail to generalize the ability to another context. For example, during lunch, your student with autism may be able to demonstrate appropriate use of a napkin, but he may not be able to demonstrate this in home economics when his class is working on table manners. Additionally, a student's behavior may be substantially different in different environments (Lang et al., 2008, 2009). It is not uncommon for parents to say, "but my child never behaves that way at home." A well-prepared and organized teacher will keep a log documenting where students perform certain skills as well as under what conditions the skills are missing. This type of assessment can help you better understand exactly where, by whom, and the other contextual variables that may be important when teaching a particular student.

PEARSON
myeducationlab

Go to the Assignments and Activities section of Topic 6: Assessment in the MyEducationLab for your course and complete the activity entitled *Using Assessment to Drive Instruction*.

Curricular and Instructional Guidelines for Students with Autism Spectrum Disorders

In this section, we outline some suggestions for organizing the curriculum and designing instruction for students with ASD. These guidelines are not exhaustive.

The curricular and instructional guidelines for students with developmental disabilities are equally applicable to students with ASD. To develop an effective instructional program for students with ASD, you should consider the key processes discussed in the following sections.

Assess Preferences

At the beginning of the school year, try to get a comprehensive picture of the students' likes and dislikes in terms of activities by conducting a preference assessment. A preference assessment form can be as simple as a piece of paper listing the items the student likes. Assess what contexts students find challenging. For example, some students might find that structured classroom tasks they complete individually are not a challenge, whereas cooperative learning might be. As part of this process, generate a list of items such as toys, foods, and activities that the students like. You can generate this list by interviewing parents and previous teachers and then tailor the emphasis to each student.

Preference assessments should be conducted at least two times during the academic year, because children's preferences change over time. Also, as you work with students, you may see changes in their preferred activities and items. This information will be invaluable when designing the classroom routine and selecting instructional strategies.

Establish a Classroom Routine

When we discussed some of the difficulties experienced by students with ASD, we noted that they may be particularly challenged when a routine is absent or unpredictable. These students may be prone to challenging behavior when placed in a new classroom situation. It is important to establish a classroom routine quickly and to communicate this routine to the student.

When first establishing the classroom routine, consider the demands of the regular classroom routine, such as what the students are supposed to do when they first enter the classroom, when they go to lunch, and when they finish their work. The routine for the student with an ASD should fit within this larger routine as much as possible. When designing the routine, teachers should consider information regarding the student's high- and low-preference activities and then design the student's routine judiciously. For example, intersperse high- and low-preference activities. Do not expect the student to spend extended periods of time engaged in low-preference activities. Low- and high-preference activities should be evenly balanced. For example, consider Erin's case presented at the beginning of the chapter. Erin did not enjoy working on sign language, and if she is required to do this task for too long, she engages in challenging behavior. However, Erin does enjoy coloring and scribbling on paper. An appropriate routine for Erin that could minimize challenging behavior might alternate brief periods of sign language work with periods of coloring.

Bob Daemmrich/PhotoEdit Inc.

Why is it important to establish a classroom routine? How do daily routines benefit students with autism spectrum disorders?

Some students may experience difficulties transitioning from high-preference to low-preference activities. In these cases it may be helpful to incorporate a neutral activity (i.e., something the child does not dislike, but is also not highly preferred) following a high-preference activity (e.g., coloring for Erin) and before a low-preference activity (e.g., sign language drills for Erin). When this is done, the child is not being asked to give up something they enjoy to do something they hate, but instead this eases the transition and may also reduce the likelihood of challenging behavior.

It is important to establish a routine as early as possible in the school year. The daily routine should be communicated to students through a daily schedule. This schedule can be presented to students in different formats. For the student with Asperger syndrome, the schedule can be written into a personal diary that the student carries with him or her. For the student with autism, the schedule could be posted on the wall with pictures attached identifying the daily activities and the times they will occur. At the beginning of each school day, you should review the activities on the schedule for that day with each individual student.

It is important to involve the student, as much as possible, in preparing this schedule. So, within the constraints of mandated classroom activities, the student could choose the sequence of activities for the day. Certain time periods may be left blank during the day. When a blank period arises, you might offer the student a choice between different activities. For example, consider Carl's case again. After English class Carl could be scheduled for a preferred activity as a reward. Carl's teacher, Mrs. Page, could offer Carl two choices of how to spend his free time, perhaps playing on the computer or looking at an insect picture book. For higher functioning students, it may be sufficient to simply offer the choices verbally. However, for some students pictorial representations of the activities may more clearly explain the choices. In these instances Carl could select the picture of the insect book to indicate his preference.

This form of active scheduling is an important antecedent intervention to enhance self-control and communication skills. It also reduces the probability of challenging behavior from students with ASD (Flannery & Horner, 1994; O'Reilly, Sigafoos, Lancioni, Edrishina, & Andrews, 2005). See Tips for Teachers 9.2 for more suggestions for working with students with ASD.

PEARSON myeducationlab

Go to the Assignments and Activities section of Topic 17, Autism Spectrum Disorders in the MyEducationLab for your course and complete the activity entitled *Picture Schedules*.

Teach Communication Skills

Communication skills are typically very difficult for students with ASD; consequently, it is essential that you develop a comprehensive plan that maps out the skills you plan to teach and how you are going to teach them. Once you have established your daily schedule for the student, it is helpful to target communication skills to teach during each activity, such as requesting preferred items or naming objects. For example, during snack time, Erin's teacher is going to teach the sign for popcorn (a preferred food) and have Erin use the sign to get her snack. Teaching in this way makes the skill relevant to the situation. A creative teacher will find a way to target at least one communication skill during every schedule activity.

Portions of the daily schedule might involve intensive instruction in communication skills using a massed trials strategy. A massed trials strategy means that the same instructional trial is repeated again and again to a predefined criterion of correct performance. For example, you might ask the child to name certain items that are presented individually on a table or to point to an item from an array of items presented simultaneously. Each trial begins with the teacher asking a question: "What is this?" or "Point to the ___." Initially, the teacher will immediately give the answer: "A doll." The student is expected to repeat the answer. As training progresses, the teacher systematically delays the answer to the question (e.g., by 2 seconds) in order to give the student the opportunity to respond independently. All of the student's correct responses receive reinforcement (reward) from the teacher. This reinforcement should be selected from the information obtained in the preference assessment described earlier. For example, if it was determined that Erin liked popcorn, using a small piece of popcorn as reinforcement during massed trials might be appropriate. Alternatively, for some children

Tips FOR TEACHERS 9.2

WORKING WITH STUDENTS WITH ASD

- *Use picture and word schedules for daily activities.* Picture schedules may have photographs or drawings that represent activities that will occur during the day. Referencing this schedule may help the child understand what is coming next and transition between activities and environments more smoothly. This type of schedule will help you introduce changes in routine slowly, and let the student know in advance that these changes are going to occur.

- *Establish routines early in the school year.* Students with ASD often rely heavily on routines. Communicate clearly about any changes in the routine, and post them in your picture schedule.

- *Learn about augmentative and alternative communication.* Students with delays in social communication often use a

different mode of communication. You may have students who use picture wallets, communication boards, or even voice output communication aids to communicate. Learn to feel comfortable using these devices.

- *Establish collaborative relationships with families.* Parents know their child best, and they can assist you when you have questions or concerns. Communicate regularly with parents so that they are aware of any changes in your class. Ask them to communicate to you about changes at home.

- *Be aware of your classroom environment.* Students with ASD may be hypersensitive to environmental conditions such as noise, lighting, and temperature. Become familiar with your individual students' needs and make adjustments to your classroom environment as needed.

Robin Sachs/PhotoEdit Inc.,

What forms of augmentative and alternative communication are available for students with autism?

physical contact (e.g., high-five or a hug) and praise may be sufficient reinforcement.

Communication skills should also be taught as part of the ongoing natural context. This type of communication instruction is often called milieu or naturalistic instruction. These instructional strategies are similar to massed trials strategies. The main difference with milieu training is that the communication training occurs when there is a natural opportunity for the child to communicate. For example, at lunchtime the child could be presented with an empty glass. You hold the container of milk. The child motions toward the glass. You then present the container of milk with the request, "I want milk please." The student repeats the phrase and is then given the milk. The consequence of the request (receiving the milk) acts as a natural positive consequence of engaging in the request. No arbitrary consequences selected from the preference assessment are necessary using this strategy. Over time, you can delay using the phrase until the natural conditions (e.g., empty glass and container of milk) elicit the request spontaneously from the student.

Children with autism often have profound language delays (Charman et al., 2003). Addressing communication difficulties is a common and often high-priority education goal. Communication can occur through gestures, facial expressions, eye blinks, and behavior, and through augmentative and alternative communication (AAC). Low-technology devices can involve pictures or drawings at which the student points to convey a message. High-technology devices can provide voice output (speech synthesizers) and can be programmed with many messages.

A communication board is one example of augmentative communication. The essential elements are the board itself and the symbols or pictures. The board can be made of sturdy paper or an actual board, or it can be a regular or simplified computer keyboard or a computer screen. The symbols or symbol systems that are selected depend on the learner and the environment in which he or she lives. Symbols should be selected according to what students need and want to communicate. In constructing communication boards, Lewis (1993) suggests that the following questions need to be addressed:

- What choices will the student be able to make?
- How will the choices be represented on the board?
- How will the student make his or her selections?
- How many choices will be available and how will they be arranged on the board?
- How will the communication board be constructed?

Figure 9.1 presents examples of common symbol systems, which include Core Picture Vocabulary (Johnson, 1985), Talking Pictures (Leff & Leff, 1978), Pic Syms (Carlson, 1984), Oakland Schools Picture Dictionary (Kirstein & Bernstein, 1981), Picture Communication Symbols (Johnson, 1985), and Blissymbols (Bliss, 1965).

The goals and strategies of communication instruction should be identical for students who do not speak and those who do speak. You will need to work closely with your speech and language pathologist to find the best AAC solution for your student. To find the best solution for your student, you need to identify your communication goals for your student and present this information to the speech pathologist as you discuss the optimal AAC device for the student in question.

The communication skills chosen for instruction will depend on such factors as the level of the student's disability and family priorities. The communication skills of many students with autism will be at what is described as a prelinguistic level. For example, the child may lead you to an area (e.g., locked cupboard) where a desired item is present (e.g., favorite toy). This leading behavior is common in autism and is often referred to as autistic leading. It is important to identify these prelinguistic behaviors and replace them with more appropriate communication skills, such as orally requesting an item, using the instructional strategies previously described. Other children may not even present with prelinguistic behaviors, appearing almost

FIGURE 9.1 — Picture Symbol Systems for Communication Boards

	Core Picture Vocabulary	Talking Pictures	Pic Syms	Oakland	Picture Communication Symbols	Blissymbols
Man						
Wash						
Want		No symbol				
Hello		No symbol		No symbol		
Happy		No symbol				
House						
Car						

Source: Glennen, S. (1992). Augmentative and alternative communication. In G. Church and S. Glennen (Eds.), *The handbook of assistive technology* (p. 100). San Diego, CA: Singular Publishing Group. Reprinted with permission.

comatose. For these students, rudimentary skills such as making and maintaining eye contact may need to be encouraged.

Because students with ASD tend not to efficiently generalize skills they have been taught, you will need to encourage generalization of the targeted communication skills in as many different environments as possible. One way to facilitate this is to involve parents as trainers. Parents spend more time with their children than you do and will have many opportunities to implement milieu or naturalistic strategies. Therefore, involving the parents in the process of teaching communication skills can be very beneficial. Parents can be effective teachers, and involving them in their child's instruction can have a positive effect on reducing the stress involved in interacting with their child.

See the Tech Tips for information on computer programs that are helpful in instructing students with ASD.

Teach Social Skills

The distinction between communication skills and social skills is a somewhat arbitrary one. In a sense, one must possess adequate communication skills in order to engage socially with others. For the purposes of this chapter, social skills include the ability to initiate appropriate social interactions, respond to social initiations from others, and terminate social interactions appropriately.

Tech TIPS

COMPUTER PROGRAMS FOR STUDENTS WITH AUTISM SPECTRUM DISORDERS

In selecting computer programs to use with students, we must look beyond the content of the program to determine whether the material is presented in a way most suited to each individual student's learning style and ability—a critical issue for learners with autism. You should consider the suggestions here in general terms rather than as specific solutions for any single individual.

Typically, because many learners with autism can process visual material better than auditory, carefully selected computer programs may help them to improve basic skills more easily on the computer than in a classroom setting. Look for educational software that is self-paced, offers clear guidelines for expectations, and requires minimal teacher assistance. Consider the following:

Boardmaker
▷ **www.mayerjohnson.com**
Many teachers have had success in using this program to help learners with autism with organization, structure, and expectations. A visual calendar can be useful, as can visual images of sequential steps for specific activities—such as

washing hands, checking out a book, or dressing to go outside in the winter. Also useful are visual signals to help the learner with transitions throughout the day—when to stop playing a game or when to put away materials. For example, prepare green (go), yellow (warning), and red (stop) signs. As the student begins an activity, give her the green sign. When the time for that activity is almost over, exchange the green sign for the yellow one, announcing that time is almost up.

Pyramid Educational Consultants
▷ **www.pecs.com**
Picture Exchange Communication System (PECS) has designed this site for use by persons with autism and related developmental disabilities. PECS has received worldwide recognition for focusing on the initiation component of communication. The PECS system employs applied behavior analysis in conjunction with the development of functional communication skills that focus on the initiation of communication and the design of effective educational environments.

---

myeducationlab

Go to the Assignments and Activities section of Topic 17: Autism Spectrum Disorders in the MyEducationLab for your course and complete the activity entitled *Social Skills*.

Go to **www.teacch.com**, the Division of TEACCH (Treatment and Education of Autistic and related Communication-handicapped Children) where you can find information and resources about various educational approaches to working with children with autism.

A person is perceived to be socially competent by others if he or she is able to interact socially in an effective manner, generalize these interaction styles across multiple social situations, and maintain such interactions over time. Social skills targeted for instruction include the following:

- Initiating conversations with others
- Responding to initiations
- Maintaining conversations
- Responding to criticism

These skills have been taught within a multitude of social contexts such as play and leisure situations (e.g., initiating interactions with peers on the playground), the home environment (e.g., responding appropriately to parent initiations), and work settings (e.g., expanding interactions with co-workers). Strategies for teaching social skills are varied and can include verbal, gesture, and physical prompts; role-play; and a variety of self-management strategies (self-monitoring, self-instruction, and self-reinforcement).

You should focus your efforts on teaching social skills to students with ASD when they possess communication skills but fail to discriminate how to use these skills effectively with peers and others. In other words, social skills interventions should be a major focus for students with autism who are higher functioning and students with Asperger syndrome. As mentioned earlier, a variety of social skills intervention strategies are available; you need to select an intervention that will be maximally effective for these students. Remember that social skills deficits occur for a number of reasons, including the inability to understand the social context, such as the intentions, feelings, and perceptions of others. Therefore, many of the popular instructional strategies that focus primarily on teaching overt social skills without teaching the person to understand the perceptions of others may not be effective.

Two social skills teaching strategies that may prove helpful with these students are **social problem solving** and **Social Story™ interventions**. Both of these intervention strategies teach the student with ASD to understand the social context in addition to responding to or behaving appropriately in that social context.

Social Problem Solving.   Social problem solving involves teaching the social skills you want your students to perform (e.g., maintaining appropriate distance from a person when initiating an interaction) as part of a generic process of engaging in social interactions. In other words, you will teach students a set of strategies to monitor or manage their own social skills in addition to the very specific social skills you want them to perform.

A number of empirical studies have examined the effectiveness of teaching social problem solving to people with disabilities (e.g., O'Reilly & Glynn, 1995; O'Reilly, Lancioni, & Kierans, 2000; O'Reilly, Lancioni, Sigafoos, O'Donoghue, Lacey, & Edrisinha, 2004; Park & Gaylord-Ross, 1989). Replicating previous research from supported employment studies, O'Reilly and Glynn (1995) taught social problem-solving skills in school settings to students with disabilities who were socially withdrawn. Students learned to initiate appropriately with teachers following training. They also generalized the skills trained to the schoolyard setting with peers. The results of this and similar studies indicate that social problem solving is a powerful strategy for teaching social skills that generalize to real-world settings and are maintained over time.

In school settings, teachers often teach these skills in an environment removed from the regular classroom context, because the training involves one-to-one rehearsal and feedback with the teacher or paraprofessional. This problem-solving strategy is taught using a combination of role-play, feedback, modeling, and verbal instruction with you or a paraprofessional. See Tips for Teachers 9.3 for guidance on how to design this instruction.

Social Story Interventions.   Social Story interventions have very similar goals to those of the social problem-solving approach. Unlike social problem solving, however, Social Stories are a relatively recent social skills intervention technique. Although some positive research on this technique has been published, more research is needed to clarify best practices in using Social Stories.

Social Story interventions are based on the premise that children with ASD are unable to interpret the social context or imagine the perspectives of others during social interactions. Additionally, social interactions may evoke challenging behavior because they are unpredictable and hence possibly aversive to students with ASD. Effective social interventions must involve teaching students to understand the social context and to perform appropriately within that specific context.

Getty Images/Photodisc

What strategies will you use to teach social skills in your classroom? What social skills are needed in a situation similar to the one pictured here?

Tips FOR Teachers 9.3

USING SOCIAL PROBLEM-SOLVING STRATEGIES

- Schedule two to three 30-minute periods during the first week of training to give the student ample exposure to the skill. Thereafter, you can provide brief feedback to the student during the regular classroom routine as he or she performs the social skill targeted during training.

- Teach the student to ask and answer a series of questions in relation to the social context in which the targeted social skill occurs.

- Teach the student to discriminate the salient social stimuli by asking himself or herself, "What's happening here?" The student must then accurately describe the social situation.

- Help the student make decisions about how to behave by asking himself or herself: "What should I do?" These prompts help the student generate a series of alternative

action plans and select the most appropriate social interaction for the current context. At this point, the student performs the overt social skill (e.g., initiating the conversation, responding to an initiation from another).

- The teacher or paraprofessional should role-play the social partner at this point of the training and give immediate feedback regarding the student's performance of the targeted social skill.

- Have the student evaluate the social interaction by asking, "What happened when I [description of how he or she behaved]?" The student is prompted to generate a description of the responses of other people in the social interaction and to evaluate whether these responses were positive or negative.

A Social Story is an individualized short story designed to clarify a particular social context, the perspectives of others in that context, and the social skills to be performed. In other words, a Social Story provides "information on what people in a given situation are doing, thinking, or feeling, the sequence of events, the identification of significant social cues and their meaning, and the script of what to do and say" (Attwood, 2000, p. 90). Social Stories are usually developed based on a series of guidelines (Gray, 2000):

- Stories should be tailored to a student's comprehension level.
- A story may consist of a series of simple sentences and/or picture cues that describe the context and provide examples of desired responses, explain the perspectives of others, and explain the rules of social engagement.
- A Social Story should provide a description of a social context and social exchange and be directive in telling the student how to behave.

Social Stories usually use role-play, modeling, and feedback immediately before the target social situation in order to facilitate acquisition and generalization of the social skills. An example of a Social Story used to reduce screaming, crying, hitting, and falling during homework for a 7-year-old student with ASD is included in Figure 9.2. This student's parents read the story aloud to him before homework (Adams, Gouvouis, VanLue, & Waldron, 2004).

Selecting Social Skills for Intervention.   Take some time at the beginning of the school year to observe how your students with ASD interact with peers and others during the school day. Cue in to such skills as their ability to initiate social interactions, to respond to others' interactions, and to terminate interactions appropriately. Carefully examine their body language. Does body language match the intent of the verbal interactions? How is their social performance during structured versus unstructured parts of the school day? By making these careful observations, you may be able to develop a list of key social deficits and the social situations in which they occur. This information will form the basis of your social skills curriculum. When designing this curriculum, you should only target individual or small numbers of social skills at a time. Intervene using a problem-solving intervention strategy and then (unobtrusively) prompt performance of the target social skills throughout the school day. Once these skills begin to improve, target another set of social skills. Remember to involve paraprofessionals (see Tips for Teachers 9.4 for additional information on working with paraprofessionals) and the students' families in training these social skills across settings, because these students do not generalize new skills without specific training.

FIGURE 9.2

Example of a Social Story Used to Decrease Challenging Behavior During Homework for Peter, a 7-Year-Old Boy with ASD

Almost every day I do my homework.

Mom and Dad help me with my homework.

Sometimes I have to do reading.

Sometimes I have to do spelling.

Sometimes I have to do math.

When homework is hard, sometimes I get upset.

When I get upset, sometimes I want to cry and scream.

Sometimes I want to fall off my chair.

Sometimes I hit the table or other things.

Sometimes I say that I don't want to do my homework.

Mom and Dad are sad when I get upset.

They are sad when I cry, scream, fall off my chair, and hit.

They are sad when I say I don't want to do my homework.

When I do my homework and it gets hard Mom and Dad will help me.

I can ask Mom and Dad for help.

I don't have to cry, scream, fall off my chair, or hit.

In a quiet voice I can tell Mom or Dad that I don't understand.

In a quiet voice I can tell Mom or Dad that I don't remember.

In a quiet voice I can tell Mom or Dad that I need help.

When I use my quiet voice Mom and Dad are happy.

Mom and Dad are happy when I use my quiet voice.

I will use my quiet voice to tell Mom and Dad that I don't understand.

I will use my quiet voice to tell Mom and Dad that I don't remember.

I will use my quiet voice to tell Mom and Dad that I need help.

Source: Adams, L., Gouvousis, A., VanLue, M., & Waldron, C. (2004). Social story intervention. Improving communication skills in a child with an autism spectrum disorder. *Focus on Austism and Other Developmental Disabilities* 19, 87–94.

Tips for TEACHERS 9.4

WORKING WITH PARAPROFESSIONALS

- *Keep your paraprofessional informed.* Students may have quirks such as having tantrums when they are touched. Inform paraprofessionals about these and other unique characteristics of your students.

- *Educate your paraprofessional.* Paraprofessionals may have limited formal education. They may benefit from some tips on working with students with ASD.

- *Create a schedule.* Use a schedule to help your paraprofessional understand your classroom. If you are out of the class, the schedule can still be followed.

- *Communicate clearly.* Just as it is important to communicate clearly with parents, you should communicate regularly with your paraprofessional so that he or she is aware of minor changes in your classroom or with your students and their families.

- *Vary responsibilities.* Paraprofessionals may become frustrated when they are expected to supervise a student in the restroom day after day. Rotate staff responsibilities so that no person gets stuck with the "dirty work" on a regular basis.

Addressing Challenging Behaviors

Many students who are diagnosed with ASD engage in challenging behaviors. **Challenging behavior** is defined as behavior by a child that results in self-injury or injury to others, causes damage to the physical environment, interferes with the acquisition of new skills, and/or socially isolates the child (Sigafoos, Arthur, & O'Reilly, 2003). Challenging behavior can include disruption, aggression, and self-injury. Disruptive behaviors that students most often exhibit include noncompliance, throwing materials, talking out of turn, and disturbing other students. **Aggression** can include any behavior that involves one student striking another (hitting, kicking, and biting). **Self-injury** includes behaviors in which a student injures himself or herself (e.g., head banging or eye poking).

Challenging behaviors are often a form of communication for students with disabilities. Specifically, students with disabilities engage in challenging behavior because it results in desired outcomes. Given their delays in language, communicating their wants and needs becomes more difficult, and thus challenging behavior becomes an effective form of communication. For example, consider Erin's case from the beginning of the chapter. Erin does not want to work on her sign language; however, she lacks the verbal ability to request a break from work. What Erin has learned is that if she engages in self-injury (head hitting), the teacher will give her a break. In this way head hitting is seen as a form of communication between Erin and her teacher in which Erin is in effect saying, "I do not want to do this." There are many possible messages that children with ASD communicate via challenging behavior. They may use challenging behavior to access a preferred item (Carl's insect book), gain adult attention, or escape from work. These consequences or outcomes of challenging behaviors are known as functions of behavior (Sigafoos et al., 2003).

Using Functional Behavioral Assessment (FBA)

You can determine the function of a student's challenging behavior by completing a functional behavioral assessment (FBA). There are three steps to an FBA (see also Tips for Teachers 9.5 for more information on how to handle challenging behavior):

1. Indirect assessments
2. Direct assessments
3. Functional analysis

Indirect Assessments.   These assessments should be completed before direct assessments. **Indirect assessments** include interviews with parents and previous teachers, as well as the completion of rating scales. These interviews and rating scales allow you to clearly describe the challenging behavior, along with some of the possible reasons for why it occurs.

Direct Assessments.   This type of assessment involves observing your student and documenting the sequence of behaviors around the challenging behavior. One example of a **direct assessment** is an ABC sequence chart. Observational assessment should be conducted

myeducation**lab**

Go to the Building Teaching Skills and Dispositions section of Topic 17: Autism Spectrum Disorders in the MyEducationLab for your course and complete the activity entitled *Using Social Supports and Social Skills Instruction.*

Tips FOR TEACHERS 9.5

MANAGING CHALLENGING BEHAVIORS

- *Understand why behaviors are occurring.* Students engage in challenging behavior for reasons, usually as a form of communication. A functional behavioral assessment will help you understand why the behaviors are occurring.

- *Be consistent.* All interventions should be implemented consistently so that the student understands what is expected on a daily basis.

- *Make sure that everyone is aware of the student's behavior intervention plan (BIP).* Challenging behaviors usually

occur in all settings. Therefore, everyone, including bus drivers, secretaries, and parents, should implement intervention components.

- *Monitor challenging behavior closely.* It may be difficult to notice when a behavior decreases from 50 times a day to 25 times a day. Use systematic data collection and analysis to monitor your student's progress.

FIGURE 9.3

An ABC Analysis

Child: Manuel
Date and Time of Observation: April 4, 9:40–11:20 AM

What happened before the behavior	Target behavior	What happened after the behavior
Teacher says, "What word is this, Manuel?"	✔	Teacher moves away and asks another student.
Teacher points to a letter and asks, "What letter is this Manuel?"	✔	Teacher moves on to a different topic with the class.
Teacher asks Manuel to open his book.	✔	Teacher does not persist but moves on to another student.

---

during those times of the day when challenging behavior is most likely to occur; it should also be conducted for approximately five school days. Because of the intensity of this observational process, it may be best for a consultant, such as a behavior or autism specialist, to conduct these observations.

An example of an ABC analysis for Manuel, a student with ASD and challenging behavior, is presented in Figure 9.3. The ABC assessment presents data on Manuel's target behavior (head hitting) between 9:40 A.M. and 11:20 A.M. (the time of day when Manuel is most likely to engage in challenging behavior) during a given school day. Each time the target behavior occurs, the teacher places a check mark in the target behavior box (center column). The teacher then describes what happened immediately before the behavior. In the final column, the teacher describes what people did in response to the student's behavior. Three incidents of the target behavior are included in Figure 9.3. You can see from this brief assessment that head hitting occurred when a task demand was placed on Manuel. When he engaged in head hitting, the task was removed. This brief assessment from this particular school day would seem to indicate that Manuel hit his head in order to communicate his desire to escape from demanding tasks.

Functional Analysis. If steps 1 and 2 do not clearly identify the function of your student's challenging behavior, you might need to seek the assistance of a behavioral specialist who can help you design and implement a functional analysis, step 3 of the FBA. A functional analysis consists of an experiment in which you manipulate one variable in your classroom to determine its effects on challenging behavior. All possible variables must be manipulated, and rates of challenging behavior must be compared across each condition. For example, if you think your student is trying to escape independent math or is trying to obtain peer attention, you have four manipulations to implement: getting out of math, not getting out of math, getting peer attention, and not getting peer attention. Because this third step of the FBA is time consuming and sometimes provokes more challenging behavior, it is often reserved for research purposes or for times when the function of behavior is not clear after steps 1 and 2 have been completed.

Using Positive Behavioral Support

In the past, teachers and parents addressed challenging behavior by attending to the form of the behavior (e.g., hitting) rather than the function (e.g., obtaining teacher attention). The intervention was implemented after challenging behavior occurred. For example, when a student hit a peer, the teacher told the child to stop hitting. Hypothetically, this reprimand was intended to teach the student that hitting was not tolerated and thus help the student learn not to hit anymore.

Research has shown that these reactive procedures are not as effective at addressing challenging behaviors as the strategy of positive behavioral supports (Sigafoos et al., 2003). Positive behavioral supports comprise several key features. First, the approach is based on the sound behavioral science of human behavior. Second, interventions must be practical and based on FBA results. Interventions are implemented in a proactive manner rather than in a traditional reactive manner and focus on teaching new skills that foster independence, improve adaptive skills, or increase effective communication. These interventions also allow individuals with disabilities to access natural communities of reinforcement. Candy and other treats are not provided following the demonstration of a new skill such as talking. Rather, an individual is taught to request pizza in the lunchroom where pizza occurs naturally. Interventions are monitored through systematic data collection and analysis to determine intervention effectiveness.

Another feature of positive behavioral supports is the consideration of social values during the assessment and intervention processes. Behavior change should be observed across all environments of the child's day; it should be durable, lasting through the school and postschool years. Behavior change should be relevant and result in concomitant improvements in social behavior.

Over the years, Horner and his colleagues have conducted a series of studies on the use of positive behavioral supports with students who engaged in challenging behavior. In these studies:

- Teachers conducted functional behavioral assessments.
- A team approach to problem solving and intervention design was used.
- Teachers implemented practical and effective interventions.
- The students were taught new skills.
- Ongoing data collection and monitoring were used.

For example, Todd, Horner, and Sugai (2000) examined a fourth-grade student who was taught to self-monitor, self-evaluate, and self-recruit teacher attention. Teaching him these skills resulted in a decrease in frequency of challenging behavior, an increase in on-task behavior, and an increase in task completion. Vaughn and Horner (1997) compared levels of challenging behavior when students received instruction during preferred and nonpreferred tasks and when teachers rather than students selected tasks. They reported that for two students, rates of challenging behavior were lower when students were able to select tasks, regardless of task preference. Last, Day, Horner, and O'Neill (1994) described an intervention in which students were taught alternative communication in place of challenging behavior. In this study, three participants engaged in challenging behavior to escape difficult tasks or to obtain preferred items. Once they were trained in an alternative communication, challenging behavior decreased and new communication increased.

You will note from this description of research on positive behavioral supports that many of the goals and strategies of positive behavioral support (e.g., to enhance self-control, choice making, communication training) were discussed earlier in this chapter. In fact, you may be able to prevent challenging behavior with many of these students if you use the strategies outlined earlier.

PEARSON
myeducationlab

Go to the Assignments and Activities section of Topic 7: Classroom/Behavior Management in the MyEducationLab for your course and complete the activity *Positive Behavior Support in the Classroom.*

Summary

- PDD includes a number of disabilities, including autism, Asperger syndrome, Rett syndrome, childhood disintegrative disorder, and PDD–NOS. Both Rett and childhood disintegrative disorder are extremely rare. ASD is a subgroup of the PDD categories and includes autism and Asperger syndrome. Both of these diagnostic categories have similar symptoms but differ in terms of the severity of expression of these symptoms.

- The core difficulties experienced by students with ASD include communication and social skills deficits or excesses and rigidity of behavior patterns. These students may also engage in challenging behavior, including self-injury, aggression, and property destruction.

- Although teachers often know who those students are that have been identified with ASD, there may be others who they suspect may need additional supports. In both cases, teachers should document student performance in the areas of language, social, academic, or adaptive behaviors. In some cases, teachers are asked to complete rating scales describing student behavior. Documenting behaviors and monitoring progress helps teachers assess students' progress.

- Key processes for effective instruction for students with ASD include assessing preferences, establishing a classroom routine at the beginning of the year, teaching communication skills, and teaching social skills.

- Many students with ASD engage in challenging behavior. You must understand when, where, and why they engage in such behaviors. This can be accomplished using the FBA process. The results of the FBA can then be incorporated into a behavioral support plan that involves teaching communication skills and modifying the curriculum to make challenging behavior less necessary for the student.

Think and Apply

1. Interview the parents and teachers of a student with ASD to identify preferences for that student. Make a list of five activities/contexts and items that the student likes and dislikes. Then identify ways in which you can incorporate student preferences into the student's instructional routine.

2. Teach a targeted communication skill to a student with ASD using the massed trials format. Then find at least five opportunities to implement the milieu intervention strategy with that same student for the same communication skill.

3. Identify two students with ASD who engage in severe challenging behavior. With their teachers, review the results of their FBA and observe the implementation of the positive behavioral support plan.

PEARSON
myeducationlab)

Now go to Topic 17: Autism Spectrum Disorders; Topic 7: Classroom/Behavior Management; and Topic 6: Asssessment in the MyEducationLab (www.myeducationlab.com) for your course where you can:

- Find learning outcomes for these topics along with the national standards that connect to these outcomes.

- Complete Assignments and Activities that can help you more deeply understand the chapter content.

- Examine challenging situations and cases presented in the IRIS Center Resources.

- Apply and practice your understanding of the core teaching skills identified in the chapter with Building Teaching Skills and Dispositions learning units.

Helping All Students Succeed in Mathematics

From Chapter 14 of *Teaching Students Who Are Exceptional, Diverse, and At Risk in the General Education Classroom*, 5/e. Sharon Vaughn. Candace S. Bos. Jeanne Shay Schumm. Copyright © 2011 by Pearson Education. All rights reserved.

$\mathcal{H}$elping All Students Succeed in Mathematics

FOCUS QUESTIONS

1. What are some of the current trends in math curriculum and instruction?

2. What are some of the reasons students with learning problems have difficulty with traditional mathematics curricula?

3. What are the recommended changes to traditional mathematics curricula and the implications of such changes for students with learning problems?

4. What teaching strategies are most important in helping all students acquire basic math skills?

5. How can teachers ensure that students understand the meaning of a mathematical operation and not just the answer to the problem?

6. How can teachers help students develop and use problem-solving strategies both in math as well as in other content areas?

Frank Siteman

INTERVIEW
ONE STUDENT'S EXPERIENCE

Shawn is an undergraduate at a small university. But unlike most first-year students, he is 21 years old, not 18. Since Shawn was very little, his parents have known he was not like the other children in the family or other children they knew. He was extraordinary in many ways and had problems in other ways. These problems were apparent when Shawn started school. Although few subjects were easy for him, all subjects were easier than math.

Through elementary and high school, Shawn received poor grades in mathematics, but not because of a lack of effort on his part. Shawn says, "No matter how much I studied, I just did not get it. When I say I can't do math, I mean it's not that I'm not trying, it's that it just really doesn't make any sense to me." Shawn recalls that in fourth grade he had a teacher who seemed to really understand his challenges with math and who worked hard to help him visualize what he was doing when he was solving math problems. She used objects such as colored chips to represent ones, tens, and hundreds and tried to make math real to him. He said that these accommodations helped and improved his attitude about learning math. Overall, though, he felt that the type of intensive support for math he needed was just not available. He explains: "I was mainstreamed into classrooms where there were at least 25 other students. I think the attitude toward students, especially students with learning disabilities, is 'Why should I change my teaching style just for you?'" Shawn describes his years in school this way: "It's like somebody saying we are going to make you do this even though you don't know how to. It was so hard and frustrating all of the time."

In high school, Shawn began to advocate for himself and seek out assistance with his courses, but again he describes his math experiences as unsuccessful. Shawn's experiences with mathematics have been so negative that he currently goes to great strides to exclude math from his life. "I don't take math. I switched my major so I won't have to take math. Math is just not a part of my life."

As a student with learning disabilities, what advice would Shawn give teachers? "The reason a student is coming to you with a problem and saying that they're LD is not because they want to give you more problems in your life, it's because they want you to help them."

Introduction

The purpose of this chapter is to introduce procedures for effectively instructing students like Shawn who have extraordinary problems learning mathematics. Think about how you felt about mathematics instruction. What do you think were some of the factors that influenced how you felt about mathematics instruction? Surely the teachers you had and the way mathematics was taught had a great deal of influence on how you feel about the subject today. Unfortunately, far too few students consider mathematics an exciting subject, and many students with disabilities perform poorly in mathematics because of low expectations for success and poor instruction (Baker, Gersten, & Lee, 2002; Bryant, Hartman, & Kim, 2003; U.S. Department of Education, 2008).

Current Trends in Mathematics Curriculum and Instruction

A central topic in education is mathematics instruction. This issue has been paramount for students with learning difficulties. There is growing national concern that students across all achievement groups are not faring well in mathematics compared with students in countries such as Belgium, Canada, England, Finland, Hungary, Japan, New Zealand, Scotland, and Sweden. Some think that the mathematics performance of students in the United States is related to the way in which mathematics is taught. In fact, the National Mathematics Advisory Panel (U.S. Department of Education, 2008) indicated that mathematics instruction is broken and needs to be fixed. The most important message they provide is to put "first things first"—meaning that students need to master important skills and knowledge sequentially.

Influences on Math Instruction

Mathematics instruction has been in a state of change over the past 30 years, with considerable emphasis on developing mathematical literacy through helping students construct knowledge (U.S. Department of Education, 2008). The Mathematics Advisory Panel included the outstanding research scientists in mathematics education in the United States who met and reviewed research on effective mathematics instruction. In their lengthy report (U.S. Department of Education, 2008) the Mathematics Advisory Panel offered six recommendations including:

1. Streamline the mathematics curriculum so that only the most essential elements of mathematics instruction are taught. These essential elements include whole numbers, computational proficiency, measurement, geometry, proficiency with fractions including decimals, percentage, and negative fractions.
2. Use findings from rigorous mathematics research to (a) give students an early start in mathematics, (b) teach in ways that recognize the importance of both conceptual understanding of mathematics and fluency and automaticity in mathematical facts, and (c) recognize that persistence in teaching and learning mathematics (i.e., effort) is important, not just inherent talent.
3. Provide preservice and professional development for teachers of mathematics so that they are knowledgeable about math content as well as effective instructional practices.
4. Use both student-centered and teacher-directed instruction. Students with learning difficulties and disabilities respond positively to explicit instruction in mathematics.
5. Emphasize mathematics instruction that leads to success in algebra.
6. Read and implement findings from rigorous research on math instruction.

The professional mathematics instruction group, the National Council of Teachers of Mathematics (NCTM), has been significantly influential in defining instructional core content in mathematics. In 1989, this group set curriculum standards for the development and implementation of mathematics curricula (NCTM, 1989). Since that time, NCTM has created professional standards (in 1991), assessment standards (in 1995), and most recently, a set of standards that builds on the three previous standards documents (published in 2000) and are summarized in Figure 14.1. Since the NCTM standards were published, NCTM went one step further and created "Curriculum Focal Points," which are the topics in mathematics that are most important at each grade level. These related ideas, concepts, and skills define the key instructional practices for teachers for each grade (NCTM, 2006) and are available for each grade level from prekindergarten through grade 8. As a prospective or practicing teacher, these focal points may be useful to you as you select curriculum and design instruction for students with special needs.

You can see from reviewing the Math Standards that mathematical problem solving is a major focus of the NCTM standards. When students with disabilities or math difficulties demonstrate challenges in mathematics problems solving, it is of particular concern because it interferes with students' access to higher-level math content and with applying math skills to everyday problems.

In an effort to determine how effective mathematical textbooks are in teaching math problem-solving standards to all students, Jitendra and colleagues (2005) reviewed five mathematical textbooks to determine the extent to which they addressed NCTM's problem-solving standards. These researchers also looked at the extent to which the texts provided design features associated with improved instructional outcomes for students with disabilities (e.g., prerequisite skills, teaching examples, practice problems, review, and feedback). Most textbooks provided an adequate number of problem-solving opportunities for students. However, with respect to instructional design criteria that would enhance instruction and support learning for students with disabilities, the textbooks were rated quite low, with few textbooks meeting even three instructional design features. To best accommodate students with disabilities, these

FIGURE
14.1

NCTM Standards 2000

Instructional programs for prekindergarten through grade 12 in the following areas should enable all students to use the following concepts:

1. Number and operations
   - Understand numbers, ways of representing numbers, relationships among numbers, and number systems
   - Understand meanings of operations and how they relate to one another
   - Compute fluently and make reasonable estimates

2. Algebra
   - Understand patterns, relations, and functions
   - Represent and analyze mathematical solutions and structures using algebraic symbols
   - Use mathematical models to represent and understand quantitative relationships
   - Analyze change in various contexts

3. Geometry
   - Analyze characteristics and properties of two- and three-dimensional geometric shapes, and develop mathematical arguments about geometric relationships
   - Specify locations and describe spatial relationships using coordinate geometry and other representational systems
   - Apply transformations and use symmetry to analyze mathematical situations
   - Use visualization, spatial reasoning, and geometric modeling to solve problems

4. Measurement
   - Understand measurable attributes of objects and the units, systems, and processes of measurement
   - Apply appropriate techniques, tools, and formulas to determine measurements

5. Data analysis and probability
   - Formulate questions that can be addressed with data and collect, organize, and display relevant data to answer them
   - Select and use appropriate statistical methods to analyze data
   - Develop and evaluate inferences and predictions that are based on data
   - Understand and apply basic concepts of probability

6. Problem solving
   - Build new mathematical knowledge through problem solving
   - Solve problems that arise in mathematics and in other contexts
   - Apply and adapt a variety of appropriate strategies to solve problems
   - Monitor and reflect on the process of mathematical problem solving

7. Reasoning and proof
   - Recognize reasoning and proof as fundamental aspects of mathematics
   - Make and investigate mathematical conjectures
   - Develop and evaluate mathematical arguments and proofs
   - Select and use various types of reasoning and methods of proof

8. Communication
   - Organize and consolidate their mathematical thinking through communication
   - Communicate their mathematical thinking coherently and clearly to peers, teachers, and others
   - Analyze and evaluate the mathematical thinking and strategies of others
   - Use the language of mathematics to express mathematical ideas precisely

9. Connections
   - Recognize and use connections among mathematical ideas
   - Understand how mathematical ideas interconnect and build on one another to produce a coherent whole
   - Recognize and apply mathematics in contexts outside of mathematics

10. Representation
    - Create and use representations to organize, record, and communicate mathematical ideas
    - Select, apply, and translate among mathematical representations to solve problems
    - Use representations to model and interpret physical, social, and mathematical phenomena

authors suggest that teachers will need to provide more specific and explicit instruction with additional examples as well as specific feedback.

Think about your own mathematics instruction when you were in school. Was the emphasis on worksheets and learning computation, or was it on problem solving and activities? Math educators suggest that students need to learn both and that an early emphasis on critical skills such as mathematical computational fluency is important, especially with opportunities to understand the computations conceptually and to apply them (U.S. Department of Education, 2008). In other words, it is not important to pick either mathematical computation or problem solving and application—students need to learn both.

Math Proficiency

The National Research Council (NRC) has conducted an examination of U.S. mathematics education from kindergarten through graduate study. This joint activity was conducted by the Mathematical Sciences Education Board, the Board on Mathematical Sciences, the Committee

FIGURE 14.2

The National Council of Teachers of Mathematics Recommendations

- Do not alter curricular goals to differentiate students; change the type and speed of instruction.

- Make mathematics education student oriented, not an authoritarian model that is teacher focused.

- Encourage students to explore, verbalize ideas, and understand that mathematics is part of their lives.

- Provide opportunities on a daily basis for students to apply mathematics and to work problems that are related to their daily lives. Relate what they are learning to real-life experiences.

- Teach mathematics so that students understand when they can estimate an answer and when they need to compute an exact answer.

- Teach problem solving, computer application, and use of calculators to all students.

- Teach students to understand probability, data analysis, and statistics as they relate to daily decision making, model building, operations, research, and application to computers.

- Shift from relying primarily on paper-and-pencil activities to use of calculators, computers, and other applied materials.

on the Mathematical Sciences, and the National Research Council. The extensive report resulting from the work of these committees not only outlines problems in mathematics education but also charts a course for remedying them. The suggestions that relate to students with learning and behavior problems are presented in Figure 14.2.

In addition to the guidelines in Figure 14.2, the National Research Council (2001) indicates that "mathematical proficiency" is the essential goal of instruction. What is mathematical proficiency? The aspects of mathematical proficiency are described here. As you read them, consider how you might integrate these ideas into your instruction for students with disabilities. Think about how you might document whether students are making progress.

- *Conceptual understanding* refers to understanding mathematic concepts and operations.
- *Procedural fluency* refers to being able to accurately and efficiently conduct operations and mathematics practices.
- *Strategic competence* refers to the ability to formulate and conduct mathematical problems.
- *Adaptive reasoning* refers to the thinking about, explaining, and justifying mathematical work.
- *Productive disposition* refers to the ability to appreciate the useful and positive influences of understanding mathematics and how one's disposition toward mathematics influences success.

Despite this plea for additional emphasis on problem solving, computation is still an essential component of the mathematics curriculum. Some feel that students with learning problems potentially have the most to lose as the curriculum shifts away from computation and toward an emphasis on problem solving and teaching students to think mathematically, thus the recent focal points for mathematics instruction (NCTM, 2006) provide an opportunity for teachers to identify the critical elements of instruction for their grade level and to determine whether students have mastered the previous focal points. This emphasis on the high-priority skills and practices at each grade level will ensure that the National Mathematics Advisory Panel's recommendation (U.S. Department of Education, 2008) to do first things first and to do the most important things at each grade level—not everything—can be accomplished.

For example, in fourth grade, the focal points (NCTM, 2006) emphasize that students demonstrate quick recall of multiplication and division facts and are very fluent with whole number multiplication. Fourth graders are also supposed to demonstrate understanding of decimals and the connection between decimals and fractions as well as an understanding of area and how to determine the area of two-dimensional shapes. How can James Frist, a fourth-grade teacher with two students with disabilities, consider these math focal points for all of the students in his class including his students with disabilities? Following are some guidelines to help James:

- Students with disabilities may be slower and require more practice, but they are not necessarily less accurate. Consider that the students with disabilities may need more time to complete the problem.
- Students with disabilities may need more support (e.g., additional instruction), to have the problem read to them, guidance about the key ideas to focus on, and reminders about which operation to use. At the same time, however, they should have access to learning the same focal points in mathematics.

- When students work in pairs or groups, it is not uncommon that the students with disabilities are assigned passive and unimportant roles where they have little opportunity for learning and participating. Consider ways to alter this practice and to include them more actively in partner or group work.
- Students with disabilities may not have adequate fluency with basic math facts and may need additional practice and opportunities to acquire this proficiency.

Understanding why your students are having difficulty learning math will help you to better meet their needs. The following sections offer specific information about why students struggle.

Difficulties in Learning Mathematics

Students with behavior disorders, mental retardation, learning disabilities, and attention problems typically score below their same-age peers on measures of math achievement (Zentall & Smith, 1993). Some of their difficulties in mathematics relate to understanding the problem. In other instances, they lack the computation skills to adequately complete the problem. Typically, students with disabilities have difficulties with both math facts and procedures (Barnes et al., 2006). Interestingly, not all of their difficulties in mathematics relate to their knowledge of math; some reflect other problems such as memory, difficulty in considering math problems from a "reasonable" perspective, poor calculation skills, number reversals, and difficulty understanding operation signs (Bryant, Hartman, & Kim, 2003).

What kinds of difficulties in mathematics do students with disabilities have? How can teachers help students with these kinds of difficulties?

Despite the significant difficulties many individuals with disabilities have with mathematics, they do not report lower self-perceptions of their math skills than average-achieving students (Montague & van Garderen, 2003).

Students who have both math and reading disabilities are more at risk than students with math disabilities alone (Jordan & Hanich, 2003). This is because students with both reading and math disabilities have additional problems associated with processing symbols and text (Bryant, Bryant, & Hammill, 2000; Bryant, Hartman, & Kim, 2003).

Developmental Arithmetic Disorder

Students with developmental arithmetic disorder have significant difficulties learning arithmetic—difficulties that are unexpected given the students' overall cognitive functioning and academic performance in other subject areas. For example, Shawn, the student introduced at the beginning of this chapter, demonstrated a significant arithmetic disorder. His performance in arithmetic was unexpectedly low given his overall cognitive performance. His difficulty in mathematics was also long lasting, not related to an area of mathematics or a particular teacher. Good teaching is likely to help students with developmental arithmetic disorder but probably not enough to ensure grade-level performance.

Nonverbal Math Difficulties

Johnson and Myklebust (1967) were the first to introduce the notion of nonverbal math disabilities. They were referring to a small group of students who displayed good reading and verbal expression but extreme difficulty with mathematics. Other problems associated with students who display nonverbal mathematics problems include the following:

- Social immaturity
- Disorientation
- Deficits in visual, motor, and self-help skills
- Problems estimating distance and time

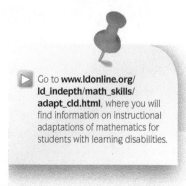

Go to **www.ldonline.org/ld_indepth/math_skills/adapt_cld.html**, where you will find information on instructional adaptations of mathematics for students with learning disabilities.

Bob Daemmrich Photography, Inc.

Saje, a third-grade student with disabilities, was a successful reader but demonstrated significant difficulties in mathematics and was really a puzzle to his teacher, Theresa Ramirez. She could not figure out why, despite Saje's high verbal expression and good vocabulary, he continually mixed up old and new rules. He not only had problems in math but also was frequently inattentive and disorganized and avoided responsibility. No matter how often she reminded Saje to keep his math paper neat, the papers he turned in had frayed edges, had numbers all over the place (instead of problems written in neat columns), and were covered with eraser marks and holes. Theresa asked the special education teacher how to help Saje. The special education teacher worked with Saje, administered some tests, and explained to Saje's classroom teacher that he had a nonverbal math difficulty.

Although math would always be challenging for Saje, the special education teacher suggested some things that the classroom teacher could do to help Saje:

1. First, she taught only one mathematical principle at a time until Saje became masterful and fluent with that principle.
2. She used word games, songs, and other verbal activities to enhance instruction.
3. She devised organizational aids such as graph paper with large boxes that Saje could use to write numbers.
4. She provided Saje with devices such as computers and tape recorders as alternatives to pencil and paper.

Students who demonstrate nonverbal math difficulties are capable of acquiring meaningful understanding of mathematics and solving mathematical problems. Providing effective instructional accommodations such as the ones provided for Saje can improve their mathematical performance not only in your class, but in the future as well.

Effective Math Instruction for All Learners

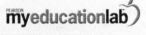

Go to the Assignments and Activities section of Topic 10: Content Area Teaching in the MyEducationLab for your course and complete the activity entitled *Mathematical Concepts*.

Students can display poor math performance for several reasons. The one that can be most readily corrected is the inappropriate or inadequate instruction in mathematics that many students receive. Many professionals believe that the math difficulties among students with learning problems are compounded by ineffective instruction. Most teachers know how they learned to compute math problems but are not aware of alternative ways to compute them (e.g., they memorized successfully multiplication tables but are unfamiliar with adding numbers to resolve multiplication). Few teachers have procedures for using concrete approaches and how to successfully use manipulatives to teach computation. Tips for Teachers 14.1 provides a summary of guidelines for instructional practices for students with disabilities in a general education classroom.

As a general education teacher, you will also need to be prepared to meet the instructional needs of students who are mathematically gifted. There is a debate about whether to accelerate the pacing of instruction for gifted students or to provide differentiated instruction. Johnson (2000) indicated that most experts recommend a combined approach. Tips for Teachers 14.2 provides some suggestions for meeting the needs of mathematically gifted students.

Tips for Teachers 14.1

INSTRUCTIONAL PRACTICES FOR STUDENTS WITH DISABILITIES

- Select appropriate, comprehensive math content.
- Select goals that establish high expectations.
- Provide systematic and explicit instruction.
- Teach students to understand math concepts.

- Monitor the progress of students.
- Teach to mastery.
- Promote a positive attitude toward math.
- Teach students to generalize the math skills they learn.

Additional tips for teachers can be located at these websites: www.ldonline.org/ld_indepth/math_skills and www.superkids.com/aweb/tools/math

Tips FOR TEACHERS 14.2

INSTRUCTIONAL PRACTICES FOR GIFTED STUDENTS

- Give preassessments so that students who already know the material do not have to repeat it, keeping instruction and activities meaningful. In the elementary grades, gifted learners still need to know their basic facts. If they do not, don't hold them back from other, more complex tasks, but continue to work concurrently on the basics.

- Create assessments that allow for differences in understanding, creativity, and accomplishment; give students a chance to show what they have learned. Ask students to explain their reasoning both orally and in writing.

- Choose textbooks that provide more enriched opportunities. Because most textbooks are written for the general population, they are not always appropriate for gifted students. Use multiple resources. No single text will adequately meet the needs of these learners.

- Be flexible in your expectations about pacing for different students. While some may be mastering basic skills, others may work on more advanced problems.

- Use inquiry-based, discovery learning approaches that emphasize open-ended problems with multiple solutions or multiple paths to solutions. Allow students to design their own ways to find the answers to complex questions. Gifted students may discover more than you thought was possible.

- Use a lot of higher-level questions. Ask "why" and "what if" questions.

- Provide units, activities, or problems that extend beyond the normal curriculum. Offer challenging mathematical recreations such as puzzles and games.

- Provide AP level courses in calculus, statistics, and computer science, or encourage prepared students to take classes at local colleges if the supply of courses at the high school has been exhausted.

- Differentiate assignments. It is not appropriate to give more problems of the same type to gifted students. You might give students a choice of a regular assignment; a different, more challenging one; or a task that is tailored to interests.

- Expect high-level products (e.g., writing, proofs, projects, solutions to challenging problems).

- Provide opportunities to participate in contests such as Mathematical Olympiads for the Elementary School (grades 4–6), Math Counts (grades 7–8), the American Junior High School Mathematics Exam (grades 7–8), or the American High School Mathematics Exam (grades 9–12). Give feedback to students on their solutions. After the contests, use some of the problems as the basis for classroom discussions.

- Provide access to male and female mentors who represent diverse linguistic and cultural groups. They may be individuals within the school system, volunteers from the community, or experts who agree to respond to questions by email. Bring speakers into the classroom to explain how math has opened doors in their professions and careers.

- Provide some activities that can be done independently or in groups based on student choice. Be aware that if gifted students always work independently, they are gaining no more than they could do at home. They also need appropriate instruction, interaction with other gifted students, and regular feedback from the teacher.

- Provide useful, concrete experiences. Even though gifted learners may be capable of abstraction and may move from concrete to abstract more rapidly, they still benefit from the use of manipulatives and hands-on activities.

Source: Adapted from Johnson, D. T. (2000, April). Teaching mathematics to gifted students in a mixed-ability classroom. *ERIC Digest E594* (ERIC Document Reproduction Service No. ED441302). Reprinted by permission of the author.

Evaluating Mathematics Curricula

Considering the mathematical focal points by NCTM (2006) and the guidance provided by the National Mathematics Advisory Panel (U.S. Department of Education, 2008), it is likely that math curricula will be influenced and aligned with the math panel guidelines described in the section "Influences on Math Instruction." Students with disabilities and math difficulties will benefit from teachers who consider the following:

- ■ *Students have difficulty reading the information provided.* Because the reading vocabulary is too difficult and the reading level is too high, students with math difficulties are able to learn very little by reading their math books. Consequently, teachers must provide supports that make the information accessible. For example, Max Diamond, a tenth-grade math teacher, assigned several pages of reading in the math textbook as homework. Realizing that several of his students would not be able to read and understand the text adequately, Max had these pages read into a tape recorder and made the tapes and recorders available to all students in his class.

- ■ *Math concepts are often presented poorly.* Multiple concepts are introduced at one time, and information is often presented in a scattered fashion. For this reason, Dawn McQueen reorganizes the information in the math text so that she can teach computation skills to mastery rather than skipping around teaching many new ideas in 2 weeks. Dawn introduces only one concept at a time, teaching that concept until *all* students in her class (not just those with learning problems) learn it. Then she moves on to the next concept. Although Dawn follows a sequence of pages different from that presented in the book, she believes that her efforts are worthwhile because her students seem to understand better.

- *There are insufficient problems covering any one concept or operation and too few opportunities for application of knowledge learned.* The problems are not presented in enough different situations for students to learn and transfer what they know. Janice Kauffman, a sixth-grade teacher, addresses this problem by developing her own supportive materials to supplement the book. She also provides practice with problem solving, reasoning, and real-life applications that helps students transfer their knowledge to real-life settings.
- *Students often do not have the necessary prerequisite skills assumed by the text (and so the next level is too difficult).* As Margaret Gardner plans each math unit she teaches, she spends considerable time considering the prerequisite skills students need to master the concept or operation she is teaching. After identifying these prerequisite skills, she tells students directly that she is looking to see whether they know them. She prepares activities and exercises so that she knows which students do and which do not possess the skills they need to move on to the next math concept or operation.
- *The pages and organizational format of the text vary considerably and make learning from the text difficult.* Linda Saumell, having recognized this problem, walks students through the text section by section, explaining the format to them.
- *Students have difficulty transferring knowledge to real problems.* Many of the steps necessary to help students transfer what they know mathematically to selected problems are not taught explicitly and so students fail to perform correctly. With problem solving, for example, students often know how to do pieces of the problem but do not know how to assemble these pieces to correctly generalize what they know to the new problem.

To shape the mathematics curricula so that it accommodates the learning needs of all students, particularly students with learning problems, teachers need to adapt traditional math curricula to best meet the learning needs of students in their classrooms. The teachers cited above are successful in addressing inherent limitations, improving their students' potential for a positive outcome.

Adapting Instruction for Secondary Students with Math Difficulties

Older students with mathematical problems require instructional considerations to access and learn mathematics. Though the research base is better developed for teaching mathematics to younger students with learning difficulties, there are instructional practices with older students that are associated with improved outcomes. See Tips for Teachers 14.3 for some suggestions for teachers working with older students who have experienced years of challenge and frustration in learning math.

Many older students benefit from real-world problem solving that includes a gamelike experience. Shaftel, Pass, and Schnabel (2005) provide an example of a game that gives adolescent students with learning disabilities an opportunity to use a checkbook and keep track of their expenses. Teachers can create a game board on which each "space" has a real-life experience. Examples of these experiences include

- Pay rent for your apartment: $300.
- Receive your monthly paycheck of $800.
- Unexpected dental expense; pay $180.

Go to **www.ldonline.org/ indepth/math** for additional information on teaching students who struggle with math.

Each student is provided with a checkbook and checks. Students can all be given a designated amount of money at the beginning of the game. Based on where they land on the game board, they add or subtract money. After a specified period of time, the student with the most money in his or her checkbook is the winner.

Using real-world examples such as paying bills and keeping a checkbook heightens students' interest in doing math. It also shows them that there are important reasons to master math skills, as they really do need to use these skills in their every day lives.

TipsforTEACHERS 14.3

WORKING WITH OLDER STUDENTS WHO HAVE EXPERIENCED FRUSTRATIONS LEARNING MATH

- *Provide explicit instruction.* For many students, this means clearly identifying the steps in solving the problem, facilitating background knowledge and skills, and demonstrating clearly all aspects of problem resolution. One way teachers can improve explicit instruction is to determine whether they have made transparent to the learner all critical parts of solving the mathematical problem.

- *Provide clear and a sufficient number of examples; most commercial materials fall short in this area.* Students with learning difficulties benefit from more examples and nonexamples. This means showing them the application several ways. It is also useful to demonstrate a counterexample that illustrates a faulty application.

- *Give real-life applications for students.* Students with mathematical difficulties find math abstract and conceptually difficult to understand. For this reason, teachers who link the problems to real-life situations are more successful.

- *Provide ample opportunities to be successful.* Students with mathematical difficulties need not only lots of examples from the teacher, but also lots of opportunities to practice the problem-types until they master them. One of the critical difficulties experienced by students with math problems is that they never really master a problem-type before they are introduced to something new.

- *Use cooperative learning activities, but include individual accountability as a key component.* Although cooperative learning (asking students to work in small groups with three to five other students in which they all attempt to solve the same problem) may be useful for students with mathematical difficulties because it provides them ready access to able students as models and guides, it also can have the negative consequence of leaving the target student out of the learning. Unless there is a focus on individual accountability, where every student is responsible for demonstrating learning, it is possible that cooperative groups can give students with mathematical difficulties a free ride.

Adapting Basal Materials for Students with Special Needs

Teachers need to do several things to adapt basal materials. One is to select appropriate math content. There is considerable concern among educators that poor math content is a result of the **spiral curriculum**, which occurs when the same skills (e.g., mathematics skills) are woven into every year of school and students continually "relearn" the same skills in the same area. Jason, an eighth-grade student, said it this way: "It seems every year we start with multiplication and then go to division and then we learn something about fractions and then we stop. Then the next year, we do it all over again." One approach to teaching mathematics, the Corrective Mathematics Program (Engelmann & Carnine, 1992), is designed to avoid the problems of the spiral curriculum and provide satisfactory pacing of instruction.

Teachers can also use instructional design principles to assist students with learning problems in acquiring proficiency in mathematics. These design principles include (a) teaching big ideas, (b) making strategies conspicuous, (c) using instructional time efficiently, (d) making instruction on strategies clear and explicit, and (e) providing appropriate practice and review (Pressley & Harris, 2006).

A key aspect of selecting the appropriate curriculum is that it be comprehensive. A fifth-grade teacher, Mr. Lanca, reflected, "I know my curriculum should be more comprehensive than just the facts and computation, but I'm not sure what else I should teach. Also, the students seem to really need the time to learn computation." Working on other skills in mathematics does not mean that computation is left behind; in fact, computation can often be enhanced while other components of math are taught. Students need to be taught and involved in a full range of mathematics skills that include basic facts, computation, word problems, operations, problem solving, mathematical reasoning, time, measurement, fractions, and math application.

Adapting Tests for Students with Special Needs

How effective are test accommodations in mathematics for students with disabilities? The idea behind test accommodations is that individuals with disabilities profit more from them than individuals without disabilities—thus the test accommodations are more responsive to their individual needs. Elbaum (2007) reports that when mathematics tests are read aloud to students with disabilities and their performance on these tests are compared with students without disabilities, the read-aloud condition is more helpful to elementary students with disabilities than elementary students without disabilities. However, the reverse is true for secondary students with disabilities whose improved performance with accommodations is overall lower than for students without disabilities.

Using Curricular Programs for Students With Math Difficulties

Other than the basal curriculum books, math workbooks, and the curriculum guidebooks published by many state departments of education, what curriculum resources are available to teachers? The following list provides brief descriptions of some resources that are helpful for students who have difficulty learning math.

Go to **www.greatschools .net/LD/assistive-technology/ math-tools.gs?content = 949** where you will find technology to help students learn mathematics.

- **Vmath** (Voyager Expanded Learning, 2008) was developed for students in grades 3 through 8 who may need extra instruction to meet mathematics learning goals. Vmath is designed at each grade level to assess and monitor the progress of students so that through a systematic approach to instruction they can develop into independent learners in math and help students meet grade-level goals in math.
- The **Corrective Mathematics Program** stresses direct instruction through a highly sequenced format that provides immediate feedback to students (Engelmann & Carnine, 1992). The arithmetic kits come with a detailed teacher's guide, workbooks, teaching book, and take-home sheets for homework and parent involvement. The entire program is based on behavioral principles of learning and provides explicit instructions for the teacher. The materials are designed to be fast paced with a lot of oral drill.
- The **Computational Arithmetic Program** provides 314 worksheets for teaching basic math skills to students in grades 1 through 6 (Smith & Lovitt, 1982).
- **NCTM Navigation Series** is a series of graded and topical books with CD-ROMs published by NCTM. The books focus on activities for teaching algebra, geometry, numbers and operations, and the like, based on the NCTM principles and standards.
- **Math Exploration and Applications** provides instruction, games, and manipulatives for building fluency in math skills in English and Spanish (Bereiter, Hilton, Rubinstein, & Willoughby, 1998).
- **Key Math Teach and Practice** is designed to provide remedial practice in and diagnosis of math difficulties (Connolly, 1988). Materials include a teacher's guide, a student progress chart, and a sequence chart, as well as activities and worksheets.
- **ETA/Cuisenaire** provides a variety of supplemental mathematics materials. This company specializes in math manipulatives that emphasize learning principles through hands-on learning. One of their earliest products was the Cuisenaire rods. Cuisenaire rods come in various lengths and colors and can be used to represent numbers. Students with disabilities can be taught to use Cuisenaire rods as manipulatives to facilitate their successful understanding of word problems. Over time, they are able to generalize to similar problems when the rods are not used (Marsh & Cooke, 1996).
- **Saxon Math** was designed for kindergarten through fourth grade (Larson, 2004) and eighth through twelfth grades (Saxon, 2003), addressing math concepts with an emphasis on solving math problems. Strategies for solving math problems are scaffolded through step-by-step problem solving.

Being aware of these options equips teachers with alternatives for helping all students achieve some success in math. When necessary, working with the special education teacher can help teachers identify the best programs for struggling students.

Establishing Appropriate Goals

Students and teachers who establish feasible goals in mathematics and monitor the progress of these goals are more likely to demonstrate improved success (Fuchs et al., 1992). How can teachers do this? One way is to establish goals for all students, including those with disabilities, and discuss or establish these goals with their students. Why is this important? Often the goals and expectations teachers set for students with learning problems are too low. Students benefit when they are challenged to meet realistic but rigorous academic goals.

Marie Fernandez, a middle-school teacher, realized that she often responded to students' low self-image and low motivation by setting low goals for them. She did not expect that students would be interested and work hard, and they met her low expectations. Several of the students with learning problems in her class would indicate that the work was too difficult or that there was too much work, and she would respond by lessening their load instead of thinking of alternatives. With the help of the special education teacher at her school, Marie Fernandez instituted some of the following changes:

- **Students use goal setting and self-monitoring with teacher support.** In the goal-setting process, students were asked to set realistic goals for how much work they could complete and how many problems they could solve. For example, students would determine that they would be able to complete six mathematical problems that involved multiplication of two-digit numbers with no errors in 5 minutes.

- **Teacher models and thinks aloud how to solve the problem.** Rather than giving up when students thought the problems were too difficult, Marie Fernandez began showing students how to do the problems by conducting them step by step and thinking aloud the procedures. For example, "First I read the numbers out loud and estimate how much it will be. Let's see—86 plus 22 is going to be more than 100, but not much more. Now I start on the right and add the column. Now I add the column on the left. The total is 108."

- **Teacher guides the student to solve the problem.** Thanks to the teacher's prompts and guidance, the student does not have to work through the verbalization alone. When the student has difficulty, the teacher fills in. The teacher does not do the work but guides the student through it so that he or she has accomplished the problem successfully.

- **Students have opportunities to work in small groups or alone to successfully complete the problems.** After students have succeeded in completing the problems with support from the teacher, the next step may be to have them work in small groups or pairs to complete problems before they work independently to do them. This phasing from teacher instruction to guided practice to practice with peers and then independent practice provides a scaffold so that all students can succeed.

Using Peers to Support Instructional Practice

Effective ways to facilitate learning of mathematics for students with difficulties is to engage peers in the process. One way is through peer pairing in which two students work together (usually a stronger student in math is paired with a less able student). Students are provided instruction by the teacher and then through pairs complete designated problems. The idea is that by working together they can learn to solve and practice the problems effectively (Dion, Fuchs, & Fuchs, 2007; Gardner, Nobel, Hessler, Yawn & Heron, 2007) as well as practice these skills (Fuchs et al., 1997).

Peer tutoring is effective not only for the student who is tutored, but also for the student who does the tutoring. Teaching not only helps enhance students' self-concept, but also helps them learn a great deal. Cooperative learning occurs when the teacher divides the class into small groups (ordinarily three or four students per group), usually not based on ability, and asks these groups to work together to solve problems. Maheady, Harper, and Sacca (1988) conducted a cooperative learning math instruction program for ninth- and tenth-grade students with mild disabilities. The study showed that students who participated in the cooperative teams performed better in mathematics and received higher grades than those who did not.

How can teachers guide peer tutors to help the students with whom they are paired? What makes this dynamic effective?

Bob Daemmrich Photography, Inc.

Slavin, Madden, and Leavey (1984; Slavin, 1995) designed team-assisted individualization, in which individualized instruction is provided in a cooperative learning model. Each of the four or five students in the heterogeneous learning team is assigned individualized mathematics material at his or her own level. Students on the same team help one another with problems and also manage checking and record keeping for the individualized math materials. Students work independently, but teachers teach skills to groups of students who are at the same level by pulling them from various teams.

Using Response to Intervention: Identifying Students Who Need Help in Math

Math, like reading and writing, is an academic area where response to intervention (RTI) can be implemented. One of the best ways to use RTI in mathematics is to screen students for math difficulties and then to provide them with early and intensive intervention to ensure their progress. There are several measures that can be used to determine students' early math knowledge (Clarke & Shinn, 2004; Fuchs et al., 2007):

1. ***Number identification.*** Students are asked to identify orally numbers between 0 and 20 when these are presented randomly on a piece of paper.
2. ***Number writing.*** Students are asked to write a number between 1 and 20 when the number is provided to them orally.
3. ***Quantity discrimination.*** Students are asked to identify which of two numbers is the larger (or smaller).
4. ***Missing number.*** Students are provided with a string of numbers and are asked to identify the number that is missing.
5. ***Computation.*** Students are asked to complete computations that are representative of their grade level. Students are provided 2 minutes to complete as many problems as possible.

Many of the same principles that apply to the use of RTI in reading also apply to math, including

- *Screening*—students can be screened to determine whether they have math problems in numeracy, math calculations, and/or problem solving.
- *Evidence-based math*—schools and districts can ensure that the math instruction for all students is based on the best research available.
- *Interventions*—when students have difficulties that are not adequately addressed through the evidence-based math program in the classroom, additional instruction through short-term interventions (10–20 weeks) can be implemented.
- *Progress monitoring*—students' progress in the classroom and in interventions can be documented to ensure that they are staying on track and meeting curriculum benchmarks.

Assessment and Progress Monitoring

Effective math instruction involves checking students' work frequently and providing feedback. When students demonstrate math difficulties, their progress needs to be assessed by their classroom math teacher approximately every 2 weeks, and if students are not progressing adequately, accommodations including reteaching and guided practice need to be provided to ensure success. The math assessments used should align with the instructional curriculum.

Students in teacher Alex Chinn's fifth-grade class were asked to complete a worksheet to practice a new skill he had taught them for using dollar signs and decimal points in subtraction problems. Alex told the students to complete only the first problem. After they completed the problem, they were to consider whether the answer made sense and whether dollar signs and decimal points were used correctly. If so, they were to place a *C* next to the problem. If they were not sure whether the problem was correct, they were to mark it with a question mark (?); and if they thought the problem was wrong, they were to use a star (*). Alex moved quickly from student to student, checking the first problem and providing them with feedback and reinforcement: "Jacob, you were right, you did have the problem correct. Maxine, what are you unsure about? Now, look at it again. What do you think? Yes, that's right, it's correct. Beth, let's do this problem together." The teacher then guides the student by facilitating problem completion and then provides additional opportunities for the student to do similar problems independently.

Being a Model in Math.   Most of the time, a positive attitude toward math comes from effective instruction and the interest the teacher shows in mathematics. Tips for Teachers 14.4 offers suggestions for promoting positive attitudes toward math.

TIPS FOR TEACHERS 14.4

PROMOTING POSITIVE ATTITUDES TOWARD MATH

- Provide multiple opportunities for success.

- Select real-world problems that address issues of importance to the students.

- Be certain that students have the prerequisite skills to adequately solve the problem.

- Teach students to chart their progress—success is the best motivator.

- Provide calculators and other tools to support success.

- For complex problems, ask students to solve the problem in steps so that they get feedback as they proceed.

- When appropriate, encourage students to work with partners.

Diagnosing Students' Learning Needs in Mathematics.   When students have persistent difficulties in math that continue after teachers have made adequate instructional accommodations, teachers may need to provide further diagnosis to pinpoint the students' math learning needs. Jana is a first-year special education teacher. She is fortunate to work in a middle school with three other special education teachers who have been working at the school for several years and are used to team teaching. Jana's school administrator asked her whether she would be comfortable teaching mathematics to all of the special education students. Because she is pretty good at mathematics herself, Jana thought this arrangement would give her an opportunity to learn to teach one content area very well. She quickly realized that her first task would be to determine the performance levels in mathematics of all her students. She also realized that she needed to select a measure that would tell her what students knew and did not know and also how they compared with other students in their grade. Although there is general information on the IEP about the student's math performance, she wanted more precise, diagnostic information.

There are a number of ways in which Jana can obtain the information she needs to develop instructional programs for her students. One of the first questions Jana needs to address is whether she has the time to give an *individually administered assessment* or whether she needs to use a group administered measure. For students with special needs, individually administered measures yield the most information for teachers. Second, Jana needs to decide whether the measure is designed for students in the age range of the students she is teaching. Table 14.1 provides a list of mathematics measures, states whether they are group or individually administered, and lists the age range for which they are appropriate.

How can teachers best make decisions about whether students are learning mathematics effectively? Also, how can teachers monitor the progress of their students so that they can document the rate and progress students are making in mathematics? Perhaps the best way to determine student progress is to implement curriculum-based measurement (CBM), which is a method of determining whether the student is learning the curriculum that is taught. Teachers prioritize the most important skills students need to learn each week and then assess students prior to and following instruction. These tests can be group administered, teacher developed, and take as little as a few minutes to administer. Based on the findings from the pretest, teachers can identify what they need to teach all students and what they need to teach some of the students. Posttesting at the end of the week tells the teacher who needs additional instruction. There is considerable and growing evidence that when teachers use CBM to monitor their students' progress and to adjust their instruction accordingly, students make gains at much more rapid rates than when CBM is not used (Stecker & Fuchs, 2000).

What is CBM for math? Simply stated, it is a way of documenting the extent to which the student is learning the critical elements you have targeted in the curriculum. To illustrate, consider the case of Ricky, a fifth-grade boy with learning and attention problems, who is struggling with math. His goals for the next 10 weeks are (a) to know all subtraction facts up to 100 automatically, (b) to quickly be able to do addition with regrouping word problems, and (c) to be able to use basic measurement terms such as *inches, feet,* and *yards* appropriately. Ricky's teacher, Mr. Rojas, pretested Ricky on all 100 subtraction facts in random order, timing him while he completed the worksheet. He then showed Ricky how to graph his

TABLE 14.1 — Measures to Assess Mathematics Performance

TEST NAME	HOW ADMINISTERED	AGE/GRADE APPROPRIATE	OTHER INFORMATION
Comprehensive Math Assessment	Group	Grades 2–8	Based largely on the National Council of Teachers of Mathematics' critical elements in mathematics instruction
Diagnostic Achievement Battery	Individual	Most grade levels	Provides normative data on student performance but not specific information for identifying strengths and weaknesses
Wide Range Achievement Test	Individual or Group	Most grade levels	Provides normative data on student performance but difficult to identify students' needs for instruction
Woodcock Johnson III Tests of Achievement	Individual	Most grade levels	Provides normative data on student performance but may not provide adequate information for designing instruction
Test of Early Mathematics Ability	Individual	Ages 3–9	Provides information to assist with designing and monitoring instruction
BRIGANCE Diagnostic Comprehensive Inventory of Basic Skills—Revised	Individual	Prekindergarten–grade 9	Provides information to assist with designing and monitoring instruction
Comprehensive Mathematical Ability Test	Individual	Grades 1–12	Provides information to assist with designing instruction
Key Math—Revised	Individual	Grades 1–12	Provides information to assist with designing instruction
Test of Mathematical Abilities	Individual	Grades 3–12	Provides information to assist with designing instruction
Math—Level Indicator: A Quick Group Math Placement Test	Group	Grades 4–12	Takes approximately 30 minutes, and because it is group administered, it quickly determines the performance levels of a large group of students. The problems are based on the NCTM standards.

Source: Bos, C. S. & Vaughn, S. (2006). *Strategies for teaching students with learning and behavior problems* (6th ed.). Boston: Allyn & Bacon.

performance in two ways: first, by graphing how long it took him to complete the worksheet, and second, by graphing the number of problems correct. Together they agreed that he would take a version of this test once every week to determine whether he could decrease the amount of time he needed to complete the test and increase the number of problems he got correct. Next, they established a schedule of work assignments and practice sessions. His teacher followed a similar procedure with measurement and problem solving to determine what Ricky knew and what he needed to know, and then he established a simple graph that Ricky could complete to monitor his progress. Ricky and his teacher frequently discussed Ricky's progress and modified assignments and instruction to facilitate his learning.

As a teacher, you may want to consider using a computerized application of CBM procedures, which is available for mathematics as well as for spelling and reading (Fuchs, Fuchs, & Hamlett, 1990). Remember, CBMs should be easy to administer, cost efficient, and sensitive to small changes in learning (Kamee'enui et al., 2005).

Assessing Students' Number Sense

One promising practice for monitoring the progress of young children in mathematics and identifying children who have mathematics difficulties or disabilities is by assessing their "number sense." Number sense refers to whether a student's understanding of a number and its use and meaning is flexible and fully developed. In terms of assessment, number sense is particularly important because it assists teachers in determining which students currently have mathematical difficulty; it also serves as a predictor for students who may have learning difficulties in the future.

Several counting measures for students' beginning math skills (ages 4–8) can be used as effective screening tools for students with mathematic difficulties or used to monitor students' progress in this area.

- Count to 20. This is a beginning-level skill requiring students to count to 20, recording which numbers were known in the correct sequence and which ones were not.
- Count by 3 and 6. This skill requires students to count from a predetermined number, say 5, in increments of 3 or 6. Teachers record the accuracy and speed with which students perform this task.
- Count by 2, 5, and 10. This skill requires that students count by the designated number—2, 5, or 10—in increments up to a specified number, such as 20 for 2s, 30 for 5s, or 100 for 10s.

Teachers are interested in assessment to help them determine what students know and what they need to know. Assessing students' number sense can also tell teachers how students compare with others at their same age or grade level. Finally, appropriate assessments allow teachers to monitor students' progress and regularly make effective instructional decisions that influence students' performance.

Helping Students Improve in Math

The most important thing to remember as a teacher is to begin with the concrete and then move to the abstract when you are teaching new math concepts or when a student is having difficulty learning a math concept. Because all students have had opportunities to interact with objects, the process makes sense to them. By using examples from the manipulation to develop problems and to write them numerically, you bridge the gap between the abstractness of mathematics and students' need to learn the information concretely. You might start instruction using elements that contribute to systematic and explicit instruction, which include (Christenson, Ysseldyke, & Thurlow, 1989; Fuchs & Fuchs, 2003; Fuchs et al., 2008)

- The teaching strategy of demonstration–prompt–practice (see Tips for Teachers 14.5).
- Explicit instruction that not only involves highly organized step-by-step presentations related to the specific target skill, but also provides information about why learning this skill facilitates student learning.
- Assurance that students understand the directions and the task demands. Periodic checks are necessary to determine whether students understand the directions, and the teacher must monitor students' progress.
- The systematic use of learning principles. This refers to maintaining and using positive reinforcement, providing varied practice, and ensuring motivation.
- The use of everyday examples that are understandable and make sense to a wide range of youngsters based on their own experiences.
- Clearly articulated models with scripted examples of how these models can be used to promote instruction.

Go to **www.aplusmath.com/ Worksheets** where you can create worksheets for various math concepts.

Tips FOR TEACHERS 14.5

PROVIDING FEEDBACK THAT ENHANCES STUDENT LEARNING

Teachers are often reluctant to give feedback to students with disabilities, wondering whether they will do more damage than good. Specific feedback helps students learn when it is provided with teaching the student as the goal. Consider the following:

- Provide feedback informing students that their response is not accurate and cue them as to what is wrong. Give students an opportunity to try again. Recognize positively if students are successful in the next try. If not successful, provide even more instruction with another opportunity to demonstrate success.

- Remind students of what they know and have done successfully in the past that is related to the problem. Encourage them to use previous knowledge to solve the new problem.

- Ask students to monitor their problem resolution and reinforce them for checking and monitoring their learning.

- Provide readily available answers and feedback so that students wait a minimal amount of time after completing problems to know what they did right and what needs to be redone.

What can teachers do to ensure that students will improve their math performance? Baker, Gersten, and Lee's (2002) synthesis of the research suggests the following:

- Collect ongoing progress monitoring data to identify what students are learning and how quickly they are learning.
- Have peers assist one another in learning, applying, and reviewing math problems.
- Use explicit and systematic instruction in all elements of mathematics, including computation and problem solving. This type of instruction guides students through problems and calculations rather than relying on students to "figure it out" independently.
- Provide parents with information on how their children are performing and engage them as supporters and motivators for their children's progress in mathematics.

Math Manipulatives. Learning the language of mathematics is an important skill for all students. Peterson, Mercer, and O'Shea (1988) examined the effectiveness of a three-stage teaching sequence on students' abilities to learn place value. The sequence included going from concrete to semiconcrete and then to abstract teaching strategies. In the *concrete* stage, the mathematical concept was taught by using manipulative objects such as pegs. In the *semiconcrete* stage, pictorial representations were used for instruction. In the *abstract* stage, only numbers were used. Students who used this three-step process for learning place values significantly outperformed a control group. Tips for Teachers 14.6 shows another way to help students move from the concrete to the abstract.

Teaching for Comprehension. Teach students to understand math concepts. Most instruction is provided to ensure that the answer is correct, the math computation has been accurately completed, or the math fact is memorized. Additional emphasis on ensuring that students understand the math process needs to be included in the math curriculum. Jan Hughes, a third-grade teacher, continually asks students to say in their own words what she has just said. During math problem solving, she often asks students to work in groups of three to write story problems that go along with an operation she has just taught. She continually thinks about ways to make the mathematics she teaches "real" to students. The following section describes ways to check for comprehension in math instruction.

Silver Burdett Ginn

What procedures can teachers develop for using concrete approaches and manipulatives in mathematics instruction? What instructional strategies work for helping students move from the concrete to the abstract?

Tips FOR TEACHERS 14.6

HELPING STUDENTS MOVE FROM CONCRETE TO ABSTRACT LEARNING

- *Concrete.* Provide manipulative and interactive opportunities to integrate the new mathematical concept. For example, use pictures, blocks, rods, or other representations to demonstrate understanding of the answer. Encourage students to use both oral and written language to relate to the new mathematical vocabulary and concept.

- *Pictorial.* Represent the mathematics problem with pictures. Provide the problem and have students interpret it and draw pictures to represent it.

- *Linking.* Encourage students to talk about what they have learned and to explain it to others. By recording or

demonstrating what they have learned in meaningful ways, they can link their language to the mathematical algorithm.

- *Symbolic.* Have students demonstrate knowledge about the symbols by talking about them and demonstrating through drawing, pointing, or replicating the meaning of the symbol or algorithm.

- *Abstract.* Have students teach the steps for computing or problem solving with alternative solutions, and then solve problems in new and creative ways without using concrete or pictorial representations.

Checking for Comprehension: The Case of Trinette.   Be certain that students understand the *meaning* of an operation, not just the answer. Students who have memorized the facts by rote often operate with little understanding of what they are doing. For example, Trinette was asked to write the answer to the following math problem:

$$3 \times 2 =$$

Answering correctly, she wrote 6. But when Trinette's teacher asked her to illustrate the problem with pictures of flowers, this is what Trinette drew:

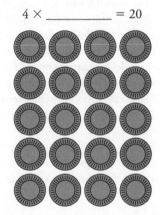

Trinette demonstrated that she did not understand the problem, although she had successfully memorized the answer and her facts.

The following drawing illustrates how rows of chips can be used to illustrate multiplication. For example, ask, "How many fours make twenty?" "Fours are placed on the board _____ times."

$$4 \times \text{_____} = 20$$

Other ways to check for comprehension include having students "talk aloud" about what is involved in solving a problem. Instead of letting them merely *read* the problem, ask them to *explain* what it means. For example, 63 – 27 could mean that someone had 63 pieces of gum and gave 27 pieces to a friend. Another strategy is to have one student explain the process to another student by using block manipulatives. For example, 24 + 31 is the same as adding 4 one-block pieces to 1 one-block piece and 2 ten-block pieces to 3 ten-block pieces. Some teachers use vocalization or have students close their eyes and use noises to illustrate operations. To illustrate multiplication, for example, the teacher and student might tap to indicate groups of six.

Using Constant Time Delay Procedure.   Constant time delay is a procedure for teaching math facts that provides for the systematic introduction of teacher assistance. This nearly errorless technique employs a controlling prompt to ensure the successful performance of the student (Gast, Ault, Wolery, Doyle, & Belanger, 1988; Stevens & Schuster, 1988). In general, the procedure involves presentation of a stimulus (e.g., a word or math fact), after which the student is allowed a specific amount of time (e.g., 3 seconds) to provide the correct answer (e.g., read the word or answer the fact). If the student does not respond within the time allowed, a controlling prompt (typically a teacher modeling the correct response) is provided. The controlling prompt is a cue that ensures that the student will respond correctly (i.e., the word name or the answer to the problem is modeled). The student then repeats the teacher's model. Although correct responses before and after the prompt are reinforced, only correct responses given before the prompt count. The effectiveness of the constant time delay procedure has been demonstrated with a variety of academic skills, students, and instructional arrangements as demonstrated in the 60-Second Lesson (Mattingly & Bott, 1990; Schuster, Stevens, & Doak, 1990; Stevens & Schuster, 1987; Wolery, Cjybriwsky, Gast, & Boyle-Gast, 1991).

60 Second LESSON
Using the Constant Time Delay with Math Facts

Ask a small group of students struggling with multiplication facts to join you at a small table.

• Show each student separately a math fact allowing 3 seconds for them to respond.

• If they respond correctly within that time period, give them positive feedback.

• If they either respond incorrectly or not quickly enough, you can say, "The answer to 4 X 7 = 28. Can you say the problem and the answer?

Providing Correction and Feedback.   Immediate correction and feedback are essential to the success of students with math difficulties. Saying, "Orlando, the first six problems are correct, and then the third row is all wrong. Please redo them." is an example of insufficient feedback. Teachers often tell students which problems are correct and which are wrong and hope that this feedback is adequate. For students with learning problems, it is not. They need more sustained interaction to help them acquire not only the skills for identifying what they did wrong, but also the procedures for how to do it differently. The teacher must analyze the problem and also obtain sufficient information from the student to determine why the problem was not done correctly. A better model for correction and feedback follows: "Orlando, point to the problems you think are correct. Think about each problem before you point." (The teacher positively reinforces Orlando as he points to problems that are right.) "Yes, those are all correct. You did an excellent job with those. You started on the right, added them correctly, carried numbers when you needed to."

When students are first learning a math concept or operation, teachers need to provide a great deal of assistance to ensure that students perform correctly. Over time, teachers need to systematically reduce the amount of help they give students.

Providing Practice

Practice is important if students are to exhibit high levels of accuracy consistently and across multiple problem types. Mastery occurs when students meet expectations for accuracy and speed in different types of problems. In operations, mastery refers to the ability to use multiple algorithms to solve an operation so that students truly learn (rather than memorize). Denise, a ninth-grade student, expresses her frustration this way: "I never seem to be able to really learn anything. Just when I feel like I'm starting to get it, we move on to a different thing. I wish I could just stay with something until I really get it." As a teacher, you need to know when there are students like Denise who need additional support.

Counting by Numbers.   Students are taught to "count by" numbers, beginning with 2, 10, and 5, and then 3, 4, 6, 7, 8, and 9. This is done by group counting, singing the numbers in sequence, writing the numbers, erasing some numbers in the sequence and having students fill them in, and having students work on worksheets with the count-by sequences.

After students have learned to count by numbers, they can apply the strategy to multiplication by using the following steps:

1. Ask students to point to the number they can count by.
2. Make hash marks to represent the number on the other side of the multiplication sign.
3. When you count by the number, point to each of the hash marks. The last number said when you reach the end of the hash marks is the answer to the problem.

Games.   Games can be an important way for students to learn mathematics skills. Larson and Slaughter (1984) provide the following suggestions for using games in mathematics instruction:

■ *Choose games that reinforce present instruction.* Be sure that the selected game reinforces much of what students already know.

- *Consider the complexity of the game* so that students do not spend more time learning the game's procedures and rules than they spend learning the math-related material.
- *Foresee potential problems associated with games,* such as disruptive behavior and shouting out.
- *Provide an answer key if an adult is not available.*
- *Play at least one round of the game with students* to ensure that they understand the rules and procedures and are acquiring the mathematics skills desired.
- *Use aides or parent helpers to monitor the games.*

Strategies for Helping All Students Acquire Basic Math Skills

Mathematics instruction once focused on the acquisition of the basic math skills, saving problem solving for later in the math curriculum. We now realize that teaching basic skills and problem solving must be coordinated from the beginning of math instruction. Key components of basic math skills include the following:

- Prenumber
- Numeration
- Place value
- Fractions

Prenumber Skills

Many young students with learning problems come to school without certain basic prenumber skills necessary for initial success in mathematics. Sonya Perez, a first-grade teacher, described Malcolm in this way: "When he came to my class, he knew how to count to 10, but he didn't know what he was doing. He didn't know what the numbers meant. As far as he knew, he could have been saying his ABCs." She realized that he first needed to learn one-to-one correspondence.

One-to-One Correspondence. Students demonstrate understanding of one-to-one correspondence when they are able to determine that each object corresponds to another object. For example, when a student puts out cereal bowls for himself, his sister, and his mother, he learns that each bowl represents one person. Early humans used one-to-one correspondence to keep track of their accounts. For example, a man might put a rock in a bucket to represent each bag of grain he gave to a neighbor. The following activities can be used to teach one-to-one correspondence:

- *Use everyday events to teach one-to-one correspondence.* Allow students with difficulties in this area to pass out materials. "Allison, please get one pair of scissors for each student in your group. Naja, you need to have a chair for each member of your group. How many chairs are there? How many more do you need?"
- *Use objects when you work with small groups of students who need help with one-to-one correspondence.* Give each student 10 small blocks. Place 3 blocks in the center. Say, "I want you to place a block next to each one in the center. As you place a block, I want you to say the number. I will do the first one, and then you do what I did."
- *Give students a set of cards with pictures on each card.* Ask students to put the correct number of objects (e.g., pegs) on top of each number card. Reverse the task by giving objects to students and asking them to put the correct picture card next to the objects.

Classification. Classification, the ability to group or sort objects based on one or more common properties, is an important prenumber skill because it focuses students, making them attend to the common properties of objects and reduce large numbers of objects to smaller groups. Classification can be by size, color, shape, texture, or design. Most students are naturally interested in sorting and think that activities related to this prenumber skill are fun. Examples of such activities follow:

- Provide students with a bag of miscellaneous articles that vary in size, shape, and color. Ask students to sort the articles any way they like into an empty egg carton or empty plastic containers. After they finish, ask them to tell you the rules for sorting their articles.

After they have had a chance to listen to others, give them a chance to sort the articles again and to explain their rules for sorting.

- Provide students with an empty egg carton and a box of small articles. Ask students to sort the articles by a single property, such as color. Now ask them whether there is another way in which they might be able to sort the articles. For example, ask them to consider size, texture, and so on.
- Ask students to work in small groups, and provide them with a bag of articles. Ask one student to sort several of the articles by a property. Then ask other students in the group to guess the property that qualifies the articles for the group.
- Use pictures for sorting tasks. Good pictures include ones that represent animals, foods, plants, and toys.
- Board games and bingo games can be played by sorting or classifying shapes, colors, and pictures.

Seriation.   Seriation, the ability to rank objects according to the degree to which they possess a certain common characteristic, is similar to classification in that it depends on the recognition of common attributes of objects but differs from classification in that the order in which objects are placed depends on the extent to which each object possesses the attribute. For example, seriation can occur by length, height, color, or weight. Sample activities for teaching seriation follow:

- Give students a long piece of string. Ask them to cut the string into pieces of various lengths. Then ask them to put the lengths in order from shortest to longest. Now ask students to work in groups of three. Have them use those same piles of string to create one long seriation, from shortest to longest. Continue to ask students to work in different groups to sort the string sizes.
- Ask students to work in groups of eight. In these groups, ask them to put themselves in order from shortest to tallest. Now ask them to put themselves in order from longest to shortest hair. Continue asking students to put themselves in seriation based on different attributes.
- Using a peg with various sizes of rings, ask students to put the rings on the peg from largest to smallest.
- Fill jars of the same size with different amounts of sand or water and ask students to put them in order.

See Activities for All Learners later in the chapter for more activities.

Working with Numeration

Numeration is the understanding of numbers and their manipulations. Do not assume that because students can count or identify numbers that they understand the value and the meaning of the numbers. This is a mistake that many teachers and parents make.

Understanding numerals is an extremely important basic concept, one that throws many children into mathematical confusion early. A good example is Michelle, whose early experiences with math were positive. She learned to say, read, and write numbers with little or no difficulty. In first and second grade, she mastered addition and subtraction facts and did these problems easily. When Michelle was asked to do problems that involved addition with regrouping (adding numerals and then converting them to tens, hundreds, thousands etc.), her lack of knowledge of numerals and their meaning quickly became evident. Following are examples of the way Michelle did some problems:

$$27 + 15 = 312$$
$$49 + 36 = 715$$

As you can see from Michelle's answers, she remembered her math facts, such as $7 + 5$ and $2 + 1$, or $9 + 6$ and $4 + 3$, but did not understand what the numbers meant. Michelle added 7 plus 5 to get 12 and then 2 plus 1 to get 3 resulting in the answer 312; however, Michelle did not understand the importance of place value nor did she "check" her answer by estimating a reasonable answer and determining if she was even close.

Understanding numeration and place value is necessary for progress in computation. Like Michelle, many students fail to make adequate progress in math because they do not understand the meaning of the numerals and the place value with which they are working. For example, students who understand the meaning of the numerals 25 and 17 would be less likely to make the following conceptual error:

$$25 - 17 = 12$$

Estimating. Many students with learning difficulties in math do not have a sense of how much a certain amount really is—what it means to have five dollars, for example, or how many eggs are in a dozen, or about what 15 and 15, added together, should equal. These students cannot check their answers to determine how far off they are because they do not have a good idea of what an answer that makes sense would be.

Why is extra practice in estimation and other basic math skills important for students with math difficulties? How can instruction in those skills be modified for students with learning problems?

Estimating is something that can be done throughout the day and throughout the curriculum. For example, start the day by asking students to estimate how many children are absent. Estimation can be included in subject matters as well. You can use estimation in science, social studies, and even with art projects.

Students who do not understand the real meaning of numerals have difficulty applying computation to everyday problems. For example, when Michelle's teacher posed the following problem, Michelle did not understand how to begin to find the answer: "Let's pretend that you had three one-dollar bills and you were going to McDonald's to buy lunch. Let's pretend that your hamburger costs 89 cents, your French fries cost 74 cents, and your medium-sized Coke costs 69 cents. How much money would you have left to spend?"

Mistakes occur when students attempt problems that are entirely too difficult for them or when they do not understand the idea behind the problem. In such cases, the solutions students provide are totally unreasonable given the problem. One of the best ways to help students who demonstrate this problem is to continually ask them to think about the problem and estimate what their answer probably will be. For example, before computing the problem 24 plus 73, ask students what they would estimate the answer would be. If students have difficulty even identifying a reasonable response, help them round up or down the two numbers so they are easier to estimate. In the previous problem, students can round up 24 to 25 and 73 to 75. That way they can guess that the answer will be very close to 100. When students are taught to consider what a reasonable answer should be, they are better able to catch their mistakes. These problems are particularly severe for students with disabilities who demonstrate low understanding of mathematical problems and the meaning of numbers (Lucangeli, Coi, & Bosco, 1997).

Understanding Regrouping. Regrouping refers to converting from tens to ones or hundreds to tens, etc., so that borrowing can occur. Many children have difficulty with regrouping. Regrouping errors are less likely to occur when students understand numeration. Following are examples of regrouping errors:

$$39 + 27 = 516$$
$$56 - 18 = 42$$
$$41 - 24 = 23$$

Examine the errors students make and use the information to provide instruction. For example, some students subtract the smaller number from the larger number regardless of the problem. These students need practicing reading the entire number and determining which number is larger. Practicing reading numbers and stating which one is bigger or smaller may be helpful to them. Furthermore, students who consistently make errors in regrouping can practice subtracting smaller numbers (e.g., single digit numbers) until they can do so automatically and correctly before doing more complex numbers.

Understanding Zero. Students need to understand that zero is a number and means more than "nothing." In the number 30, for example, students need to understand that the number zero is a placeholder. For the number 306, students need to understand that there are 0 tens and that zero is serving as a placeholder.

Understanding Place Value

Before students can understand place value, they must understand numeration. Students who know the meaning of numbers will have far less difficulty understanding place value. For example, if a student knows what 56 actually means, then when someone talks about the tens place equaling 50, the student will not be confused. When someone talks about the ones place equaling 6 ones, the student will understand what is meant.

Grouping by Ones and Tens. To teach grouping, start with manipulatives (buttons, sticks, and blocks are useful), then pictures, and then numbers. Ask students to practice grouping by ones and tens. Students can also develop a table to record their answers, as follows:

HUNDREDS	TENS	ONES	NUMERALS
1	3	1	131
1	2	3	123
1	4	5	145

Use "ten blocks" and "single blocks" to represent numerals. For example, 35 can be represented as follows:

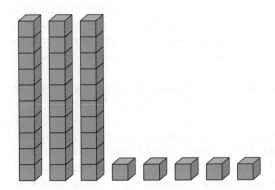

Naming Tens. Teach students to identify numerals by the number of tens. For example, 6 tens is 60, 4 tens is 40, 8 tens is 80, and so on. Give students opportunities to count by tens and then name the number. For example, "Count by tens three times." "10, 20, 30." "Count by tens seven times." "10, 20, 30, 40, 50, 60, 70." Also give students opportunities to draw picture diagrams that represent the place values of tens and ones and to identify the number.

Place Value Beyond Two Digits. When students can accurately group and identify numbers at the two-digit level, introduce them to three- and four-digit numbers. It is a good idea to be certain that students have mastered the concept of two-digit place value before you introduce numerals and place value. Give students plenty of opportunity to group, orally name, and sequence three- and four-digit place values.

Because place value is a skill taught during the primary grades, older students who have not adequately learned the skill will have difficulty with computation and word problems and may have little opportunity to learn place value. Many of the games and activities designed to teach place value are aimed at young children and are less appropriate for older students. Tips for Teachers 14.7 provides sources of numbers that may be useful for teaching place value to older students.

Learning Fractions

Although often thought of as one of the more difficult mathematical skills, fractions are actually introduced early in the mathematics curriculum. Children between the ages of 3 and 5 discover fractions when they begin to cook. "Pour in ½ cup of milk and ⅓ cup of raisins" is often a youngster's introduction to fractions. Sharing—as in "Give half of your cookie to your sister"—is also a good way for children to discover fractions.

TIPS FOR TEACHERS 14.7

SOURCES OF NUMBERS FOR TEACHING PLACE VALUE TO OLDER STUDENTS

- An odometer
- Numbers from students' science or social studies texts
- Numbers from school population (e.g., number of first-year students, sophomores, juniors, seniors, and so on)
- Population data from town, county, state, or country
- Financial data page from the newspaper

The teaching of fractions, mirroring that of other computations, proceeds from concrete to abstract. Many manipulative aids can be used to teach fractions: colored rods, cardboard strips and squares, blocks, fractional circle wheels, cooking utensils such as measuring cups and spoons, and any unit divider (e.g., egg cartons and muffin pans).

Students with learning problems are unlikely to learn fractions, however, unless they are taught directly and systematically (Engelmann, Carnine, & Steely, 2005). Such teaching includes the following:

- **Systematic practice in discriminating among different problem types.** Students with learning disabilities and behavior problems often confuse algorithms when they compute fractions. For example, when adding fractions the denominator stays the same as in ¼ plus ¾ = ¾ or 1. However, when dividing with fractions the denominator changes.
- **Separation of confusing elements and terminology.** Because much of the language of learning fractions is unfamiliar and confusing, students are more likely to learn fractions successfully when the language and concepts are clearly explained and illustrated.
- **Use of a wide range of elements to illustrate each concept.** Students have a difficult time generalizing beyond the number of examples provided by the teacher; therefore, by providing many different examples, you help students understand.

The teaching sequence for fractions, which ensures that each student can do certain work, follows:

1. **Manipulate concrete models.** Students must use fraction blocks and pegs and use instruments that require understanding of fractions (such as measuring cups, spoons, and rulers).
2. **Match fractional models.** Students must match halves, thirds, and fourths. One way to do this is to think about the role of fractions when dividing food such as pizza or pieces of cake.
3. **Point to fractional model when the teacher names a fraction.** When the teacher says "half," the student selects a model of "half" from several answers.
4. **Name fractional units when the teacher selects it.** When the teacher points to a fractional unit such as a "fourth," the student names it.
5. **Draw diagrams or use manipulatives to represent fractional units.** When the teacher says or writes fractional units such as "whole," "half," and "third," the student uses manipulative drawings to represent these units.
6. **Write fraction names when given fractional drawings.** When the teacher shows the student a picture of a fractional unit, the student writes the name of the fraction.
7. **Use fractions to solve problems.** Fractions are very helpful for dividing the cost of a bill when eating out or when dividing food such as a pie.

Strategies for Helping All Learners Acquire and Use Computation Skills

The emphasis on problem solving from NCTM (2000) does not mean that students do not need to learn math computation. In fact, students will be unsuccessful problem solvers if they spend too little time on math computation. You can help students with special needs, who often have difficulty with math computation, by addressing the following issues that present obstacles for these students.

Go to **www.superkids.com/aweb/tools/math,** where you can create worksheets on addition, subtraction, multiplication, division, fractions, and more. There are also games available on the site.

Patterns of Common Computation Errors

The computation errors that students make fit certain patterns. Rourke (1993) identifies common types of mechanical arithmetic errors, described in the following sections. Tips for Teachers 14.8 has suggestions for helping students learn computational techniques.

Tips FOR TEACHERS 14.8

TEACHING STUDENTS COMPUTATIONAL STRATEGIES

1. *Use doubles.* Students know that $2 + 2 = 4$, $3 + 3 = 6$, and $5 + 5 = 10$. With this basic information, they can easily compute related facts. For example, if $3 + 3 = 6$, what is $3 + 4$? Yes, it is one more.

2. *Count on.* Students do not need to resort to counting from 1 to solve math facts. They can learn to count on from the largest numeral in an addition fact. For example, $8 + 3$ means counting on 3 more from 8, for a sum of 11. Students learn to count on 3 more from 8: "9, 10, 11." The answer is the last number they say after they have counted on the correct number. Students can use this same principle for subtraction. For example, when asked to solve the following problem:

$$8 - 3 =$$

they now count backward from eight, "7, 6, 5." Again, the last number is the answer.

3. *Use the commutative idea.* With addition and multiplication, the order of the numbers does not matter—it always yields the same answer. For example, $3 + 4 = 7$ and $4 + 3 = 7$. With multiplication, this is also true: $4 \times 6 = 24$ and $6 \times 4 = 24$. Give students many opportunities to use this principle to be sure they understand and apply it.

4. *Think one more or one less than a known fact.* When students know a math fact, teach them that they also know related math facts. For example, Guido knew that $6 + 7 = 13$. When he was faced with the problem $6 + 8 = $ _____, he panicked. When his teacher told him that 8 is one more than 7, thus the answer is one more than $6 + 7 = 13$, he was able to solve the problem quickly. Pictures such as the following can help to illustrate the principle:

$5 + 5 = 10$ ♥♥   ♥♥
          ♥♥ + ♥♥ =
          ♥   ♥

$5 + 6 = $ ♥♥   ♥♥
          ♥♥ + ♥♥ =
          ♥   ♥♥

$5 + 4 = $ ♥♥   ♥♥
          ♥♥ + ♥ =
          ♥   ♥

5. *Using tens.* Students can learn that $10 + $ any single-digit number merely changes the 0 in the 10 to the number they are adding to it, as in the following examples:

$$10 + 4 = 14$$
$$10 + 8 = 18$$

6. *Using nines.* There are two strategies students can apply to addition facts that involve nines. First, they can think of the 9 as a 10 and then subtract 1 from the answer. In the following example, the student is taught to "think" of the 9 as a 10:

$$
\begin{array}{ccc}
9 & \text{think} & 10 \\
+6 & & +6 \\
\hline
& & 16 - 1 = 15
\end{array}
$$

Second, students can think that whenever there is a 9 in an addition problem, the answer in the ones column is always one less than the number they are adding to the 9. For example:

$$
\begin{array}{ccc}
9 & 8 & 9 \\
+4 & +9 & +6 \\
\hline
13 & 17 & 15
\end{array}
$$

7. *Counting by twos, threes, fours, fives, and tens.* Beginning with 10, teach students to count by the number. This can be done with individual students or with a small group. It is sometimes helpful to develop a rhythm to the counting sequence:

$$10-20-30-40-50-60-70-80-90-100$$

After students can count by tens to 100, ask them to count aloud by 10 from two points other than 10 and 100. For example, "Count aloud from 20 to 80." After students have learned to count by tens, they should be taught to count by fives and then by twos, threes, and fours. Being able to count by multiples helps in addition, multiplication, and division. Multiplication facts can be taught by interpreting 3×4 as counting by threes four times. Division facts, such as 8 divided by 2, can be interpreted as "How many times do you count by twos before you reach 8?"

8. *Relationship between addition and subtraction and between multiplication and division.* After students learn addition facts, they can be shown the relationship between the addition fact and subtraction. For example, students who know $7 + 6 = 13$ can learn the relationships between the known addition fact and the subtraction fact, $13 - 7 = $ _____. Whenever possible, reinforce this principle as students are working: "You know $8 + 4 = 12$, so $12 - 4$ must be _____." Give students known facts and ask them to form subtraction problems. These sample relationships can be used to teach multiplication and division facts.

Sources: Adapted from Bley, N. S., & Thornton, C. A. (2001). *Teaching mathematics to students with learning disabilities*; Thornton, C. A., & Toohey, M. A. (1985). Basic math facts: Guidelines for teaching and learning. *Learning Disabilities Focus, 1,* 44–57; and Thornton, C. A., Tucker, B. F., Dossey, J. A., & Brazik, E. F. (1983). *Teaching mathematics to children with special needs*. Menlo Park, CA: Addison-Wesley.

Spatial Organization.   Mistakes in spatial organization are those that occur because students misalign numbers in columns. These mistakes can occur when students copy problems incorrectly or as they solve problems. One way to help students correct misaligned numbers is to tell them to draw vertical lines through their numbers to ensure that ones, tens, and hundreds are all in the right place. Another way to help is to provide graph paper with large squares so that students can write the numbers in boxes and more easily align them.

Visual Detail.   Mistakes involving visual detail occur when students misread one aspect of the arithmetic problem—misreading a minus sign as a plus sign, for example, or disregarding a dollar sign. Because many of the problems that occur in mathematics can be easily corrected by the student, teach students to stop and reread the problem and their answers before they go to the next problem to be sure that they neither misread nor omitted something.

Procedural Error.   Procedural error occurs when students misapply a procedure from one arithmetic operation to another. For example, a student learns that $5 \times 5 = 25$, and when asked to complete the problem $5 + 5$ misapplies information from multiplication and writes the answer 25.

Failure to Shift Operations.   A failure to shift operations occurs when students fail to move to another operation after completing one operation. This occurs in word problems that involve more than one step, such as subtraction and addition. To help students who demonstrate this problem, ask them to reread the problem and tell you whether more than one operation is involved. Ask them to identify the types of operations involved and to provide an example of each one. Ask them to tell you how they will monitor their process and to determine how they will ensure accuracy in switching from one operation to the next.

Motoric Problems.   Mistakes resulting from motoric problems can occur when the students' writing is so difficult to read that it leads to errors in arithmetic. Many students with learning problems demonstrate such poor writing ability that it interferes with their ability to successfully perform arithmetic computations. These students have difficulty not only writing their numbers but also reading them. They often mistake their fives for threes, their twos for threes, and so on. Therefore, their calculations may be accurate, according to their interpretation of the number, but the answers are wrong because they have mistaken the number.

Memory Problems.   Mistakes resulting from memory problems occur when students forget or misremember a fact that leads to an error in arithmetic calculation. As a teacher, you can help students with learning problems by providing them with adequate time and frequent opportunities to rehearse and learn arithmetic facts.

Difficulty with Zero.   Difficulty with zero can lead to mistakes that occur when students do not understand the multiple meanings and uses of zero. Many students with learning problems learn that zero means "nothing," and they never really understand that zero is a number or the role of zero as a placeholder. The best way to help students who have difficulty with zero is to ensure that they understand how zero can be used as a placeholder. To facilitate understanding and adequate use of zero, you can teach a mini lesson to a small group of students who demonstrate difficulty with this concept such as the one described in the 60-Second Lesson.

60 Second LESSON

The Meaning of "Zero"

In a 60-second lesson the teacher might indicate that the term *zero* has several meanings.

• "What is one of the meanings of *zero*?" "Yes, zero means 'nothing'."

• "If you have zero candy, you have no candy."

• "A different meaning of zero is as a placeholder when we are writing numbers. For example, in the number 100, the zeros

tell us that the number is a LOT more than 1." The teacher can then delete the zero at the end of the number 100.

• The teacher then asks, "What number is this? Yes, the new number is 10. The zero at the end tells us that the number is more than 1 but a lot less than the previous number 100."

The teacher can then add additional examples.

Computation and Calculators

There is a preponderance of evidence that calculators assist in the acquisition of mathematics achievement for students with learning problems. Reviews of the calculator research have drawn the following conclusions:

- Calculators for instructional purposes do not impede the acquisition of basic skills. In fact, calculators can increase skill acquisition.
- The advantages of using calculators are more obvious for problems that include computation than for problem solving.
- Students who use calculators on criterion tests produce higher achievement scores than students who do not.
- Studies indicate that students do not develop a negative attitude toward math because of calculator use. In fact, calculators improve students' attitudes toward mathematics.
- It is appropriate to introduce calculators at the same time that the paper-and-pencil methods are taught.
- Students can develop their own complex problems and then solve them with use of the calculator. This also serves to increase their self-concept about math skills.

Students are more likely to be persistent in solving math problems and have a better attitude toward math when they use technology supports (Cawley, Foley, & Doan, 2003). Tech Tips provides examples of some of these supports.

Geary (2003) and Hofmeister (1989) provide a summary of the research on math problem solving:

- Most students with significant learning problems have well-developed number concepts but do have difficulties with even simple arithmetic.
- Some generalization of problem-solving skills should be planned for and systematically taught. This generalization is most likely to occur across problems without a domain. Transfer across domains will depend on the similarity of the problem.
- It may be unreasonable to expect the majority of specific problem-solving strategies in one domain, such as ratio-based word problems, to transfer to another domain, such as geometry proofs.
- The development of practical problem-solving skills will require a considerable investment of time and explicitly taught strategies and practices.
- Teaching of problem-solving strategies should be integrated with the teaching of other content in the domain, such as computational and factual knowledge.

Understanding the research on teaching problem-solving skills to all students will better prepare you to apply effective strategies for teaching students problem-solving skills.

 *Tech* TIPS

TECHNOLOGY THAT HELPS STUDENTS SOLVE MATH PROBLEMS

Many educational software programs, with varying foci. are designed to enhance mathematics instruction. As a tool or utility, programs that offer students and teachers ease of use can be extremely helpful in accommodating all learners in your class.

MathPad and MathPad Plus and Number Concepts by Cabmium LearningTechnologies, Inc. at
▷ **http://store.cambiumlearning.com/SearchResultsHP.aspx? searchtype = Subject&sorttype = Subject&Query = Mathematics&site = itc**
These programs, designed for students K–8, enable learners to do arithmetic directly on the computer. These programs are ideal for learners who need help organizing or navigating through math problems or who have difficulty using pencil and paper with math.

AAA Math at
▷ **www.aaamath.com**
This web resource for math activities is loaded with explanations, interactive practice, and games, along with teacher resources.

Ten Tricky Tiles by Sunburst Technologies at
▷ **http://store.sunburst.com/Category.aspx?MODE = RESULTS&CATID = 3360**
This program is for young children who are developing their arithmetic and number skills. Sunburst Technologies offers numerous math programs for all ages and skill levels.

Strategies for Helping All Students Develop Problem-Solving Skills

Teaching problem-solving skills is an important aspect of effective math instruction. There are several unifying components that include

- A mathematics knowledge base.
- An application of knowledge to new and unfamiliar situations.
- An ability to actively engage in thinking processes and apply this knowledge base to problems.

Each of these components must be present in order to help all students understand how to develop problem-solving skills.

Teaching Problem-Solving Strategies to Secondary Students

Mercer and Miller (1992) have developed a procedure called FAST DRAW to teach the concrete–representational–abstract teaching principle advocated in mathematics instruction. The Strategic Math Series is the name of their program. Following is an explanation of the **FAST DRAW** strategy:

Find what you're solving for.
Ask yourself, "What are the parts of the problem?"
Set up the numbers.
Tie down the sign.
Discover the sign.
Read the problem.
Answer or draw a conceptual representation of the problem, using lines and tallies, and check.
Write the answer.

Since many students with disabilities benefit from cognitive problem-solving instruction (Alter, Wrick, Brown, & Lingo, 2008; Montague, 1992), teachers are finding a multistep process useful:

1. Read the problem aloud. If students have difficulty reading, read the problem to them.
2. Ask students to think about and identify the key words in the problem using their own words.
3. Ask students to visualize the problem or draw it.
4. Guide students in putting the key parts of the problem in their own words.
5. Help students determine a reasonable hypothesis for solving the problem.
6. Ask students to estimate an answer.
7. Provide guided instruction as students calculate the answer.

Solving algebra word problems is a challenging task for many older students with math difficulties. Cognitive strategies such as asking themselves questions (self-question), thinking aloud, providing guided practice, and using graphs to monitor their progress may be helpful. Students displayed increased abilities to solve problems and transferred their skills to other settings. The self-questions Hutchinson (1993) used included the following:

- Have I read and understood the sentence?
- Do I have the whole picture, a representation, for this problem?
- Have I written the representation on the worksheet?

In summary, when teaching story problems to students with learning and behavior difficulties, keep the following guidelines in mind (Bos & Vaughn, 2006):

- Be certain students can perform the arithmetic computation before introducing the computation in story problems.

By acquiring a good mathematics knowledge base, students learn the strategies for developing problem-solving skills.

myeducationlab

To enhance your understanding of how to use learning strategies to teach intermediate algebra, go to the IRIS Center Resources section of Topic 10: Content Area Teaching in the MyEducationLab for your course and complete Case 1: Algebra (Part 1): Applying Learning Strategies to Beginning Algebra.

- Develop a range of story problems that contain the type of problem you want students to learn to solve so that they have adequate opportunities to practice and learn the pattern of the story problem.
- Instruct with one type of problem until mastery is attained.
- Teach students to read through the word problem and visualize the situation. Ask them to read the story aloud and tell what it is about.
- Ask students to reread the story, this time to get the facts.
- Identify the key question. In the beginning stages of problem solving, students should write the key question so that it can be referred to when computation is complete.
- Identify extraneous information. Tell students to note that this information will not be used.
- Reread the story problem and attempt to state the situation in a mathematical sentence. The teacher plays an important role in this step by asking the students questions and guiding them in formulating the arithmetic problem.
- Tell students to write the arithmetic problem and compute the answer. Students can compute some problems in their heads without completing this step.
- Tell students to reread the key questions and be sure that they have completed the problem correctly.
- Ask students whether their answer is likely, based on their estimate.

What should teachers consider when they design math problem-solving activities for students with special needs? To what extent will these designs benefit other students? The instructional practices that we recommend for teaching problem solving will benefit all students. Tips for Teachers 14.8 should be helpful as you design and implement problem-solving activities for students with learning problems.

Integrating Math Problem Solving into the Curriculum

Problem solving does not have to occur only during math time; it is an interesting and fun activity to integrate into the rest of the curriculum as well. Math story problems are especially easy to integrate into the reading curriculum. How? Take stories that children are reading or books that you are reading to the entire class and change the stories so that they include numbers and problems the students need to answer.

Joan Lindquist, a third-grade teacher, asked students the following questions about a story they were reading in class: "How many friends has Marcia told us about? How many friends does Linda have? Altogether, how many friends do they have? How many more friends does Linda have than Marcia?" Teachers can also add information to the stories and then ask children to solve word problems based on the additional information provided. They can then have students work in pairs to write their own word problems from the stories they are reading and have them read their word problems to the entire class so that the class can solve them.

Word problems can be easily integrated into the social studies curriculum as well. When dates are discussed, ask students to compute how many years ago the event occurred. Ask students word problems about the age of central figures in the social studies lesson. Add numbers and information to the lesson and construct word problems. Integrating math into other content areas is an important means of promoting generalization of math concepts. See Activities for All Learners for a variety of mathematics activities suitable for all learners.

Return to the interview at the beginning of this chapter, where you met Shawn, a college student with learning disabilities who had extreme difficulty with math. What questions would you want to ask him? If Shawn were in your class, how would you implement the suggestions in this chapter to ensure that his experiences in mathematics would be as positive as possible? Remember, you *can* make a difference in students' lives.

Mathematics Activities for All Learners

Slap It!!!

Objective: To provide practice in responding quickly to math

Grades: Second through eighth grade

Materials: A set of 4-inch by 6-inch cards on which the answers to math facts are written; cards can be established as answers to addition, subtraction, multiplication, or division facts

Teaching Procedures:

1. Students and teacher stand around a small table (preferably round), and teacher shows students the cards, each with a number (the answer to a math fact). Teacher spreads the cards (approximately 10) on the table with the number side up.

2. Students are told to keep both hands on the table until the teacher says, "Go." Students who lift either hand prior to the "go" signal are eliminated from that round of competition.

3. The teacher says a computation problem, followed by the word go. For example, "6 × 7 = (go)."

4. Students slap the card that has the correct answer. The first hand on the card gets to keep the card. The student with the most cards gets to be the teacher.

Adaptations:

1. Teachers can use the same game with word problems.

2. Teachers can use more than one computation during the game.

MEASUREMENT

Objective: To reinforce understanding of perimeter and area

Grades: Third grade and above

Materials: 1-inch graph paper, scissors, teacher-made table worksheet

Teaching Procedures:

1. Have students cut out squares of graph paper of different sizes: a 1-inch square, a 2-inch square, a 3-inch square, a 4-inch square, and a 5-inch square.

2. Measure the number of small squares in each large cutout square, and complete the following table:

edges	1	2	3	4	5	6
perimeter						
area						

3. Ask, "What happens to the perimeter and area each time the edges are doubled?"

4. Have students experiment with different-size squares and then complete the table.

Source: Reprinted with permission of the publisher, Teaching K–8, Norwalk, CT 06854. From the April 1993 issue of Teaching K–8.

SUBTRACTION WITH MONEY

Objective: To introduce the concept of subtraction of three-digit numbers with regrouping, using play money

Grades: Third grade and above

Materials: Play money (20 one-dollar bills, 20 dimes, and 20 pennies for each student), place-value board for each student

Teaching Procedures:

1. Review 100 pennies = 1 dollar

    10 pennies = 1 dime

    10 dimes = 1 dollar

2. Write example on the board: $5.36

    −1.27

3. Student makes $5.36 on place-value board.

4. Teacher begins questioning: "You have 6 pennies; you have to give me 7 pennies. Do you have enough pennies?" "Can you trade something?" "That's right. 1 dime = 10 pennies. Take 1 dime from your dimes place and trade it for 10 pennies from your bank. Put the 10 pennies in the pennies place." "Now, how many pennies do you have?" "Can you take 7 pennies away? How many are left?" (Teacher writes 9 in the ones column.) "Can you take 1 dollar away? How many are left?" (Teacher writes 3 in the hundreds place.)

5. Give students ample guided practice with one trade before giving them independent practice in pairs. Encourage students to self-question while completing each step.

Modifications: When students become proficient in subtracting with one trade, provide examples of problems involving two trades.

"99"

Objective: To generalize and practice adding numbers in one's head or on paper

Grades: Intermediate to high school

Materials: (1) Playing cards; (2) paper and pencils

Teaching Procedures: Explain that the objective of this game is to add cards up to a score of 99. Establish the following rules:

    Jacks and Queens = 10
    Kings = 99
    Nines = "free turn" pass; to be used anytime
    Fours = pass
    Aces = 1
    Other cards = face value

Each player is dealt three cards. The rest of the cards go face down on a draw pile. The players take turns discarding one card from their hand face up on a discard pile and drawing one card from the draw pile to put back in their hand. As a player discards his or her card, he or she must add the number from the card to any previous score acquired up to that point in the game and give the new score out loud. Note the exception: If a player plays a nine, he or she receives a free-turn pass. If a player plays a four, he or she has to pass a turn with no score. The first player to score higher than 99 loses the game.

Source: Adapted from Bos, C. S., & Vaughn, S. (2006). Strategies for teaching students with learning and behavior problems (6th ed.). Boston: Allyn & Bacon.

THE VALUE OF NUMBERS

By Ae-Hwa Kim

Objective: To help students understand the value of numbers (1s value, 10s value, and 100s value)

Grade: Primary

Materials: (1) Popsicle sticks; (2) rubber bands to group the ice cream sticks; (3) a sign; (4) number cards; (5) three boxes to hold 1s, 10s, and 100s of popsicle sticks

Teaching Procedures:

1. Count the number of popsicle sticks.

2. Model putting a rubber band around a group of 10 sticks; then ask students to put a rubber band around each new group of 10 sticks.

3. Model putting 1s in the 1s box, 10s in the 10s box, and so on. Ask students to put 1s in the 1s box, 10s in the 10s box, and so on.

4. Show the students a sign that says "Thank you for the _____ popsicle sticks" (e.g., 157).

5. Model putting that number of popsicle sticks in the boxes; then ask students to put the number of popsicle sticks in the boxes.

6. Change the numbers on the sign again and again and allow students to practice grouping popsicle sticks according to the sign.

Source: Based on an activity by Paddock, C. (1997). Ice cream stick math. *Teaching Exceptional Children,* 24(2), 50–51.

SHOPPING

Objective: To provide practice in addition, subtraction, and comparing prices (problem solving)

Grades: Upper elementary, junior high

Materials: (1) Newspaper from which to cut out various supermarket sale ads that include price per item; mount individual items on cardboard and cover them with clear plastic or just bring the ads; (2) made-up shopping lists to hand out to the class; (3) pencil and paper

Teaching Procedures: Divide the class into small groups. Tell the students that their shopping list contains the items they will need this week. Assign each group a designated amount for groceries (e.g., $30). The object is to buy everything on the list and spend the least. Place on each desk the supermarket sale ads, each with the name of its store. Assist students in interpreting the math concepts from the advertisements (e.g., 3 kiwis for $.99). After students buy each item, they record the price and the store where they bought it. (It is easier if one student in each group buys the meats, one buys the dairy products, and so on.) When the students have bought all the items on the list, tell them to total their bills, to calculate how much money they have left over, and be ready to present the results.

Source: Adapted from Bos, C. S. & Vaughn, S. (2006). *Strategies for teaching students with learning and behavior problems* (6th ed.). Boston: Allyn & Bacon.

WORK BACKWARDS

Objective: To deepen understanding of word problems by creating a problem from the solution

Grade: Upper elementary and higher

Materials: Answer sheet, pens/crayons/manipulatives, blank sheets of paper

Teaching Procedures:

1. Show students the answer to a problem (e.g., Saul has 9 balloons left).

2. Discuss the "problem" with students. Establish that this is the answer, and they need to come up with a word problem that fits.

3. The word *left* suggests that this problem involves subtraction.

4. Brainstorm with students possible problems that fit this solution, such as "Saul had 10 balloons and he let one go. How many does he have left? Saul had 47 balloons and he gave 38 to his friends. How many does he have left?"

5. Tell students to write the algorithm (10 − 1 = 9; 47−38 = 9) and draw a picture or use manipulatives to describe the problem.

6. Give students a list of answers and have them create word problems to go with each. Adjust the level or focus on specific skills by adding additional criteria to the task. For example, word problems must involve at least one two-digit number, use division, create a two-step word problem, etc. This can be an individual, partner, or cooperative group activity.

Summary

- The current trend in mathematics instruction is to emphasize effective problem solving and to promote positive attitudes toward a broad view of mathematics, with less emphasis on rote memorization.

- Difficulties in mathematical problem solving may originate from cognitive factors, educational factors, personality factors, and neuropsychological patterns.

- Several curriculum resources are available to teachers of students who have difficulty learning math. Appropriate and specific feedback can help students better understand their mistakes in mathematics, promote student self-monitoring, and boost student self-concept. Using RTI to identify students who are struggling with math includes assessing students to determine their progress and providing appropriately intensive instructional supports for students with math difficulties or disabilities.

- Just as basic skills must be mastered before higher-order problems can be taught and understood, mathematics instruction should begin at a concrete level and gradually move to increasingly abstract levels.

- Providing instruction in computational skills (i.e., addition, subtraction, multiplication, and division) requires students not only to be able to fluently and accurately compute solutions to computational problems but also to understand the meaning of these computations.

- Teaching problem-solving skills to both elementary and secondary students with math difficulties includes ensuring that they have a knowledge base about mathematics including computation, geometry, and pre-algebra as well as how to apply this knowledge to new problems and to actively engage in thinking processes applied to problems.

Think and Apply

1. Reread Shawn's description, at the beginning of the chapter, of his experiences with math. Think of three things you would do if Shawn were a student in your elementary math class. Be sure to consider how you might motivate Shawn, what your attitude toward Shawn would be, and what instructional practices you would consider implementing.

2. Make a copy of the NCTM standards (Figure 14.1). Show them to three special education teachers and ask them for instructional considerations for applying these standards to the special education students they teach. Be sure to ask them to identify the types of needs their students have and the extent to which their needs can be met if required to adhere to the guidelines.

3. Consider RTI in math at the elementary and secondary grades separately. For elementary, identify two activities you would expect to be engaged in on an ongoing basis to successfully implement an RTI model in your classroom. At the secondary level, if you are a math teacher, what role would you have in implementing RTI?

PEARSON myeducationlab

Now go to Topic 8: Instructional Practices and Learning Strategies; and Topic 10: Content Area Teaching in the MyEducationLab (www.myeducationlab.com) for your course where you can:

- Find learning outcomes for these topics along with the national standards that connect to these outcomes.

- Complete Assignments and Activities that can help you more deeply understand the chapter content.

- Examine challenging situations and cases presented in the IRIS Center Resources.

- Apply and practice your understanding of the core teaching skills identified in the chapter with Building Teaching Skills and Dispositions learning units.

$\mathcal{D}$ifferentiating Instruction and Assessment for Middle and High School Students

From Chapter 15 of *Teaching Students Who Are Exceptional, Diverse, and At Risk in the General Education Classroom*, 5/e. Sharon Vaughn. Candace S. Bos. Jeanne Shay Schumm. Copyright © 2011 by Pearson Education. All rights reserved.

Differentiating Instruction and Assessment for Middle and High School Students

FOCUS QUESTIONS

1. What is the standards-based movement and what challenges does it bring to secondary teachers?

2. What is differentiated instruction and how can it be implemented in secondary classrooms?

3. What can you do to prepare lessons that can engage all students?

4. What procedures can you use to learn the strengths and weaknesses of your textbook and how can you differentiate reading assignments for students with reading difficulties?

5. How can you differentiate assessment to meet the needs of all learners?

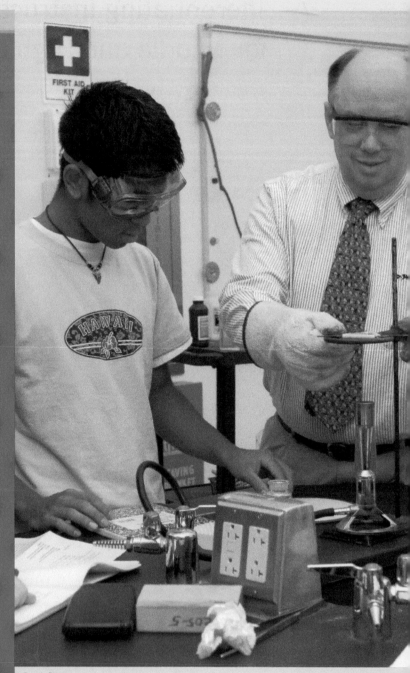

Frank Siteman

INTERVIEW
JERRY SCHUMM

Jerry Schumm is a social studies teacher at Ponce de Leon Middle Community School, an urban school that is among the most ethnically mixed in the city of Miami, Florida. He teaches approximately 175 eighth graders in six different U.S. history classes. Twelve of his students have been school-identified as having learning disabilities. Thus, Jerry's students represent a wide range of cultural, linguistic, and academic diversity. The challenge of meeting the needs of diverse learners is coupled with a challenging, fast-paced curriculum.

Jerry explains, "We are expected to provide an overview of all of U.S. history in eighth grade. Not only do we teach to demanding state standards, we also are expected to take some class time out to have students complete reading passages and questions that are similar to what they will have on their high-stakes tests. We are on block schedule—so I see each class for 100 minutes every other day. Needless to say the time rushes by and it is very tough to keep up, much less teach anything in depth."

Jerry Schumm recognizes that standards help to focus instruction and to make links with teacher-made assessments. Many of the standards in social studies are aligned with reading competencies on the state's high-stakes test. Nonetheless, trying to address all standards is daunting. As Jerry put it, "Since I took U.S. history in middle school, we've added 40 years of U.S. history. Trying to cover it all—even in a survey class—is tough. I work hard to examine the curriculum carefully, select instructional materials that are motivating and directed to the standards, and design tests and assignments that hit key ideas. I also think about what support my struggling students will need to meet standards and what more advanced students might need to stretch."

Introduction

The challenges Jerry experiences are the same that face many secondary teachers, both novice and seasoned. For many middle and high school teachers striking a balance between somewhat conflicting demands can be daunting. This chapter begins with a discussion of the standards-based movement and the challenges it brings to secondary teachers. Next, the chapter provides a definition of differentiated instruction and why it is necessary for secondary learners. It continues with concrete suggestions for preparing lessons and textbook readings that can accommodate a range of student needs. Finally, the chapter provides information about how you can differentiate assessment. In this chapter the focus is on teacher actions and activities.

Standards-Based Instruction

Like Jerry Schumm, teachers in middle and high school are often required to plan their instruction according to a set of standards determined by state or school district curriculum frameworks. An educational standard "is a statement that depicts what students should know or be able to do as a result of teaching and learning" (Conley, 2005, p. 5). Some states also adopt benchmarks or specific student behaviors that indicate they have mastered a particular standard. Figure 15.1 includes samples of standards that Jerry incorporates in his lessons.

The standards movement was ignited by the 1983 report of the National Commission on Excellence in Education titled *A Nation at Risk,* which brought public attention to the state of education in the United States. Although controversial, the report did spawn school reform and the standards movement (Marzano & Haystead, 2008; Ravitch, 1995; Resnick & Zurawsky, 2005). Standards are intended to bring coherence and comprehensiveness to curricula and serve as curricular frameworks. The National Council of Teachers of Mathematics (NCTM) was the first

FIGURE 15.1

Sample U.S. History Standards

Standard 4. The student understands United States history to 1880.

1. Knows factors involved in the development of cities and industries (e.g., religious needs, the need for military protection, the need for a marketplace, changing spatial patterns, and geographical factors for location such as transportation and food supply).

2. Knows the role of physical and cultural geography in shaping events in the United States (e.g., environmental and climatic influences on settlement of the colonies, the American Revolution, the Civil War).

3. Understands the impact of significant people and ideas on the development of values and traditions in the United States prior to 1880.

4. Understands ways state and federal policy influenced various Native American nations throughout United States history (for example, Cherokee and Choctaw removals, loss of Native American homelands, Black Hawk War, removal policies in the Old Northwest).

Source: Florida Sunshine State Standards, grades 6–8 Social Studies. Retrieved from myflorida.com February 14, 2009.

professional organization to introduce standards for the teaching of mathematics (NCTM, 1989). Since that time, professional organizations representing other content areas have developed sets of standards as well.

Since the authorization of No Child Left Behind (2001), states have adopted curriculum standards for middle and high school subjects. State and local curriculum standards are typically more detailed versions of professional standards (Darling-Hammond, 2007; Vacca & Vacca, 2008). State standards vary widely in terms of content and rigor (Peterson & Hess, 2008), so it is important that you become familiar with the standards for your subject area. Your state department of education website lists standards for the subject areas and grade levels you teach.

Advocates of standards-based on instruction cite potential benefits such as alignment with content on high-stakes tests, focused instruction, and uniformity of curriculum (Resnick & Zurawsky, 2005; Schmoker & Marzano, 1999). Proponents also pose that standards can form the basis for differentiating instruction based individual student performance in relationship to each standard (Cooper & Kiger, 2009). Critics of curriculum standards maintain that student outcomes are not necessarily rising as a result of standards-based education (Amrein & Berliner, 2002) and that authentic learning and student engagement are dwindling (Certo, Cauley, Moxley, & Chafin, 2008; Pedulla et al., 2003). Some educators and students argue that standards are too high for some students and not high enough for others (Glass, 2004; Matus, 2009; Viadero, 2007). Still others observe that because of the sometimes-excessive number of standards, content coverage is gained while in-depth inquiry is lost (Certo, Cauley, Moxley, & Chafin, 2008; Marzano & Haystead, 2008; Mastropieri et al., 2005). Gunning (2003) advises, "Although controversial and undoubtedly incorporating a number of drawbacks, the standards movement is now well established. Perhaps the best plan is to take advantage of its positive aspects . . . and work to ameliorate or eliminate its negative features" (p. 11). Tips for Teachers 15.1 provides suggestions for how to make standards-based instruction work for you.

MAKING STANDARDS-BASED INSTRUCTION WORK FOR YOU

Select—choose the standard you want to address.

1. Adopt—use the standard as is to serve as the framework for your planning.
OR

2. Adapt—adapt the standard to meet the needs of your students (e.g., teach one part of the standard, plan for adaptations for students with diverse needs).

3. Invent—use multiple resources to create innovative ways to address the standard in terms of lessons, assignments, and student assessment.

4. Assess—evaluate your approach to inform future planning.

Source: Information from Conley, M. (2005). *Connecting standards and assessment through literacy.* Boston: Allyn & Bacon.

Differentiating Instruction for Secondary Learners

Why do students in middle and high school have difficulty learning? You could answer that question by summarizing all you have learned in this textbook about different students' needs. The advent of inclusion of students with disabilities and students identified as gifted and talented in the general education classroom as well as increased cultural and linguistic diversity have initiated increased attention on how best to meet the needs of a wide range of students.

In addition to issues related to individual student differences, at the secondary level typical content-area classes pose particular problems for students. These problems include the following:

- Not all subjects are uniformly interesting to all students.
- Not all subjects are consistent with students' cultural backgrounds and prior knowledge.
- Learning in some content areas requires basic skills in reading, writing, and mathematics that some students do not have.
- The pace of instruction in some content areas is too fast for some students and too slow for others.
- The level of conceptual complexity and density in some content areas is overwhelming for some students.
- Textbooks in content-area classes can be dull and encyclopedic.
- Content-area classes require both regular homework and assignments and long-term projects.
- Taking tests is a required component of many content-area classes.

These individual differences pose challenges for secondary teachers who view themselves primarily as teachers of a specific content area (e.g., mathematics, social studies, science). Professional organizations such as the National Middle School Association and the National Association of Secondary School Principals advocate teacher preparation that includes not only solid grounding in content, but also understanding developmentally appropriate instructional practices for older learners: a balanced approach. In a joint statement, these associations and others argued, "Thomas Edison knew science, but could he have taught a class of seventh graders? Some may have considered him highly qualified, but would his students have passed a proficiency test?" (National Middle School Association, 2006, p.1). Vacca and Vacca (2008) put it this way: "Teachers who are wedded to a discipline walk a tightrope between content and process. It's a balancing act every time the attempt is made to influence what is learned (content) and how it should be learned (process)" (p. 7).

Differentiated instruction (DI) has been identified as one means to plan for individual student needs and for secondary teachers to bridge content and process. This section is organized around questions secondary teachers typically pose about DI:

- What is differentiated instruction?
- How can I differentiate assignments and homework?
- How can I plan for differentiated instruction?
- How can I accommodate students who are gifted and talented?
- How can differentiated instruction accommodate multiples intelligences?
- How does differentiated instruction relate to response to intervention?

What Is Differentiated Instruction?

The call for DI has come from a number of fields, including reading, special education, gifted education, teaching English as a second language, and multiple intelligence (Schumm & Avalos, 2009). Consequently, a number of definitions for DI have evolved and teachers often have misconceptions about what it is and what it entails. Schumm and Avalos (2009) offer the follow basic components of differentiated instruction:

- DI is both a philosophy of instructing students based on individual needs as well as instructional practices aligned with the philosophy.
- DI draws on a wide variety of practices (some research based; some not).
- DI at the secondary level can occur not only in the general education classroom, but also in advanced placement classes, resource rooms, or pull-out settings.

Carol Tomlinson, an expert in DI, offers the following definition:

A differentiated classroom offers a variety of learning options designed to tap into different readiness levels, interests, and learning profiles. In a differentiated class, the teacher uses (1) a variety of ways for students to explore curriculum content, (2) a variety of sense-making activities or processes through which students can come to understand and "own" information and ideas, and (3) a variety of options through which students can demonstrate or exhibit what they have learned. (Tomlinson, 2005, p. 1)

Components of Differentiated Instruction.   DI involves curriculum enhancement and curriculum modification (Koga & Hall, 2004). Curriculum curriculum enhancement involves no changes to the curriculum, but involves instructional strategies that promote learning for all students. For example, preteaching vocabulary and using graphic organizers are examples of curriculum enhancers.

Curriculum curriculum modification is more complex and is targeted to the individual needs of students. It includes both accommodation and adaptation. Accommodation involves no changes in curriculum requirements for students, but may make modifications to how the material is presented and what is required of the student. For example, a student with learning disabilities might listen to an audiotaped version of a science textbook rather than completing the reading assignment. The student would take the same test as his or her peers, but in an oral format. Adaptations go one step further in that curriculum requirements might be altered. For instance, if middle school students are working on a three-point essay in language arts class, a student with identified difficulties in writing may be assigned a paragraph writing activity. Accommodations and adaptations are more time consuming for teachers, but are critical for providing students with the support they need to succeed (Koga & Hall, 2004).

A learning contract is one strategy that is recommended for organizing differentiated instruction (Tomlinson, 2001). Learning contracts are particularly helpful when planning long-term assignments and research projects. With a learning contract, you identify target standards or objectives and then negotiate with students about the pathway and products they will produce to determine mastery.

Differentiated Instructing Using Flexible Grouping.   As you implement differentiated instruction in your classroom, you will want to plan for a variety of grouping patterns. Group size and membership should be flexible, with formats that change according to the goals of the lesson as well as your students' characteristics. A variety of grouping patterns can be referred to as multiple grouping formats.

At the middle and high school levels, your students may be tracked or placed in the same class by achievement level. Quite often the decision whether to track students or group them in mixed-ability classes is a school or district decision. Even in "same-ability" classes, however, you will quickly note that students in your class have a range of differences to which you need to attend.

Grouping patterns are determined by two basic variables:

1. They can be categorized by group size: whole class, small group, pairs, and single student.
2. Group composition may be homogeneous grouping (students at similar achievement levels) or heterogeneous grouping (students at a wide range of achievement levels).

Depending on the purpose of the learning activity, you can branch beyond these two basic variables and group students by interest, skills to be learned, or prior knowledge of a topic. To mix things up a bit, you may give students time to create their own small groups for activities such as discussing with classmates the books they read independently over the weekend.

For multiple grouping structures to be successful, careful planning is essential. The temptation becomes not to group at all, but instead to fall into the pattern of whole-class teaching followed by individual practice. As you think about a lesson, keep grouping in mind by asking yourself the following questions:

- What is the best group for teaching this lesson?
- What is the best group size for follow-up activities?
- What is the best composition of learners for each group with respect to student academic ability and work habits?
- What materials are needed for each group?

- Will the groups be teacher-led, student-led, or cooperative?
- What room arrangement is necessary for the grouping plan?
- When students move from one group to another, how can I ensure a quick and smooth transition?
- What issues related to students' behavior and social needs should I consider?

If you decide to have your students work cooperatively in small groups or in pairs, students may need explicit instruction in how to work together. In **cooperative learning groups**, students work together toward a common goal, usually to help one another learn academic material (Slavin, 1991). Working collaboratively, students must learn such lessons as how to give and receive help, how to listen and respond to the ideas of others, and how to complete a task as a team. Teachers cannot assume that middle and high school students automatically know how to work in groups. Most of the time, these skills need to be taught explicitly and practiced, just like skills in any other academic area.

How Can I Differentiate Assignments and Homework?

Students' success or failure in a content-area class is often based on their performance on assignments and homework. But what about students with learning and behavior problems? Should they have the same assignments and tests as everyone else? What if a student cannot read? What if a student cannot work under timed conditions?

Scott Cunningham/Merrill

What might be some advantages of working in cooperative learning groups for students with special needs? What can teachers do to ensure that all group members get the most out of their group activity?

Teacher surveys, interviews, and classroom observations indicate that teachers of all grade levels (elementary through high school) do not often make individual adaptations to homework, assignments, and tests (Ness, 2008; Schumm & Vaughn, 1991, 1992a; Schumm et al., 1995a). Constructing individual assignments and tests may not be feasible on a day-to-day basis and may not even be necessary. In this section, you learn about ways to prepare effective assignments and homework for all students.

You should already be aware of the importance of having a homework policy and communicating that policy to students and their families. But there is more you can do to make assignments clear and comprehensible. After conducting a comprehensive review of the literature, Cooper and Nye (1994) concluded that homework assignments for students with disabilities should be brief, focused on reinforcement of old material rather than new material, monitored carefully, and supported through parental involvement.

The most important aspect of making assignments is to give complete information. You need to let students know why the assignment is important, when it is due, what support they will have for completing the task, and the steps necessary for getting the job done. Having complete information helps to motivate students. The procedure in Tips for Teachers 15.2 can help you provide students with a complete set of directions.

Class assignments and homework can be adapted for special learners so that they can experience success without undue attention being brought to their learning difficulties. The key to success is to make assignments appropriate in content, length, time required to complete, and skill level needed to accomplish the task. It is also important that students know how and where to get help when they get stuck.

How Can I Plan for Differentiated Instruction?

Planning for the success of all students in your class involves careful consideration of the needs of individuals as well as those of the class as a whole. If you ask experienced teachers how they plan to meet a wide range of student needs, you are likely to get a collection of very different answers. In most cases, teachers have a single lesson or unit plan and make adaptations on the spot for individual students. The unfortunate consequence is that adaptations

Tips FOR TEACHERS 15.2

STRATEGIES FOR GIVING ASSIGNMENTS

- Explain the purpose of the assignment. Stress what you expect students to learn and why learning the skill or concept is important. Connect the skill or concept to real-life applications.

- Explain in detail the procedures for completing the assignment. Ask one or two students to summarize the procedures to check for understanding.

- Get students started by modeling one or two problems or by providing an example.

- Describe the equipment and materials needed to complete the assignment.

- Anticipate trouble spots, and ask students how they might tackle difficult parts in the assignment.

- Tell students when the assignment is due.

- Explain how the assignment will be graded and how it factors into the overall grade for the class.

- Describe appropriate ways to get help or support in completing the assignment.

- For an in-class assignment, explain your expectations for student behavior while they complete the assignment and what students who finish early should do.

- Address student questions.

become incidental, inconsistent, and (for students with disabilities) not representative of what is mandated on their IEPs.

A number of systems have been recommended for planning for differentiated instruction (see Table 15.1). The planning pyramid is an effective framework to use when planning instruction that will meet the needs of all of your students. To be

TABLE 15.1 Ways to Provide Access to Content-Area Instruction for All Learners

	SOURCE	DESCRIPTION	BENEFITS FOR STUDENTS WITH SPECIAL NEEDS
Planning Pyramid	Schumm, Vaughn, & Leavell (1994); Schumm, Vaughn, & Harris (1997)	A three-tiered framework for planning instructional units and lessons for diverse learners. Key concepts are identified and appropriate assignments and adaptations are incorporated.	Serves as a tool to integrate learning for all students and as a way for special and general education teachers to coordinate planning and instruction.
Universal Design for Learning	Hitchcock, Meyer, Rose, & Jackson (2002); Voltz, Sims, Nelson, & Bivens (2005)	A system for identifying appropriate goals, materials, methods, and assessments for all students.	Assignments and assessments are at an appropriate level of challenge. Exceptional students are viewed as participants, not outliers.
Curriculum Mapping	Hayes-Jacobs (1997); Koppang (2004)	A calendar-based system used to gather data about content, skill instruction, and assessment within and across grade levels in a school.	Specialists have a clear picture of what is going to be taught and when. Assists in planning of appropriate accommodations.
Concept Anchoring Routine	Bulgren, Schumaker, & Deshler (1994); Deshler et al. (2001)	A series of instructional methods to help students with disabilities master key concepts in the general education curriculum.	Helps students to connect new information with prior knowledge.

Sources: Koppang, A. (2004). Curriculum mapping: Building collaboration and communication. *Intervention in School and Clinic, 39,* 154–161; Schumm, J. S. & Avalos, M. A. (2009). Responsible differentiated instruction for the adolescent learner: Promises, pitfalls, and possibilities. In W. Blanton & K. Wood (Eds.) *Promoting literacy with adolescent learners.* New York: Guilford; Schumm, J. S., Vaughn, S., & Leavell, A. G. (1994). Planning pyramid: A framework for planning for diverse student needs during content area instruction. *The Reading Teacher, 47* (8), 608–615; Lenz, B. K., & Deshler, D. D. (2004). *Teaching content to all: Evidence-based inclusive practices in middle and secondary schools.* Boston: Allyn & Bacon; Rock, M. L., Gregg, M., Ellis, Edwin, & Gable, R. A. (2008). REACH: A framework for differentiated classroom instruction. *Preventing School Failure, 52,* 31–47; Rose, D. H., & Meyer, A. (2002). *Teaching every student in the digital age: Universal design for learning.* Alexandria, VA: Association for Supervision and Curriculum Development; and van Garderen, D., & Whittaker, C. (2006). Planning differentiated, multicultural instruction for secondary inclusive classrooms. *Teaching Exceptional Children, 38,* 12–20.

effective, you will need to take into consideration the degrees of learning—what and how much do you expect all, more, or some of your students to learn? Consider, for example, sixth-grade teacher Sara Hood, who used the planning pyramid to plan a two-and-a-half-week unit on Latin American countries for her middle school students. Sara has two students with learning disabilities in her class. One student, Carlos, has difficulty with decoding; another, Miriam, struggles with reading comprehension. Her state-adopted textbook is very difficult for these students, and her planning needs to include accommodations to help both students learn content.

To prepare for the lesson, Sara examined the whole unit in the textbook and chose the fundamental ideas she wanted students to learn. The bottom of the pyramid (see Figure 15.2) listed topics that all groups would research and on which all students would be tested. The middle and top of the pyramid listed student-selected material.

One major concern Sara had in planning was finding activities that would keep her middle school students involved in learning and provide Carlos and Miriam the support they needed. To address these concerns, she planned to divide the classes into mixed-ability cooperative learning groups, each of which would select a country and present what they learned to the rest of the class. Sara provided the students with a checklist with her expectations for the cooperative learning groups' oral presentations in class. In the cooperative learning groups, material was read aloud to facilitate access to the information for Carlos. Also, groups worked together to identify key information, thus assisting Miriam with comprehension.

In addition to using cooperative learning groups to facilitate differentiated instruction, Sara also planned to include differentiated assessment. In his IEP, Carlos is allowed to have tests administered orally. Thus, Sara's special education colleague administered his unit exam orally to Carlos. Miriam's IEP calls for extended time in taking tests, and the special educator facilitated that as well. Both Carlos and Miriam participated in their groups' oral presentations.

Planning is a critical component for successful differentiated instruction in the general education classroom. The planning pyramid can serve as a framework for such planning—not only for students with learning and behavior problems, but also for students who are identified as gifted and talented.

How Can I Accommodate Students Who Are Gifted and Talented?

Consider the following quotation:

Of all the students you are teaching in a given class, which group do you think will probably learn the least this year? It may surprise you to find that in a class that has a range of abilities (and which

FIGURE 15.2 Planning Pyramid for a Unit on Latin American Countries

How present-day government operates

Currency rate of exchange
Anything I haven't thought of!!!

Nobel Prize winners
20th-century rulers
Topography

Capital; major cities   Historical highlights
Latitude; longitude   Major bodies of water
Famous persons   Natural resources and industry
Birth; death rate
Currency used   Food

class doesn't?), it is the most able, rather than the least able, who will learn less new material than any other group. (Winebrenner & Espeland, 2000, p. 1)

How can this occur?

Think about Rick, a tenth-grade student who knows all the vocabulary for an English test at the beginning of the week. He gets a grade of 100% on the test, but has he learned anything?

Think about Mina, a sixth-grade student who is a voracious reader and is particularly interested in astronomy. She skims the chapter in her general science textbook, quickly gets its gist, and realizes that the content is basic and boring. The class lecture does not go beyond answering the end-of-chapter questions. Mina does not have the opportunity to share what she really knows and "tunes out" during class discussion. She gets a grade of 70% on a chapter test because she simply doesn't care about "proving" what she knows.

Think about Caroline, an eighth-grade student who has known all about the eight parts of speech since third grade. Even if she had forgotten the eight parts of speech in third grade, it wouldn't have mattered because they were also taught in fourth, fifth, sixth, and seventh grades. She gets a grade of 100% on a grammar unit test, but has she learned anything?

Think about Thaddeus. Thaddeus loves to draw and does so constantly at home and at school. Unfortunately, he would rather draw than do anything else, and his teacher frequently reprimands him for "doodling" rather than completing assignments.

You've got the picture. Frequently, students who are gifted or talented and other high-achieving students already know the material being covered in the general curriculum. Can you imagine spending 7 hours a day, 5 days a week, school year after school year, reviewing information you already know? Can you imagine having genuine artistic talent and not having the opportunity to develop that talent or to share it with others? Can you imagine drilling on standards that you have already mastered (Glass, 2004; Viadero, 2007)?

Go to **www.hoagiesgifted.org** where you will find Hoagies' Gifted Education page, which includes online resources for students, parents, and teachers.

Characteristics of Students Who Are Gifted and Talented. As a classroom teacher, you'll need to recognize the characteristics of students with extraordinary gifts and talents so that you can help identify students for special services and provide appropriate instruction for gifted students who are members of your class. There is disparity among states in terms of how giftedness is defined, how students are identified for gifted education services, and how services are provided (pull-out programs, full-time programs, inclusion programs) (Hallahan, Kauffman, & Pullen, 2009). There is a clear trend toward increased inclusion of students who are gifted and talented in the general education classroom (Van Tassel-Baska, Quek, & Feng, 2007). Thus, it is important that you investigate local policies and understand your role in identifying students with special gifts and talents and designing instruction that meets their needs.

What you should also be aware of is that the gifted population is very diverse (Soller, 2003). Part of this diversity is due to definitional differences and local criteria for admission to gifted programs (Stephens & Karnes, 2000); part is due to individual differences (Robinson, Zigler, & Gallagher, 2000); and part is due to the degree of giftedness (Ziegler & Heller, 2000).

Underidentified High-Achieving Students. Another group that is of particular interest to many general education teachers is that of high-achieving students who are not identified for special programs. Frequently, teachers will notice a child with extraordinary talents and abilities who might not meet state or school district criteria to qualify for a special program. It becomes the general education teacher's responsibility to provide such children with the support, encouragement, and stimulation they need to feel productive and successful.

Table 15.2 provides an overview of characteristics of gifted and talented students and instructional suggestions for addressing those characteristics. As you can see, some characteristics relate to academic factors, whereas others refer to social and emotional factors. It is important to note that not all gifted or talented students demonstrate every one of these characteristics; there is a wide range of individual differences in the physical, academic, social, and behavioral traits of students who are gifted and talented.

As a general education teacher, you'll want to become familiar with policies and procedures for identifying and instructing students who are gifted and talented. In addition, you'll want to learn about what resources are available to you and to your students. You'll also want

TABLE
15.2

Classroom Strategies and Adaptations for Gifted Students

CHARACTERISTICS OF GIFTED AND TALENTED STUDENTS	CLASSROOM STRATEGIES AND ADAPTATIONS
Advanced vocabulary for chronological age	• Develop word relationship skills (e.g., analogies, homonyms, etc.). * • Encourage use of wide variety of words. • Suggest keeping a journal of "word of the day" or "word of the week." * • Provide experiences in second language learning. *
Outstanding memory; possesses lots of information	• Teach ways to summarize information. • Work on specific product development. * • Provide exhibition space for student products. * • Allow for oral reports before the class. * • Provide unstructured activities, allowing the student to choose the medium of expression. *
Curious; asks endless questions ("Why?" "And then what?")	• Plan exploratory, interdisciplinary curriculum. * *
Operates on higher levels of thinking than same-age peers; is comfortable with abstract thinking	• Emphasize thinking strategies, problem solving, creative solutions, and decision making within the context of specific subject areas. * * • Teach debating skills. * • Regularly include open-ended, higher-order thinking questions in classroom discussions.
Has many interests, hobbies, and collections	• Develop interest-group assignments that enable gifted students to work together with others who share similar interests. * * • Encourage and provide time to pursue free reading based on student interests. * • Create centers where students select topics and work together on projects that require several types or levels of skills. * *
May have a passionate interest that has lasted for many years (example: dinosaurs)	• Encourage reading biographies and autobiographies of individuals who shared interests in common with the student. * • Use outside resources to help students develop their talents. * * • Find mentors.
Intense; gets totally absorbed in activities and thoughts	• Allow some time for uninterrupted reading and thinking. • Teach time-management skills. • Teach strategies for transitioning from one task to another. • Give a 5-minute warning when it is time to wind down one task and start another.
Strongly motivated to do things of interest; may be unwilling to work on other activities	• Adapt assignments to focus on in-depth work on most difficult aspect of assignment and to skip easiest components. • Provide interesting things to do if student finishes assignment before others in the class.
Prefers complex and challenging tasks to "basic" work	
Catches on quickly, then resists doing work, or works in a sloppy, careless manner	• Create open-ended, self-paced assignments. * * • Help students set their own high, yet realistic, outcomes for assignments that vary in complexity. * * • Co-create a "contract" for completion of assignments signed by teacher, parent, and student.
Comes up with "better ways" for doing things; suggests them to peers, teachers, and other adults	• Set expectations for working collaboratively with peers, teachers, and other adults. • Model appropriate ways of offering suggestions for "better ways" of doing things. • Teach leadership skills. • Recognize ideas when appropriate and expand and elaborate on them.
Aware of global issues that are uninteresting to many age-level peers	• Develop a reading list of books, journals, and magazines to foster interest in global issues. • Provide support in conducting informal research using print and nonprint sources.
Sophisticated sense of humor; may be "class clown"	• Set guidelines for appropriate timing of humor in the classroom. • Encourage student to explore the use of humor in a variety of genres.

* Information from *Teaching gifted kids in the regular classroom* by Susan Winebrenner. Copyright 1992. Used with permission from Free Spirit Publishing, Inc., Minneapolis, MN (800) 735-7323. All rights reserved.

* * Information from *Excellence in educating gifted and talented learners* by Joyce Van Tassel-Baska. Copyright 1998.

Go to **www.nagc.org**, the National Association for Gifted Children website, where you will find resources for educators, parents, and students who are gifted and talented.

to learn about policies related to acceleration and enrichment. Acceleration refers to the procedure of moving them quickly through the grades or through the curriculum. With the idea that some students might not be socially ready for the demands of acceleration to higher grades, enrichment evolved as an alternative to acceleration. Gifted education programs in the United States have varied in their emphasis on acceleration or enrichment. In some cases, programs in general education have elected to incorporate elements of both.

There are several approaches to DI for gifted students suggested in the literature. Two commonly recommended approaches for general education classrooms are curriculum compacting and the Parallel Curriculum Model.

Curriculum Compacting. Experts in the field of gifted education suggest that general education teachers work cooperatively with teachers in gifted programs to compact the general education curriculum for gifted students (Reis & Renzulli, 2005). Research indicates that gifted and high-achieving students may already know 40% to 50% of concepts and skills at the outset of a lesson (Reis & Purcell, 1993). Curriculum compacting provides students with the opportunity to demonstrate what they already know about a subject. Teachers can then eliminate content that is repetitive or review for students, replacing it with advanced learning experiences. To assess what your students know, see the 60-Second Lesson.

Curriculum compacting is a three-step identification process:

1. What the student already knows about a topic
2. What a student needs to learn
3. What adaptations or activities are appropriate for facilitating student learning

Parallel Curriculum Model. Tomlinson, Kaplan, Renzulli, Purcell, Leppien, and Burns (2001) developed a framework for differentiated instruction called the Parallel Curriculum Model (PCM). PCM takes into consideration four curriculum design components:

1. Core Curriculum—key concepts to be learned
2. Curriculum of Connections—making interdisciplinary linkages
3. Curriculum of Practice—supporting students in learning to think like a practitioner
4. Curriculum of Identity—helping students make personal meaning and clarification of what they are learning

The parallel curriculum components can be used together, separately, or in various combinations depending on the teacher's goals. Like the planning pyramid, PCM forces teachers to think about what is important to learn and how to facilitate instruction for a wide range of student needs.

Although DI is a viable way to accommodate individual differences, the National Association for Gifted Children (2005) also offers some cautions and comments about the

60 Second LESSON

ASSESSING PRIOR KNOWLEDGE

When you begin a new unit or topic, you need to find out what your students already know and what they need to learn. Finding out what students know will help you plan differentiated lessons and think about accommodations you might need for students with special needs. Some teachers skip this very important step because they don't want to take the time to construct a pretest. Here are some efficient ways to assess prior knowledge:

1. One quick way to assess prior knowledge (a way that takes little preplanning) is "most difficult first" (Winebrenner, 1992). In a list of tasks organized by relative difficulty, identify the most difficult tasks and have students who are willing to take the challenge do them

first. Allow students who demonstrate mastery to go on to a self-selected task. Students who are gifted or high achieving frequently get bored with undue repetition and practice. "Most difficult first" can help to circumvent this problem.

2. Put three or four structured questions that relate to the core of a lesson on the board or an overhead transparency. Have the students respond in writing to the questions.

3. Free recall is another way to assess prior knowledge. Provide students with the topic of the lesson and have them generate as many ideas as they can about the topic within a brief time limit.

practice. Differentiated instruction should not mean "just more work" for advanced students. It should offer opportunities for both acceleration and enrichment. Thus, differentiated instruction holds great promise, but involves careful planning and ongoing evaluation.

How Can Differentiated Instruction Accommodate Multiple Intelligences?

In his book *Frames of Mind* (1983), Howard Gardner proposes the theory of multiple intelligences. Gardner suggests that human beings are capable of exhibiting intelligence in seven domains: linguistic, logical–mathematical, spatial, musical, bodily–kinesthetic, interpersonal (i.e., discerning and responding to the needs of others), and intrapersonal. Later, Gardner identified an eighth intelligence, the naturalistic, which consists of the ability to, "recognize, categorize and draw upon certain features of the environment (Gardner, 1999, p. 48). Gardner (2006) has also suggested a ninth intelligence, the existential, which refers to the ability to identify big issues and fundamental life questions.

What determines the number of individuals in the student population who are identified as academically or creatively exceptional? What groups tend to be underidentified and why?

Traditional intelligence tests tap only linguistic and logical–mathematical intelligence. Gardner advocates a revamping of assessment procedures to evaluate all eight areas in ways that are sensitive to culture, age, gender, and social class (Checkley 1997; Gardner & Hatch 1989). Assessment needs to investigate skills that are needed to survive in society, not skills associated with the ability to succeed in a school setting. Gardner and his colleagues have developed assessment procedures aligned with multiple intelligence theory through their Project Zero and Project Spectrum at Harvard University. The main tenet of Gardner's theory to remember when planning educational programs is the responsibility to help all students realize and enhance their potential and strengths by showing children joy and interest in learning while helping them with the mastery of skills and curriculum (Gardner, 2006).

Gardner explains that the approach does not mean that teachers "need to create nine different lesson plans. Instead, design rich learning experiences that nurture each student's combination of intelligences" (Moran, Kornhaber, & Gardner, 2006, p. 22). Classroom applications of the theory have emerged (e.g., Armstrong, 2003; Christodoulou, 2009; Stanford, 2003), and there is emerging evidence that the approach results in higher engagement and motivation among minority students (Williams, 2009). Key to the implementation of multiple intelligence theory are differentiated assessment and instruction using thematic units as a vehicle. Students can tune into learning through multiple channels.

How Does Differentiated Instruction Relate to Response to Intervention?

Response to intervention (RTI) at the middle and high school levels offers challenges not inherent at the elementary level. First, students at secondary levels are more likely to be placed in departmentalized settings. Second, scheduling problems can inhibit time for Tier 2 and Tier 3 instruction. Third, the pacing of instruction is much more rapid with little time for review or reteaching. Much is to be learned from research and practice about how best to provide tiered instruction for middle and high school students (Mastropieri & Scruggs, 2005). Because students in middle and high schools settings may remain undiagnosed for special services, ongoing research in this area is warranted.

Much of what you read in this chapter about differentiated assessment and instruction can be incorporated into Tier 1 strategies. The steps you take to address individual needs through implementation of evidence-based strategies can form the foundation for RTI.

Because RTI in secondary settings is in its infancy, caution in implementation is warranted. You'll want to familiarize yourself with the legal requirements of RTI, engage in professional

Go to the Assignments and Activities section of Topic 8: Instructional Practices and Learning Strategies in the MyEducationLab for your course and complete the activity entitled *Incorporating Multiple Intelligences into the Classroom.*

development to learn more about tiered instruction and progress monitoring, and develop strong communication with your peers (Canter, Klotz, & Cowan, 2008). You'll also want to know how Tiers 2 and 3 are implemented at your school and how and when student progress monitoring occurs (Burns, 2008). At the middle and high school levels, identifying and addressing student needs may offer students their last chance.

Preparing Engaging Lessons for Middle and High School Students

Jerry Schumm is known for his wardrobe. He has costumes for most periods of history that he teaches. As he tells his students, "I don't want you just to learn history, I want you to feel history. I want you all to plug in!" Jerry knows that keeping adolescents engaged takes a big bag of tricks that he replenishes frequently. This section provides ideas for expanding your bag of tricks by (a) using prelearning activities, (b) using graphic organizers, (c) creating listener-friendly lectures, (d) giving demonstrations, and (e) facilitating student participation.

Using Prelearning Activities

Prelearning activities are strategies that teachers use to activate students' prior knowledge and to preteach vocabulary and concepts—essentially, to prepare students to learn. Lauren Lopez, who teaches ninth-grade science, describes her students as follows:

> Some of my students have traveled all over the world; others have never left their neighborhood. Some of my students have had solid instruction in science in the elementary grades; others have had none. The time I spend with prelearning activities sets the stage for learning and helps build common vocabulary. It saves lots of reteaching time.

Like Lauren, you can use purpose-setting activities and preteaching vocabulary to help students prepare to learn new information.

Purpose Setting. **Purpose-setting activities** provide students with a reason for completing a reading assignment or for listening to a lecture. Setting a purpose for learning helps to guide the reading and listening process and helps students improve the depth of their comprehension. Purpose-setting activities are important for all learners but particularly for students with motivational and attentional problems. Although teachers often set a purpose for reading or listening, students can engage in purpose setting as well (Gunning, 2010). Tips for Teachers 15.3 provides guidelines for setting a purpose before you give a lecture or a reading assignment.

Tips FOR TEACHERS 15.3

SETTING A PURPOSE FOR A LESSON

- Keep the purpose brief, but make it powerful. Students become more actively involved in listening, reading, or participating in a classroom activity when they have a reason for doing so.

- Set a single purpose. When students are given too many purposes, they can lose their focus.

- Make certain that the purpose statement is not too narrow in scope and that it does not reveal too much content, which can actually inhibit comprehension.

- Have a regular purpose-setting routine. For example, write the purpose for learning on the board or demonstrate how the purpose was set.

- After reading, begin discussion with a reiteration of the purpose for reading.

- Help students learn how to set their own purposes. Talk about the importance of setting a purpose and how to develop purpose statements.

- Keep the written purpose statement in full view of students while they are participating in a class activity. Some students may need to be reminded about the purpose of the lesson.

Source: Blanton, W. E., Wood, K. D., & Moorman, G. B. (1990). The role of purpose in reading instruction. *The Reading Teacher, 43*(7), 486–493.

Preteaching Vocabulary.   In recent years, vocabulary instruction has taken a front seat in research and practice (Pearson, Hiebert, & Kamil, 2007). Before beginning a content-area unit or lesson, you can help students gain a better understanding of what they are about to read or hear through direct preteaching of a few key words. Teaching too many new technical vocabulary words can confuse students. Preteaching is helpful for all students, particularly those with limited prior knowledge of the topic.

In selecting the words you are going to preteach, begin by identifying the key concepts you want students to learn in a unit or lesson (McCoy & Ketterlin-Geller, 2004). Next, identify the key vocabulary related to the concept that would be most helpful for your students to learn up front. If you are experienced with the content of the unit or lesson and if you have spent time getting to know your students and their background, this selection should be relatively easy.

Chiappone (2006) lists seven principles of excellent vocabulary instruction:

1. Develop awareness of the stages of word knowledge.
2. Build experiential background for students.
3. Relate word learning to students' backgrounds.
4. Develop depth of meaning through multiple sources and repeated exposures.
5. Foster appreciation and enthusiasm for word learning.
6. Teach strategies to build independent word learning.
7. Teach words in context.

Keeping these principles in mind, use a wide variety of methods and materials to preteach vocabulary. Some examples include semantic feature analysis, the key word method, and graphic organizers.

Using Graphic Organizers

One set of tools that Rita Menendez uses almost daily is graphic organizers. Vacca and Vacca (2005) describe a graphic organizer as "a diagram that uses content vocabulary to help students anticipate concepts and their relationships to one another in the reading material. These concepts are displayed in an arrangement of key technical terms relevant to the important concepts to be learned" (p. 271). Rita explains that she uses not only a variety of graphic organizers but also a variety of materials. "Sometime I just use the white board, sometimes the SmartBoard or PowerPoint, and sometimes overhead transparencies." Rita then adds, "Starting a lesson with a graphic organizer helps, but refining the organizer as we read or listen and using the organizer as a tool for reviewing what we have learned [are] important as well."

For students with learning disabilities and other students with reading comprehension difficulties, graphic organizers provide a visual representation of key ideas in the text and the relationships among those ideas. Using lines, arrows, and flow charts, graphic organizers can help students conceptualize key ideas. Kim, Vaughn, Wanzek, and Wei (2004) conducted a synthesis of the research on the use of graphic organizers for teaching reading comprehension to students with learning disabilities. Twenty-one articles (published between 1963 and 2001) were identified, coded, and analyzed for statistical significance. Most of the studies were conducted with students in intermediate and secondary grades. In general, the researchers found support for the use of graphic organizers in terms of student outcomes on teacher-made or researcher-made tests. Use of graphic organizers appeared to assist in learning material in typical classroom instruction. What remains to be discovered is whether this comprehension tool can be used to improve student outcomes on standardized tests.

Semantic Maps.   Providing students with visual representations of concepts and vocabulary to be learned is a powerful prelearning tool, particularly for special learners. One visual tool that is commonly used in prelearning activities is a semantic map (Irwin, 2007; Pearson & Johnson, 1978), a visual aid that helps students see how ideas are related to one another and to what students already know.

Lists of words prepared in advance by the teacher or generated by students through teacher-guided brainstorming are placed on the board. After discussing the meanings of the words, students discuss how to cluster the words and work together to develop a map to represent visually the relationships that exist among the ideas. For example, Figure 15.3 shows a semantic map for the words for a chapter on Egypt. Students can use the map as a listening or

FIGURE 15.3

Example of a Semantic Map

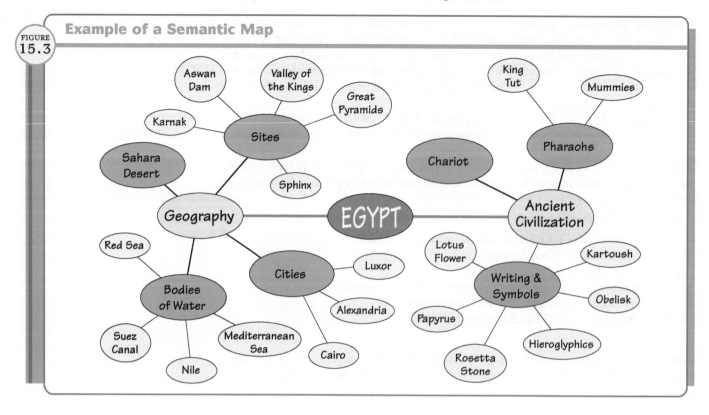

reading guide. The map can also serve as a framework for postlistening and postreading discussions and as an aid for studying for tests or quizzes.

Concept Diagrams. Concept diagrams (Lenz & Deshler, 2004) are another way to introduce a lecture or reading assignment. A concept diagram (see Figure 15.4) is similar to a semantic map, but also helps students determine the definitions, characteristics, examples, and nonexamples of a concept.

Concept diagramming is time consuming. Select concepts with care. Choose those that are pivotal to the curriculum and that students need to understand thoroughly. See Tips for Teachers 15.4 for recommendations for creating concept diagrams.

Timelines. Timelines can be used to provide students with a way to visualize and sequence content-area information as they read, listen, and discuss. They can be used in math (e.g., sequences of

 **TEACHERS 15.4**

CREATING CONCEPT DIAGRAMS

- Identify major concepts to teach.

- List important characteristics of the concepts. Think about whether each characteristic is always present, sometimes present, or never present.

- Locate examples and nonexamples of the concept.

- Construct a definition of the concept by naming the superordinate concept, its characteristics, and the relationships among characteristics.

- Introduce the concept diagram to students using an advance organizer.

- Elicit a list of key words or ideas that relate to the concept.

- Explain or review the parts of the concept diagram and their intended use.

- Name and define the concept with students.

- Discuss characteristics that are always present, sometimes present, and never present in the meaning of the concept.

- Discuss examples and nonexamples of the concept.

- Link the examples and nonexamples to the characteristics.

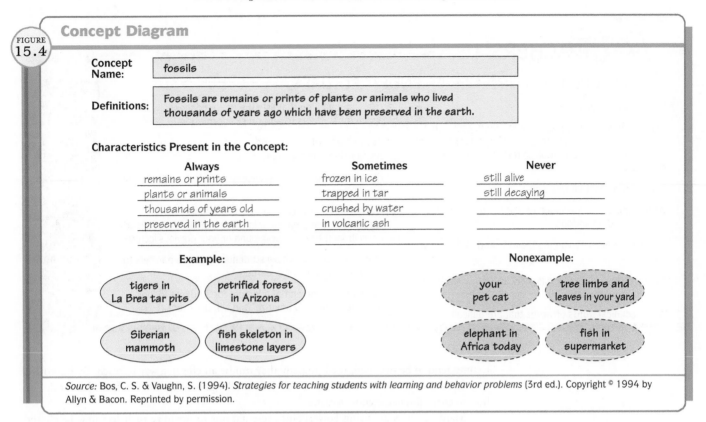

Source: Bos, C. S. & Vaughn, S. (1994). *Strategies for teaching students with learning and behavior problems* (3rd ed.). Copyright © 1994 by Allyn & Bacon. Reprinted by permission.

events in word problems), science (e.g., seasons of the year), reading (e.g., biographies or story plots), and art (e.g., timeline of classic art) and as a study skills tool (e.g., assignments for the month and activities needed to complete each assignment) (Fry & Kress, 2006). Timelines can be more than simple listings of facts on a horizontal black line (Kelly & Clausen-Grace, 2007). They can be illustrated or include photographs as well.

Creating Listener-Friendly Lectures

When using computer software or navigating Internet sites, people talk about them as being "user-friendly." When teachers, like website developers, keep the audience in mind and anticipate points of potential difficulty, the product is user-friendly. Listener-friendly lectures are lectures structured to facilitate listening and learning. Such lectures are not only well organized, but also help students discern what is most important and connect new ideas to what they already know. Well-designed lectures are particularly beneficial for students with learning disabilities, English language learners, and listeners with relatively limited language skills and/or little prior knowledge of the content.

The goal of lectures is to enhance student understanding. One key to enhancing understanding is instructional clarity—the clear, direct, explicit presentation of information. McCaleb and White (1980) list the following five components of instructional clarity:

1. *Understanding*—connecting new information with what students already know
2. *Structuring*—providing a clear format for the presentation, one that students can follow easily
3. *Sequencing*—arranging a presentation in a logical order
4. *Explaining*—defining key terms and providing examples as necessary
5. *Presenting*—delivering material in an articulate and lively manner with correct pacing, and using visual aids and multimedia as necessary

In all classroom presentations, clarity should be your goal. Clarity is important for all students but particularly for students who have difficulty with language or organizational skills or who have little prior knowledge of a topic. Instructional clarity is particularly important during lectures. Giving lectures is often necessary to generate interest in a topic, to provide information that is not included in textbooks, or to clarify or embellish textbook information. Although

TIPS FOR CREATING LISTENER-FRIENDLY LECTURES

- Use advance organizers.

- Use cue words or phrases to let students know what information is important (e.g., "It is important that you know," "The key information to remember is," "In summary").

- Repeat important information.

- Write important information on the board, the transparency, and a handout.

- Stress key points by varying the tone and quality of your voice.

- Number ideas or points (e.g., first, second, next, then, finally).

- Write technical words or words that are difficult to spell.

- Use a study guide that lists the major concepts, with space for students to add other information.

- Use pictures, diagrams, and semantic maps to show relationships among ideas.

- Provide examples and nonexamples of the concepts you are discussing.

- Ask questions or encourage discussion that requires students to relate the new information to ideas they already know (from their own background or your previous lectures).

- Stop frequently and have students work with partners to discuss what they have learned.

- Allow time at the end of a lecture for students to look over their notes, summarize, and ask questions.

lectures tend to be overused, used properly they can be an effective way to teach. By improving your lectures, you help students improve their note taking. See Tips for Teachers 15.5 for tips on how to create listener-friendly lectures.

Many teachers are using PowerPoint presentations to organize their lectures. Leigh and Johnson (2004) recommend the following:

- When preparing PowerPoint presentations, give careful attention to font size and color and background color. The goal is for all students to be able to read the print clearly, even if they are sitting at the back of the room.
- Carefully plan the amount of information you provide on each slide—not too much information, not too little.
- When presenting the slides, don't go through them too quickly, particularly if students do not have handouts of the slides.

While giving lectures, use cues to help students become more active listeners and better note takers (see Figure 15.5).

Another way to make your lectures more friendly is to use the pause procedure (Armbruster, 2009; Ruhl, Hughes, & Gajar, 1990). The **pause procedure** is a technique that helps students learn more from lectures. During logical breaks in a lecture (approximately every 10 minutes), the teacher pauses for 2 minutes. During that time, teachers have pairs of students compare their notes to make certain that key concepts have been recorded. Students also ask each other questions to check for understanding. At the end of the 2 minutes, ask students whether they have any questions or concepts that need further discussion or clarification. After this quick monitoring for student understanding, the lecture continues.

Giving Demonstrations

Demonstrations can be used to show students how to perform a skill, complete a task, or solve a problem. Demonstrations can be for the whole class, small groups, or individual students. They can be preplanned or can occur on the spot as part of interactive planning when students need more explanation. The key to demonstrations is that they must engage students, especially passive learners who will watch your demonstration and then forget every step of it. The important thing is to get students involved and thinking about what you are doing.

As with any lesson, before you give a demonstration be sure to set a purpose, define key vocabulary, and provide an overview or advance organizer of the presentation, including key things to observe (Good & Brophy, 2007). Also provide guidelines for student participation during the presentation. Should they take notes? Should they ask questions before, during, or after the demonstration (Good & Brophy, 2007)?

Using Cues When Giving Lectures

FIGURE 15.5

Use the following list of cues to help students learn how to listen and watch for important information. Encourage students to listen and watch for additional cues and add them to the list. When integrating a content unit with a unit on note taking, you can place on a handout or post on a wall chart the information presented in this activity.

Type of Cue	Examples
Organizational cues	"Today, we will be discussing . . ."
	"The topic I want to cover today . . ."
	"There are (number) points I want you to be sure to learn . . ."
	"The important relationship is . . ."
	"The main point of this discussion is . . ."
	Any statement that signals a number or position (e.g., first, last, next, then)
	"To review/summarize/recap, . . ."
Emphasis cues: verbal	"You need to know/understand/remember . . ."
	"This is important/key/basic/critical."
	"Let me repeat this, . . ."
	"Let me check, . . . now do you understand?"
	Any statement repeated.
	Words are emphasized.
	Teacher speaks more slowly, loudly, or with more emphasis.
	Teacher stresses certain words.
	Teacher spells words.
	Teacher asks rhetorical question.
Emphasis cues: nonverbal	Information written on overhead or board.
	Information handed out in study guide.
	Teacher emphasizes point by using gestures.

Note: For more information, see Suritsky, S. K. & Hughes, C. A. (1996). Notetaking strategy instruction. In D. D. Deshler, E. S. Ellis, & B. K. Lenz (Eds.), *Teaching adolescents with learning disabilities* (2nd ed., pp. 267–312). Denver: Love.

After the demonstration, ask students to summarize the steps, or have one or two students repeat the demonstration for the class. Rivera and Deutsch-Smith (1988) offer an additional strategy for giving demonstrations to students with learning problems: the **demonstration plus model strategy**. To use this strategy, after completing your demonstration by following the steps outlined in the preceding paragraph, add these two steps:

1. After the students have viewed the demonstration, have a student perform each step, verbalizing each step as you did.
2. Have all students complete additional practice exercises independently, using the steps.

You can also improve a demonstration by describing your thinking as you move through the demonstration. Teacher **think alouds** are a metacognitive strategy used to model how to think and learn (Block & Israel, 2004; Oczkus, 2009). Think alouds are most frequently used to model reading processes, but they can also be used to model thinking during a demonstration. Davey (1983) listed the following five powerful uses of think alouds:

1. Making predictions or showing students how to develop hypotheses
2. Describing your visual images
3. Sharing an analogy or showing how prior knowledge applies
4. Verbalizing confusing points or showing how you monitor developing understanding
5. Demonstrating fix-up strategies (p. 45)

Facilitating Student Participation

As you have seen, student engagement can be fostered through cooperative learning groups and involvement in hands-on learning activities.

This section includes additional suggestions for facilitating participation of all students in your class through two common content-area practices: questioning and discussion.

Questioning. When Grace Demming did her college field experience in urban high schools in the late 1990s, one of the most frequent instructional patterns she observed was questioning routines. Teachers asked questions; students gave answers. Grace remarked, "It was like watching a tennis match—back and forth; back and forth." Searfoss and Readence (1989) refer to the typical exchange that goes on in a classroom as *ping-pong discussion*. The teacher asks questions and students answer, back and forth. When teachers "serve the ball" only to students who are most capable of supplying the answer, other students become mere spectators.

Meichenbaum and Biemiller (1998) talk about the "art of questioning" and compare it to a dance: "each partner needs to be attuned to the other, following the other's lead" (p. 153). Questioning is important for helping you to monitor student understanding of content and also for understanding how students are processing what they learn. Good and Brophy (2007) write about the "diagnostic power" of questioning. Questioning can also be used to scaffold and support student learning.

Asking simple yes/no questions or "guess what I'm thinking" questions has little diagnostic value in the classroom. Effective questioning strategies include the following:

- Distribute questions evenly among all students.
- Make certain that questions are clearly stated.
- Ask a variety of question types—lower and higher order questions.
- Ask all kinds of students all kinds of questions.
- Give students specific feedback about their answers.
- Let students explain why an answer is right.
- Let students explain their thinking when they get an answer wrong.
- Sequence the questions in such a way that they provide structure for learning.
- Ask questions in a nonthreatening, natural way.
- Encourage students to ask questions of you and of one another.
- Make questions relevant to students and to real-world applications.

One of the most important aspects of question asking is wait time (Rowe, 1974). No one likes to be put "on the spot." Giving students 3 to 5 seconds to think about an answer results in more thoughtful answers, more elaborated responses, and greater likelihood of participation from a wide range of students. There are benefits to asking fewer questions and giving students more time to give thoughtful answers (Zwiers, 2008). See the 60-Second Lesson for more suggestions for questioning strategies.

60 Second LESSON

TECHNIQUES FOR TEACHING QUESTION ANSWERING

Scaffolded questioning: When a student answers a question incorrectly, rather than giving the student the correct answer or moving on to another student, provide scaffolded questioning to promote student learning. Scaffolded questioning is not asking questions that lead to the answer you have in your head. Rather, scaffolded questioning is a set of sequenced prompts that begin with general questions and then provide increased guidance. The goal is not just for the student to arrive at the right answer; it is also to help students learn strategies for problem solving and answering questions. Some examples of scaffolded questions are:

- What information do you need to answer this question?

- Do you need me to repeat the question?

- What are some key words in my question? How can the key words help you answer the question?

- Look at the graphic organizer we started at the beginning of the lesson. What information in the graphic organizer can help you answer the question?

Group responding: When reviewing material for a test or when helping students develop fluency in answering the question, group responding can be helpful. Choral or group responding occurs when the teacher asks the whole class a question and the entire class responds simultaneously. Group responding should be used judiciously because it is more difficult to monitor individual student responses.

Sources: Irwin, J. W. (2007). *Teaching comprehension processes* (3rd ed.). Boston: Allyn & Bacon; and Meichenbaum, D., & Biemiller, A. (1998). *Nurturing independent learners: Helping students take charge of their learning.* Newton, MA: Brookline Books.

Discussions.   When done well, classroom discussions can be stimulating for students and for teachers as well. However, leading classroom discussions can be challenging for teachers (Ezzedeen, 2008; Wolsey & Lapp, 2009; Zwiers, 2008). Effective classroom discussions involve not only setting a positive classroom environment that encourages participating and risk-taking, but also planning a great deal (Zwiers, 2008). The goal is to engage students in vibrant discussions (Bean, 1985), in which student participation is high, students' thinking is stimulated, and students have opportunities to connect what they are learning to their personal knowledge and experience. Vibrant discussions help students learn how to express ideas, justify positions, listen to the ideas of others, and ask for clarification when they don't understand (Kauchak & Eggen, 1993; Zwiers, 2008).

Your role in a discussion is that of moderator and encourager. As a moderator, you help the group to establish a focus and stay on the topic. As an encourager, you engage reluctant participants and make certain that students are free to express their points of view. To encourage vibrant discussions, try the alternatives to traditional questioning in Tips for Teachers 15.6 (Dillon, 1979).

The discussion web (Alvermann, 1991) is a graphic aid to help students prepare for classroom discussions in content-area classes. As Figure 15.6 shows, the discussion web is designed to help students examine both sides of an issue. It is appropriate for elementary and secondary students and can be used before and after lectures.

Alvermann suggests the following procedure for implementing the discussion web:

What qualities are present in a vibrant discussion group? How can discussion skills be directly taught?

- Prepare students for reading or listening by introducing key vocabulary, activating prior knowledge, and setting a purpose for reading.
- After students have read a selection or listened to a lecture, introduce the discussion web with a provocative question. For example, after giving a lecture about the First Amendment, you could ask, "Should rap music be censored?" Provide time for students to discuss the pros and cons of the issue in pairs and complete the discussion web as a team. Students should take turns filling in as many "Yes" and "No" statements as the team can generate.
- Regroup pairs of students into teams of four students, who then compare their discussion webs and build consensus on an answer to the question.
- Have the group select and record the strongest argument and the reason for their choice.
- Have a spokesperson from each group take 3 minutes to report the results, and give individual students with dissenting or unrepresented points of view an opportunity to state their positions.
- Assign students an individual activity in which they write a position statement about their point of view on the issue.

 EACHERS 15.6

TECHNIQUES FOR STIMULATING DISCUSSION

- *Declarative statements.* Provide information to which students can respond or react.

- *Declarative restatements.* Summarize student comments.

- *Indirect questions.* Ask questions that begin "I wonder . . ." or "What would happen if . . ."

- *Imperatives.* Make statements that encourage students to tell more about what they were thinking or to provide examples.

- *Student questions.* Invite students to ask questions of one another.

- *Deliberate silence.* Give everyone time to think and to gather their thoughts.

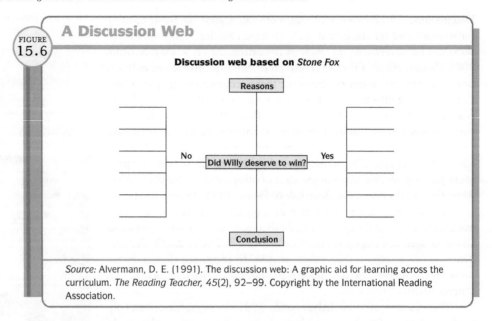

FIGURE 15.6

A Discussion Web

Discussion web based on *Stone Fox*

Source: Alvermann, D. E. (1991). The discussion web: A graphic aid for learning across the curriculum. *The Reading Teacher, 45*(2), 92–99. Copyright by the International Reading Association.

The discussion web provides a structure for *critical thinking*—examining both sides of an issue carefully before making a judgment.

Effective Content-Area Reading Instruction for Middle and High School Learners

In your academic career you've developed strategies for navigating textbook reading assignments. Lots of practice and, perhaps, some direct instruction on how to read and learn from text have helped you along the way. For many students, textbooks can be labor intensive (Stahl, 2004; Wood, Lapp, Flood, & Taylor, 2008). This is certainly true for students who struggle with reading, but can also be true for some usually high-achieving students who have not learned approaches for efficient and effective textbook reading. This section shows you how to become familiar not only with the strengths and weaknesses of your textbook, but also with the ways in which students interact with and respond to the text. This section also contains effective techniques for making textbook adaptations for special learners.

Familiarizing Yourself with the Textbook

As a classroom teacher, you might not have the opportunity to select the textbook that is used in your content-area classroom. Typically, state selection committees decide on a limited number of state-adopted textbooks from which school districts can choose. At the district level, the list is shortened by a district committee. At the school level, grade- or committee-level teams frequently choose the textbook. Chances are, you will inherit a textbook that someone else has chosen for you. To familiarize yourself with your textbook, you need to consider text-based factors that contribute to the many challenges students encounter with textbook reading: readability level and friendliness level.

Go to **www.lexile.com** to learn more about the Lexile Framework™ for Reading.

Readability Level.   Traditionally, a textbook's level of difficulty is gauged by its readability level, expressed as a grade level. For example, you might hear a teacher say, "This science book is intended for 10th graders, but the readability level is 11th grade." Readability levels are determined by applying to the text one or more readability formulas (e.g., Dale & Chall, 1948; Fry, 1977; Raygor, 1977). Such formulas are based on sentence complexity (measured by sentence length) and word difficulty (measured by word length and frequency). Keep in mind that readability levels are overall estimates of the textbook level of difficulty and that within each textbook some passages might vary—in some textbooks as much as three or four grade levels.

Another way to estimate the level of difficulty of a text is by Lexile levels. The Lexile Framework® for Reading estimates the student's reading level and a text's readability level. If a student has the same Lexile level as the Lexile level of a text, the student should be able to read the book with 75% accuracy. Lexile scores range from 200L (beginning readers) to 1700L (advanced readers).

Your teachers' manual will report the readability level and/or Lexile level of your text. Why is this important to know? Fran Hampton teaches 10th-grade biology. Some of her students are students with learning disabilities, some are English language learners, and a few are garden variety poor readers who have not been placed in special services. The reading levels of her students range from about 4th-grade level to 12th-grade level. The textbook has a stated readability level of 10th grade. Thus, Fran needs to make adaptations to the textbook to promote learning for all students in her classroom.

Friendliness Level.   In addition to the readability level of your textbook, you should also become familiar with the text features included in your text that can support readers. **Friendly text** or **considerate text** is written and formatted in such a way that information can be extracted easily and support is available when the reader does not understand (Armbruster & Anderson, 1988; Singer, 1986). The degree to which text is considered friendly or considerate to the reader is determined by the number of features included in the text that promote learning (such as headings and subheadings, vocabulary in boldface type, and chapter summaries).

Familiarize yourself with the textbook you plan to use, and learn to recognize friendly text features that support student learning as well as areas in which you will need to intervene. Friendly text has *organization, explication, conceptual density, metadiscourse,* and *instructional devices.*

- *Organization* is sequence in which the author presents information in the text. Organization includes the general structure of the text as well as consistency and connectedness of ideas.
- *Explication* is how the author explains ideas and teaches the reader. Explication includes necessary background information and examples.
- *Conceptual density* is the number of new vocabulary terms or concepts the author introduces.
- *Metadiscourse* is the degree to which the author "talks" to the reader. Metadiscourse includes direct explanations of how to learn from the text and how to connect ideas from one part of the text to another.
- *Instructional devices* are the number of learning tools the author provides. Examples of learning tools are a table of contents, marginal annotations, and a glossary.

At the beginning of the school year, Fran Hampton does a textbook walk-through with her students. She holds a class discussion about the friendly text features in their book and brainstorms about ways students can use those text features to prepare for class discussions, labs, and tests.

Understanding How Students Interact with and Respond to Text

As you examine the textbook you will be using, you should anticipate how you will need to supplement it. The ultimate judge of the readability and friendliness of a textbook is the reader. The **FLIP chart strategy** helps students learn to evaluate text on their own (Schumm & Mangrum, 1991). ("FLIP" stands for **F**riendliness, **L**anguage, **I**nterest, and **P**rior knowledge.) By filling out forms like the one shown in Figure 15.7, students learn what is comfortable for them individually as readers. After students have completed the FLIP chart, you can learn (through class discussions and individual conferences) what is difficult for them in terms of text friendliness, language, interest, and prior knowledge. Students with reading and learning problems especially need to learn how to talk about the textbook and any problems they have with it. Classroom discussions based on the FLIP chart strategy also help students think as a group about effective strategies for coping with text they find difficult.

Making Textbook Adaptations

Suppose you learn that the textbook is too difficult for some of your students. What will you do? Research indicates that most content-area teachers seldom implement many adaptations for a number of reasons (Schumm & Vaughn, 1992a; Schumm, Vaughn, & Saumell, 1992).

myeducationlab

To enhance your understanding of how to provide effective reading instruction for high school students, go to the IRIS Center Resources section of Topic 9: Reading Instruction in the MyEducationLab for your course and complete Module 20: PALS: A Reading Strategy for High School.

The FLIP Chart

FIGURE
15.7

Title of assignment _____

Number of pages _____

General directions: Rate each of the four FLIP categories on a 1–5 scale (5 = high). Then determine your purpose for reading and appropriate reading rate, and budget your reading/study time.

F = Friendliness: How friendly is my reading assignment?
Directions: Examine your assignment to see if it includes the friendly elements listed below.

Friendly text features

Table of contents	Index	Glossary
Chapter introductions	Headings	Subheadings
Margin notes	Study questions	Chapter summary
Key terms highlighted	Graphs	Charts
Pictures	Signal words	Lists of key facts

1_____ 2_____ 3_____ 4_____ 5

No friendly text features   Some friendly text features   Many friendly text features

Friendliness rating _____

L = Language: How difficult is the language in my reading assignment?
Directions: Skim the chapter quickly to determine the number of new terms. Read three random paragraphs to get a feel for the vocabulary level and number of long, complicated sentences.

1_____ 2_____ 3_____ 4_____ 5

Many new words;   Some new words;   No new words;
complicated sentences   somewhat complicated sentences   clear sentences

Language rating _____

I = Interest: How interesting is my reading assignment?
Directions: Read the title, introduction, headings/subheadings, and summary. Examine the pictures and graphics included.

1_____ 2_____ 3_____ 4_____ 5

Boring   Somewhat interesting   Very interesting

Interest rating _____

P = Prior knowledge: What do I already know about the material covered in my reading assignment?
Directions: Think about the title, introduction, headings/subheadings, and summary.

1_____ 2_____ 3_____ 4_____ 5

Mostly new information   Some new information   Mostly familiar information

Prior knowledge rating _____

Overall, this reading assignment appears to be at:

☐ a comfortable reading level for me

☐ a somewhat comfortable reading level for me

☐ an uncomfortable reading level for me

First, adapting textbooks takes time, and teachers' time for planning and preparing for instruction is already limited. Second, textbook adaptations often slow down instruction, and teachers cannot cover as much material as they would like. Third, some teachers think that making adaptations for the few students who need them is not fair to the high-achieving students who are ready to work at a faster pace. Fourth, some teachers feel that they do not

TEACHERS 15.7

GUIDELINES FOR ADAPTING CONTENT-AREA TEXTBOOKS

Substitute the textbook for students who have severe word-recognition problems:

- Audiotape textbook content.
- Read textbook aloud to students.
- Pair students to master textbook content.
- Use direct experiences, films, videotapes, recorders, and computer programs as substitutes for textbook reading.
- Work with students individually or in small groups to master textbook material.

Simplify the textbook for students whose reading level is far below that of the textbook used in class:

- Construct abridged versions of the textbook content or use the publisher's abridged version.
- Provide students with chapter outlines or summaries.
- Use a multilevel, multimaterial approach.

Highlight key concepts for students who have difficulty comprehending textbook material:

- Preview reading assignments with students to orient them to the topic and provide guidelines for budgeting reading and study time.
- Provide students with a purpose for reading.
- Provide an overview of an assignment before reading.
- Structure opportunities for students to activate prior knowledge before starting a reading assignment.

- Introduce key vocabulary before assigning reading.
- Develop a study guide to direct learning.
- Summarize or reduce textbook information to guide classroom discussions and independent reading.
- Color-code or highlight textbooks.
- Reduce length of assignments.
- Slow down the pace of reading assignments.
- Provide assistance in answering text-based questions.
- Demonstrate or model effective reading strategies.
- Place students in cooperative learning groups to master textbook content.
- Teach comprehension-monitoring techniques to improve ongoing understanding of text material.
- Teach students to use graphic aids to understand textbook information.

Increase idea retention for students who have difficulty with long-term memory:

- Structure postreading activities to increase retention of content.
- Teach reading strategies to improve retention.
- Teach students to record key concepts and terms for study purposes.
- Teach memory strategies to improve retention of text material.

Source: Schumm, J. S. & Strickler, K. (1991). Guidelines for adapting content area textbooks: Keeping teachers and students content. *Intervention in School and Clinic,* 27(2), 79–84. Copyright © 1991 by PRO-ED, Inc. Reprinted by permission.

---

have the training they need to make adaptations (Hall, 2005; Mallette, Henk, Waggoner, & Delaney, 2005). Fortunately, with professional development and use of a broadening array of instruction resources, teachers can make the adaptations students want and need (Cantrell, Burns, & Callaway, 2009). Tips for Teachers 15.7 lists textbook adaptations you might consider, three of which are discussed here in greater depth: text highlighting, multiliteracies, and listening to learn.

Text Highlighting. Students with comprehension problems have difficulty sifting out important information. Underlining or highlighting key points in the textbook can help students attend to the most salient information (Santa, Havens, & Valdes, 2004; Wood & Wooley, 1986). As you read the textbook, highlight the information you think is most important. Then student or adult volunteers can use your book as a guide to highlight the same information in books for students with reading and learning disabilities. Keep in mind that this is an intermediate step. Students should also be taught how to highlight and identify key information on their own (Santa et al., 2004). You can use cooperative learning groups to support students in learning how to draw salient information from textbooks. Students can work collaboratively to develop text coding or "text graffiti" systems using colored pens and sticky notes (Buehl, 2009).

Multiliteracies.   After you and your students have taken a careful look at your textbook, you might realize that you will need to go beyond the textbook to provide your students with alternative reading material. Living in a digital age requires students to learn skills for dealing with multiples sources of information or **multiliteracies** (Bean, Readence, & Baldwin, 2008; Burniske, 2008; Wood et al., 2008). "No longer can we refer to traditional books alone as text. Now the term *text* has expanded to include print, graphic novels, art, music, digital and visual media, technical writings, popular culture such as music and television programs and characters, and Internet texts (webpages, blogs, instant messaging for example)" (Wood et al., 2008, p. 6).

Although Fran Hampton uses the textbook for her core curriculum, like more and more content-area teachers, she has begun using trade books (both fiction and nonfiction) and other reading materials (e.g., magazines and journals) to supplement content-area textbooks. Trade books and other alternative reading sources can be used to spark interest and to help students develop lifelong reading habits. In addition to informational books, she also uses historical fiction, biographies, and autobiographies as part of her planning to make the study of biology alive and relevant. Because informational trade books at lower readability levels have been produced in recent years, it's possible to locate books on the same theme at varying levels as a basis for classroom discussion (Fitzpatrick, 2008). Regardless of how you choose to integrate trade books in content-area instruction, try to select (or help your students select) books that are engaging and that will grab their interest, and don't forget to share your own enthusiasm for reading and learning beyond the textbook.

Fran has not limited herself to traditional print media. She encourages students to use the Internet. Fran identifies appropriate websites and creates inquiry-based activities based on web content. Students work in teams in the school's computer lab to complete the activity and then later to engage in class discussion about what they learned. She also encourages her students to use **cybaries**, or cyber libraries, to find links to websites that can be useful in their research (e.g., *Nettrekker*). As Fran puts it, "I'm continuing to keep an open mind about multiliteracies, but do so with caution. On the one hand my students are increasingly more tech savvy and motivated to use digital resources. On the other hand, I want to ensure that we use safe Internet practices." See Tech Tips to learn about some supporting technology.

Listening to Learn.   For over 60 years the nonprofit organization Recording for the Blind & Dyslexic (RFB&D) has provided audiobook library services for students who have difficulty with traditional texts. The organization offers recorded books in both CD-ROM and downloadable versions to assist students who are blind, have low vision, or have learning disabilities.

Go to **www.cast.org**, the website of the Center for Applied Special Technology, where you will learn more about gaining access to the general education curriculum through technology.

TechTips

USING TECHNOLOGY TO SUPPORT LEARNING IN CONTENT AREAS

Learners with difficulties in reading and comprehending written text often experience failure in content-area classes such as social studies and science. Although learners may be receiving support in their reading and writing skills, they also need support in their content-area classes. There are many programs online that you can use in the classroom or that students can use on their own. Consider some of the following:

On-line science museum by the Smithsonian at
▷ **www.smithsonian.org/**
The Smithsonian Institution home page, with extensive links to art, design, history, culture, science, and technology collections, is a treasure trove of information for students looking to learn about content areas that will enrich their knowledge base.

Cast e-reader by CAST, Inc. at
▷ **www.cast.org**
This website uses the universal design framework for accommodating all learners. Using a wide array of technologies and media, this site allows educators to assess all students accurately and to provide instruction that will meet students' needs.

Bookshare by Benetech at
▷ **http://www.bookshare.org/**
For students with visual, learning, or physical disabilities, this site is an online library that provides access to online books, periodicals, newspapers, and textbooks. Once students provide proof of their disability, they may become eligible to become members of Bookshare.

SUGGESTIONS FOR RECORDING READING ASSIGNMENTS

- Instead of recording an entire chapter verbatim, read the key sections and paraphrase the less important sections.

- Code the text so that readers or listeners will know whether the person on the tape is reading or paraphrasing.

- Provide a short advance organizer on the tape to help students get ready to read and listen.

- Insert questions that readers or listeners can stop to think about.

- Remind readers or listeners to stop periodically to think about what they have read.

- Use a natural tone of voice and a comfortable reading rate. Have students experiment with recorded texts to see whether they comprehend better with or without the accompanying printed text.

Their expanded website offers information for how to access recorded materials and suggestions for implementing them in your classroom.

With the advent of portable media players, audiobooks are increasingly popular and acceptable to students. Students can listen to the books in a listening center in classrooms, resource rooms, school libraries, or at home. If the material is not available through RFB&D, Tips for Teachers 15.8 provides suggestions for recording reading assignments.

Boyle and colleagues (2002) recommend pairing the listening of recorded text with other learning strategies to get maximum results. In particular, they recommend the SLiCK sequence to structure learning from recorded text. The steps in the SLiCK strategy are as follows:

- **S**et up the CD-ROM playback machine.
- **L**ook ahead or preview the printed chapter and any organizational aspects of the CD-ROM to identify headings, subheadings, and key words.
- **C**omprehend the recorded text through careful listening and reading along with the text.
- **K**eep notes from text for further review and to prepare for tests and classroom discussions.

Effective content-area reading instruction coupled with listener-friendly lectures can serve as the foundation for students' success in middle and high school. Activities for all Learners includes additional ideas you can use to promote student learning in secondary grades.

Another key element that determines student success or failure is student assessment. But what about students with learning and behavior problems? Should they have the same assessments and tests as everyone else? What if a student cannot read? What if a student cannot work under timed conditions? In the next section, you'll learn about key ideas in thinking about differentiating assessment.

Differentiating Assessment

In classrooms that include highly diverse learners, differentiated assessment should go hand in hand with differentiated instruction. Learners may have different assessment needs. For example, some children with challenges in learning basic skills may need more intensive and frequent progress monitoring than others. For children who are English language learners or students with disabilities, testing accommodations such as extended time may be appropriate. Differentiated assessment involves to use of formal assessments and informal measures (Chapman & King, 2004; Wormeli, 2006b). It also involves accommodations and adaptations to meet individual needs. Tomlinson (2003) identifies four ways that assessment and instruction can be linked:

1. Preassessment is necessary to find out what each student knows and needs to learn.
2. Ongoing assessment is needed to monitor student learning during instructional units and to make adjustments as necessary.
3. Teachers identify multiple ways for students to demonstrate what they have learned.
4. Students become actively engaged in setting instructional goals and in self-assessment in meeting those goals.

CONTENT-AREA INSTRUCTIONAL ACTIVITIES FOR ALL LEARNERS

CONVERSATIONAL DISCUSSION GROUPS

Objective: To help students become comfortable in classroom discussions

Grades: Middle school and above

Teaching Procedures: The idea behind conversational discussion groups is that discourse about reading assignments and lectures should be more like conversations. Authentic oral language experiences with peers can be particularly helpful for English language learners (Wolsey & Lapp, 2009). Discussion groups can be held after reading a book or other selection, listening to a lecture, hearing a guest speaker, or viewing a video in class. There are three steps to implementing conversational discussion groups:

1. *Introduce/review rules.* Before dividing students into conversation groups, either introduce or review rules. You will need to determine rules in advance or perhaps have the group generate rules related to etiquette for speaking in a group, participation, staying on task, and behavior.

2. *Lines of thought.* During the discussion time, the teacher presents students with three questions—one at a time. When students finish with one question, the teacher goes to the group to hear and respond to their answer and then gives a second question. Questions are related to background knowledge, summarizing the story or lecture, and making personal reactions or reflections.

3. *Debriefing.* Students then spend some time reflecting on and evaluating their experiences in the conversational discussion group. The reflection is guided by three questions: (a) How did we go about getting our answers today? (b) How did we do? and (c) What can we do to improve next time?

Depending on the group of students, they may need more or less teacher direction and

modeling in how to discuss what they have read or heard. The real goal of conversational discussion groups is to get beyond a formalized structure and to encourage students to have productive, personally meaningful discussions with their peers.

Sources: O'Flahavan, J. F. & Stein, C. (1992, December). The conversational discussion groups project. In K. Jongsma (Chair), *Understanding and enhancing literature discussion in elementary classrooms*. Symposium conducted at the 42nd Annual Meeting of the National Reading Conference, San Antonio, TX; and Wolsey, T. H. & Lapp, D. (2009). Discussion-based instruction in the middle and secondary school classroom. In K. D. Wood & W. E. Blanton (Eds.), *Literacy instruction for adolescents: Research-based practices* (pp. 368–391). New York: Guilford.

JIGSAW PUZZLE METHOD

Objective: To help students work cooperatively to learn content-area material

Grades: Middle school and above

Materials: Expert sheets

Teaching Procedures:

1. Select a unit of material for students to learn that can be broken up into four sections. For example, a social studies chapter on Italy might be broken up into imports and exports, natural resources, famous sights, and native foods.

2. Assign students to four different "expert" groups. The members of each group are responsible for learning the material in their assigned section—they must become experts.

3. Allow expert groups enough time to complete "expert sheets." Expert sheets are handouts you have prepared for students to record important information they have learned.

4. Prepare a quiz (two or three questions) that each group member must pass to truly become an expert. Students who do not pass the test can work with you or

with group mates to learn the information. You can decide whether students can use their expert sheets to take the quiz.

5. Move the students into their jigsaw groups. A jigsaw group consists of one expert from each of the four different groups.

6. Each expert then teaches the content he or she learned to members of the jigsaw group.

Source: Aronson, E. & Patnoe, S. (1997). *The jigsaw classroom: Building cooperation in the classroom* (2nd ed.). New York: Addison-Wesley/Longman; and Paratore, J. R., & McCormack, R. L. (2009). *Grouping in the middle and secondary grades: Advancing content and literacy knowledge.* In K. D. Wood & W. E. Blanton (Eds.), *Literacy instruction for adolescents: Research-based practices* (pp. 420–441). New York: Guilford.

SEND A PROBLEM

Objective: To help students learn content-area material

Grades: Middle school and above

Materials: Index cards

Teaching Procedures:

1. Students work individually to generate questions about a reading assignment or lecture.

2. Students record their questions on the front of an index card; they record answers on the back of the same card.

3. Students are assigned to work in groups of three or four to review the questions and answers for accuracy of the answers. Answers are revised if needed.

4. The stack of question cards is then passed to another group of students. Members of the group take turns asking and answering questions.

5. The process of passing continues until time is up or until all groups have had the opportunity to review the cards of every group.

This section begins with a discussion of formal assessment including high-stakes testing and teacher-made tests. It continues with ideas for informal or alternative assessment including suggestions for engaging secondary students in self-assessment. The chapter concludes with ideas for assigning student grades.

Preparing Students for High-Stakes Tests

The passage of the No Child Left Behind Act mandated large-scale assessment for all students, including students with disabilities and English language learners. High-quality instruction that is direct and focused on concepts to be learned, clarification of student misunderstandings, attention to level of difficulty of assignments, and support to guide problem solving are some of the best ways to promote student achievement (Vaughn, Gersten, & Chard, 2000).

Implementation of high-stakes tests varies considerably, especially among those students who qualify for accommodations. Other than providing high-quality instruction, how teachers prepare students for taking high-stakes tests depends on the nature of state-identified standards and the format of the examination used (Katsiyannis, Zhang, Ryan, & Jones, 2007). Tips for Teachers 15.9 provides questions that can guide your thinking about how to prepare students for high-stakes tests in content areas such as science and social studies. At the middle and high school levels, some content areas are not included in statewide assessments. Nonetheless, teachers in all subject areas are increasingly being provided with professional development and resources to align their teaching in a way that promotes student achievement on tests in reading, writing, and mathematics. Tips for Teachers 15.9 also provides questions you can ask curriculum leaders in your school.

Your state, school district, and school may have policy statements and procedures for appropriate and ethical ways to prepare your students for high-stakes tests. As a classroom teacher, you should become familiar with those policies and procedures. You will also want to find out what adaptations or exam alternatives are available for which individual students in your class may be eligible (Wasburn-Moses, 2003).

PEARSON
myeducationlab

Go to the Assignments and Activities section for Topic 6: Assessment in the MyEducationLab for your course and complete the activity entitled *High Stakes Testing*.

Tips FOR TEACHERS 15.9

QUESTIONS THAT WILL GUIDE YOU IN PREPARING STUDENTS FOR HIGH-STAKES TESTING IN CONTENT AREAS

- What state standards are designated for students in my grade level?

- How are state standards aligned with district and school requirements?

- What materials do I have that are aligned with the standards?

- What is the format of the state exam?

- Are there resources available to help me design my teacher-made exams to align with the format of the state test?

- Does my state or district maintain a website with resources that can assist me in planning, assessment, and instruction?

- When students do not seem to be making progress on state standards, what classroom interventions can I implement?

- When classroom interventions do not work, are there resources for my students at the school or district level for more intensive intervention?

- How can I integrate standards into my ongoing teaching to keep students motivated and engaged?

- What accommodations or alternative assessments are available for students with disabilities or those who are English language learners?

Here are some questions you can ask of curriculum leaders in your school:

- What is the format of high-stakes tests in our state?

- What types of questions can I include in my class discussions and tests that support question formats used on state examinations?

- What formats for writing assessment are used on state assessments? What ways can I incorporate those formats into my assignments and tests?

Helping Students Develop Test-Taking Strategies

There is growing evidence that helping students develop test-taking strategies can enhance performance on high-stakes tests (Carter, Hughes, & Wehby, 2005). Keeping local requirements in mind, Thurlow, Elliott, and Ysseldyke (2002) suggest three general ways a teacher can help students prepare for high-stakes tests: test approach skills, test-taking skills, and test preparedness.

1. **Test approach skills** are skills that can help students get physically and mentally ready for exams. Sending flyers home to parents about the importance of sleep and nutrition can help prepare students physically. Miyasaka (2002) emphasizes the importance of reducing test anxiety. Teaching test-taking and test preparedness skills will help alleviate student anxiety. However, the positive attitude you set in your classroom is vital for the reduction of anxiety. Talk with your school counselor about students who seem to have an unusually high level of anxiety about the examination.
2. **Test-taking skills** are skills that students use during the examination (Flippo, Becker, & Wark, 2009). You can help students develop test-taking skills by providing suggestions for taking specific types of tests (multiple-choice, true/false, matching, short-answer, essay) and by teaching testing vocabulary. Table 15.3 presents cue words related to essay examinations that can help middle and high school students construct better answers on open-ended items on high-stakes tests.
3. **Test preparedness skills** are skills related to knowing both the general content and the format of the test. Critics of high-stakes tests point out that teachers are reduced to "teaching to the test" and that instruction becomes stilted and narrow. Gulik (2003) warns, "A teacher should not engage in instruction that addresses only those portions of knowledge included on the test" (p. 2). Many teachers find this easier said than

---

TABLE 15.3

Instruction Cue Words for Answering Essay Questions

CUE	MEANING	CUE	MEANING
Analyze	Break into parts and examine each part.	List	Provide a numbered list of items or points.
Apply	Discuss how the principles would apply to a situation.	Outline	Organize your answer into main points and supporting details. If appropriate, use outline format.
Compare	Discuss differences and similarities.	Prove	Provide factual evidence to support your logic or position.
Contrast	Discuss differences and similarities, stressing the differences.	Relate	Show the connections among ideas.
Critique	Analyze and evaluate, using criteria.	Review	Provide a critical summary in which you summarize and present your comments.
Define	Provide a clear, concise statement that explains the concept.	State	Explain precisely.
Describe	Give a detailed account, listing characteristics, qualities, and components as appropriate.	Summarize	Provide a synopsis that does not include your comments.
Diagram	Provide a drawing.	Trace	Describe the development or progress of the idea.
Discuss	Provide an in-depth explanation. Be analytical.		**Add your own instruction cue words and definitions!**
Explain	Give a logical development that discusses reasons or causes.		
Illustrate	Use examples or, when appropriate, provide a diagram or picture.		
Interpret	Explain and share your own judgment.		
Justify	Provide reasons for your statements or conclusion.		

Source: Adapted from Bos, C. S. & Vaughn, S. *Teaching students with learning and behavior problems* (4th ed., p. 326). Boston: Allyn & Bacon. Copyright © 2006 by Pearson Education. Reprinted by permission of the publisher.

done. Guthrie and Wigfield (2000) offer suggestions for making connections between standards, test content, and student motivation:

- **Learning and knowledge goals.** Set core learning goals that are co-developed by the teacher and the students.
- **Real-world interactions.** Make connections between the academic curriculum and the personal experiences of learners.
- **Interesting subject content.** Students will devote effort, attention, and persistence to topics that are enjoyable and intriguing.
- **Strategy instruction.** Provide direct instruction, scaffolding, and guided practice.
- **Praise and rewards.** Give informative compliments that make learners feel a sense of accomplishment and pride in their work.

Teacher-Made Tests. Tests are the primary means teachers use to determine whether students have learned new concepts and can apply them. Regular classroom tests can be teacher made, department or district made, or come from supplemental textbook materials. If you use department-made, district-made, or textbook-made exams, read the exams thoroughly to make sure the content is representative of what you have covered in class or in reading assignments. It is a good idea to take the tests yourself as a way of reviewing test content. One of the primary steps you can take is to create student-friendly tests.

Tests are also a way to find out what students need to learn and what they have learned. Pretests can be used to identify what students already know about a topic and help you plan for differentiated instruction. Tests can also be used for ongoing monitoring of student progress and for outcomes at the end of a lesson or unit. The best way to discover what students have learned is to construct student-friendly tests, adapt test administration and scoring as necessary, consider alternatives to testing (such as assessment portfolios), and teach test-taking skills.

Student-friendly tests are considerate to the test taker in content and format. The content has been covered in class or assigned readings, and students have been told explicitly that they are responsible for learning it. The format is clear and easy to understand. To construct student-friendly tests, you must first decide what skills and concepts to include. The lesson and unit planning pyramids can be particularly helpful here; to complete them, you decide which concepts are most important and prioritize those concepts for instructional purposes. You know what you want all, most, and some of your students to know, and you have told them your expectations. You can cover those skills and concepts on the test. Avoid asking trivial questions (Conderman & Koroghlanian, 2002).

In a test format, directions should be clear and unambiguous, and items should be legible and properly spaced. Students should have sufficient room to place their answers and specific guidelines if answers are to be written on a separate sheet (Salend, 1994). Attention to format is important for all students but particularly for those who have difficulty reading and taking tests and those who are anxious about test taking. Tips for Teachers 15.10 provides some suggestions for teacher-made tests.

Even with student-friendly tests, students with learning problems may have difficulty reading tests, working within time constraints, or resisting distractions during a test. Other special learners may have physical needs that inhibit performance on a test (they may tire easily, for example). As you decide which, if any, adaptations to use, consider the material to be covered by the test, the test's task requirements (e.g., reading, taking dictation), and the particular needs of special learners. Consult with the special education teacher and other specialists in your school to get advice about the most appropriate adaptations for individual students. Tips for Teachers 15.11 provides suggestions for making adaptations for students with special needs.

Alternative Assessments. In addition to tests, alternative assessments can be used for preassessment, ongoing monitoring, and assessment of student outcomes at the end of a lesson or unit. The idea with alternative assessments is to offer students variety in terms of how they can demonstrate what they have learned and can do. The following are some examples of alternative assessments:

- Audiotapes, videotapes, CD-ROMs, photographs
- Teacher, peer, and self checklists
- Lists of books read
- Lists of accomplishments

WRITING EFFECTIVE TEST QUESTIONS

True/False Questions

- Test one idea.

- Write items without any qualification.

- Avoid using negatives.

- Avoid items that are obviously true or false.

- Write items of the same length.

- Write an equal number of true and false items.

Multiple-Choice Questions

- Write direct questions.

- Make the stem longer than the choice.

- Avoid using *all* or *none* choices.

- Arrange choices in logical order.

- Avoid clues within the item or test.

- Avoid using negatives.

- Write items of the same length.

- Scatter the correct choices equally.

Matching Questions

- Use homogenous lists.

- Place longer phrases in the left column.

- Include more responses than premises.

- Arrange response in a logical order.

- Restrict the number of matches to 10 or fewer.

Source: Conderman, G., & Koroghlanian, C. (2002). Writing test questions like a pro. *Intervention in School and Clinic, 38,* 83–87. Copyright 2002 by PRO-ED, Inc. Reprinted with permission.

TESTING ADAPTATIONS

- Teach students test-taking skills.

- Give frequent quizzes rather than only exams.

- Give take-home tests.

- Test on less content than the rest of the class.

- Change types of questions (e.g., essay to multiple choice).

- Use tests with enlarged print.

- Use black-and-white copies (versus dittos).

- Highlight key words in questions.

- Provide extra space on tests for answering.

- Simplify wording of test questions.

- Allow students to answer fewer questions.

- Give extra help preparing for tests.

- Give the actual test as a study guide.

- Give practice questions as a study guide.

- Give open-book and note tests.

- Give tests to small groups.

- Give extended time to finish tests.

- Read test questions to students.

- Allow use of learning aids during tests (e.g., calculators).

- Give individual help with directions during tests.

- Allow oral instead of written answers (e.g., tape recorders).

- Allow answers in outline format.

- Allow word processors.

- Give feedback to individual students during test.

Source: Jayanthi, M., Epstein, M. H., Polloway, E. A., & Bursuck, W. D. (1996). Testing adaptations: A national survey of the testing practices of general education teachers. *Journal of Special Education, 30,* 99–155.

- Samples of home learning
- Goals statements and record of goal attainment
- Journals and self-reflections
- Graphs of individual student progress
- Copies of passages read fluently

Both tests and alternative assessment artifacts can be organized into an assessment portfolio. **Assessment portfolios** are collections of work samples that document a student's progress in a content area (Wormeli, 2006a). You can use portfolios to provide tangible evidence of student performance over a period of time. Portfolios can include writing samples of all stages of the writing process and in all genres. Suggestions for developing assessment portfolios are included in Tips for Teachers 15.12.

Assessment portfolios can be organized according to subject-area standards that students need to master. Students can gather evidence that demonstrates their progress in meeting standards and benchmarks. Thus, students can become actively engaged in self-assessment. For this to happen, students need to be aware of academic goals, criteria for mastery, and what constitutes adequate evidence (Andrade & Valtcheva, 2009; McMillan & Hearn, 2008). Checklist and self-reflection prompts can be used to get students actively engaged in gauging their progress in meeting goals (Wormeli, 2006a). Although secondary students can become actively involved in monitoring their performance, their assessment should only represent a small portion (perhaps 5%) of their grade (Andrade & Valtcheva, 2009).

Grading

Perhaps few other topics related to differentiated assessment and instruction generate more discussion than grading. Teachers, administrators, parents, and students struggle with what is fair in terms of individual student rights, equity among all students in the classroom, and accountability to state and local standards (Nunley, 2006; Wormeli, 2006a). Even though local policies are in place that address grading issues, there are no easy answers as to what is fair and equitable for all students.

In general, when differentiating assessment and grading, keep in mind what you want your students to know and be able to do to demonstrate mastery of a standard. The pathway that students take to mastery may be very different (Nunley, 2006). One way to make your expectations

Tips for Teachers 15.12

DEVELOPMENT OF ASSESSMENT PORTFOLIOS

- Develop a portfolio plan consistent with your purposes for the assignment.

- Clarify what work will go into portfolios.

- Start with only a couple of different kinds of entries and expand gradually.

- Compare notes with other teachers as you experiment with portfolios.

- Have as a long-term goal the inclusion of a variety of assessments that address content, process, and attitude goals across the curriculum.

- Make portfolios accessible in the classroom. Students and teachers should be able to add to the collection quickly and easily.

- Develop summary sheets or graphs that help to describe a body of information (e.g., "I can do" lists, lists of books read, or pieces of writing completed). Let students record these data when possible.

- Work with the student to choose a few representative samples that demonstrate the student's progress.

- Review portfolios with students periodically (at least four times during the school year). The review should be a time to celebrate progress and to set future goals.

- Encourage students to review portfolios with a classmate before reviewing with the teacher. Students should help make decisions about what to keep.

- In preparation for a parent conference, have students develop a table of contents for the portfolio.

Source: Radencich, M. C., Beers, P. C., & Schumm, J. S. (1993). *A handbook for the K–12 reading resource specialist* (pp. 119–120). Boston: Allyn & Bacon.

HELPING STUDENTS USE RUBRICS

Objective: To help students learn to use rubrics effectively

Grades: Grades 6 and above

Teaching Procedures: To complete this activity, you will need a rubric and some student work samples. Give the students examples of high-quality work, average work, and less than satisfactory work, and have them complete the following **RUBRIC** process:

Read the rubric and the material to be graded.

Use the rubric to give an initial score.

Bring a buddy to help you rate again.

Review the material together.

Identify and award the scores together.

Check the scores again.

Source: Jackson, C. W., & Larkin, M. J. (2002). RUBRIC—Teaching students to use grading rubrics. Teaching Exceptional Children, 35, 40–45.

and grading guidelines clear to students is through the use of rubrics or scoring guides. Such tools are increasingly being used to give students explicit information about expected performance on tests and assignments (Whittaker, Salend, & Duhaney, 2001; Wormeli, 2006a). Rubrics are of two general types: analytic rubrics (process-oriented instruments that break an activity into component parts) and holistic rubrics (product-oriented instruments used with parts that are interrelated) (Jackson & Larkin, 2002). Although the construction of rubrics does take some time, they typically streamline the grading process. Rubrics also make your expectations more tangible for students and their parents. Activities for All Learners provides a strategy to help secondary students become proficient in the use of rubrics.

Summary

- Since the authorization of No Child Left Behind (2001), states have adopted curriculum standards for middle and high school subjects. It is important that you become familiar with the standards for your subject area in the state where you plan to teach.

- Differentiated instruction (DI) has been identified as one means to plan for individual student needs. DI is both a philosophy of instructing students based on individual needs as well as instructional practices aligned with the philosophy.

- Content-area teachers can use prelearning activities such as purpose setting, preteaching vocabulary, and graphic organizers to improve students' comprehension and depth of learning. Student participation in class can be improved through the planning and implementation of well-structured questions and vibrant discussions.

- Textbook adaptations include study guides, highlighting, and alternative reading materials. You can become familiar with the strengths and weaknesses of your textbook by evaluating its subject matter content, readability level, and friendliness level. One way to learn how your students interact with and respond to the textbook is to use the FLIP chart.

- In classrooms that include highly diverse learners, differentiated assessment should go hand in hand with differentiated instruction. Differentiated assessment involves use of formal assessments and informal measures such as surveys, rubrics, checklists, projects, and home learning activities.

Think and Apply

1. Now that you have read this chapter, think about how Jerry Schumm met the challenges he faced in content-area instruction. What practices did he use? What additional strategies would you use in your own class?

2. On your department of education website, locate the instructional standards for your state in a subject area you plan to teach. Identify three standards and think about what

challenges the standards might pose for high-, average-, and low-achieving students; for students with learning and behavior problems; for students who are English language learners; and for students who are gifted.

3. Work in a cooperative learning group to brainstorm the potential pitfalls of differentiated instruction and how you might overcome those pitfalls in your middle or high school classroom.

myeducationlab

Now go to Topic 6: Assessment; Topic 8: Instructional Practices; and Learning Strategies; and Topic 9: Reading Instruction in the MyEducationLab (www.myeducationlab.com) for your course where you can:

- Find learning outcomes for these topics along with the national standards that connect to these outcomes.
- Complete Assignments and Activities that can help you more deeply understand the chapter content.
- Examine challenging situations and cases presented in the IRIS Center Resources.
- Listen to Teacher Talk to hear how one teacher holds high expectations for her students with severe disabilities.
- Apply and practice your understanding of the core teaching skills identified in the chapter with Building Teaching Skills and Dispositions learning units.

Chapter 6

A Metacognitive Model for Teaching and Learning

After reading this chapter, you will be able to:

1. Explain the importance of metacognitive skills and knowledge to academic success
2. Relate the role of metacognition in the formation and mediation of attributions, efficacious beliefs, motivation, and strategy use
3. Describe how teachers can utilize their understanding of metacognitive knowledge, skills, and strategies to create independent learners
4. Discuss methods for integrating metacognitive and cognitive strategies instruction into the curriculum
5. Compare and contrast instructional methods and materials in a metacognitive framework for learning with those of a traditional teaching model

A RATIONALE FOR UNDERSTANDING STUDENT AND TEACHER ACADEMIC DIFFICULTIES

Some suggest that although Americans are more highly educated than ever before, they are not necessarily *better* educated. Thus, "The Nation's Report Card," compiled by the National Assessment of Educational Progress (NAEP, 1996, 2005), provides evidence that many students who graduate from high school lack the basic academic literacy skills necessary to successfully complete college. This trend has not changed in any meaningful way since 1971 (U.S. Office of Educational Research and Instruction [OERI], 2002). Logan (1976) concluded that most students, including both high school and college, scored low in critical thinking. Research conducted by Keeley, Browne, and Kreutzer (1982) found that 40% to 60% of the participating seniors, when asked to read a passage and identify an example of a flaw in logic, ambiguity, or misuse of data, could not do so even when the passage contained several such errors. In 1996, NAEP data indicated that only 39% of the 17-year-old students assessed could find, understand, summarize, and explain relatively complicated information they read, while only 6% could synthesize and learn from specialized reading material.

The percentage of students graduating high school who write adequately is even lower, at 31% (NAEP, 1996), with only 2% categorized as writing well. Research further indicates that students can start an assignment but only about 83% have the skills and knowledge to finish (NAEP, 1996). A report issued by the U.S. Department of Education in March of 2002 suggests that although there have been improvements in reading and writing scores, they have not been sustainable. The long-term trend in assessment data gathered by NAEP indicates little meaningful change in students' basic reading and writing abilities since 1971 (OERI, 2002). Concerns regarding students' poor academic performance is not, however, the exclusive domain of educators. Leaders of business and industry are also noting that students graduating from our nation's schools are not adequately prepared to meet their employment needs. Specifically, they complain that many of their employees have great difficulty working independently, solving complex problems, thinking critically, and making decisions in unstructured situations (Rojewski, Schell, Reybold, & Evanciew, 2004).

Although many people have a proprietary interest in effecting student learning, educators are ultimately responsible for students' educational outcomes. To improve student learning, teachers must answer two key questions. The first and perhaps most important question requires us to define or establish the cause of the problem: Do we attribute ineffectual student outcomes to the educational system, the classroom teacher, or the student? Successfully identifying the problem leads to the next question: How do we use this knowledge to inform teaching?

To address these questions, we will utilize a metacognitive framework for learning in the belief that it provides a clearer understanding of the problems associated with student learning. This chapter consists of three sections (1) the relationship between metacognition and learning, (2) a metacognitive framework for learning, and (3) metacognition in the classroom.

In the following case study, Akeem and his teacher are engaged in a typical classroom scenario. Follow along as Akeem attempts to learn the science content his teacher is presenting. What teaching and learning strategies are Akeem and his teacher employing to facilitate learning?

Akeem, an 11th-grade student, sits attentively in his science class trying to follow the teacher's lecture on the effects of secondhand cigarette smoke on the human body. The teacher is using the analogy of a person trapped in a burning building, forced to inhale smoke for an extended period. The smoke from both the fire and the cigarette contain many harmful chemical agents—carcinogens and toxins. To illustrate her point, the teacher asks the class to recall an article she read to them on the health problems reported by firefighters and volunteers working to rescue survivors after the terrorist attack on the World Trade Center.

Akeem recalls the article, the subsequent discussion in class, and the chapter in his science textbook he studied the night before on the relevance of environmental toxins to public safety. He remembers that during the class discussion someone mentioned many workers were complaining of respiratory problems following the attack. Health officials believed these were the result of inhaling smoke and fumes from the burning buildings.

Akeem struggles to make the connection to the teacher's analogy. To his dismay, he realizes that he did not understand what he had read in the text, making listening to the discussion especially important. He tries to increase his concentration on the teacher's explanation, but he is just not interested. Further impairing his attempts to concentrate are the two students behind him whispering about college entrance exams on Saturday. The teacher's use of the cigarette-smoking analogy is acting as a distraction also; it reminds him of an acquaintance's continued attempts to get him to smoke. He worries that if he does not smoke he will be excluded from future social activities with this person and the popular group he represents; perhaps they will not mind if he chooses not to smoke and include him anyway. Thinking about what the teacher is discussing becomes even more difficult as he remembers the funeral he attended last summer. Akeem's uncle died of cancer. Akeem is worried that the chemicals used at the factory where his uncle worked caused his death. He is concerned for other family members who are still working and living near there.

Akeem decides to redouble his efforts to concentrate; he is finally able to filter out all of the distractions. He slowly realizes that maybe his mother's concerns and the conflicting feelings surrounding his new friends may be useful in understanding the teacher's lecture if he focuses his attention specifically on the two experiences as they relate to toxins in the environment. The teacher interrupts his insight by announcing a pop quiz. Akeem experiences a sinking feeling in the pit of his stomach: He knows that he did not understand the lesson, making it unlikely he will perform well on the quiz. His average for the course will undoubtedly fall to a D. He wonders if he will have the grades necessary to gain acceptance to the college he wants to attend.

If we were to analyze this scenario utilizing a metacognitive framework for learning, we would see that the student and teacher are both using metacognitive strategies to facilitate learning. The thoughts and feelings experienced by Akeem as he attempts to direct his own learning are metacognitive in nature; for example, when he acknowledges that he is not interested in the topic under discussion, when he recognizes he does not understand the material he read in the textbook or the class discussion, he is exhibiting metacognitive skill in that he is monitoring his thinking relative to the cognitive task before him. Akeem's conscious attempts to modify his thinking by blocking out distractions that are interfering with his ability to concentrate are also metacognitive, as is his plan to use his memories of past events to inform his learning. Many students, even ambitious ones, do not share Akeem's metacognitive ability (Ediger, 2005).

The teacher in the vignette is also utilizing metacognitive strategies as tools to facilitate student learning. She gives the students several examples of instances where toxins in the environment had a detrimental effect on the health of the public. She tries to establish a relationship between secondhand smoke and the potential threat of environmental toxins, issued from a variety of sources, to public safety. Metacognitively, she knows her efforts to make meaningful connections will enhance understanding and recall for most students.

Today, however, her efforts have met with mixed results. Although Akeem has begun to understand her point, it is too late for him to use his newly emerging understanding on the quiz. Research tells us her success as a teacher and Akeem's success as a student might improve if she taught the lesson using both cognitive and metacognitive strategies. How can the teacher present the information in a way that is more likely to facilitate students' understanding and recall of the concepts?

It is a widespread misperception that effort alone can improve student outcomes. Thus, it is commonly suggested that if the teacher and/or student only worked harder, we could expect a different outcome. Could it be that both teacher and student are not trying hard enough? Research suggests that simply working harder is not the answer to improving outcomes in either case. While effort is necessary to learn, effort alone is not sufficient to ensure academic success. It is only when effort is combined with the appropriate tool or cognitive strategy that an improved outcome can be expected. Unfortunately, because of underlying deficits in metacognitive knowledge and skills, teachers and students often do not choose the most appropriate tools, or if they do, they tend to use them inefficiently. As we will discuss later in this chapter, each must learn to use both metacognitive and cognitive strategies to ensure academic success. This instructional approach, more commonly referred to as teaching process and content, requires that teachers understand the process by which students learn and then use that metacognitive knowledge to plan in a way that will enable students to learn academic content.

To illustrate, let us reconsider Akeem's situation. Suppose the teacher had introduced the lesson to the class by pointing out the utility of having a PLAN (see Figure 6.1) for learning the content. She models the PLAN metacognitive framework for learning, demonstrating how students can use a graphic organizer as a tool for making abstract concepts and ideas more concrete. The graphic organizer depicts visually how the new information relates to students' prior knowledge, real-life situations, class discussions, articles they read, and what is in their textbook. Would Akeem have grasped the concepts more quickly if his teacher had taught the lesson using this instructional model? The research suggests he might have.

The metacognitive method of teaching process and content differs from methods generally adopted by teachers in that the metacognitive strategies are taught before the cognitive strategies. The metacognitive strategy then serves as a framework that supports student learning, structuring the learning process and directing tool use. In other words, metacognitive knowledge regulates and guides academic problem solving. As an instructional methodology, a metacognitive framework for learning is not widely utilized by classroom teachers. This is troubling, since metacognitive knowledge and skills are necessary components of academic literacy (Baker, 1989; Markman, 1985; Otero & Campanario, 1990; Randi, Grigorenko, & Sternberg, 2005; Spencer & Logan, 2005; Weaver, 1995).

Academic literacy refers to the knowledge, skills, and strategies that students need to ensure success across reading, writing, listening, studying, and critical-thinking

This metacognitive PLAN provides a framework from which various process options are used to access content:	Goal
P Pinpoint your goal	• Science/math
Precisely identify content/social/general objective	• Social studies/history
Picture success	• Music/art/theater
Pursue confidently	• Language arts
L Look at your options	• Classroom management
List strategy or tool options	• Effective instruction
Let experience guide choices	**Process Options: Teacher**
A Analyze progress	• Universal Design for Learning
Adjust if necessary	• Project-based learning
Admit if not working & pick again	• Strategies instruction
N Note results, refer to your goal	• Collaboration
Now think of other areas where this strategy could be used	**Process Options: Student**
Note your success, attribute to appropriateness of process choice. Congratulate yourself: good choice!	• Graphic organizers
	• Learning strategies
	• Social skills strategies
	• Technology

FIGURE 6.1 Metacognitive Framework for Learning
Source: Spencer, S. (2009). Unpublished course material. Center for Pedagogy, Winthrop University.

processes (Nist, 1993). For example, research indicates that children who are fluent readers display metacognition knowledge and skills relative to reading, viewing it as a problem-solving activity, and employ a variety of strategies while reading (Brenna, 1995; Randi et al., 2005). In practical terms, this means metacognitive knowledge and skills include and direct knowledge of strategies for planning one's reading and writing activities, monitoring comprehension or writing, rereading if necessary, taking notes when studying, proofreading written drafts, and modifying strategy use to improve outcomes. This is a prototypical example of how successful students learn: They learn by applying metacognitive knowledge and skills to learning academic content. Conversely, research suggests that students who are not successful lack the prerequisite metacognitive knowledge and skills necessary to become independent learners (e.g., Borkowski Carr, Rellinger, & Pressley, 1990; Borkowski & Muthukrishna, 1992; Brown, 1987; Gaskins & Elliot, 1991; Randi et al., 2005).

Earlier in this chapter, we asked that you consider two questions as you read: Why are students not learning, and what is causing the problem? You are no doubt beginning to hypothesize that many of the academic problems experienced by students in our schools are metacognitive in nature. To assist you in fully addressing these questions, the following section will provide additional insight into the construct of metacognition and its educational implications for student learning and classroom practice.

THE RELATIONSHIP BETWEEN METACOGNITION AND LEARNING

Defining Metacognition

When asked to define metacognition, most teachers and teacher candidates quickly reply that it is "thinking about thinking." When asked what that means, however, few have an answer. Defining metacognition and understanding the role it plays in learning may not be simple; however, metacognitive ability may be one of the most important factors underlying student and teacher success.

Over 30 years ago, Flavell (1971) introduced the concept of metacognition. His theory relied heavily upon constructivism; that is, what we remember are meaningfully organized events, or schemas (Flavell, 1985). As has the work of Piaget, contemporary research in cognitive psychology and information processing has contributed substantially to the base of research from which metacognitive theory has grown (e.g., Atkinson & Shiffrin, 1968; Brown, 1987; Belmont & Butterfield, 1969; Newell, Shaw, & Simon, 1958).

Flavell (1971) believed metacognition described a person's conscious ability to manage and monitor the input, storage, search, and retrieval of the contents of his or her memory, positing that metacognition functions to both monitor and regulate cognitive actions related to problem solving or goal attainment (Flavell, 1976). Drawing on the work of Piaget, he theorized that metacognitive ability begins in children at about age 6 or 7, emerging gradually in a stage-wise progression as the result of environmental affordances and maturation. As metacognitive knowledge and skills develop, the child learns to identify situations in which information deemed as potentially useful at some point in the future is consciously and purposefully stored. The child further learns to conduct deliberate, systematic searches to update this information, thereby maintaining a store of current data that are available for retrieval and application when necessary. Flavell (1976) theorized:

> Assuming cognitive development progresses typically, by adolescence children will have experienced six cognitive-developmental trends: (a) increases in information-processing capacity, (b) increases in domain-specific knowledge, (c) concrete and formal operations, (d) the ability to engage in quantitative thinking, (e) the acquisition of metacognitive knowledge and experiences, and (g) improvement of the cognitive competencies the child already possesses. (p. 1003)

He further suggested that it is during the concrete operations stage of cognitive development that the abilities of the adolescent begin to differentiate from those of the child. It is during this 7- to 11-year period that the child develops the ability to put thoughts into classes, seriating them and relating them to corresponding experiences, thoughts, and ideas—operations referred to as first-order operations or concrete operations. Flavell, Miller, and Miller (2002) suggested that:

> Metacognitively sophisticated children . . . are like busy executives, analyzing new problems, judging how far they are from the goal, allocating attention, selecting a strategy, attempting a solution, monitoring the success or failure of current performance, and deciding whether to change to a different strategy. (p. 393)

The transformation from concrete to formal operations is complete when the child begins to formulate thoughts as propositions and then proceeds to operate further upon them, making various kinds of logical connections between them (implications, causality, junction, disjunction, etc.). Formal operations, then, are really second-order thoughts intentionally performed upon the results of prior cognitive (first order) thoughts. For example, if cognitive thoughts involve perceiving, understanding, and remembering, then metacognitive thoughts involve thinking about one's own perceiving, understanding, and remembering. As mentioned earlier, we commonly refer to this process as "thinking about thinking."

From a developmental perspective then, the research concerning metacognition indicates that the "meta" basic competencies are available to individuals from an early age (Schneider, 1998). The rate at which metacognitive knowledge and ability develops and the degree of proficiency attained vary by individual, dependent on factors such as genetics, environment, and experience. In this chapter, the focus will be on experience, in particular the effects of educational experience on metacognitive development.

HOW DOES ONE ACQUIRE METACOGNITIVE KNOWLEDGE?

Flavell (1979) suggested that metacognitive knowledge develops as a result of an individual's understanding of the learning process and the variables that affect learning. This knowledge is specific to understanding oneself as a learner, general knowledge of the learning process, and the ability to consciously use that knowledge (Flavell, Green, & Flavell, 1995). Metacognitive knowledge consists of (a) personal knowledge regarding one's own and others' thinking, (b) task knowledge requiring that different types of tasks demand different types of cognitive abilities, (c) strategy knowledge wherein one is aware that cognitive and metacognitive strategies can enhance learning and performance, and (d) an understanding that contextual or environmental knowledge can affect cognitive ability. As you read, note how the various components that make up metacognitive knowledge overlap; they are interactive and interdependent.

Personal Knowledge

Personal knowledge consists of the beliefs or knowledge an individual has regarding the process of thinking (Flavell, 1979). One can have thoughts and feelings about oneself as a learner, or make comparisons between people or groups as learners, or one can have thoughts regarding how people process information in general. The knowledge one has about oneself as a learner provides insight into personal variables that influence performance. It involves accessing information stored in long-term memory, such as recognizing what makes specific tasks easy or difficult for you, and knowledge of cognitive strategies and metacognitive strategies necessary to accomplishing those tasks. For example, we can see our case-study student Akeem demonstrating metacognitive insight. He recognizes that his inability to concentrate on the teacher's lecture is due to competing thoughts about family and friends, and he subsequently attempts to block out these thoughts. He is demonstrating personal knowledge of himself as a learner by choosing strategies to offset these factors based on this metacognitive knowledge. Knowledge of oneself as a learner develops over time. It differentiates successful students from those who face academic failure (Gaskins & Elliot, 1991).

Just as students use personal knowledge of themselves to facilitate their learning, teachers must utilize their personal metacognitive knowledge regarding how people learn in general and how student learning can vary individually and across classes if they are to ensure successful student outcomes. Consider once again the case study of Akeem. His teacher is demonstrating metacognitive ability when, recognizing that the new concepts she is introducing are difficult to comprehend, she plans to use strategies that will facilitate learning. Her plan involves using a strategy in which students relate the new information she is presenting on the effects of secondhand cigarette smoke on the human body to concepts she had previously taught; that is, the smoke-associated respiratory problems of firefighters working during the terrorist attacks on the World Trade Center. She knows that when students associate new concepts with those they have previously learned, it is easier for them to assimilate, recall, and apply new information in the future to other settings with similar task demands.

This teacher's ability to make effective strategy choices is the result of the additive effect of reflecting on how her individual students and/or groups of students learn. Flavell (1979) would have categorized the type of metacognitive knowledge exhibited by Akeem's teacher as an "understanding of the learning game." As for students, metacognitive insight such as this develops over time, via observational, experiential, and affective interactions with task, context, and strategy variables (Flavell, 1979).

Strategies Knowledge

Strategies knowledge categorically contains an individual's awareness and understanding of the mental tools available to undertake metacognitive and cognitive tasks. Both kinds of strategic knowledge are important because they positively correlate with increases in academic performance and motivational beliefs and may compensate for lack of content knowledge (Paris & Winograd, 1990). Strategic knowledge and skills can differentiate good students from those who are at risk for academic failure. Flavell (1979) made a qualified distinction between cognitive and metacognitive strategies:

> The main function of a cognitive strategy is to help you achieve the goal of whatever cognitive enterprise you are engaged in. In contrast, the main function of a metacognitive strategy is to provide you with information about the enterprise or your progress in it. (p. 106)

Cognitive strategies are the worker bees of the mind: They perform the intellectual work decided on by the metacognitive bosses. Once automatized, these strategies are referred to as skills. Examples of cognitive skills include rehearsing, inferring, comparing, predicting, and analyzing. As we mentioned earlier, although cognitive skills are important, teaching must emphasize metacognitive skills because, contrary to popular belief, while cognitive strategies are necessary, they are not sufficient to ensure learning (Sternberg, 1986a, 1986b). Table 6.1 provides suggestions for coaching students to think metacognitively. Teaching these skills is important because without the metacognitive boss skills, the cognitive strategies would lie inert in long-term memory, much as books in a library lie dormant until a reader acts upon the stored information (i.e., opens a book and reads it) to create new knowledge.

Cognitive strategies are intended only to provide students with a tool for understanding the hierarchical, stepwise order in which to perform a particular task (i.e., a means to an end); they alone do not give students the skills they need to be successful if taught independent of the metacognitive strategies (Spencer & Logan, 2005). Flavell (1979) explained the relationship as follows: "cognitive strategies are invoked to make cognitive progress, metacognitive strategies to monitor it." If there are to be any long-term benefits, cognitive strategies instruction must depend, at least in part, on training at both the metacognitive and the cognitive levels, otherwise they will sit idle in the library of one's mind.

TABLE 6.1 Cognitive Coaching

Questions to Regulate Thinking and Retrain Faulty Attributions

In your role as thinking coach, consider providing questions to prompt or guide student thinking and facilitate metacognitive development. Providing feedback to students is critical. Teach students to ask questions such as these to retrain faulty attributions, increase efficacious beliefs, motivate students to engage in learning, and promote the development of critical-thinking skills in students:

- Did I identify a goal?
- If I did not correctly identify the goal, what could I do differently to make sure I correctly identify the goal next time?
- What was my plan for successfully completing the assignment?
- Did I choose a strategy that allowed me to meet my goal? If I answered yes, where could I use this strategy with success for other assignments?
- If the strategy I chose did not work, can I identify the reasons why?
- Taking the reasons why the strategy did not work into consideration, what other strategies would have been more appropriate?
- Did I remember to monitor my progress using the strategy I chose? If yes, how did I do this? If no, how could I have done this?
- Did I remember to toss the strategy out and choose again if the strategy was not working?
- Did I remember that frustration or lack of success means that I need to toss out the tool I am using and choose again?
- Did I remember to ask for help if I wanted it?
- Did I set guidelines to determine whether I was making progressing toward my goal?
- If I was not making progress toward my goal, did I remember to make a modification to my original plan and chose another strategy? How can I remind myself to do this next time?
- Did I remember to evaluate the effectiveness of my choices to determine if this approach was successful?
- If I was successful, did I remember to remind myself my success is due to my appropriate choice of strategies or tools to get the job done?
- If I was not successful the first time, did I remind myself it is because I did not choose the appropriate tool, that all I had to do was simply choose again until I found the right one for the job?
- What did I like or not like about using the strategy?
- Is there another subject or type of assignment where you could use this strategy successfully?

Source: Spencer, S. (2009). Unpublished course material. Center for Pedagogy, Winthrop University.

Schools have included cognitive strategies instruction in their curriculum for years, but traditionally it has failed to ensure acquisition and generalization of content knowledge (Spencer & Logan, 2005). You may recall hearing students remarking, "I do not know how to do this . . ." when, in fact, the strategies or tools necessary to complete the assignment independently are within sight lying at the learning center or clearly posted on the classroom wall.

Now consider how similar this situation is to the classroom teacher who laments, "I do not know how to teach this child," when books of cognitive strategies lie within grasp on the bookshelf gathering dust, a forgotten remnant from the last professional development workshop. Students and teachers alike often have no idea how to proceed, even if the requisite tools are within their reach. In both cases, they have not acquired the metacognitive skills needed to perform a cognitive task. Everyone needs metacognitive and cognitive strategy knowledge. It enables us to regulate the flow of cognitive information and exert active control over the thought processes involved in learning (Borkowski, Carr, & Pressely, 1987; Paris & Winograd, 1990).

Metacognitive knowledge underlies students' and teachers' understanding that success, both academic and social, is dependent upon conscious, effortful behavior directed toward monitoring and modifying the variables affecting learning (Borkowski et al., 1990; Carr & Jessup, 1997; Sternberg, 1986a, 1986b). It is, therefore, of the utmost importance to understand how to develop and apply metacognitive knowledge.

As an example of how educators can develop metacognitive and cognitive knowledge in their classrooms, refer to the scenario in the previous section in which Akeem's teacher revised her teaching to include the PLAN metacognitive framework for learning (see Figure 6.1) to teach her students how to learn academic content. PLAN supports the development and application of metacognitive knowledge in that it teaches students and teachers how to plan, monitor, modify, and evaluate their learning and teaching. For example, Akeem's teacher demonstrated how students could more effectively learn the new content if they used a graphic organizer to make abstract concepts and ideas more concrete. However, the graphic organizer is but one of many cognitive strategies available. Student must learn that there are factors other than personal knowledge that influence one's strategy choices, one of which is task knowledge.

Task Knowledge

Task knowledge is metacognitive knowledge applied by learners to solve specific problems. Knowledge of task variables includes knowledge about the nature of the task as well as the type of processing demands it will place on the individual. Constructivist and metacognitive theory provide a framework from which to explain how task knowledge is developed and applied in educational contexts (e.g., Bruner, 1974; Dewey 1997a, 1997b; Flavell, 1971, 1976, 1985; Neisser, 1967; Piaget, 1972, 1990; Vygotsky, 1986; Vygotsky & Vygotsky, 1980).

These theoretical approaches indicate that we actively construct task knowledge and skills via assimilation and accommodation of new information into previously existing schemas, thereby developing new task-general and task-specific knowledge upon which we may act to solve task-related problems (Huitt & Hummel, 2003). For example, over time a student develops task knowledge relative to homework in general, math homework in particular, and more specifically math homework involving fractions in Mr. Pacheco's class, etc.

Task-associated knowledge is heavily dependent upon a metacognitive model for problem solving and prior knowledge (Price & Driscoll, 1997). A comparison of successful learners with unsuccessful learners indicates successful learners use this mental model to interpret and react to new tasks based on existing schemas. Considering that a learner's metacognitive knowledge and problem-solving ability can grow with each new experience, he or she can over time become more adept at solving academic task-related problems with each assignment, each class, and each classroom activity.

The quality of students' individual and collective experiences with academic tasks can affect their metacognitive development and may account for the difference between successful and unsuccessful learners' ability to work independently (Flavell, 1971, 1976, 1985; Piaget, 1990). If students inaccurately interpret or do not understand task demands (i.e., the assignment), for example, they are unlikely to select appropriate strategies to complete that task successfully (Flavell, 1971, 1976, 1985; Piaget, 1990). Over time, successful learners develop more complex schema in a particular subject area, whereas unsuccessful learners over time fall behind, become frustrated, and end up being dependent on others to explain the tasks. Successful learners' schemata include information regarding experiences with the subject, including perceptions of ability, attributions related to past successes and failure, strategy knowledge, and a metacognitive problem-solving model for completing the task (Flavell, 1971, 1976, 1985). Unsuccessful learners' schemata, by comparison, do not include such information. These learners are not adept at metacognitive self-appraisal and do not understand why they cannot learn. They often falsely attribute their inability to learn to a lack of intelligence or something else outside of their control.

Consider again our case-study student Akeem's interpretation of the situation in his science class as he heard the teacher announce a test and realized he was unprepared. He accurately appraised the task variables, considered the personal and strategy variables affecting learning, and concluded that his inability to come up with a strategy for filtering out the competing thoughts had made it impossible for him to concentrate on the teacher's lecture. As a result, he was not able to access his prior knowledge on related topics and make the connections required to understand the new concepts. Prior experience and accurate self-appraisal of the task demands led him to anticipate that he would not do well on the test; he accurately attributed his poor performance to an inability to filter out competing thoughts about family and friends. Successful learners like Akeem generally function better in any given academic domain than unsuccessful learners with no schema or an inadequate schema (Huitt & Hummel, 2003; Piaget, 1972, 1990).

The successful learners' schemata enhance problem-solving ability by facilitating interpretation and reaction to new information, which contributes to the quality of their metacognitive problem solving. Schemata development is dependent on a student's ability to make accurate metacognitive self-appraisals. Unsuccessful learners often experience inaccuracies in metacognitive self-appraisal. This is particularly problematic because the ability to appraise one's use of cognitive knowledge and experiences is necessary to accurately identify the goal of an assignment, develop plans for reaching the goal, monitor and modify cognitive activity relative to successfully completing the task, and evaluate task outcomes (Flavell, 1971, 1976, 1985). Inaccurate self-appraisal, if not modified, can act on cumulative perceptions of strategy choice, the ability to detect and correct faulty cognitions, and the ability to generalize prior experience across tasks with similar demands (Borkowski et al., 1990; Flavell, 1971, 1976, 1985). Inaccurate appraisals can also result in faulty attributions that, if left untreated, can lead to lowered efficacious beliefs, lowered motivation, and the development of learned helplessness (Borkowski et al., 1990; Brophy, 1987).

Students with well-developed metacognitive skills rarely make faulty attributions relative to their academic performance. Their analysis of task demands takes into consideration expectations or beliefs stemming from past successes or failures

(Borkowski et al., 1990; Brophy, 1987). This knowledge then directs their efforts as they attempt to anticipate the effect of prior knowledge on attributions, efficacious beliefs, and motivation, allowing them to act strategically. As you can see, the transformative nature of the metacognitive variables associated with learning, in particular the affective components related to faulty attributions (i.e., efficacious beliefs, motivation, learned helplessness), can determine task-related behavior (Borkowski, 1992; Borkowski et al., 1990).

Contextual or Environmental Knowledge

Contextual or environmental variables also affect students' metacognitive and cognitive knowledge, accounting for developmental and individual differences in students (Crane, 1996; Hartman & Sternberg, 1993; Paris, Newman, & Jacobs, 1985). Of interest to teachers is the role of nonacademic contexts (e.g., the home environment) and academic contexts (i.e., the classroom environment) in both student learning and teacher success. Among these variables, the quality and type of interactions between children and parents, and between students and teachers, are particularly important because these two contexts significantly affect an individual's development, retention, and transfer of metacognitive and cognitive skills and knowledge (e.g., Dickinson, 2001; Lonigan & Whitehurst, 1998; Pellegrini & Bjorklund, 1997; Stone & Conca, 1993).

It may surprise some that among nonacademic factors, parent–child interactions contribute a reported 75% to the child's intellectual development, whereas the mother's intelligence accounts for only approximately 25% of intellectual development (e.g., Crane, 1996; Dickinson, 2001; Lonigan & Whitehurst, 1998; Stone & Conca, 1993). Stone and Conca (1993) found the parent–child interactions involving children who demonstrate greater verbal intelligence were different in several ways from those involving children who demonstrated lesser degrees of verbal intelligence. For example, the parents of children who demonstrated greater verbal fluency had a greater number of conversational exchanges, used language to establish cause–effect relationships, set boundaries, provided prompts to encourage thought, provided instructions and explanations, and encouraged analysis. In comparison, the parents of the less verbally proficient children engaged in fewer conversational exchanges with their children. Their interactions were also qualitatively different in that they often provided fewer cognitive and linguistic challenges. These parents tended to have lower expectations for their children and in general were more likely to believe that children are passive recipients of knowledge (Stone & Conca, 1993).

Teachers may not find this research or its implications surprising, but many teachers are surprised at the findings of researchers examining the quantity and quality of teachers' interactions with students who are low achievers. Studies indicate trends and patterns among teacher–student interactions that mimic those of parent–child interactions (e.g., Brophy, 1992; Stone & Conca, 1993). For example, teachers tend to call on low achievers less often, allow them less time to respond, or provide them with the answer rather than provide scaffolding to elicit an improved response. Comparisons further indicate that teachers and parents alike tend to criticize low achievers more frequently when they respond incorrectly, praise them less often when they respond correctly, and provide less accurate and less detailed feedback during interactions. In general, teachers and parents provide low-achieving students with quantitatively and qualitatively different feedback as compared to high-achieving students (Stone & Conca, 1993).

This line of research contributes greatly to our ability to understand variations in students' cognitive and metacognitive knowledge and skills. The foundation for metacognitive development begins in the home, where during conversations with parents they learn how to think critically and how to use what they are learning to solve task-related problems. For example, imagine two parents watching a child building a block tower. They observe the child make a poor choice for the foundation of the tower: The size of the block the child chose is inappropriate, leading the parents to suspect the tower of blocks will become unstable and eventually fall to the floor. Parent 1 does not intercede but waits for the collapse of the tower and then uses this as an opportunity to help the child figure out why the tower fell. This parent discusses the range of options available to the child, thinking through the resultant outcomes. Parent 2 does not intercede either. However, after the tower collapses, this parent reacts very differently. This parent rushes over, scolds the child for yet another error in judgment, and then quickly demonstrates how to build a tower and walks away.

Similar scenarios occur in classrooms each day as teachers knowingly watch children make mistakes. Teachers can either perpetuate the cycle begun at home and complete the task for the student or show the student how to solve the problem for him- or herself. The teacher who understands why the student is having difficulty, and who correctly attributes the student's failure to underlying metacognitive deficits, will react very differently than the teacher who does not understand student learning. For example, two teachers announce spelling tests. One teacher suggests that students who did poorly on last week's test should study harder if they expect to pass the upcoming test. The other teacher demonstrates metacognitive insight, suggesting that anyone who did not perform well on last week's test study smarter. This means understanding that failing a test is not a sign of a lack of intelligence; it simply indicates a poor choice of study strategies. Thus, the teacher reminds the students that everyone makes a poor choice from time to time, but the trick is learning to choose the strategy that works best. Students consider a list of possible strategies as the teacher demonstrates how to make an appropriate choice.

What are the educational and societal implications? Studies indicate that many students do not have access to an environment at home or at school that is conducive to developing the metacognitive skills and knowledge necessary to ensure academic success (Langley, Wambach, Brothen, & Madyun, 2004; Nist, 1993; Pierce, 1998). Students across all grade levels and academic contexts exhibit metacognitive deficits. These deficits underlie many reading, writing, and critical-thinking problems and the affective variables that influence motivation (Pierce, 1998).

Illustrating this point, universities and colleges report growing numbers of students enrolling in developmental courses (Langley et al., 2004; Nist, 1993; Pierce, 1998). Of particular concern to the field of education, if not society, are college students who plan to teach but who have difficulty with basic academic literacy skills and deficiencies that are metacognitive in nature. The question is, will low-achieving students develop metacognitive knowledge and skills if neither parents nor teachers teach them? Principals report that teachers often do not know what to do when students fail to learn. Can teachers who do not understand how to learn effectively teach others how to learn?

METACOGNITIVE REGULATORY PROCESSES

To be an effective learner, you must efficiently operate, coordinate, and apply metacognitive and cognitive knowledge and skills. To be an effective teacher, you must be cognizant of this process and understand it well enough to teach it to others. Although there may be instances where metacognition is unconscious, it is primarily a function of effortful conscious manipulation and activation of information and processes (Fernandez-Duque, Barid, & Posner, 2000; Schunn & Dunbar, 1996).

Metacognitive processes are complex and sophisticated, exist in varying degrees of proficiency, and do not necessarily develop naturally. These skills include metacognitive activity related to planning (e.g., conflict resolution or resource allocation), monitoring (e.g., error detecting), and modifying (e.g., inhibitory control and error correction) the resources associated with cognition (Nelson & Narens, 1990; Reder & Schunn, 1996).

To illustrate these metacognitive regulatory processes, refer once again to Akeem. While listening to the teacher's lecture, Akeem lost his train of thought or failed to understand what the teacher was saying. He recognized that he has failed to comprehend, he correctly identified conflicting thoughts as the cause of the problem, but he did not correct the problem in time to pass the test. If he had had more time, would Akeem have the metacognitive skills and knowledge necessary to regulate his thinking and bring about the desired outcome? Would he have the metacognitive insight to know how to regulate his thinking about the learning task? If he had had more time, would Akeem have been able to identify the problem and construct a plan, choose a strategy to control his intrusive thoughts, monitor the effectiveness of the strategy, and modify that plan if necessary, all in time to perform well on the test? The answer is yes, because while not all students develop metacognitive knowledge naturally, they can learn it.

Students can fail to engage their metacognitive regulatory skills or experience impaired metacognitive regulatory ability due to environmental disadvantages, as previously noted (e.g., socioeconomic status, inadequate instruction, and ineffectual parental exchanges), or disability. As you will recall from Chapter 2, metacognitive and cognitive deficits, while having different causes, manifest similarly in the classroom and often place students at risk for academic failure. Students generally exhibit a limited awareness of the usefulness of specific cognitive strategies and take qualitatively different approaches to reading, math, and concept learning tasks (Ehri, Nunes, Stahl, & Willows, 2001; Torgesen, 1993; Wolf, Bowers, & Biddle, 2000). Students with metacognitive deficits may not recognize the value of strategy use and, as a result, do not use cognitive strategies even when they are available to them, or may continue to use ineffective strategies even when they prove ineffective (Gerber, 1983; Short & Ryan, 1984; Swanson, 1989; Wong, 1994). These students often do not use systematic plans for approaching problems and may have difficulty identifying relevant details (Swanson, 1989).

Students may be at risk academically because of limited flexibility—that is, they are unable to shift between strategies for reasons similar to those demonstrated by students with learning disabilities (Meltzer, 1993). For instance, a student may choose to prepare for a spelling test by writing the spelling words five times each. If the student were an inefficient learner due to metacognitive deficits, the student would not monitor, modify, or evaluate the usefulness of the study strategy and would associate poor performance with a poor strategy choice. Unfortunately, the student would not associate failure with a poor strategy choice and would inappropriately continue using a study strategy that was ineffective, this time writing the words 10 times in preparation for the next week's spelling test. This student would in all likelihood fail the test again and remain confused as to why this happened when he had studied harder the second time. Students who are ineffective learners do not realize effort alone does not provide the desired result.

Successful students, on the other hand, understand that their success is the result of pairing effort with the appropriate strategy or tool for the job; they study smarter, not harder. If you compare a student with metacognitive insight to the ineffective learner cited above you would see that the former monitors the effectiveness of the study strategy. If the strategy is not facilitating recall of the spelling words, the student will not continue to use it but will modify his choice, choosing another study strategy rather than persisting in the use of one that is not working. This student could demonstrate further metacognitive insight by choosing an alternative study strategy based on previous success with a strategy in another class that had similar testing or task demands (Meltzer, Solomon, Fenton, & Levine, 1989; Swanson, 1987, 1989; Wong, 1994).

As you are no doubt beginning to see, a lack of metacognitive and cognitive flexibility can affect the transfer of learning between academic domains and may account for poor generalization of learned strategies. Students with metacognitive deficits have insufficiently developed schemata, which impairs their ability to decode, encode, and manipulate information, which may place them at risk (Ehri et al., 2001; Torgesen, 1993; Wolf et al., 2000). Plainly put, it is difficult for these students to learn because they have a poor knowledge base to build on, or draw from, and if they had one would not know how to use it to accomplish their goals. Think of the students' knowledge base as a bank account. If the students understand learning, they make wise choices daily, learning from each task they undertake and banking that experience, like daily knowledge investments. Their knowledge base grows with each investment and can support almost any expenditure or solve any problem that arises.

Extrapolating from the banking example, consider students' knowledge base regarding academic content such as reading, and see how students without a metacognitive deficit can become more and more skilled at reading. They learn to recognize letters and words automatically, which frees them up to apply what they have learned in other classes to comprehending the text under consideration. They are in effect freeing up more and more processing capacity for comprehending the meaning of what they read (Hunt & Ellis, 1999). By comparison, students with metacognitive deficits have not learned to recognize the letters and words automatically; they must devote an inordinate amount of time and processing capacity to the decoding process itself. They are unable to draw upon metacognitive knowledge to help them solve the problem because they have had limited success with similar tasks in other settings. As a result, they have less energy available to engage in the metacognitive activity necessary to comprehend the text (Ceci, 1985; Felton & Wood, 1989; Kistner & Torgesen, 1987; McDougall, Borowsky, MacKinnon, & Hymel, 2005; Torgesen, 1993). They truly do not know what to do; they do not know how to regulate their own thinking to meet the classroom demands associated with learning. The educational implication of metacognitive deficits, regardless of the cause, is a lack of understanding of the learning process (Ceci, 1989).

Metacognitive regulatory problems can and do cause students with and without disabilities to experience academic difficulty. For example, an inability to simultaneously engage in metacognitive and cognitive thought may account for problems in coordinating the many varied cognitive processes involved in reading, writing, problem solving, and learning (e.g., perception, memory, language, strategy use, and attention) (Mazzoni & Nelson, 1998; Stone & Michaels, 1986; Swanson, 1989). Although students may not develop metacognitive knowledge naturally, they can learn it.

A METACOGNITIVE FRAMEWORK FOR LEARNING: IMPLEMENTING YOUR TEACHING PLAN

Growing numbers of students are experiencing learning problems, which makes teachers' jobs difficult. However, the job becomes less difficult when the students have similar learning problems. That is, having many students with different learning problems is far more challenging than having many students with a similar learning problem. As you will recall, metacognitive deficits explain many of the learning problems demonstrated by students in the high-incidence category; in addition, a lack of metacognitive insight accounts for many of the ineffective educational decisions teachers make.

The inability to make effective educational decisions is the most common and most disadvantageous characteristic associated with metacognitive deficits. Teachers and students who are effective learners understand that success is dependent on their ability to apply what they know. As a result, they are planful and goal oriented and choose the tools or strategies that will lead to goal attainment. Successful problem solvers periodically monitor progress toward their goal, modify their plan if necessary, and evaluate the outcome of their plan relative to improving their learning and teaching. Effective teachers and students are good problem solvers who understand the ability of well-chosen strategies to facilitate learning and educational decision making. They do not have to depend on others to solve their problems. While not everyone develops this ability naturally, it can be learned.

The PLAN strategy (see Figure 6.1) is a metacognitive strategy that both teachers and students can use to structure educational decisions, learning in the process how to become independent learners. It provides a systematic approach to teaching and learning content that combines strategic processes and metacognitive knowledge of the variables that affect learning (i.e., person, task, strategy, and context). The PLAN strategy provides students and teachers a common language, which facilitates communication and fosters a collaborative classroom environment where students and teachers can actively work together to solve academic and social problems.

Implementing the PLAN Strategy

To demonstrate how the PLAN strategy is used to guide problem solving, we will apply it to the vignette in which Akeem and his teacher are working on a science lesson. The teacher will need to make several important academic decisions before she can begin teaching the lesson.

The first decision she must make is critical: She must pinpoint her goals for herself and her students. From the case study, it appears her goal is for students to understand the relationship between secondhand smoke and the potential threat of environmental toxins from a variety of sources to public safety.

The next step in the PLAN strategy asks the teacher to look at her options. She must decide which instructional strategies or tools she will choose to meet her stated goal. We will assume this teacher is a reflective practitioner, which means she will demonstrate metacognitive insight, critical thinking, and reasoning when making her decisions. She will base her choices on knowledge of how students learn from a variety of assessments and research-based instructional methods. She will reflect on instructional methods that have worked well in the past, given similar task demands. She may also choose to collaborate with other educators before making a final decision to teach the lesson using a lecture format.

The third step in the PLAN strategy requires Akeem's teacher to analyze progress by periodically monitoring or analyzing her movement toward the goal. If she sees that the instructional methods she has chosen are not achieving the desired results, she will make another selection. Often when a teaching method is unsuccessful, teachers falsely assume they need to try harder or the student needs to try harder. Success is not a matter of effort alone; effort with the appropriate strategy or tool is what leads to successful outcomes for both students and teachers.

Let us further examine Akeem's scenario and assume he and his classmates performed poorly on the pop quiz the teacher gave. If his teacher is monitoring students' progress, the poor grades could cause her to reflect on the academic goals and methodological choices she made previously. Based on what she knows about concept development and learning, she may choose to abandon the straight lecture format she currently utilizes, choosing instead to modify her teaching methods to include the use of graphic organizers, which she knows are well researched and noted for improving students' ability to understand abstract concepts (Ellis, 2004). Upon further reflection, the teacher may choose to modify her original instructional goals and method wanting her students to develop as independent learners.

To realize her goal, Akeem's teacher could decide to abandon traditional teaching methods, choosing to discontinue her role as lecturer, simply providing information, expecting rote recall and recitation of facts. In her reconceptualized role, the teacher becomes a *thinking coach*, someone who acts as a facilitator working with students to construct meaning and promote critical-thinking and problem-solving skills. As a thinking coach (see Table 6.1), she would work collaboratively with students on authentic problem-solving activities that provide opportunities for developing knowledge and skills necessary to become independent learners. If Akeem's teacher chose not to monitor her progress toward her goals, she would continue teaching the content using ineffective methods, not realizing a simple methodological modification would solve her problem. She would, in effect, be dependent on others to help her solve classroom problems.

The fourth step in the PLAN strategy asks teachers and students to note the results of their educational decisions. Akeem's teacher needs to evaluate her strategy choices. Did the instructional methods she chose lead to the desired outcome? Can she employ these methods in other classes where she desires similar outcomes? Did her students develop critical-thinking skills and a greater degree of independence as learners, and are they more metacognitively aware?

Regardless of the outcome, evaluation is a necessary part of any educational plan. Choices that lead to successful outcomes and those that do not conclude successfully should be analyzed to determine utility for future situations with similar task demands. We do not always know how we got something right. Consider the computer. How often have you gotten a result and not been able to repeat it because you do not know what you did to reach the desired outcome? It is important to determine both why something went well and why it did not for future success.

Success and planful use of strategies are highly correlated; therefore, it is important for teachers to point out to students that success is dependent on making appropriate choices. Educators must emphasize the point that academic successes and/or failures are due to the educational choices we make, and nothing more. Many people who have met with repeated academic difficulty falsely attribute their lack of success to something outside their control and eventually give up in frustration. Frustration should be a signal that the choice you made is not working; the strategy is inappropriate for the task. The lesson here is rather than working harder with the same tool, work smarter. Discard a strategy that does not work and choose another.

METHODS FOR SOLVING INSTRUCTIONAL PROBLEMS

If teachers and students are to exercise control over their own learning they must understand that there is more than one way to solve a problem or complete a task. If you refer to the PLAN strategy, you will see examples of various options available to teachers and students for reaching differing goals (e.g., graphic organizers, strategic instruction). As explained earlier, students and teachers often do not consider the options available to them. Akeem's teacher chose to use graphic organizers to solve her problem. Graphic organizers are appealing for two reasons; they are well researched and have universal appeal (Ellis, 2004). Graphic organizers effectively increase learning and promote higher-order thinking across student groups (i.e., students who are gifted intellectually, students with learning disabilities, students with mild learning problems).

Graphic Organizers

Graphic organizers promote higher-order thinking skills through visual representation of concepts, visual organization of concepts, and visual depiction of the structural relationships between concepts. They affect meaningful learning by decreasing processing loads, making abstract concepts that were previously overt covert and recognizable. Graphic organizers are intended to make an abstract concept easier to understand by helping the learner organize and interpret new incoming information, and they work particularly well to develop prior knowledge. They act as a framework upon which the learner can integrate the new material into a more familiar structure. Additionally, they also facilitate the generalization of conceptual knowledge across academic domains.

Creating a graphic organizer involves the following steps:

1. Choose a text or lesson. (This strategy work equally well across content areas and grade levels where conceptual learning is emphasized.)
2. Decide what the students are to focus on while they read or listen (e.g., character analysis, cause and effect, sequences and cycles, or hierarchal analysis). This will determine the format of the graphic organizer to be used (pyramid, fishbone, story map, time line, Venn diagram, etc.)
3. Determine the detail necessary to represent the concept and/or relationship. Providing too many details in a graphic organizer may confuse students more than it clarifies ideas for them.

4. Review the graphic organizer with students. Do not assume that students will automatically understand it. Provide students with an explanation of the ideas in the graphic organizer and how they relate to one another. Explain how the graphic organizer will support their efforts to comprehend the text that they will be listening to or reading.

In summary, graphic organizers aid the development of higher-order thinking skills by teaching students to identify details and major concepts, recognize patterns, and make decisions about relationships (Ellis, 2004). They support schema development, enabling students to connect new information to existing relevant information across academic domains. Such generalization leads to an expanded knowledge base. Further, there is ample evidence that the use of graphic organizers promotes independent learning (Ellis, 2004).

Strategic Instruction

Strategic instruction is another excellent option for promoting independent learning, problem solving, and higher-order thinking. In general, a strategy is a tool, plan, or method students and teachers can use to accomplish a task. Strategies are systematic, hierarchical, stepwise progressions that when followed lead to task completion. Two types of strategies are referred to in this text—cognitive and metacognitive.

Cognitive strategies function as tools; they tend to be task specific, allowing you to manipulate information such as taking notes, asking questions, or composing a paragraph. Metacognitive strategies function to monitor tool use. Metacognitive strategies are regulatory in nature; they are strategies that a student uses when planning, monitoring, and evaluating learning or cognitive strategy performance.

Mnemonic strategies are a type of learning strategy proven by years of research to facilitate the recall of information learned in school (Mastropieri & Scruggs, 1997). For example, learning strategies help students complete academic tasks by telling them how to learn academic content. Many students have difficulty recalling information for a test or remembering vocabulary words. Mnemonic strategies work by creating meaningful connections where none exist. For learning to be effective, some type of connection must be established between the new information students are to learn and what they already know. It would be more powerful to capitalize on existing connections, but in their absence, mnemonics are very useful for helping recall of information. Keyword associations and acronyms are both examples of mnemonic strategies with which most people are familiar.

1. Keyword associations are useful for helping students learn spelling or vocabulary words. Learners are required to make a connection between the new word and a visual image they create involving a related word. The image then serves as the key to remembering the new word. For example, a student studying mathematical concepts could remember the difference between horizontal and vertical lines by picturing a horizontal line stretching across the horizon. Keyword associations work best when the student vividly pictures the association (associations that are ridiculous or unusual may aid in recall). For example, to ensure the student remembers the association for differentiating between horizontal and vertical lines, we could enhance the image by making the line stretch across a tropical horizon dotted with palm trees, sailboats, and sparkling blue water. Keyword associations are most effective when learners generate the keyword associations themselves, rather than having them provided by a teacher or textbook. Students who experience difficulty making up their own keywords can benefit from having the teacher model the process, gradually transferring more responsibility to the learner.

2. Acronyms are abbreviations in which each of the letters stands for the first letter in a list of words to be recalled. For example, many people are familiar with the acrostic used to remember the Great Lakes: HOMES (Huron, Ontario, Michigan, Erie, and Superior). Acrostics can also help students remember lists of words when the first letter of each word is used to form a sentence. For example, many people learned the order of the planets with the acrostic My Very Educated Mother Just Served Us Nine Pizzas (Mercury, Venus, Earth, Mars, Jupiter, Saturn, Uranus, Neptune and Pluto), and My Dear Aunt Sally has helped many students recall the proper order of mathematical operations (*m*ultiply and *d*ivide before *a*dding and *s*ubtracting). Strategies such as these support skills and knowledge development in academic areas and are important to student learning. For example, they can teach students organization, note taking, test-taking and study skills, reading comprehension, decoding, math, and writing processes.

STRATEGY SETS, INTERVENTION, AND PROGRAMS

The literature abounds with descriptions of strategy sets, strategy interventions, and strategy programs that make learners aware of what they are to do to complete specific tasks. These strategies employ acronyms to help students remember the steps they are to use when completing writing, reading, and other academic tasks. The Learning Toolbox Web site, developed by researchers at James Madison University, features strategy sets appropriate for middle and high school students. In addition to a complete array of strategies, there are assessment questionnaires students and teachers can use to identify areas of need and strategy lists that match the area of need with appropriate strategy choices. The site is interactive, providing students, parents, and teachers with step-by-step instructions and videos for supporting student learning and increasing independence—in particular, facilitating collaborative efforts, providing homework support, and improving instructional delivery. For additional information on this site, consult the appendix entry for this chapter.

Perhaps the most widely known strategies intervention program is the Strategic Instruction Model (SIM) developed by Donald Deshler, Jeanne Schumaker, and their colleagues at the Center for Research on Learning (CRL) at the University of Kansas. Among the learning strategies developed by the CRL are word identification, paraphrasing, self-questioning, sentence writing, and vocabulary learning strategies. This model of strategies instruction is systematically delivered and embedded into core curriculum courses. The steps of SIM are as follows (Boudah & O'Neill, 1999; Schumaker & Deshler, 1992).

1. *Pretest:* Measure students' skills prior to training and obtain their commitment to learning.
2. *Describe:* Explain the steps of the strategy, where the strategy can be applied, and how the strategy will be beneficial to students.
3. *Model:* Demonstrate how to use the strategy by "thinking aloud" while applying the strategy to content material.

4. *Verbal practice:* Students memorize the strategy steps and key usage requirements.
5. *Controlled practice:* Ensure student mastery of the strategy using simplified materials in controlled settings.
6. *Grade-appropriate practice:* Ensure student mastery of the strategy in situations similar to those in the student's general education classrooms.
7. *Post-test:* Measure students' skills following training.
8. *Generalization:* Help students apply strategies in general education and nonacademic settings.

The RAP strategy (Schumaker & Deshler, 1992) is one example of a SIM strategy a teacher might employ if he or she wanted to improve students' reading comprehension. The steps of the RAP strategy are: *R*ead the paragraph; *a*sk yourself, "what are the main ideas?"; and *p*ut it in your own words.

To illustrate, suppose that at the beginning of the year, an English teacher explains that being able to paraphrase a story is important because paraphrasing helps with comprehension and is required to write reports, answer questions, and discuss ideas. The teacher shares the steps of the RAP paraphrasing strategy with students and models how to paraphrase *Romeo and Juliet* to complete different types of learning tasks. The teacher then has students participate in class activities and assignments, requiring them to practice paraphrasing text and use the information. The teacher continually evaluates and provides feedback to encourage high-quality paraphrasing. Finally, to promote generalization, the teacher suggests other academic and nonacademic areas with similar task demands where the strategy might be used (Schumaker & Deshler, 1992). Teaching for generalization is not only utilitarian but also serves to motivate students to think strategically.

Metacognitive Strategies

Metacognitive strategies direct the use of cognitive strategies. The two must therefore be used interactively, forming a pair of several strategies that are used in tandem to accomplish a learning task. For example, if a student is asked to read a book and write a report, she would use a metacognitive strategy such as SODA (see Table 6.2) to plan and monitor the use of cognitive writing strategies. The first step in writing a composition, or any task, is identifying the goal. The students asks themselves what they are being asked to do. The students plans by thinking about the audience, who will be reading what is written (e.g., what do they need or want to know), and what their expectations are. The students then consider the advantages and disadvantages of the various strategies options for completing the task and select the one most likely to lead to a successful outcome. When making their strategy choices, students consider personal, task, and strategy knowledge that will affect successful task completion, such as intent, prior knowledge of the subject, and motivation. Previous experience is also considered—which strategies have proven effective in previous learning situations with similar task demands. This information collectively informs the students' final strategy choice.

Where many students fail is they do not metacognitively monitor the implementation of their strategy choices, making modifications if necessary. Monitoring may include several mini-stages: looking back while writing to make sure they follow the outline (or deciding to abandon parts of the outline) or laying aside the composition for a day and then rereading it with a fresh eye. The student might use the COPS strategy

TABLE 6.2 SODA: Solve Problems!

When anyone, whether a teacher or a student, first begins to develop his or her metacognitive ability, a framework for the process can be helpful. The collaborative problem-solving strategy SODA (situation, options, advantages, disadvantages), outlined here, can be used by groups and individuals (such as teachers, students, and families) to develop a plan, solve a problem, or make a decision.

Situation: Describe the problem or situation you
are trying to figure out.

Options: Describe three different strategies or   1.
suggestions you can use to solve the problem you   2.
have described.   3.

Disadvantages are things you don't like about the   Option #1:
options you have identified.   a.

Tell at least two disadvantages for each of the   b.
options you identified.
                                                       Option #2:

                                                       a.

                                                       b.

                                                       Option #3:

                                                       a.

                                                       b.

Advantages are things you like about the options   Option #1:
you have identified.   a.

Tell at least two advantages for each of the   b.
options you identified.
                                                       Option #2:

                                                       a.

                                                       b.

                                                       Option #3:

                                                       a.

                                                       b.

Review the advantages and disadvantages of the   Option #1:_____
options you wrote down. Check the option that   Options #2:_____
gives you the most advantages and least   Options #3: _____
disadvantages.

Survey the results: Always evaluate the work you did by asking:

• Remember to monitor your progress toward the   1. Did you reach your goal?
  goal.   2. Are there any other situations where you can use
• If the solution you chose is not working, modify   the SODA strategy to help you solve a problem.
  by trying one of your other options.   3. Write them down.
                                                       4. Don't forget to congratulate yourself when you
                                                          did a good job.
                                                       5. Remember you were successful because you
                                                          chose the right strategy.

Source: Reprint permission being sought from Allyn & Bacon.

(Shannon & Polloway, 1993) to check to make sure capitalization, organization, punctuation, and spelling are correct before proceeding.

Sophisticated learners move metacognitively back and forth between the three stages—thinking and planning, writing for a while, rereading to see how they are doing, thinking of how to fix mistakes or add new information, writing again, and so on, until they are finished.

Last, they evaluate their educational decisions. Students reflects on whether the strategies they chose led to successful task completion; in this case, if the teacher approved of the book report. Evaluation also entails generalization of knowledge learned from this task. An effective learner identifies other classes that might have similar requirements and makes the connection between successful strategy use in the current situation and applicability across other academic content with like demands.

GUIDELINES FOR TEACHING STRATEGICALLY

In Table 6.3 you will find guidelines for teaching strategically, including methods for integrating strategies instruction into the curriculum. The TAKE CHARGE strategy, developed by the author, provides information useful for successfully teaching academic content using metacognitive and cognitive strategies or processes. The strategy provides a metacognitive framework for learning that the teacher can use to structure each lesson regardless of the content, highlighting that the learning process is the same whether teaching or learning math, science, or reading. The steps of TAKE CHARGE are as follows:

1. Teach both the learning process and content.
2. Authenticate the usefulness of the strategy by providing a rationale for why students should choose to use them to facilitate learning.
3. Think aloud so students can see/hear how successful thinkers operate to solve a learning problem.
4. Engage students so they learn to think aloud as they work through a problem.
5. Critical-thinking skills are developed via strategy use—teach students to self-evaluate.
6. Happiness is choosing your strategies wisely—teach students to equate success with strategy use.
7. Attitude is key—encourage students to develop a "can do" relationship with learning.
8. Reinforce the link between strategy use and success, because nothing motivates like success.
9. Goal setting is to be encouraged as a method for increasing positive learning outcomes.
10. Effort is not everything: Work smarter, not harder.

METACOGNITION IN THE CLASSROOM: THE IMPACT OF BELIEFS ON TEACHING AND LEARNING

If research indicates strategic instruction (i.e., cognitive and metacognitive) is beneficial to student learning, why do teachers generally report a lack of willingness to utilize it and other forms of differentiated instruction (e.g., Dembo & Gibson, 1984; Schumm &

TABLE 6.3 TAKE CHARGE: Guidelines for Teaching Strategically

1. Teach process and content.
   - Explicitly teach students how to learn and think critically using metacognitive and cognitive strategies.
   - To ensure student success using cognitive strategies, it is necessary to introduce the concept of strategy use in general first using a metacognitive strategy, such as SODA (see Table 6.2) or PLAN (Figure 6.1).
2. Authenticate by providing a rational for why they should choose to use strategies.
   - While we know strategic thinking accounts for the difference between academic and social success and failure, students often do not.
   - Ineffective learners by their very nature typically do not understand this, which explains why they frequently give up in frustration rather than try again. They feel they have no control over learning outcomes.
   - Demonstrate this principle by relating stories, either personal or those of others, that illustrate the point. It is important to validate strategy use.
3. Think aloud so students can see/hear how successful thinkers operate to solve a problem.
   - It makes the covert thought process accessible to students. Consider having students listen and watch as you demonstrate your thought processes. For example, you might begin with a graphic organizer to introduce a lesson on the Watergate investigation. Think aloud as you process through the lesson.
4. Engage students to think aloud as they work through a problem.
   - By having learners reflect on their thought processes aloud either during or after task completion, you will provide an opportunity to identify and correct faulty cognitions.
   - Do this whether student outcomes are successful or unsuccessful. Often students do not know how they got the correct answer, making it unlikely that will be able to repeat the success independently.
5. Critical-thinking skills.
   - Provide opportunities that facilitate analytical ability and reasoning skills. For example, ask students to keep an informal journal of their thinking as they attempt assignments. This activity will allow the students and the teacher to overtly evaluate thought processes that are generally unavailable for examination. This activity can also provide opportunities to make modifications to faulty cognitions in a timely manner.
   - In the journal, students record the process or steps they went through to complete a given assignment or task. Journaling is a formative assessment method that allows the teacher to monitor, modify, and evaluate student thinking. The teacher uses questions designed to stimulate student thinking (see Table 6.2) about their thought processes.
   - The teacher acts as a thinking coach to guide the student through a discussion of the contents of their journal.
   - Students who are experiencing academic difficulty may need to discuss their journal after each assignment to allow the teacher to correct faulty cognitions or eliminate faulty attributions before they can develop. Students learning to overcome learned helplessness, in particular, will need more support initially.
   - Formative feedback teaches students how to monitor, modify, and evaluate their thinking by scaffolding as they reflect on their thought processes. This is a critical aspect of helping students to

TABLE 6.3 (*Continued*)

become independent self-directed learners. The extra effort and time teachers spend providing formative feedback is well teaching.

6. Happiness is choosing your strategies wisely!
   • Banish frustration—teach students to attribute their success or failure to their choices rather than factors outside their control, such as a perceived lack of intelligence, bad luck, or lack of teacher support.
   • Teach students to monitor strategy use, to modify before becoming frustrated, how to avert failure, and to reinforce efficacious beliefs as a part of your strategy to retrain faulty attributions.
   • Attribution retraining is needed to end learned helplessness. It motivates and creates positive efficacious beliefs.

7. Attitude is key—encourage students to develop a "can do" relationship with learning.
   • Part of the attribution retraining process is developing and strengthening students' efficacious beliefs regarding school.
   • This is a vital step in the process of becoming a self-directed independent learner because efficacious beliefs drive behavior.
   • Students must realize they can control their own destiny by making appropriate choices.

8. Reinforce the link between strategy use and success, because nothing motivates like success.
   • Linking success with strategy use gives students control. Students who are in control no longer feel a sense of helplessness.
   • If necessary, set up a situation where students are successful—make it clear that success is attributable to appropriate strategy choices and a lack of success is attributable to nothing more than an inappropriate choice.
   • Acceptance of this premise provides for the continued development of efficacious beliefs, which in turn motivates students to put forth the effort necessary to learn.

9. Goal setting is to be encouraged.
   • It takes time to develop metacognitive proficiency—maintain students' motivation by reinforcing each successive approximation toward the goal.
   • Make learning authentic—it motivates. Encourage students to establish big goals and big dreams. Consider having students bring in photographs of people they admire, lifestyles they would like to establish, and careers of interest them. Collaboratively analyze the skills and knowledge students must acquire to reach their goals. Show them how setting goals is the way to realize their dreams; choosing the right strategies or tools is how they get there.

10. Effort is not everything: Work smarter, not harder.
    • If students or teachers are frustrated, it is likely they have made an inappropriate strategy selection and are perseverating. In all likelihood, they have forgotten to monitor and modify their plan of action. Model strategic learning for students—toss out teaching methods or learning strategies that frustrate you both and choose again!

Source: Spencer, S. (2009). Unpublished course material. Center for Pedagogy, Winthrop University.

Vaughn, 1991, 1992; Showers & Joyce, 1996; Soodak & Podell, 1993; Vaughn & Schumm, 1995)? Moreover, why have these beliefs and the accompanying educational practices not changed appreciably over the past decade despite educational reform efforts (Mittelhauser, 1998; Peterson, 2002; Schumm & Vaughn, 1991; Scruggs & Mastropieri, 1996; U.S. Department of Education, 2000)? Examination of this problem reveals that teacher beliefs more than any other factor may account for this phenomenon. In the following sections of the text, we will examine the link between teacher's beliefs, educational decision making, and metacognition.

Teachers' Efficacious Beliefs Affect Instructional Decisions

Although teachers sometimes attribute control of their behavior to external factors such as lack of time and support and so on, cognitive social learning theory and research suggest that internal factors may actually account for their professional decisions. Albert Bandura (1986) noted that people regulate effort in accordance with the effects they expect their actions to have, in which case teachers' beliefs, rather than the actual consequences of their actions, will direct their classroom behaviors. That is, teachers' efficacious and attributional beliefs regarding their ability to accommodate students with disabilities and other diverse learning needs will dictate their actions (Borkowski, 1992; Dembo & Gibson, 1984; Showers & Joyce, 1996; Soodak & Podell, 1993, 1994). The predictive quality of the relationship between efficacious beliefs, attributions, motivation, and underlying metacognitive knowledge and skills may provide an explanation of teachers' unwillingness to accept responsibility for students who are having academic difficulty (Dembo & Gibson, 1984). Understanding this relationship could not only positively affect future teacher's instructional practices but also improve student academic outcomes.

Bandura (1977, 1986) proposed that our behavior is determined by both general outcome expectancy and a sense of self-efficacy. Self-efficacy is related judgments (i.e., metacognitive self-assessments) of how well we can execute courses of action required to deal with prospective situations (Bandura, 1986). Efficacy as it pertains to teaching is conceptualized as existing along two dimensions—teaching efficacy and personal teaching efficacy (Ashton & Webb, 1982). The dimension of personal teaching efficacy measures teachers' beliefs in their personal abilities to instruct students, while the dimension of teaching efficacy measures teachers' beliefs about the ability of effective teaching in general to influence student learning (Gibson & Dembo, 1984).

The construct of self-efficacy explains teachers' behavior by establishing a relationship between teachers' educational beliefs, specifically the subconstruct personal teaching efficacy, and teacher planning, instructional decisions, and classroom practices (Pajares, 1992; Soodak & Podell, 1993; Woolfolk, 1998; Woolfolk & Hoy, 1990). To illustrate the point, if Akeem's teacher were strong in both variables of efficacy she could be expected to believe that all of her students could learn. She would realize that lack of success in the classroom is due to a mismatch between student needs and instructional demands. She would thus persist longer with students having academic difficulty, provide different types of feedback, tend to use elements of direct instruction, and respond to students in an active, assured manner (Gibson & Dembo, 1984).

Teachers with weak personal teaching efficacy and strong teaching efficacy would react very differently. If we apply Bandura's theoretical predictions we would see that even if Akeem's teacher has strong general teaching efficacy and believed all students can learn regardless of factors such as family, background, and IQ, she would not persist in the face of academic difficulty unless she believed they could perform the necessary activities (Gibson & Dembo, 1984). As you may have noted, the behaviors exhibited by Akeem's teacher resemble the phenomenon of learned helplessness found in students with learning disabilities.

That is, students with learning disabilities and teachers alike appear to give up in difficult academic situations after repeated failure accompanied by faulty attributions (i.e., inaccurate metacognitive assessment) (Soodak & Podell, 1993, 1994). For example, teachers can and do attribute the failure of students to forces outside their control (e.g., lack of training or time, student lack of intelligence, or family factors; Soodak & Podell, 1993, 1994) just as students with learning disabilities do (luck, teacher, etc.). Soodak and Podell (1993, 1994) found that 62.7% of teachers studied attributed lack of student success to problems in the home, and only 2.7% attributed learning problems to their instructional style. Teachers additionally reported that they lack the knowledge, skills, and confidence necessary to plan and implement adaptations for students who are at risk or who have disabilities (Vaughn & Schumm, 1995). However, research indicates that even when teachers do claim to be skillful in using various adaptations, they often do not use them in the classroom (Schumm et al., 1994). Why does this happen? How can we as educators use this knowledge to inform our professional practice?

Perhaps as research and theory suggest, teachers do not make adaptations and accommodations for students with diverse learning needs because they do not believe their efforts will be successful (Bandura, 1986; Gibson & Dembo, 1984). Teachers' beliefs and expectations are relevant because they directly influence the expenditure of effort, such as decision making, planning, persistence in a failure situation, and the selection of professional skills and knowledge they will acquire (Gibson & Dembo, 1984; Pajares, 1992). Thus, faulty attributions or inaccurate metacognitive assessment may account for a perceived lack of control over academic outcomes, lack of motivation, lack of persistence, and a lack of planful strategic behavior in teachers and students (Borkwoski, 1992; Soodak & Podell, 1993; Torgesen & Licht, 1983).

Successful students and teachers in general metacognitively assess or analyze classroom situations correctly. They attribute their success and/or failure to factors within their control, such as effort, advantageous choices or inappropriate choices, and planful strategic behavior. They understand how to use metacognitive knowledge and skills to solve classroom problems. They are motivated to put forth the necessary effort to act, to self-direct their learning behaviors by setting goals, monitoring, and evaluating the effectiveness of cognitive and metacognitive endeavors. They will discard an ineffective strategy in favor of one with which they have previously experienced success, given similar task demands, rather than perseverating, which can lead to lowered efficacious beliefs, faulty attributions, and learned helplessness.

WHEN TEACHERS AND STUDENTS GIVE UP: RETRAINING FAULTY ATTRIBUTIONS

Faulty assumptions about the learning process, as we have seen, can inaccurately lead individuals to mistake causality for educational actions and attribute outcomes to external forces. An external locus of control often results in a sense of powerlessness; students and teachers may feel unable to control their own academic destinies. These feelings (i.e., meta-experiences) and subsequent beliefs may lead to the development of learned helplessness, which, over time, can cause each to give up on teaching and or learning in frustration (Maier & Seligman, 1976). To break the cycle of learned helplessness and motivate students to learn and teachers to teach strategically, we must understand the problem.

Learned helplessness as it affects students and teachers is the result of faulty metacognitive regulatory activity among three components—strategic knowledge, self-regulation, and the motivational beliefs associated with strategy use (Borkowski, 1992). Individuals who have given up educationally due to learned helplessness do not understand the value of strategic behavior and therefore are not motivated to use it to solve classroom problems (Gaskins & Elliot, 1991). They do not understand the value of strategy use because they have not learned to regulate the thinking, teaching, and learning processes. The ability to do so is metacognitive in nature.

Metacognitive knowledge and skills enable us to develop an internal locus of control, wherein we realize that control over our learning is the result of combining cognitive strategy knowledge and knowledge of the metacognitive processes (Borkowski, Estrada, Milstead, & Hale, 1989). Specifically, the two types of knowledge are used procedurally, forming a mental model or schema from which to reason that being strategic is the key to successfully solving problems. This leads to an increased sense of self-efficacy, or confidence in one's ability to act in a way that will lead to goal attainment. Correctly attributed successes or failures serve to motivate both teacher and student.

When this knowledge does not develop naturally, attributions must be explicitly retrained to accurately equate academic successes with effort and the use of appropriate tools (i.e., strategic effort) rather than to luck, family, or lack of intelligence (Borkowski, 1991). Enjoyment of the learning and/or teaching process will increase when teachers and students become more metacognitively aware, attributing success to strategic events, wherein motivation increases as successes increase; motivation then acts as a catalyst, energizing the strategic processes, thus starting the cycle anew with the advent of the next problem to be solved (Brophy, 1987; Borkowski & Muthukrishna, 1992).

Attribution Retraining Methods

Attribution retraining begins by reconceptualizing the teacher's role. The teacher is no longer simply a purveyor of information; the teacher is a thinking coach (see Table 6.1). In your role as thinking coach, consider providing questions to prompt or guide student thinking that will facilitate metacognitive development. When teachers ask questions such as these, students can see overtly how experienced thinkers process information, how they approach solving an academic problem.

The TAKE CHARGE strategy (see Table 6.3) suggests that this process can be facilitated by asking students to keep a journal of their thought processes as they undertake tasks. Provide a notebook or computer on which students can record and analyze the actions they take to complete given tasks. This method provides the teacher with a valuable tool with which to monitor student thinking and attribution retraining. It provides students an opportunity to think about how they approach learning, to develop the ability to self-regulate and self-assess. As they become more proficient at thinking and develop the ability to ask themselves questions, faulty attributions are retrained, efficacious beliefs increase, and students become more confident in their ablity to succeed in the classroom, which in turn motivates them to engage in learning. In addition to the thinking journal, the TAKE CHARGE strategy offers other methods that teachers can use to promote the development of positive attributions, such as providing rationales for strategy use, thinking aloud to make covert processing accessible, and the importance of goal setting.

Last, it is important to remember to provide feedback to students and link success to strategy use. Specifically, make students aware that success is the result of appropriate strategy choices, and a lack of success is nothing more than a poor strategy choice. If a student or teacher makes a poor choice, simply choose again. Everyone makes inappropriate choices; they learn to analyze and learn from these mistakes. Making this connection for students is vital to attribution retraining. If left out, students and/or teachers may perseverate and perpetuate the negative learning cycle.

Metacognitive strategies retrain faulty attributions. Earlier in the chapter, we discussed the PLAN strategy (see Figure 6.1) and the SODA strategy (see Table 6.2). The PLAN strategy acts as a framework for learning from which all of these strategies can be integrated across all grade levels. These strategies provide teachers and students a common language and framework from which to both access and deliver academic content and social skills instruction. They are appropriate choices when selecting strategies for supporting attribution retraining. The instructional methods and cognitive theory upon which they are based can promote the acquisition, maintenance, and generalization of both content knowledge and metacognitive and cognitive strategy knowledge and skills (Borkowski, 1992; Flavell et al., 2002; Hartman & Sternberg, 1993; Spencer & Logan, 2005).

Summary

Teachers have chosen, or have been directed to use, instructional programming based on a traditional one-size-fits-all model. This method of teaching tends to foster discrete fact-based learning and dependence, which is qualitatively different from the higher-order knowledge they and others report as valuable. Thus, teachers' and students' lack of success may be due to ineffective instructional choices and ineffectual programming options—not a lack of effort, as some think.

Although ineffectual programming options may not account for all instances of lack of effort, it could account for continuing frustration with student performance, loss of efficacious beliefs, and motivation attributed inaccurately by teachers to student-centered problems. A metacognitive model of instruction could eliminate contextual mismatches that can account for student learning. An educational environment such as this takes into consideration the strengths and needs of both the teacher and the students. This model draws upon educational research and theory that indicates intellectual performance, both cognitive and metacognitive, is influenced by an interaction between the classroom environment and ones beliefs (e.g., Borkowski, 1992; Flavell et al., 2002; Hartman & Sternberg, 1993; Logan et al., 1999; Logan & Stein, 2001; Spencer & Logan, 2003, 2005).

If you understand how learning occurs, you can change it. As you have read, educators often do not know how to affect change where student learning is concerned. Teachers, just as those they teach, are not immune to metacognitive deficiencies. As professionals, we have not always learned from our mistakes; sometimes we try to solve our problems before properly identifying them. Teachers as students may perseverate, using ineffective strategies until the result is repeated failure that leaves many teachers with an unwillingness to persist in the face of demanding classroom situations. Like students, we can exhibit symptoms of learned helplessness.

Can this situation be avoided? It would seem so. Teachers are students as well as teachers, therefore, they can learn how to "think"—learn how to learn. Adequate instructional opportunities for students today and for future generations depend on all students having the opportunity to develop and apply metacognitive skills and knowledge. Our ability to learn how to solve educational problems depends on it. We must learn how to learn, so that we can teach others how to learn.

References

Ashton, P., & Webb, R. (1986). *Making a difference: Teachers' sense of efficacy and student achievement.* New York: Longman.

Atkinson, R. C., & Shiffrin, R. M. (1968). Human memory: A proposed system and its control processes. In K. W. Spence & J. T. Spence (Eds.), *Psychology of learning and motivation* (2nd ed.). New York: Academic Press.

Baker L. (1989). Metacognition, comprehension monitoring, and the adult reader. *Educational Psychology Review, 1,* 3–38.

Bandura A. (1977). *Social learning theory.* Upper Saddle River, NJ: Prentice Hall.

Bandura A. (1986). *Social foundations of thought and action: A social cognitive theory.* Upper Saddle River, NJ: Prentice Hall.

Belmont, J. M., & Butterfield, E. C. (1969). The relations of short-term memory to development and intelligence. In L. C. Lipsitt & H. W. Reese (Eds.), *Advances in child development and behavior* (4th ed., pp. 29–82). New York: Academic Press.

Borkowski, J. G. (1992). Metacognitive theory: A framework for teaching literacy, writing, and math skills. *Journal of Learning Disabilities, 25,* 253–257.

Borkowski, J. G., Carr, M., & Pressely, M. (1987). "Spontaneous" strategy use: Perspectives from metacognitive theory. *Intelligence, 11,* 61–75.

Borkowski, J. G., Carr, M., Rellinger, L., & Pressley, M. (1990). Self-regulated cognition: Interdependence of metacognition, attributions and self-esteem. In B. J. Jones & L. Idol (Eds.), *Dimensions of thinking and cognitive instruction* (pp. 53–92). Hillsdale, NJ: Lawrence Erlbaum Associates.

Borkowski, J. G., Estrada, M. T., Milstead, M., & Hale, C. A. (1989). General problem-solving skills: Relations between metacognition and strategic processing. *Learning Disability Quarterly, 12,* 57–70.

Borkowski, J. G., & Muthukrishna, N. (1992). Moving metacognition into the classroom: "Working models" and effective strategy teaching. In M. Pressley, K. R. Harris, & J. T. Guthrie (Eds.), *Promoting academic competence and literacy in school* (pp. 477–501). San Diego, CA: Academic.

Boudah, D. J., & O'Neill, K. J. (1999). Learning strategies (ERIC/OSEP Digest #E577). Reston, VA: *ERIC Clearinghouse on Disabilities and Gifted Education.* (ERIC Document Reproduction Service No. ED433 669). Retrieved January 11, 2006, from http://www.ericdigests.org/2000-2/learning.htm

Brenna, B. A. (1995). The metacognitive reading strategies of five early readers. *Journal of Research in Reading, 18*(1), 53–62.

Brophy, J. (1987). *Motivation in the classroom.* East Lansing: Michigan State University Institute for Research on Teaching.

Brophy, J. (1992). Probing the subtleties of subject-matter teaching. *Educational Leadership, 49*(7), 4–8.

Brown, A. L. (1987). Metacognition, executive control, self-regulation, and other more mysterious mechanisms. In F. E. Weinert & R. H. Kluwe (Eds.), *Metacognition, motivation, and understanding* (pp. 65–116). Hillsdale, NJ: Lawrence Erlbaum Associates.

Bruner, J. (1974). *Toward a theory of instruction.* Cambridge, MA: Harvard University Press.

Carr, M., & Jessup, D. L. (1997). Gender differences in first-grade mathematics strategy use: Social and metacognitive influences. *Journal of Educational Psychology, 89*(2), 318–328.

Ceci, S. J. (Ed.). (1985). *Handbook of cognitive, social, and neuro-psychological aspects of learning disabilities, Vol. 1.* Hillsdale, NJ: Lawrence Erlbaum Associates.

Ceci, S. J. (1989). On domain-specificity . . . more or less: General and specific constraints on cognitive development. *Merrill Palmer Quarterly, 35*, 131–142.

Crane, J. (1996). Effects of home environment, SES, and maternal test scores on mathematics achievement. *Journal of Educational Research, 89*(5), 305–314.

Dembo & Gibson, (1984). Teacher efficacy: A construct validation. *Journal of Educational Psychology, 76*, 569–582.

Dewey, J. (1997a). *Experience and education.* New York: MacMillan.

Dewey, J. (1997b). *How we think.* New York: Dover.

Dickinson, D. (2001) *Beginning literacy with language.* Baltimore: Paul H. Brookes.

Ediger, M. (2005). Struggling readers in high school. *Reading Improvement, 42*, 34.

Ehri, L. C., Nunes, S. R., Stahl, N., & Willows, D. M. (2001). Phonemic awareness instruction helps children learn to read: Evidence from the National Reading Panel's meta-analysis. *Reading Research Quarterly, 36*(3), 250–287.

Ellis, E. S. (2004). *What is the big deal about graphic organizers?* GraphicOrganizers.com. Retrieved February 5, 2006, from http://www.graphicorganizers.com/Sara/ArticlesAbout/Q&A%20Graphic%20Organizers.pdf

Felton, R. H., & Wood, F. B. (1989). Cognitive deficits in reading disability and attention deficit disorder. *Journal of Learning Disabilities, 22*, 3–13.

Fernandez-Duque, D., Baird, J. A., & Posner, M. I. (2000). Executive attention and metacognitive regulation. *Consciousness and Cognition, 9*, 288–307.

Flavell, J. H. (1971). First discussant's comments: What is memory development the development of? *Human Development, 14*, 272–278.

Flavell, J. H. (1976). Metacognitive aspects of problem solving. In L. B. Resnick (Ed.), *The nature of intelligence.* Hillsdale, NJ: Lawrence Erlbaum Associates.

Flavell, J. H. (1979). Metacognition and cognitive monitoring: A new area of cognitive-developmental inquiry. *American Psychologist, 34*, 906–911.

Flavell, J. H. (1985). *Cognitive development* (2nd ed.). Upper Saddle River, NJ: Prentice Hall.

Flavell, J. H., Green, F. L., & Flavell, E. R. (1995). Young children's knowledge about thinking. *Monographs of the Society for Research in Child Development, 60*(1) (Serial No. 243).

Flavell, J. H., Miller, P. H., & Miller, S. A. (2002). *Cognitive development* (4th ed.). Upper Saddle River, NJ: Prentice Hall.

Gaskins, I. W., & Elliot, T. T. (1991). *Implementing cognitive strategy instruction across the school: The Benchmark manual for teachers.* Cambridge, MA: Brookline Books.

Gerber, M. M. (1983). Learning disabilities and cognitive strategies: A case for training or constraining problem solving? *Journal of Learning Disabilities, 16*(5), 255–260.

Gibson, S., & Dembo, M. H. (1984). Teacher efficacy: A construct validation. *Journal of Educational Psychology, 76*(4), 569–582.

Hartman, H. J., & Sternberg, R. J. (1993). A broad BACEIS for improving thinking. *Instructional Science, 21*(5), 400–425.

Huitt, W., & Hummel, J. (2003). Piaget's theory of cognitive development. *Educational Psychology Interactive.* Valdosta, GA: Valdosta State University. Retrieved July 1, 2005, from http://chiron.valdosta.edu/whuitt/col/cogsys/piaget.html

Hunt, R. R., & Ellis, H. C. (1999). *Fundamentals of cognitive psychology* (6th ed.). Boston: McGraw-Hill.

Keeley, S. M., Browne, M. N., & Kreutzer, J. S. (1982). A comparison of freshmen and seniors on general and specific essay tests of critical thinking. *Research in Higher Education, 17*, 139–154.

Kistner, J., & Torgesen, J. K. (1987). Motivational and cognitive aspects of learning disabilities. In A. E. Kasdin & B. B. Lahey (Eds.), *Advances in clinical child psychology.* New York: Plenum.

Langley, S., Wambach, C., Brothen, T., & Madyun, N. (2004, Fall). Academic achievement motivation: Differences among underprepared students taking PSI general psychology course. *Research in Teaching in Developmental Education.* Retrieved July 1, 2005, from http://www.findarticles.com/p/articles/mi_qa4116/is_200410/ai_n9465339/pg_3

Logan, G. H. (1976). Do sociologists teach students to think more critically? *Teaching Sociology, 4*(1), 29–48.

Logan, K. R., & Stein, S. S. (2001). The research-lead teacher model: Helping general education teachers with classroom behavior problems. *Teaching Exceptional Children, 33,* 10–15.

Logan, K. R., Stein, S. S., Nieminen, P., Wright, E. H., Major, P., & Hansen, C. (1999). *The research-lead teacher model: Gwinnett county public school's model for bridging the gap from research to practice.* Retrieved November 13, 1999, from http://www.lsi.ukans.edu.jg/bluelogan.htm.

Lonigan, C. J., & Whitehurst, G. J. (1998). Relative efficacy of parent and teacher involvement in a shared-reading intervention for preschool children from low-income backgrounds. *Early Childhood Research Quarterly, 13,* 263–290.

Maier, S. F., & Seligman, M. E. P. (1976). Learned helplessness: Theory and evidence. *Journal of Experimental Psychology: General, 105,* 3–46.

Mastropieri, M. A., & Scruggs, T. E. (1997). Best practices in promoting reading comprehension in students with learning disabilities: 1976 to 1996. *Remedial and Special Education, 18*(4), 197–213.

Markman E. M. (1985). Comprehension monitoring: Developmental and educational issues. In S. F. Chipman, J. W. Segal, & R. Glaser (Eds.), *Thinking and learning skills: Vol. 2 Research and open questions* (pp. 275–291). Hillsdale, NJ: Lawrence Erlbaum Associates.

Mazzoni, G., & Nelson, T. O. (1998). *Metacognition and cognitive neuropsychology: Monitoring and control processes.* Mahwah, NJ: Lawrence Erlbaum Associates.

McDougall, P., Borowsky, R., MacKinnon, G. E., & Hymel, S. (2005). Process dissociation of sight vocabulary and phonetic decoding in reading: A new perspective on surface and phonological dyslexias. *Brain and Language, 92,* 185–203.

Meltzer, L. J. (1993). Strategy use in students with learning disabilities: The challenge of assessment. In L. J. Meltzer (Ed.), *Strategy assessment and instruction for students with learning disabilities: From theory to practice* (pp. 93–139). Austin, TX: Pro-Ed.

Meltzer, L. J., Solomon, B., Fenton, T., & Levine, M. D. (1989). A developmental study of problem-solving strategies in children with and without learning disabilities. *Journal of Applied Developmental Psychology, 10,* 171–193.

Mittelhauser, M. (1998). *The outlook for college graduates, 1996–2006: Prepare yourself.* Washington, DC: U.S. Department of Labor Bureau of Labor Statistics. Retrieved July 3, 2005, from http://www.pueblo.gsa.gov/cic_text/employ/3college/3college.htm

National Assessment of Educational Progress (NAEP). (1996). *Trends in academic progress.* Washington, DC: Author. Retrieved July 1, 2005, from http://nces.ed.gov/pubsearch/pubsinfo.asp?pubid=1999452

National Assessment of Educational Progress (NAEP). (2005). *Condition of education.* Washington, DC: Author. Retrieved July 1, 2005, from http://nces.ed.gov/programs/coe/

Neisser, U. (1967). *Cognitive psychology.* New York: Appleton-Century.

Nelson, T. O., & Narens, L. (1990). Metamemory: A theoretical framework and new findings. In G. H. Bower (Ed.), *The psychology of learning and motivation.* New York: Academic Press.

Newell, A., Shaw, J. G., & Simon, H. A. (1958). Elements of a theory of human problem solving. *Psychological Review, 65,* 151–166.

Nist, S. (1993, Fall–Winter). What the literature says about academic literacy. *Georgia Journal of Reading,* 11–18.

Otero J. C., & Campanario J. M. (1990). Comprehension evaluation and regulation in learning from science texts. *Journal of Research in Science Teaching, 27,* 447–460.

Pajares, M. F. (1992). Teachers' beliefs and educational research: Cleaning up a messy construct. *Review of Educational Research, 62,* 307–332.

Paris, S. G., Newman, R., & Jacobs, J. E. (1985). Social contexts and functions of children's remembering. In C. Brainerd & M. Pressley (Eds.), *The cognitive side of memory* (pp. 81–115). New York: Springer-Verlag.

Paris, S. G., & Winograd, P. (1990). How metacognition can promote academic learning and instruction. In B. F. Jones & L. Idol (Eds.), *Dimensions of thinking and cognitive instruction* (pp. 15–51). Hillsdale, NJ: Lawrence Erlbaum Associates.

Pierce, W. (1998). *Understanding students' difficulties reasoning: Perspectives from several fields.* Retrieved July 5, 2005, from http://academic.pg.cc.md.us/~wpeirce/MCCCTR/underst.html

Pellegrini, A. D., & Bjorklund, D. F. (1997). The role of recess in children's cognitive performance. *Educational Psychologist, 32,* 35–41.

Peterson, K. D. (2002). Positive or negative: A school's culture is always at work, either helping or hindering adult learning. *Journal of Staff Development*, 23, 3.

Piaget, J. (1972). *The psychology of the child*. New York: Basic Books.

Piaget, J. (1990). *The child's conception of the world*. New York: Littlefield Adams.

Price, E., & Driscoll, M. (1997). An inquiry into the spontaneous transfer of problem-solving skill. *Contemporary Educational Psychology, 22*, 472–494.

Randi, J., Grigorenko, E. L., & Sternberg, R. J. (2005). Revisiting definitions of reading comprehension: Just what is reading comprehension anyway and what is the relationship with metacognition? In S. E. Israel, C. Collins-Block, K. L. Bauserman, & K. Kinnucan-Welsch (Eds.), *Metacognition in literacy learning: Theory, assessment, instruction, and professional development* (pp. 149–199). Hillsdale, NJ: Lawrence Erlbaum Associates.

Reder, L. Y., & Schunn, C. D. (1996). Metacognition does not imply awareness: Strategy choice is governed by implicit learning and memory. In L. Y. Reder (Ed.), *Implicit memory and metacognition*. Mahwah, NJ: Lawrence Erlbaum Associates.

Rojewski, J. W., Schell, J. W., Reybold, E., & Evanciew, C. E. P. (2004). Perceived structure of advanced cognitive skills for adolescents with learning disabilities. *Journal of Industrial Teacher Education, 32*, 4. Retrieved July 4, 2005, from http://scholar.lib.vt.edu/ejournals/JITE/v32n4/rojewski.html#Berryman1992#Berryman1992

Schneider, W. (1998). The development of procedural metamemory in childhood and adolescence. In G. Mazzoni & T. O. Nelson (Eds.). *Metacognition and cognitive neuropsychology: Monitoring and control processes* (pp. 1–21). Mahwah, NJ: Lawrence Erlbaum Associates.

Schumaker, J. B., & Deshler, D. D. (1992). Validation of learning strategy interventions for students with learning disabilities: Results of a programmatic research effort. In B. Y. L. Wong (Ed.), *Contemporary intervention research in learning disabilities: An international perspective* (pp. 22–46). New York: Springer-Verlag.

Schumm, J. S., & Vaughn, S. (1991). Making adaptations for mainstreamed students: General classroom teachers' perspectives. *Remedial and Special Education, 12*, 18–27.

Schumm, J. S., & Vaughn, S. (1992). Plans for mainstreamed special education students: Perceptions of general education teachers. *Exceptionality, 3*(2), 81–96.

Schumm, J. S., Vaughn, S., Haager, D., McDowell, J., Rothlein, E., & Saumell, L. (1995). General education teacher planning: What can students with learning disabilities expect? *Exceptional Children, 61*(4), 335–352.

Schunn, C. D., & Dunbar, K. (1996). Priming, analogy, and awareness in complex reasoning. *Memory and Cognition, 24*(3), 271–284.

Scruggs, T. E., & Mastropieri M. A. (1996). Teacher perceptions of mainstreaming/inclusion, 1958–1995: A research synthesis. *Exceptional Children, 63*(1), 59–74.

Shannon, T. R., & Polloway, E. A. (1993). Promoting error monitoring in middle school students with LD. *Intervention in School and Clinic, 28*, 160–164.

Short, E. J., & Ryan, E. B. (1984). Metacognitive differences between skilled and less skilled readers: Remediating deficits through story grammar and attribution training. *Journal of Educational Psychology, 76*(2), 225–235.

Showers, J., & Joyce, B. (1996). The evolution of peer coaching. *Educational Leadership, 53*(6), 12–16.

Spencer, S. S., & Logan, K. R. (2003). A school based staff development model that bridges the gap from research to practice. *Teacher Education and Special Education, 26*, 51–62.

Spencer, S. S., & Logan, K. R. (2005). Improving students with learning disabilities ability to acquire and generalize a vocabulary learning strategy. *Learning Disabilities: A Multidisciplinary Journal, 13*, 87–94.

Soodak, L., & Podell, D. (1993). Teacher efficacy and student problem as factors in special education referral. *Journal of Special Education, 27*, 66–18.

Soodak, L. C., & Podell, D. M. (1994). Teachers' thinking about difficult-to-teach students. *Journal of Educational Research, 88*, (1), 44–51.

Sternberg, R. J. (1986a). Inside intelligence. *American Scientist, 74*, 137–143.

Sternberg, R. J. (1986b). *Intelligence applied*. New York: Harcourt Brace Jovanovich.

Stone, A., & Michaels, D. (1986). Problem-solving skills in learning disabled children. In S. J. Ceci (Ed.), *Handbook of cognitive, social and neuropsychological aspects of learning disabilities: Vol. I*. Hillsdale, NJ: Lawrence Erlbaum Associates.

Stone, C. A., & Conca, L. C. (1993). The origin of strategy deficits in children with learning disabilities: A social constructivist perspective. In L. Meltzer (Ed.), *Strategy Assessment and Instruction*. Austin, TX: Pro-Ed.

Swanson, H. L. (1987). Information-processing theory and learning disabilities: An overview. *Journal of Learning Disabilities, 20*, 3–7.

Swanson, H. L. (1989). Strategy instruction: Overview of principles and procedures for effective use. *Learning Disability Quarterly, 12*, 3–14.

Torgesen, J. K., & Licht, B. (1983). The learning disabled child as an inactive learner. Retrospect and prospects. In J. D. McKinney & L. Feagans (Eds.), *Topics in learning disabilities* (pp. 3–32). Baltimore: Paul H. Brookes.

Torgesen, J. K. (1993). Variations on theory in learning disabilities. In G. R. Lyon, D. B. Gray, J. F. Kavanagh, & N. A. Krasnegor (Eds.), *Better understanding of learning disabilities: New views from research and their implications for education and public policies* (pp. 153–170). Baltimore: Paul H. Brookes.

U.S. Department of Education. (2000). National longitudinal transition study-2. Menlo Park, CA: SRI International. Retrieved July 4, 2005, from www.nlts2.org/reports/2007_08/nlts2_report_2007_08_complete.pdf.

U. S. Department of Education Institute of Education Institute of Education Sciences. (2002). *The nation's report card*. Washington, DC: Author. Retrieved September 5, 2005, from http://nces.ed.gov/pubsearch/pubsinfo.asp?pubid=2003529

United States Office of Educational Research and Instruction (OERI). (2002). *Report on national literacy trends*. Retrieved July 1, 2005, from http://www.ed.gov/offices/OERI/SAI/

Vaughn, S., & Schumm, J. S. (1995). Responsible inclusion for students with learning disabilities. *Journal of Learning Disabilities, 28*, 264–270, 290.

Vygotsky, L. (1986). *Thought and language*. Boston: MIT Press.

Vygotsky, L., & Vygotsky, S. (1980). *Mind in society: The development of higher psychological processes*. Cambridge, MA: Harvard University Press.

Weaver C. A. (1995). Monitoring of comprehension: The role of text difficulty in metamemory for narrative and expository text. *Memory & Cognition, 23*, 12–22.

Wolf, M., Bowers, P., & Biddle, K. (2000). Naming speed processes, timing, and reading: A conceptual review. *Journal of Learning Disabilities, 33*, 322–324.

Woolfolk, A. (1998). *Educational psychology*. Boston: Allyn & Bacon.

Woolfolk, A. E., & Hoy, W. K. (1990). Prospective teachers' sense of efficacy and beliefs about control. *Journal of Educational Psychology, 82*(1), 81–91.

Wong, B. Y. L. (1994). Instructional parameters promoting transfer of learned strategies in students with learning disabilities. *Learning Disability Quarterly, 17*, 110–120.

Chapter 8

Integrating Technology to Meet Student Needs

After reading this chapter, you will be able to:

1. Recall and explain important terms related to the field of assistive technology

2. Explain who would benefit from using assistive technology devices to enhance their learning

3. Identify team members and their roles and responsibilities in developing IEPs, IFSPs, and IWRPs

4. Understand the assessment process using the SETT framework

5. Discuss how funding for assistive technology is determined and obtained

6. Evaluate the appropriate uses of hardware and software accessibility devices for communication, reading, writing, and mathematics

7. Reflect on the importance of assistive technology as a means for providing all learners access to the curriculum

From Chapter 8 of *Planning Effective Instruction for Students with Learning and Behavior Problems*, 1/e. Rebecca B. Evers. Sue S. Spencer. Copyright © 2011 by Pearson Education. All rights reserved. Chapter opening photo copyright © Anthony Magnacca/Merrill.

Most of us have used assistive technology often without realizing it, such as when walking into a business with automatic doors or reading closed-captioned television screens in health clubs, but to people who have physical, sensory, or cognitive impairments, assistive technology is critical, as they may be unable to accomplish everyday tasks and enjoy recreational activities independently without it.

A PARADIGM SHIFT IS UNDERWAY

Educational services for students with exceptional learning needs have changed considerably since the passage of the first special education law in 1974. The way services are provided is influenced by legislation and a changing philosophy and approach to individuals with exceptional needs. This is due in part to a shift in the social consciousness of our society. Passage of the Americans with Disabilities Act (1990) played a large role in making the general public aware of the needs of persons with disabilities. As never before, we are made aware in our daily lives that there are persons with exceptional needs—when we ride our bicycle up a curb cut, note the Braille on an elevator keypad, or see real people with disabilities and actors portraying characters with disabilities on television programs such as *West Wing, Sesame Street,* and *Blind Injustice.* We can watch portrayals of persons with exceptionalities in movies like *Rain Man, What's Eating Gilbert Grape,* or *I Am Sam,* and the news media regularly call our attention to special cases of persons with special needs who have overcome great challenges or done great things. In short, we are more aware of the diversity of the human condition than in any previous time in our history.

Another important factor that has helped make people with special needs visible in our society is the inclusion movement in our schools. No doubt many readers of this text had classmates with exceptional needs during their public school experience. Your awareness and sensitivity to their needs influenced your general perceptions of persons with exceptional needs. Further, the reauthorizations of the Individuals with Disabilities Education Improvement Act (IDEA-04) and the Assistive Technology Act of 2004 demonstrate a public awareness of and willingness to meet the needs of citizens with disabilities.

All of these factors have created a shift in public and professional attitudes that has led to the growth of the independent living movement. Just as the inclusion movement worked to achieve greater access to the public schools, the independent living movement is working for greater access to information and even more inclusive practices in schools. Beyond the educational setting, it is working for equal employment opportunities and access to the same goods and services as other citizens have.

A shift in thinking about persons with special needs who could benefit from assistive technology has taken place as well. This important paradigm shift has gone from looking at the person as defective (i.e., failing to perform or as having a deficit) to looking at the person as trying to perform within a fragmented system of resources with limited access to information or a lack of fit with the environment. This technology/ecology way of thinking about persons with exceptional learning needs has been put into practice by the proponents of Universal Design for Learning (UDL) and implemented by many in the field of assistive technology. The basic premise is this: If we give the person who is attempting a task the proper tools and suitable workspace, he/she will be able to complete the task in a satisfactory manner. To make this possible, we need to be aware of the proper tools and how to make the workspace or classroom environment a user-friendly place to work and learn.

Teachers, related services professionals, administrators, and family members often think that assistive technology (AT) is only for persons with physical, sensory, or severe cognitive disabilities. An overriding purpose of this chapter is to change that way of thinking. King (1999) wrote of the constraints of AT use, that devices for a specific task are seen as only for that task, in part because we are not able to see past the obvious intended use to a personal vision for using the device. In this chapter you will be challenged to think about AT as a routine part of your teaching methods, to include AT as one of the UDL options in every lesson you plan, and to recognize that AT can be used by all students with exceptional needs, not just a select few.

DEFINING ASSISTIVE TECHNOLOGY

Who Uses Assistive Technology?

There are an estimated 44 million Americans with disabilities today. These are persons who have a limitation of activity that could make them viable candidates for AT. This composes the single largest minority group ever defined, eclipsing the elderly (37 million), Hispanics (44 million), and African Americans (37 million) (U.S. Census Bureau, 2009). Furthermore, the population is extremely heterogeneous, including persons who are young and old, rich and poor, and of any gender, race, religion, or ethnicity. In fact, there is a strong likelihood that many readers of this book may need AT in their own future.

This also means that there is a high probability that any educator at any level of schooling from early childhood care centers to the highest graduate levels may work with a person who uses AT. Most certainly, this means that teachers of the 5 million students with disabilities in P–12 public schools are likely to work with a student who uses or could benefit from AT. At this point, we have limited scientifically collected data on the actual number of school-aged AT users. As this book is being written, data collection is underway at the National Assistive Technology Research Institute (NATRI) at the University of Kentucky, but without such definitive information, it is safe to say that potentially every student with an IEP (Individualized Education Program) could use assistive technology.

What Is Assistive Technology?

Assistive technology can be a device or service that can be used as a tool by a person with a disability to achieve, maintain, or improve a function of daily life, including meeting educational goals and objectives. In addition, as educators we should remember that AT does not only mean a *device* but a *service* as well. Comparison of the AT Act of 2004 and IDEA-04 definitions of *assistive technology*, AT devices, and AT services are provided in Figure 8.1. You may note that these definitions are very similar and all define AT as any device that is assistive to a person who is trying to complete a task, whether it is a task for a daily living activity or learning.

In their discussion of what constitutes AT, Watts, O'Brian, and Wojcik (2004) pointed to disagreement in the field about including instructional applications as AT.

The following definitions are from H.R. 4278: The Assistive Technology Act of 2004 (see previous mention in Chapter 1 of this text).

Assistive Technology is defined as product, appliance, apparatus, or device utilized as an assistive technology device or assistive technology service (§3.3). **IDEA-04** does not include this definition.

An *Assistive Technology Device* is defined as "any item, piece of equipment, or product system whether acquired commercially off the shelf, modified, or customized, that is used to increase, maintain, or improve functional capabilities of individuals with disabilities" (Section 3, part 4). **IDEA-04 adds** "The term does not include a medical device that is surgically implanted, or the replacement of that device" (§300.6).

"Assistive Technology Service" means any service that directly assists an individual with a disability in the selection, acquisition, or use of an assistive technology device. Such term includes

  (A) the evaluation of the assistive technology needs of an individual with a disability, including a functional evaluation of the impact of the provision of appropriate assistive technology and appropriate services to the individual in the customary environment of the individual;
  (B) a service consisting of purchasing, leasing, or otherwise providing for the acquisition of assistive technology devices by individuals with disabilities;
  (C) a service consisting of selecting, designing, fitting, customizing, adapting, applying, maintaining, repairing, replacing, or donating assistive technology devices;
  (D) coordination and use of necessary therapies, interventions, or services with assistive technology devices, such as therapies, interventions, or services associated with education and rehabilitation plans and programs;
  (E) training or technical assistance for an individual with a disability or, where appropriate, the family members, guardians, advocates, or authorized representatives of such an individual;
  (F) training or technical assistance for professionals (including individuals providing education and rehabilitation services and entities that manufacture or sell assistive technology devices), employers, providers of employment and training services, or other individuals who provide services to, employ, or are otherwise substantially involved in the major life functions of individuals with disabilities; and
  (G) a service consisting of expanding the availability of access to technology, including electronic and information technology, to individuals with disabilities (Section 3: part 5: A-G) **IDEA-04** includes A–F with slightly different wording but similar meanings; however, the special education law does not include item G in their definition of AT service.

FIGURE 8.1 Definitions from the AT Act of 2004 Compared with IDEA-04

Sources: Information from the Council of State Administrators of Vocational Rehabilitation (2004); Mandlawitz (2006).

They included the following definition of AT: "a cognitive prosthesis that can replace an ability that is impaired" (p. 43). Further, they cited an Office of Special Education Programs letter of clarification that states "there is no defined list delineating what can and cannot be considered assistive technology" (p. 43). Thus, professionals in schools have considerable freedom when defining and selecting AT for their students' use and for instructional purposes.

Also, AT has been defined by levels, types, and categories. Levels of AT devices are distinguished between *no-tech, low-tech*, and *high-tech*, and types are applications that are *transparent, translucent,* and *opaque*. Categories are determined by the use or task performed by the device or software.

LEVELS *No-tech* refers to items that may be used by anyone to more easily accomplish a particular task. No-tech items might include handheld magnifiers, highlighters, sticky notes, cushioned pens and pencils, book stands, and slanted clipboards. Typically, low-tech involves the application of ergonomics—that is, the science of making the space or task more comfortable for or accessible to a person. Low-tech usually refers to less complicated AT devices such as customized hand tools, work space modifications, and off-the-shelf devices such as adjustable lamps or cushioned chairs. Finally, high-tech usually refers to specialized computer software and electrical and electronic devices such as computers and handheld hardware, augmentative communication boards, and environmental control systems (see Figure 8.2).

TYPES Technology may be considered *transparent* (King, 1999) if the device uses icons or signs that are easily understood or may be guessed. For example, the printer icon (a graphic that resembles a printer) used in virtually every word-processing program is readily understood and therefore provides transparency. A device may be *translucent* (King, 1999) if the user may be able to guess how to use it but needs some background knowledge to fully understand how to operate the device. For example, while we may guess how to use a new cell phone or digital camera, we might not be able to take advantage of all the options without reading the owner's manual and practice with special features. Finally, devices are defined as *opaque* (King, 1999) when users must be

No/Low Tech --> / <--High Tech
Variety of pens and pencils
Pencil grips
Outline
Graphic organizers
Templates
Prewritten words/phrases
Dictionaries
Spell checkers
Thesauruses
Electronic dictionaries
Touchscreen
Macros (fewer keystrokes)
Word processor with spelling and grammar check
Slowing the rate of the keys
Alternative keyboards
Alternative input devices: switches, head pointers
Word prediction software
Voice recognition software
Speech output: screen and Web readers
Translation to sign language or Braille output

FIGURE 8.2 AT Continuum from No/Low- to High-Technologies That Are Specifically Related to Written Expression

Source: Information from Watson (2005).

taught specific information to adequately use them. For example, the first time most of us might attempt to use a copier to make a double-sided, stapled, hole-punched booklet we would need to have specific instructions to find our way through the menu and put the paper in correctly.

CATEGORIES   King (1999) and others have divided AT into 10 essential categories:

1. Augmentative and alternative communication (AAC)
2. Adapted computer access
3. Devices to assist listening and seeing
4. Environmental control
5. Adapted play and recreation
6. Seating and positioning
7. Mobility and powered mobility
8. Prosthetics
9. Rehabilitation robotics
10. Integration of technology into the home, school, community, and place of employment (p. 17)

The above list covers AT that is generally seen as being useful to persons with physical, sensory, and severe cognitive disabilities. Professionals in the field of AT also include devices and software that will also benefit persons with high-incidence disabilities. For example, the Center on Disabilities (at California State University, Northridge) include AT for persons with learning disabilities in their AT training program. Bryant and Bryant (2003), Male (2003), and others describe a variety of technologies that enhance access for all learners with exceptional needs to information and academic instruction as assistive technology. (See Table 8.1 for more information on the categories and purposes of AT.)

SELECTING ASSISTIVE TECHNOLOGY

The steps to selecting AT applications and devices include assembling the team that will make the decisions, assessing the skills and needs of the AT user, training the student and support persons, evaluating AT effectiveness, supporting student use, and, finally, determining who has financial responsibility for the purchase of selected AT. In the following section, we will look at each of these steps in more detail.

Step 1: Assembling the Team

Selecting appropriate AT solutions requires a collaborative team approach. Therefore, selecting appropriate team members is essential (see Figure 8.3 for a list of team members). This team will consider all the possibilities and determine how best to incorporate appropriate technology into the Individualized Family Service Plan (IFSP) for young children, Individualized Education Program (IEP) for school-age students, or the Individualized Written Rehabilitation Plan (IWRP) for transitioning students.

To accomplish these tasks, the team must have the full participation and mutual understanding of all members and encourage creative, inclusive solutions. For example, including the student and his family in the decision-making process is extremely

TABLE 8.1 Purposes of Assistive Technology

| Author | Purposes | |
	General	Educational
Ashton, 2000	Body support, protection, and positioning problems Communication problems Education and transition problems Environmental interaction problems Existence problems Sports, fitness, and recreation problems Travel and mobility problems	
Behrmann, 1994		Accessing reference materials Cognitive assistance Modified materials Note taking Organizational tools Productivity tools Writing tools
Beigel, 2000		Academic Communication Psychomotor Social
Blackhurst & Edyburn, 2000	Body supports, protection, and positional problems Communication problems Education and transition problems Environmental interaction problems Existence problems Sports, fitness, and recreation problems Travel and mobility problems	
D. P. Bryant, Bryant, & Raskind, 1998		Listening Math Organization/memory Reading Writing
Clinton, 1993	Cognitive and academic abilities Expressive and/or receptive language Fatigue factors Physical abilities Positioning in relation to the device Vocational potential	

(Continued)

TABLE 8.1 Purposes of Assistive Technology (*Continued*)

| Author | Purposes | |
	General	Educational
Edyburn, 2000		Academics Daily living Leisure/recreation Program accessibility Study skills
Hutinger, Johanson, & Stoneburner, 1996	Cognition Communication Motor skills Social and emotional development	
Lueck, Dote-Kwan, Senge, & Clarke, 2001	Daily living Educational Occupational Recreation and leisure Social-emotional relations	
Parette & Murdick, 1998	Assistive listening Electronic Communication Environmental access Independent living Leisure/recreation Mobility Positioning Visual	
Quenneville, 2001		Academic achievement Organization Fostering social skills
RESNA, 1992	Assistive listening Augmentative Communication Computer access Computer-based Instruction Environmental controls Mobility Physical education, Recreation, leisure, and play Positioning Self care Visual aides	

Source: Information from Watson (2005).

The following includes just some of the people who may make up the team for any AT intervention and a brief description of each role.

- **Teachers**—both special and general education teachers can contribute information on classroom setting and instructional demands, barriers to the student's academic performance, and participate in the assessment, training, and follow-up processes. Most important, however, is that they will reinforce use of the AT in their classrooms and do any reteaching that may be needed.
- **Student & family members**—should be full collaborating partners in the process of evaluating and selecting AT. Because families may not be informed about appropriate AT devices, teachers may need to educate them so that everyone is on the same page. As the user, students should be included in the selection to ensure that any devices meet their individual needs. Families can ensure that students receive support and encouragement to use or practice with the device outside the school setting. Further, families can be helpful advocates in acquiring and funding issues.

Not every school or district has an AT specialist. If the district where you work does, here is what you might expect that person to provide for the team

- **Assistive technology specialist (ATS)**—individuals trained to conduct assessments of students' needs as well as capabilities to use various AT devices and provide the training for students, family members, and teachers who will be using or supporting use of a specific device. In addition, the practitioner may collaborate with a variety of other professionals to bring information to the team during the selection and training process. These can include:
  - **Physician**—will be required to write a prescription for assistive devices that meet medical needs and must be used during the school day. This is especially true if funding is provided by an insurance company or Medicaid/Medicare.
  - **Assistive technology supplier (ATS)**—can provide commercially available assistive technology devices that require personalized fitting or special accessories, such as wheelchairs, hearing aids, eye glasses, and specialty magnifiers.
  - **Audiologist**—may be a physician or specialist who can assess needs and recommend devices for students with a hearing impairment.
  - **Designer/fabricator**—may be an AT professional or the maintenance person at the school who can build personalized accessories such as blocks to raise desks, ramps, accessible door/cabinet handles, or other features that will support student accessibility.
  - **Funding agency**—commonly called third-party payer, can assess written justification, prescription, or grant application for AT devices and services for adherence to regulations or company manual. This may be an insurance company, community organization, or Medicaid/Medicare.

- **Occupational therapist (OT)**—can provide information about the student's functional skills, including gross motor skills and muscle control of different body parts, and may provide training or adapt devices as appropriate.
- **Physical therapist (PT)**—can provide information about the student's muscle strength, range of motion, flexibility, balance, and coordination. The PT plans and implements exercises to improve physical function and trains individuals in use of assistive devices such as wheelchairs and prosthetic devices.
- **Speech language pathologist (SLP)**—can provide information about the student's speech and language problems, evaluate the potential use of communication devices, and recommend types of specialized communication aids and techniques.

FIGURE 8.3 Team Members Who Might Be Part of the AT Assessment Process

- **Social worker**—can provide information about the student's total living situation and how the use of AT may impact the culture of the family. The social worker can be a valuable resource about community organizations and resources for funding and can act as the liaison for the team.
- **Psychologist**—can provide information about the student's potential for learning and using AT.

When the student is planning or making the transition from school to employment or postsecondary education, the team may include:

- **Vocational rehabilitation counselor (VRC)**—can provide information about the student's potential to hold a job, assist with identification of tools necessary to obtain, and execute essential functions of the job. This counselor would be involved in similar ways with students who are moving to postsecondary educational settings. Most important, the VRC can include AT in the Individual Written Rehabilitation Program (IWRP) that will be used if the student plans to use VR services.

This is in no way an inclusive list of team members, as teams must be constructed to meet the needs of individual students and special circumstances. For example, in a school situation, bus drivers, media center personnel, cafeteria workers, paraeducators, and others who have daily contact with a student may need to be involved in providing information or receiving training.

FIGURE 8.3 Team Members Who Might Be Part of the AT Assessment Process (*Continued*)
Sources: Information from the Alliance for Technology Access (1996); Bryant & Bryant (2003); Center on Disabilities at California State University, Northridge (2002); Male (2003).

important to, among other things, ensure that technology use is supported. One of the keys to achieving successful technology outcomes is the use of a collaborative approach throughout the technology intervention, starting with identification of needs. When involved, students will contribute important information about their goals, interests, dislikes, priorities, and the practical aspects of their living situation. Further, by participating in this collaborative process, they share the responsibility for achieving a good match between themselves and the technology solution.

Step 2: Assessing Skills and Needs

Three assessment concepts have been identified for selection: *ecological*, *practical*, and *ongoing* (Bryant & Bryant, 2003).

ECOLOGICAL   Teams should consider all environments where the student performs tasks (Watts et al., 2004). In schools, examples of environments would include classrooms (self-contained or inclusion), library/media centers, science labs, occupational skills workrooms, and gymnasiums. Home environments where students might be doing homework should be considered. In the community, examples of environments would include public libraries and field trips sites. Work environments should also be considered for students in work-study programs. Finally, all extracurricular and recreational opportunities such as after-school clubs, Scouts, and sports should be considered.

Data about the student's environments should be collected from the student, family members, teachers, paraeducators, coaches, peers, and related services professionals.

Multiple means of data collection may be used, such as observation of the student interacting the environment, paper/pencil surveys and rating scales, and interviews. The key consideration is that information be collected from as many people within the student's environments as possible.

PRACTICAL   Buying AT that is not appropriate because it is too difficult for the student to use or unsuitable for the environment is wasteful of time, effort, and funds. Evaluating the practical use of AT prior to purchase can decrease instances of AT abandonment. During the selection process, students and teachers need opportunities to use and personally evaluate the hardware and software being considered (Long, Huang, Woodbridge, Woolverton, & Minkel, 2003). Decision making when selecting AT must be grounded in the everyday practicality of the device within the actual environment where the student works.

Obtaining AT for pre-purchase evaluations in school settings can present practical problems, but solutions are available. Methods for obtaining AT to use in these situations include contacting state assistive technology projects and searching the Internet. State AT projects maintain demonstration labs, and most will lend AT to schools for evaluation and training purposes (see discussion of AT projects in the Funding section of this chapter). The AT specialist or district office can contact the sales department of AT suppliers and vendors regarding availability of AT for evaluation and training. Finally, some software companies offer free 30-day-trial copies on CD or for download from their Web sites.

ONGOING   AT is meant to enhance users' learning experience and help them perform tasks that they might not be able to do otherwise within their environment. Therefore, as students learn and are required to demonstrate advanced levels of a task, perform new tasks, or change environments, the requirements for AT may change as well, so ongoing assessment is essential to providing optimal AT and AT services. For example, a second-grader may require only a simple calculator that performs basic mathematical calculations, but as the student advances in grade levels so do the mathematical calculations he is required to perform. At some point, a basic calculator will not meet the student's skill level or needs and a calculator that performs the functions required by new tasks must be selected. This will be true for both hardware and software that the student uses. Ongoing assessment is required to ensure that student skills and needs are known and supported.

Decision-Making Models

A variety of models for assessing and selecting AT devices exist within the AT literature (Table 8.2). Among these, we have chosen the SETT (Table 8.3) model for several reasons. One reason is that it is widely acknowledged as an excellent model (Bryant & Bryant, 2003). In addition, SETT contains the features viewed as important in the educational assessment literature, such as a comprehensive ecological approach; team problem-solving, strength-based assessment, ongoing longitudinal approach, student involvement, documentation, and student outcomes (Watts et al., 2004). Further, the SETT model includes the three assessment components we noted above (Bryant & Bryant, 2003): ecological, practical, and ongoing.

TABLE 8.2 Models for Assessing and Selecting AT

Author	Steps
Bryant & Bryant (2003)	• Consider various contexts. • Consider strengths and weakness. • Consider technology experience. • Consider technology characteristics. • Consider the person–technology match.
Cook & Hussey (2002)	Human, Activity, Assistive Technology (HAAT) model considers • The skills of the individual • The task that the person is expected to perform • The context or constraints on the activity
Harden & Rosenberg (2001)	• Conduct student observations. • Conduct student interview. • Review IEP goals. • Observe and assess the environment. • Obtain family input.
Institute for Matching Person and Technology (2002)	Matching Person and Technology (MPT) model considers • The environment • The users' preferences • Functions and features of the AT
Long et al. (2003)	• Recognize the problem. • Evaluate of the need. • Assess barriers, identify AT & AT services. • Consider AT menu. • Match AT and AT service to need. • Select AT, identify training needs. • Secure suppliers. • Secure funding for AT & AT services. • Implement AT. • Follow up.
Zabala (2002)	• Conduct intake/referral. • Identify student needs. • Identify desired outcomes. • Develop and nurture team members. • Conduct skills assessment. • Conduct device trials. • Revisit desired outcomes. • Procure device. • Begin implementation of AT. • Conduct follow-up/follow-along.

Sources: Information from Bryant & Bryant (2003); Cook & Hussey (2002); Harden & Rosenberg (2001); Institute for Matching Person and Technology (2005); Long et al. (2003); Zabala (2002).

TABLE 8.3 Using the SETT Framework to Facilitate Team Discussions

S = Skills	• What are the skills we know the student is unable to perform in all environments?
	• Are there other special needs?
	• What are the student's current abilities?
	• How does the student manage learning tasks now?
	• How does the student manage the physical environment now?
E = Environment	• What is the physical arrangement of the environment?
	• What setting demands are found in the environment?
	• What types of materials and equipment are used here? (For example, PE, math, or science classrooms have unique equipment.)
	• Are there accessible issues in the environment?
	• Are there attitudes and expectations of teacher, staff, and others that should be considered when selecting AT?
T = Tasks	• What are the instructional demands of the curriculum or teacher in each instructional situation?
	• What tasks occur in the student's natural environments that enable progress?
	• What tasks are required for active involvement in these environments?
T = Tools	Based on skills needed to perform required tasks and student's present capabilities to function in all environments:
	• Brainstorm possible AT applications (no, low, and high).
	• Select the most promising for a trial use.
	• Plan specifics of the trial period (including ways success will be assessed).
	• Collect data on success.

Sources: Information from Center on Disabilities (2002); Male (2003); Watts et al. (2004).

However, the most important feature of SETT is the collaborative nature of this framework. As discussed earlier, many professionals may be involved, each with his or her own professional points of view. SETT provides a structure that allows a diverse group to share expertise and work together to plan with the student. In an interview, Zabala, the developer of SETT (Bryant & Bryant, 2003, p. 28), reported that she asks team participants to spend the first few minutes of a meeting jotting down on sticky notes the five most important things the team should know about the student, environments where the student works or lives, and the tasks frequently required in these environments. Then Zabala invites the participants to place their sticky notes on poster paper under the appropriate heading. This activity allows the group to learn about the student quickly.

THE SETT FRAMEWORK SETT stands for Student, Environment, Tasks, and Tools. Within the framework, individuals work collaboratively to increase the team's collective knowledge about (a) the student, (b) the environment in which AT will be used, and (c) the tasks that must be preformed in that environment and to (d) select the most appropriate tools for those tasks (see Figure 8.4 for definitions).

SETT components include, but are not limited to the following:

Skills that are typically found in general and special education environments:

- Motor
- Cognitive, including memory and attitude
- Language and processing
- Sensory

Environments where the student is typically required to perform:

- School (self-contained or inclusion)
- Community (library, field trips)
- Work (for students in transition programs)
- Recreation (Scouts, after-school clubs, PE, sports)
- Home (doing homework)

Tasks typically performed in the above environments:

- Academic tasks of reading, writing, and assessment of learning
- Use of classroom equipment and tools (pens/pencils, paper, sports equipment, art and music equipment)
- Organization (notebooks, projects, homework, work schedules)
- Participation in activities requiring spoken word
- Using research resources (library, Internet, etc.)
- Using teaching materials (handouts, textbooks, maps, etc.)
- Use of standard technology applications (keyboard, monitor, mouse, storage devices, and printers)

Tools that may be applicable:

- No-technology solutions that may work
- Low-technology tools that may work
- High-technology tools that may work

FIGURE 8.4 Definitions of SETT Components

Sources: Information from Center on Disabilities at California State University, Northridge (2002); Watts et al. (2004).

The SETT framework and the sticky-note activity provide a structure for educators, parents, and students to collaborate and discuss AT devices and services that are a given student needs. For example, the IEP team may think that the student needs to word process written work but is not sure what hardware application is best. By discussing the student's skills and capabilities to function without a computer, the places a computer will be used, and the tasks to be performed in that environment, the team can decide if a desktop, laptop, or handheld computer would best meet the student's skills and needs. This will also eliminate the purchase of an expensive device that cannot be used in all environments or is more opaque (complex) than the student can readily use. See Table 8.3 for questions that facilitate team discussions and decision making.

Step 3: Training

Giving educators and related service providers, students, and their families training and opportunities to try the AT before implementation is crucial. Such opportunities reduce the problem of underuse, misuse, and abandonment of the AT device (Long et al., 2003). In addition, when all the professionals involved understand the device, how it works, and how to use it effectively in the classroom environment, they are more likely to accept and support its use. Lack of training is a major barrier to implementation of AT in the classroom (Hutinger, Johanson, & Stoneburner, 1996; McGregor & Pachuski, 1996).

In this phase of the assessment, a good working relationship with knowledgeable vendors and suppliers is critical. These are most knowledgeable about the equipment or software and its features and your school district requirements. Further, suppliers and vendors who have working relationships with your school district will be more willing to loan items for evaluation.

Step 4: Evaluation of AT Effectiveness

The first assessments and evaluation of AT use should be performed soon after delivery of the AT device, ideally within the first month. This is a time to check that student, family, and teachers are satisfied with it and that the system is working effectively. Follow-along assessment is just as important and is a long-term commitment to the student's use of AT. Follow-along assessments should occur regularly, as often as every 2 to 3 months during the first year of AT and before each IEP meeting during the student's academic career. As noted previously, the goal of follow-up and follow-along assessments is to ensure that the AT continues to meet the student's skills and needs and is being used to the fullest potential. Throughout this period, the team can determine if additional training is needed and if the stated goals for AT use are being met.

Ongoing evaluation can help reduce the occurrence of AT device abandonment. This is a serious problem and should be a concern during the assessment and selection process. A growing body of research on the abandonment of assistive technology illustrates the complexity of the interface between a person and a device (King, 1999). One overarching factor is failure to consider the student user's preferences in AT selection. The rate of device abandonment ranges from as low as 8% to as high as 75% (Center on Disabilities, 2002). On average, about one-third of all devices are abandoned. This issue must be addressed when selecting the team. As noted earlier in this chapter, being inclusive when selecting the team maximizes acceptance of whatever AT is selected. And most certainly, it is vital to include the student user whose skills, needs, and preferences are being considered. Most of the abandonment occurs within the first year, especially within the first 3 months, as users learn relatively early whether a device works for them (Center on Disabilities, 2002). In short, ongoing and early evaluations of AT effectiveness are essential to make certain that the selected AT meets the student's skills and needs, is used to the fullest potential, and is not abandoned.

Step 5: Supporting Student Use

In Steps 1–4 we mentioned the importance of the student user's role in the selection of AT use, in particular, the importance of matching the student and the AT for skills and needs. In this section we will discuss factors that affect the use of AT and may lead to abandonment during the transitional stage to full acceptance and use of the AT. This process of becoming accustomed to using and being seen using the AT can be difficult. For example, the human factors of culture, age, gender, and literacy (King, 1999) constitute student preferences. While the student is the primary focus of AT selection, we cannot ignore the cultural beliefs and customs that may affect acceptance and use of AT.

Student preferences based on cultural beliefs and customs must be honored by not forcing students to use AT that they do not believe in or cannot accept (King, 1999). For example, devices and software that were developed for a specific age can be problematic if these are not also age appropriate for the student under consideration. Thus, software developed primarily for early-childhood or elementary-age students would not be age appropriate for an adolescent, regardless of the student's skill level. Taking the time and effort to find age-appropriate AT is essential for acceptance by the student (King, 1999). Giving careful consideration to these issues will help support students and avoid early abandonment as they become accustomed to their new AT.

Two final considerations during AT selection are service and replacement of AT that is broken or requires maintenance or updating. King (1999) suggested three measures: (1) teaching the student alternative backup methods for accomplishing the task for which the AT was being used, (2) obtaining devices that can be repaired or replaced easily, and (3) knowing the warranty policies before you purchase. Lengthy disruptions in AT use can lead to abandonment, which may exacerbate the effects of the disability and tax the recourses of a school district (Long et al., 2003).

So far in this section we have discussed assembling the team that will make AT decisions, assessing the skills and needs of the AT user, training the student and support persons, evaluating AT effectiveness, and supporting student use. The final step is the determination of financial responsibility for providing the AT.

Step 6: Responsibility for Providing AT

The sources for funding and how to access these sources are important aspects of the selecting process for all teachers to understand. Frequently students are denied AT applications and devices because school teams are concerned about costs to the school district and parents are unable to afford the device. Therefore, understanding that neither the school nor parents must be responsible for funding all AT devices needed in school settings will help in the decision process. Further, understanding the application process for third-party funding will support collaborative efforts across school, healthcare providers, and community agencies and will increase the likelihood that students will have the AT needed to have full access in school environments.

WHAT IS THE SCHOOL'S RESPONSIBILITY FOR PROVIDING AT DEVICES AND SERVICES? Devices and services we commonly classify as AT have been within the scope of a free appropriate public education (FAPE) since the initial enactment of federal special education legislation (Pub. L. 94-142) in 1975. Further, subsequent special education laws state clearly that representatives of the school district must consider AT during every IEP and, if AT is determined appropriate, provide or pay for AT devices or services. Under special education law, schools have always been required to provide adaptive equipment, augmentative communication devices, typewriters, tape recorders, word processors, Braille versions of print materials, auditory trainers, wheelchairs, and other types of devices and services to students who need them. In addition, over the years other decisions and policy letters have established some core principles related to AT device funding, as outlined below.

According to a U.S. Department of Education (USDOE) policy letter, known as the "Goodman Letter," schools are prohibited from refusing to consider AT devices and services as part of the IEP process (National Information Center for Children and Youth with Disabilities, 1991). The USDOE established policy even though the special education law (Pub. L. 94-142) did not use the term *assistive technology*. Therefore, when IDEIA-04 added terms defining AT devices and services, no new benefits were added but existing regulations were merely clarified. In addition, these regulations made an express connection between provision of AT devices and services and three components of a FAPE—special education, related services, and supplementary aids and services (National Information Center, 1991).

The latest revision that reauthorizes and amends IDEIA-04 was signed into law in December of 2004. The 2004 reauthorization made only one change related to AT. In the definition (Sec. 602(1)(B)) of the term *assistive technology device*, the law states that a device does not include surgically implanted medical device or replacement of such a device. This exception arose in part from a concern, based on a recent due-process hearing, that school districts might be held responsible for providing cochlear implants for children with hearing impairments (Mandlawitz, 2006). No other substantial changes to assistive technology portions of the 1997 law were made in the 2004 reauthorization; therefore, all previous provisions of 1997 still apply to AT. Briefly, the law is clear that AT is not a school district option. When needed by a student with disabilities, it must be provided.

Obtaining AT Funding from Third Parties

Local education agencies are not required to fund all assistive technology devices, especially when devices are not related directly to the FAPE or are related to medical conditions. Inability to provide or obtain funding for AT devices can be frustrating for school districts, teachers, and families of students with disabilities (Erickson, 1998). Funding remains a primary deterrent to acquisition of assistive technology (Male, 2003). Therefore, it is imperative that all parties involved be aware of the laws and regulations that permit, for example, Medicaid and Medicare funds to be used for AT devices. In addition, educators and related service providers should understand how to obtain funding from sources in their community. Resolving the funding problem requires a creative and innovative collaborative problem-solving approach involving professionals, families, and the community.

MEDICAID   Recipients of Supplemental Security Income (SSI), Aid to Families with Dependent Children (AFDC), and In-Home Supportive Services (IHSS) automatically receive Medicaid. In addition, some students may qualify under one of the federal poverty-level programs (Erickson, 1998).

AT under the Medicaid program is generally classified as medical supplies, durable medical equipment or prosthetic or orthotics equipment and will require prior approval. Each state is allowed to establish a definition for medical necessity, therefore it is important to know how a given state defines the term and to be able to argue that the equipment or services needed come within the definition (U.S. Department of Health and Human Services, n.d.).

In all instances, technology and service must be considered medically necessary. A commonly used definition requires proof that the device is necessary to preserve bodily functions essential to activities of daily living or to prevent significant physical disability. Certainly, educators and families may assert that the FAPE is an activity of daily living for school-age children and youth. By contrast, items promoting comfort or well-being alone are covered only if their primary purpose satisfies the first criterion. The federal courts have determined that the question of medical necessity should be determined by the individual's treating physician, not agency personnel or even Medicaid physician consultants.

Teachers and members of IEP teams can request that families ask their health provider to determine if devices selected at the IEP meeting fall into any of the Medicaid categories of medically necessary AT. Collaboration between schools and healthcare providers can improve the prospects that students receive appropriate AT needed.

MEDICARE Medicare is a federal health insurance program for aged and disabled persons. Entitlement to Medicare services is not based on an individual's financial status (Social Security Administration, 2001). Students may be entitled to benefits under Medicare if they have received 24 months of Social Security Disability Insurance (SSDI) benefits or 24 months of railroad retirement disability benefits (42 U.S.C. §426(b)) (Sheldon & Hart, 2004).

Medicare, just as Medicaid, covers AT devices and services only when necessary and reasonable for the treatment of an illness or injury or to improve the functioning of a malformed body member (see 42 U.S.C. §1395y(a)). Devices may include prosthetic devices, durable medical equipment, crutches or walkers, and wheelchairs, including power chairs, customized chairs, and power-operated vehicles such as tri-wheelers, when considered appropriate, and diagnostic tests (Part B coverage). Medicare does not cover devices that are solely for educational purposes, such as augmentative and assistive communication devices, braillers and Braille texts, and eyeglasses and contacts (U.S. Department of Health and Human Services, 2004). Physicians are responsible for completing and submitting the proper forms to the Social Security office and must establish that the requested equipment (a) is medically necessary, (b) is part of the beneficiary's course of treatment, (c) has a potential functional outcome, and (d) is the least expensive appropriate equipment available. Certainly, educators can support the physician argument that the functional outcome is a free, appropriate education. Teacher support can include observational data and samples of student work completed with and without the device. Thus, if an assistive augmented communication (ACC) device is the only means available for a student to communicate effectively, it may be considered a Medicaid benefit. In fact, every Medicare beneficiary from 1993 to 2001 was successful when appealing the Medicare decision not to fund ACC (Sheldon & Hart, 2004). Persons eligible under Medicare have the right to challenge any decision that they believe to be wrong by requesting an administrative hearing. Each state is required to provide an opportunity for the applicant to explain why he or she disagrees with a denial of requested technology. An unfavorable decision can be appealed to state or federal court.

VOCATIONAL REHABILITATION While Department of Vocational Rehabilitation (VR) services do not cover students until they have graduated from public school, vocational rehabilitation personnel may become involved with students during their transition planning process. At this time, AT should be discussed with the rehabilitation counselor and included in the student's Individualized Written Rehabilitation Plan (IWRP). Once a student has transitioned to the VR Department, AT devices and services related to postsecondary education and employment become the responsibility of that agency (Sheldon & Hager, 1997).

Private Insurance, State Resources, Foundations, and Community Organizations

PRIVATE INSURANCE Families of students who do not qualify for Medicaid or Medicare may be willing to purchase AT with their own funds or apply for funding through their private health insurance companies. Students may come to school with AT purchased by families and ask for permission to use the appliance in general education classrooms or for an accommodation permitting the appliance be written into IEP. Educators should be mindful that while families may agree to purchase AT, they may not be required or coerced to do so (Male, 2003).

STATE RESOURCES Each state and territory in the United States has an Assistive Technology Project Center funded with federal grant money from the Assistive Technology Act. These centers have up-to-date information on AT resources, including funding sources within each state. Some projects list resources available on their Web sites. These projects may also offer lending programs that allow students and teachers to evaluate an AT device before it is purchased. School personnel and persons with disabilities are able to visit their state's project center to learn and gain hands-on experiences with AT. Finally, project center personnel are invaluable resources regarding AT and welcome sharing their knowledge. (You can find your state project's Web site with an online search.)

FOUNDATIONS AND COMMUNITY ORGANIZATIONS Most major corporations and businesses, including banks, retailers, and manufacturers, have foundations that provide scholarships, grants, and awards for philanthropic purposes, including public school programs. You can find information about grants, scholarships, and gifts by visiting the corporate Web site or calling the local branch office.

Community organizations that have philanthropic missions include Shriners, Lions, Moose, and Rotary Clubs. These organizations' members may be able to access funds through their foundations. In addition, many organizations aligned with specific disabilities have foundations that provide or loan funds to purchase AT; some have programs that buy back and sell used equipment. Their Web sites list contact information as well as information about AT services they offer.

Additional sources are vendors and suppliers of AT. A number of these vendors and suppliers are provided in the resource list at the end of this chapter. While they may not supply funding, they often have information about funding sources and may offer support in applying for grants. Finally, social workers, counselors, and AT specialists in school districts may have working relationships with the foundations and organizations within a local community or state for other purposes, so they are often a good place to start when searching for funding.

Whether students qualify for AT from their school district, Medicaid, Medicare, a private organization, or a combination of funds from several sources will depend on the proactive teamwork of all parties involved in the process. To be successful, teams must collaborate on a plan to seek multiple funding sources, research information on how each organization determines funding, and who makes the funding decisions (Male, 2003). Such intensive teamwork makes close collaboration between the family, school, physician(s), funding sources, and suppliers absolutely vital. In conclusion, taking time to complete the steps necessary in forming a team, selecting appropriate AT, and obtaining funding are imperative to providing full access to the standards-based curriculum in classrooms.

AT APPLICATIONS FOR INSTRUCTION

As you learned in the beginning of this chapter, AT is rather broadly defined, making it impossible to provide comprehensive coverage of the full range and depth of the topic in one book chapter. In this section of the chapter, we will discuss the categories of AT that teachers are likely to find or need in school settings to teach content knowledge to students with exceptional needs. Examples of specific hardware and software programs will be given to illustrate what is available. Based on the mandate for teachers and students to meet state and national standards, the emphasis will be on providing AT applications that will allow students with exceptional needs full access to the curriculum and the materials used to teach that curriculum. The ultimate goal of using AT in the classroom is to support students so that they can become increasingly independent, empowered learners. Some examples of technology that are remedial and tutorial in nature may be offered if these also support content learning, but that is not the main focus. The discussion will begin with ensuring barrier-free access to computers and then move to specific AT applications for specific instructional tasks.

Barrier-Free Access to Assistive Technology

Computer access can mean the difference between success and failure in academic classes for many students with disabilities. As noted in the chapter on UDL, the first step in planning instruction should be to assess the barriers to learning found in the learning environment. In keeping with that philosophy, AT provides opportunities to remove a variety of barriers to learning, and the first barrier that should be removed to create a UDL learning environment is any barrier presented by computer hardware. Students who may encounter barriers to computer use are described below (Center on Disabilities, 2002).

- *Students with physical limitations* may not have the quality of movement in their limbs or trunks of their bodies necessary to use a standard keyboard and mouse. Some students may need a pointing device or an alternative keyboard, such as a one-handed or on-screen keyboard.
- *Students with limited cognitive abilities* may not be able to use standard computer equipment. For example, the standard keyboard has many keys that may confuse, overwhelm, or confound the student. Providing keyboards with less crowded configurations, different arrangement of the keys, keys for specific actions, or keys with simple switches may be best for some students.
- *Students with visual impairments* may not have sufficient vision to read a standard keyboard or monitor screen. Some students may need screen magnifiers, screen readers, Braille translators, and Braille printers.
- *Students with hearing impairments* may not have sufficient hearing to view Web sites with spoken language, such as videos. In fact, if they are young American

Sign Language (ASL) users, they may not have sufficient Standard English reading skills for some Web sites. In addition, some students may need on-screen captions or headphones to remove background noise.

- *Students who experience problems with receptive or expressive language processing or production (e.g., MR or LD) or who are not proficient Standard English users* will have difficulty reading or processing what they read. Some students may need voice activated-software, screen readers, or digital language translators.

What Are the Barriers to Computer Use?

As you learned in the previous chapter, access to information and learning materials is a primary goal of the UDL. Using a similar philosophy, we think of AT as an accessibility tool that provides students with exceptional learning needs access to the world of information and school curriculum and permits them to demonstrate learning and engage, interact, and communicate with others. However, although using technology while teaching can provide a richer experience, certain barriers may limit or prevent the use of computers for some students. Certain applications facilitate computer access through interface or input, output, and processing tools (see Table 8.4 for examples of these interface devices). The Center on Disabilities defines these devices as enhancements and alternatives to keyboards, mouse, monitor, or printer. Enhancing, altering, or bypassing is accomplished by hardware, software, system tools, or a combination of the three (Center on Disabilities, 2002). Information about specific applications for interface, input, and output is available from assistive technology specialists, occupational and physical therapists, vocational rehabilitation counselors, and the Internet. See Figure 8.5 for directions to find alternative input and processing that is standard on all computers.

ASSISTIVE TECHNOLOGY FOR SPOKEN COMMUNICATION

Think back over the last 24 hours and make a list of all the times and ways that you communicated with another person (or a surrogate, such as a phone answering machine). Who did you communicate with? What was the purpose of the communication? If it was formal communication, what skills did you use? If it was informal, what skills did you use? Do those skills overlap? Now consider how you might communicate if you could not use speech. Communicating is so much a part of our day that we do not even notice when we are communicating, but what about persons who do not have the physical capacity to speak, and those who cannot hear the voices of others? In this section we will discuss how AT can facilitate communication for persons with speech and hearing impairments.

What Is Communication?

This section briefly reviews information about communication that you may have learned in other courses and suggests ways to apply this knowledge when selecting appropriate AT for students.

We generally communicate in a variety of ways each day; for example, we use *expressive language* in the forms of spoken and written language, as well as gestures and facial expressions (body language). We communicate using *receptive language* when we read, listen, or interpret the body language of others.

TABLE 8.4 How Do We Interface (Input/Output) with a Computer?

Input		
Device	**Types**	**Possible Features**
Keyboards	• On-screen cursor control/pointer systems • Alternative keyboards • Voice recognition software • Eye gaze • Mind control • Switches	<u>Physical Adjustments</u> • Slant board • Key guards • Pads and supports • Keyless <u>Electronic Adjustments</u> • Sticky keys • Slow keys • Rearrange keys • Mouse keys <u>Layouts</u> • QWERTY • ABC • AEIOU • Frequency • Number • Custom • Right hand/left hand • Software specific • Person specific

Cursor controls and pointing systems	• Mouse
	• Trackball
	• Joystick
	• Paddles
	• Head mice
	• Touchscreen/window
	• Touchpad/glide pad
		Can
		• Control mouse speed
		• Be shaped to fit hand
		• Have more than one button
		• Be programmed with scripts and macros
		• Controlled by
		  ○ head movements
		  ○ touching monitor
		  ○ using windows

Output		
Device	**Types**	**Possible Adjustments**
Visual	Displays	• Font type • Contrast • Size
	Indicators	• Button tags • Label cues
	Hard copy	• Print formats/methods • Printers

TABLE 8.4 *(Continued)*

Input		
Device	**Types**	**Possible Features**
Auditory	Software enhancement	• Text enlargement
		• Screen enlargement
	Feedback	• Key beep
		• Character echo
	Speech	• Synthesized speech
		• Digitized speech and sound
	Sound system	• Headphones
		• Hearing devices
Tactual	Braille text	• Optical to tactile
	Software enhancement	• Text to Braille
		• Braille-to-text-conversion

Processing		
Device	**Types**	**Methods**
Rate enhancement (increase productivity rate)	Word prediction	Use software such as Co:Writer by Don Johnston.
	Abbreviation expansion	Create macros in computer software to type a word or phrase based on abbreviation typed by user.
	Word/phrase supplements	Use overlays that include words or phrase that type when one overlay key is hit.
	Macros	Use software built-in macro feature (see Tools in Word and use Help to teach you how) OR use built-in keyboard strokes to complete tasks in document.
Layout	Keyboard	Select a keyboard that is most suited to user's age, ability, and task to be completed.

The components or skills of language necessary for effective communication include the following:

- *Listening* involves obtaining meaning from what we hear. In fact, the act of listening is our ability to gain meaning from the spoken word. In other words, how many words, types of words, and types of syntactic structures can we understand?
- *Speaking* is the production of meaningful sounds such as words, including the number and types of words produced as well as the types of sentence structures used.
- *Semantics* refers to the content of language, which is the meaning and precision of the words we use. Speakers who use good semantics have a rich, deep vocabulary and are able to use complex sentence structures.

Computers that use the Microsoft operating systems have built-in accessibility tools that can be helpful to users with disabilities. These are free and can be used easily by most students who are able computer users.

To find these items:

1. Go to Start
2. Once you have opened the new window, click on All Programs (or whatever will take you to your programs).
3. Find and click on Accessories.
4. Find and click on Accessibility. At this point you should see a list of items to use.
5. Find and click the on-screen keyboard. You can use the keyboard if you open a word-processing program.
6. Open the Magnifier so that you can use it to read what you wrote.
7. Open the Narrator so that you can read what you wrote.

FIGURE 8.5 What Is on Your Computer?

- *Syntax* is refers to using the rules of a language; for example, knowing where to place adjectives and adverbs, proper use of nouns and pronouns, and so on.
- *Morphemes* are the smallest bit of language that can stand alone with their own meaning. They must be used properly to achieve semantic proficiency.
- *Phonology* is the ability to hear the sounds used in a language and to use them correctly in words. (*Phonological awareness* is the ability to identify those sounds and to manipulate them.)
- *Pragmatics* is the use of language with purpose or to achieve a purpose. We speak to request, inform, assist, greet, comfort, and a variety of other reasons.

Persons with communication disorders are not proficient enough in one or more of the above skills to communicate their needs or wishes. If the first six skills are not developed appropriately, students will not be able to accomplish the last—which is purposeful speech. Students who may encounter barriers when communicating are described below (Hallahan & Kauffman, 2003).

- *Students with limited physical or cognitive abilities* may have a communication disorder as the primary disability or secondary disability; for example, impaired speech may be a side effect of cerebral palsy, stroke, or traumatic brain injury. Other students may have communication difficulties related to autism and severe expressive language disorders.
- *Students with hearing impairments, including deaf/blind,* may not have enough hearing to understand spoken language. Further, students who have experienced hearing loss since birth may not have sufficiently clear spoken language to communicate with others. During the training and acquisition of spoken language, AT can support communication and social interactions with others.

Communication devices were among the first AT devices used in public schools and were used before regulations required AT in classrooms. The speech-language therapist and the audiologist will most likely take leading roles in assessing, selecting, and training steps in the team decision-making process. The next sections provide information about the major categories of AT available for persons with speech, language, and hearing impairments.

Augmented and Alternative Communication (ACC) Systems

While many people view speech as the only form of communication, as noted above, there are other modes of communication, including facial expressions, gestures, body language, and eye gaze. Each of us communicates our thoughts and moods via these modes as do persons who are not verbal. Educators need to observe, accept, and enhance the communication methods preferred by their students. Further, an ACC system will only be one part of an individual's communication system, and the other areas cannot be ignored (see section on unaided communication below).

The three primary functions of ACC systems are to (1) serve as a substitute for the vocal mode of communication, (2) supplement vocal communication for the person who has difficulty with formulation or intelligibility, and (c) facilitate communication with emphasis on intelligibility, output and organization, and general skills (Bryant & Bryant, 2003). We typically divide communication devices into two categories: aided and unaided. We will begin with the unaided, but the discussion of this topic will be very brief as the focus of this chapter is AT.

Unaided Communication

As you might think, *unaided communication* refers to methods that do not use external equipment or devices but use body parts, usually arms and hands. Print communication can be used with students who have learned to read and write enough language to express their needs and preferences. However, this is time-consuming and cumbersome, since this method requires paper, pencil, and a writing surface. Three common forms of unaided communication include sign language, education sign systems, and gestural language codes.

- *Sign language* is a primary communication system for persons who have hearing impairments. Recently teachers have found American Sign Language (ASL) to be useful in communicating with persons who have severe communication problems that have nothing to do with deafness, such as autism.
- *Education sign systems* were developed to improve movement from using sign language to reading Standard Written English grammar. One example of an educational sign system is Signing Exact English, which is composed of about 4,000 signs and includes common prefixes, suffixes, and inflectional endings.
- *Gestural language code* is a third form of sign language and uses finger spelling to communicate. American Manual Alphabet is the most commonly used finger-spelling system and is one of the forms of communication used by persons who are deaf and blind (e.g., Annie Sullivan taught this to Helen Keller).

Learning and teaching one of these unaided communication methods to students who use AT communication devices would serve as a backup system should the device need to be repaired or replaced.

Aided Communication

Aided communication can take one of two forms, either non-electronic or electronic. We will discuss the non-electronic briefly, again because the emphasis of this chapter is on technology.

NON-ELECTRONIC COMMUNICATION   Aids include language boards, communication books, and alphabet boards, to name a few. Often these devices are made by teachers and/or family members on a printer using communication board software or by drawing freehand symbols. Communication boards (e.g., Mayer-Johnson in the resource list in the Appendix) are designed to best meet the specific needs of the person and their modes of communication. If the person is able to spell, for example, the board may consist of the alphabet and some phrases to speed up communication. Such phrases could include "May I have a drink of water?" or "My name is Becky." Others who do not spell well may need symbols to represent ideas they are trying to communicate. These could be symbols of family members, comments, questions, wants and needs, and so on.

For individuals who need more communication messages than a single communication board will hold, another option is a communication book (e.g., see Mayer-Johnson in the resource list in the Appendix). Communication books may be constructed in a notebook with multiple pages for each communication set. For example, there might be a page each for school, home, recreation, restaurants, and other settings frequented by the user. Some books are organized by categories of speech. For example, there would be a page for people, verbs, places, and greetings. These types of communication systems require more cognitive and physical skill than a single language board.

Non-electronic communication devices should not be looked at just as a backup to an electronic system. For many, a non-electronic device is sufficient and there is no need to pursue a more expensive electronic device.

ELECTRONIC ACC SYSTEMS   Electronic communication devices range from something as simple as a two-location device that provides yes and no buttons to a device that is a fully functional laptop computer. As with all areas of AT, it is important to match the needs of the consumer to the features of the device. Providing a $7,000 multifunctional AAC device to a child who is only developmentally ready to say her name and answer yes or no questions would seem pointless. This is exactly the type of situation that can lead to abandonment, as mentioned earlier.

Any computer can serve as an augmentative communication device by installing communication software, but this type of system is not for everyone. While a laptop will enable the user to use software (such as word processing in addition to a variety of communication software), using computers in this manner can cause problems. For example, laptop computers lack the durability of most dedicated communication systems and therefore are not suitable for young children or persons whose disability may cause them to drop things. Also, computers do not respond well to spills or drool. Many AAC manufacturers test their equipment for durability and seal surfaces so that spills or drool will not affect operation.

A number of small commercially available communication devices are suitable for student use in the classroom. These devices can record words, phrases, music, different languages, and just about anything else a student might want to use. They can be simple, with one stored word or phrase, or complex, with hundreds of prerecorded words, phrases, and sentences.

The Say-It! SAM Communicator (Words+) is an example of electronic devices that use digitized speech systems. Devices using digitized speech work like tape recorders: Teachers or friends can record words, phrases, music, sound effects, and whatever else the user might want. There is little room for spontaneous communication when using these devices because all speech is prerecorded, but one advantage to these programmable devices is that they allow speech input in languages other than English.

Synthesized speech (or text-to-speech), on the other hand, allows the user to communicate spontaneously, as well as speak stored words or phrases. Although still awkward sounding in many cases, the quality of synthetic voices has improved as has the selection of voice types. Examples of voice output communication aids are the DynaVox (Sunrise Medical) and IntelliTalk 3 (IntelliTools).

Communication Devices Used by Persons Who Are Deaf

One final consideration in the discussion of communication is the ability to hear others speak. Persons with hearing impairments experience differing levels of hearing capabilities from no hearing, garbled hearing, to loss of hearing in certain tonal ranges (Friend, 2005).

Assistive listening systems (ALS) are frequently used in public schools to amplify the teacher's voice for students who are hard of hearing. You may have seen persons using these devices at theaters and during religious services or other public events. Essentially, ALS are amplifiers that bring sound directly into the ear. The speaker wears a microphone, and the listener wears headphones. Sound is transmitted wirelessly throughout the room from an antenna to the headphones. The headphones separate the sounds, particularly speech, from background noise.

Traditional hearing aids are electronic, battery-operated devices that amplify and change sound to allow for improved communication. Hearing aids receive sound through a microphone, which then converts the sound waves to electrical signals. The amplifier increases the loudness of the signals and then sends the sound to the ear through a speaker. Below we will briefly look at the most common hearing aids as well as the pros and cons for children.

- In-the-ear (ITE) hearing aids fit completely in the outer ear and are used for mild to severe hearing loss. The case, which holds the components, is made of hard plastic. ITE aids can accommodate added technical mechanisms such as a telecoil, a small magnetic coil contained in the hearing aid that improves sound transmission during telephone calls. ITE aids can be damaged by earwax and ear drainage, and their small size can cause adjustment problems and feedback. They are not usually worn by children because the casings need to be replaced as the ear grows.
- Behind-the-ear (BTE) hearing aids are worn behind the ear and are connected to a plastic ear mold that fits inside the outer ear. Sound travels through the earmold into the ear. BTE aids are used by people of all ages for mild to profound hearing loss. Poorly fitting BTE ear molds may cause feedback, a whistle sound caused by the fit of the hearing aid or by buildup of earwax or fluid. Children typically use BTE aids because the ear molds can be adjusted easily as the child grows.

- Canal aids fit into the ear canal and are available in two sizes. The in-the-canal (ITC) hearing aid is customized to fit the size and shape of the ear canal and is used for mild or moderately severe hearing loss. A completely-in-canal (CIC) hearing aid is largely concealed in the ear canal and is used for mild to moderately severe hearing loss. Because of their small size, canal aids may be difficult for the user to adjust and remove and may not be able to hold additional devices, such as a telecoil. Canal aids can also be damaged by earwax and ear drainage. These are not typically recommended for children.
- Body aids are used by people with profound hearing loss. The aid is attached to a belt or a pocket and connected to the ear by a wire. Because of its large size, it is able to incorporate many signal processing options, but it is usually used only when other types of aids cannot be used.
- Cochlear implants are electronic devices designed for persons who have severe to profound losses of hearing. The implant bypasses the outer and middle ear by sending auditory signals directly to the inner ear, where useful information is sorted from random sounds and sent to the auditory nerve. (At present, cochlear implants are a source of controversy in the deaf community and may not be an acceptable AT device for all students who are deaf.) In the earlier section, we noted that a student's cultural beliefs may affect how he or she views or accepts AT, and this appears to be true of using cochlear implants. Some members of the deaf community are opposed to implants because they see the implants as an attempt to eradicate deafness and therefore the deaf community, but the implant providers and many parents of children who are deaf consider implants as an opportunity for their children to participate in mainstream society (National Association of the Deaf, n.d.). As a final note, this is one of the AT exceptions noted in IDEA-2004, because school districts may not be required to fund cochlear implants.

Spoken communication can be augmented and supported with a variety of AT, from an easy-to-construct and inexpensive set of pictures on a communication board to complex electronic voice output communication aids and hearing aids.

ASSISTIVE TECHNOLOGY FOR WRITTEN COMMUNICATION

Results of research on effects of word processing on the quality and quantity of P–12 student writing are mixed (Roblyer, 2003). Most differences were attributed to the researcher's choice of software, students' prior experience and writing abilities, and types of writing instruction. Use of a word-processing system appeared to have positive effects on student writing when used in the context of good writing instruction and when students were given opportunities to learn word-processing procedures prior to the research study. Therefore, understanding the writing process and providing guidance to students who experience difficulty in producing age-appropriate written products is just as important as providing the AT for the physical production of writing work.

The Writing Process

Written communication is a complex task that involves both process and mechanics. Process consists of organizing ideas gathered from research or personal knowledge (imagination for creative writing) into a coherent product. Mechanics include spelling, handwriting, punctuation, and capitalization as well as an understanding the complexities of syntax and semantics.

Many students with disabilities have a lower level of age-appropriate spelling, capitalization, and punctuation skills than their peers. Problems with basic writing skills require these students to spend a majority of their writing time on mechanics rather than acquiring the skills needed for high-level writing processes. For example, students who are not good spellers use only words that they can spell, which can lead to short sentences void of descriptive words. The same is true for sentence structures; if a student is unsure about punctuation or complex grammar constructs, she will produce short, choppy sentences. Naturally, when students expend all of their energy on the mechanics of writing, they are less likely to produce written products that demonstrate higher-level thinking about a topic or concept. Finally, students who experience difficulties with handwriting skills due to psychomotor deficits or a physical disability expend all their energies on the visual aspects of the written product, which can be physically as well as mentally exhausting.

Other students with disabilities may experience problems with planning, acquiring information, and organizing their thoughts. These are skills needed for writing the creative stories often required in elementary school or completing research papers and projects at the middle and high school levels in most content areas. Often these students are unable even to begin a project because the task seems so overwhelming to them.

There are assistive technologies available that can take away these concerns for mechanics, handwriting, and organizing skills. With appropriate AT, the product becomes the focus of the student's efforts, not the process.

Students who may encounter barriers during the writing process are described below (Hallahan & Kauffman, 2003). To construct effective writing instruction and independent practice that allows students to learn and demonstrate their knowledge, teachers should recognize barriers and plan instructional activities in which barriers are removed.

- *Students with specific writing disorders* may be referred to as having a written expression language deficit. Because writing involves several brain areas and functions, the brain networks for vocabulary, grammar, hand movement, and memory must all be in good working order. Thus, a writing disorder may result from problems in any of these areas.
- *Students with hearing impairments* may have written expression difficulties. Students who learn ASL at an early age often experience many of the same language acquisition and usage problems with Standard English as do students who are not native speakers of English (consider that ASL is their first language and Standard English is their second language).
- *Students with visual impairments* experience access problems when producing written products and usually have difficulty acquiring useful handwriting skills. They may be able to write by hand, but their ability to produce large quantities of written work may be limited. In addition, Braille users, like ASL users, may have acquisition and usage problems similar to students who are English language learners. Braille uses a series of contractions that stand for common letter combinations; this can be confusing during elementary years when students are learning both Braille contractions and the spelling of Standard English words.

- *Students with ADHD* may experience difficulties with the attention and organizational processes required to write effectively. Whether they have inattentive or hyperactivity type of ADHD, students will have difficulty maintaining attention required for planning, researching, and writing.
- *Students with physical disabilities* that limit use of their fingers, hands, and arms will experience difficulty with the physical requirements for handwriting. For example, students may have problems that limit their ability to hold conventional writing instruments, produce readable handwriting, or use handwriting for extended periods of writing required for essay questions on exams or in-class writing.

In this section we will discuss a variety of AT devices, including hardware and software, that will support learning and production of written products. Generally, these AT applications work for most of the students described above. For example, you will learn about speech recognition software that may be appropriate for students with LD, visual impairments, and physical disabilities.

One of your tasks as a member of the IEP team will be to decide which AT application would be most useful for an individual user. The IEP team should decide which specific AT application is most useful for an individual student. However, cost and availability are considerations, and several AT applications will be helpful additions to purchase AT and can support the learning of all students in your classroom. Computers and software applications have become commonplace additions in many classrooms and can remove barriers to learning for a very wide variety of students with and without disabilities.

Digital graphic organizers can help students organize their ideas or research information into a written product. Inspiration (see Inspiration in the resources section of the Appendix) is a software program that allows users to construct graphic organizers to complete a variety of tasks, and organizing a writing project is one of those tasks. Kidspiration is an option for younger users.

Word processors with auditory feedback combine a word-processor software package with a software package that reads information on the computer screen, giving users a way to independently edit and correct their work. There are several word-processing applications on the market with integrated text-to-speak capability. For example, Write OutLoud (see Don Johnston Company in the resources section of the Appendix) software reads what the user is writing as he writes, so that he may correct errors immediately. Write OutLoud To-Go is a version that is packaged with the AlphaSmart 3000 (more information is provided later in the Appendix), so students can use the computer version in the general education class or computer lab and then take the AlphaSmart version to continue the work in the resource room or at home.

Word prediction software works within any word-processing program to allow students to select the correctly spelled word. One example of this type of software is Co-Writer Solo Edition (see Don Johnston Company in the Appendix) with FlexSpell, which allows for phonetic spelling and topical dictionaries that include words from across the curriculum. Thus, it provides students with the supports they need to write what they know and what they're learning. Co-Writer can also be packaged with the AlphaSmart 3000.

Symbol-supported writing programs allow students to write stories and communicate with pictures. Writing with Symbols 2000 (see Mayer-Johnson in the Appendix) is an example of this software, which contains over 8,000 pictures to support student writing.

Speech recognition systems, also known as voice-activated software, allow students to use any word-processing or spreadsheet program to dictate information, which is then automatically converted to text. This can be an extremely useful tool for individuals who have writing difficulty, regardless of the reason. One stand-alone speech recognition application is Dragon Naturally Speaking (see ScanSoft in the Appendix). Naturally Speaking performs computer functions as well, such as opening and closing software programs, opening and saving documents, and making corrections within documents.

AlphaSmart products include the AlphaSmart 3000, Neo, and Dana. These devices are similar to laptop computers but are considerably less expensive. Each device differs in features, but all include a word processor, calculator, and spell- and grammar-check capabilities. Each allows for eight separate files to be password protected, permitting multiple users on each device. The Dana also offers wireless Internet connectivity. The Neo AlphaSmarts have an almost limitless list of uses in the classroom and for homework.

Handheld computers are portable, small enough to be held in the hand. The most popular handheld computers are those that are specifically designed to provide personal information management functions for to-do lists and to keep a calendar and address book. The Notes function of these devices can be used to take notes in class or during reading assignments.

Some students with limited hand use or eye–hand coordination problems may find the small keypad and stylus difficult to use. Add-ons such as Thumbpads and larger keyboards may be purchased to help students with word processing. Seiko has offered a solution to the small keyboard problem by replacing the keyboard with an electronic pen (see SmartPad in the resources section). The SmartPad allows handwritten notes to be uploaded into the handheld computer. Then the notes are moved to a computer for permanent storage. Software is also available that allows the notes to be edited and saved. This hardware and software offers an alternative to handwritten notes in science and mathematics classes, where drawing and labeling are frequent tasks.

Digital spellers and thesauruses can be software or stand-alone devices that allow the user to look up a word or meaning with or without speech feedback. The only prerequisite is that the user must be able to type in the word. Spellers and thesauruses are available from Franklin Electronic Publishers (for more information, see the resources section). In addition to the stand-alone spellers, most word processors have a spell- and grammar-checking function. Teaching students to use the spell checker, rather than having it turned on, helps them learn to be self-sufficient and take ownership for checking their work. Finally, Merriam-Webster offers a free online dictionary and thesaurus (http://m-w.com/). Students can look up a word and by clicking on an icon can also hear the word. However, if the word is misspelled the dictionary will provide a list of possible correct words for the student. While learning content and completing assignments, students can be working on spelling skills with one of the following programs.

- Simon S.I.O. (Don Johnston) is a spelling program that helps students sound and find out the word they want to spell.
- Show Me Spelling (Attainment Company, Inc.) teaches functional spelling of up to 500 words.

Note taking is another area of difficulty for students with attention, writing, and spelling problems. For some the processes required to attend to the teacher's words interfere with their ability to complete the task of note taking, or they become so stressed by trying to spell correctly that they miss the next thing the teacher says; or they simply can't tell what is important and should be written in the notes. One frequently use accommodation is to tape the lecture using the devices described below.

Analog/digital recorders are useful for a variety of tasks that students with exceptional needs have to complete, recording reminders or notes, recording lectures, and capturing spoken information before actually trying to write it. Full-size tape recorders have the advantage of being inexpensive, but they have the disadvantage of being bigger and bulkier to handle. Microcassette recorders are much more compact and still allow about the same amount of record time as the larger format, but this format does have disadvantages, such as difficulty finding specific points on a taped lecture and that saving recorded tapes requires storage space. Finally, tapes are easy to misplace or break.

A digital recorder uses an integrated circuit to record and hold sound. This allows for random access to the stored information as opposed to sequential access on tape-based systems we have used in the past. Digital systems enable the user to access stored information much easier and faster because recordings can be uploaded to any computer as a voice file and accessed for years to come. This also means that the student no longer needs the recorder to access the information.

Additionally, manufacturers supply software that allows the voice file to be uploaded, saved, and listened to later. This means the file can be saved to a disk or burned to a CD so the student or a transcriber can easily transport the file to any computer. Most MP3 players, iPods, PDAs, and newer cell phones also record voice files. And best of all, you can download voice files to those personal devices. No one will know if the student is listening to a lecture or music, which eliminates some of the stigma felt by students with disabilities and AT use that makes them stand out in the classroom.

ASSISTIVE TECHNOLOGY FOR READING

Reading difficulties are associated with the tasks of reading individual words, sentences, and/or paragraphs and with comprehension of what was read. Causal factors may include the inability to comprehend and organize information presented in print format, decode words, track lines on the printed page, or integrate new knowledge with previously learned knowledge.

Students who may encounter barriers when reading (Hallahan & Kauffman, 2003) are described below. Print materials are a primary source for providing information in classrooms via books, teacher-made materials, Web sites, and so on. Inability to read these materials constitutes a substantial barrier for students who have reading difficulties. Teachers should recognize the barriers presented below so that they can provide alternative ways for students to access print materials.

- *Students with specific reading disorders* may be referred to as having a visual receptive language disorder. Just as with writing, reading involves several brain areas and functions, and the brain networks for vocabulary, comprehension, organization, and memory must all be in good working order. In addition, students with auditory processing disorders may not develop the phonic awareness needed to decode unfamiliar words. A reading disorder may result from problems in any of these areas.

- *Students with hearing impairments* also may have reading difficulties. Students who learn ASL at an early age often experience many of the same vocabulary and reading comprehension problems with Standard English as do students who are English language learners (consider that ASL is their first language and Standard English is their second language).
- *Students with visual impairments* experience barriers to reading print materials. These students may need large print, Braille, or auditory sources to replace print texts and to read their computer screen and Internet materials. In addition, Braille users, like ASL users, may have some acquisition and usage problems similar to students who are ESOL. Braille uses a series of contractions that stand for common letter combinations; this can be confusing during elementary years when students are learning both Braille contractions and the spelling of Standard English words.
- *Students with ADHD* may experience difficulties with the attention and organizational processes required during the reading process. Whether they have inattentive type or hyperactivity type of ADHD, students will have difficulty maintaining attention required for decoding and comprehension, and recall tasks may be difficult. These students need help to learn methods for blocking distractions and organizing information for comprehension and recall tasks.
- *Students with physical disabilities* that limit use of their fingers, hands, and arms will experience difficulty with the physical requirements for reading, such as turning pages and taking notes. Physical limitations may impede their ability to hold conventional print materials.

We will now discuss a variety of AT devices, including hardware and software, that can remove barriers in the reading process experienced by the students described above. For example, you will learn about recorded books, electronic textbooks, text-to-speech software, and Internet resources that may be appropriate for a majority of the students noted above. The IEP team should decide which specific AT application is most useful for an individual student, but cost and availability are considerations, and several AT applications will be helpful additions to purchased AT and can support the learning of all students in your classroom.

SPELLERS, DICTIONARIES, AND THESAURUS   In the section on writing, we discussed these AT devices. These learning supports are useful for reading tasks as well because they allow students to look up words they do not know or cannot pronounce independently.

Quicktionary Pens (Reading Pens) scan a single word or a complete line of text and recognize printed fonts (6–22 point), even if the text is bold, italic, underlined, or inverted. The pen speaks and spells words and lines of text and can provide definitions. Finally, words are highlighted on a small screen as they are spoken so that the student can follow along.

Stand-alone text readers such as the Kurzweil 3000 (Kurzweil Educational Systems, Inc.) and WYNN3 (Freedom Scientific) are software programs that read whatever is presented on the screen. These packages include optical character recognition (OCR), the ability to scan printed pages and convert them into electronic text. Speech synthesis enables the scanned text to be read aloud in a variety of voices and at variable speeds. Both programs can read documents saved in word-processing programs or as PDFs and

Web pages from the Internet. They offer features that allow users to highlight text and create outlines from the highlighted text. Both contain an extensive dictionary, thesaurus, and spelling/grammar check. Each also has capabilities for electronic test taking. That is, teachers can enter digital copies of tests so that student can take multiple choice and fill-in-the-blank or answer essay questions. These are very powerful programs that promote independence and support learning for students with exceptional needs. The primary disadvantage to these programs is the cost, but once loaded on a computer multiple users can take advantage of their features.

Accessing the Internet with screen readers can be easy and free. The Technology Act requires that government agencies and federally funded companies and projects must be accessible. Several software developers who are dedicated to open-source information and Web accessibility for all readers have developed safe software for free downloads. This software (Code-it and Browse Aloud) allows users to read Web sites that have been made accessible. At this time, not all Web sites can be read in this manner, but more are being added. In addition to reading Web pages, Browse Aloud developers have created a software program that reads PDFs. (PDF Aloud: This software provides an alternative to expensive stand-alone screen readers, but it is less powerful and accurate than Kurzweil and WYNN3. For download information, see AT resources in the Appendix.)

Audio books or CDs are common AT applications for students who cannot use print materials. Audio books are available for fiction, nonfiction, and educational textbooks. Generally, the special education department in a school is responsible for ordering textbooks for students who are included in general education classes, but this can be a time-consuming process, so collaboration between teachers is essential here. There are a number of sources for audio books, and understanding the process is important for all teachers.

The Library of Congress maintains a free audio library for persons with visual and physical impairments as well as persons with a reading disability. Commercially published fiction and nonfiction books may be obtained from the Library of Congress by completing an application that requires a physician to certify the disability. Once the application is approved, books can be ordered at the user's local public library. Books are delivered and returned free of charge to the user. Students with disabilities in public schools are eligible for this free library service, but book availability is subject to the same issues as any library book. This means that novels and other books required for classroom assignments should be ordered well ahead of the need.

Educational textbooks must be acquired from other sources, as the Library of Congress does not carry textbooks. Recording for the Blind & Dyslexic, a supplier of such educational materials, had 98,000 titles in literature, history, math, and science from kindergarten through postgraduate and professional levels. If a required book is not in stock, they will record any text not in their inventory.

A special CD player is available that allows students to search textbooks and mark their place in the book. These features are especially valuable for students who are reading more than one book during the school day, but the CD player adds an additional cost to the purchase. There is a one-time application fee and a yearly membership fee for this service. For contact information and other recorded book sources, see AT resources in the Appendix.

PUBLISHER'S EDITIONS OF ELECTRONIC TEXTBOOKS Many publishers of educational textbooks are now providing electronic editions of their print books. These are available free to any student in any school, so long as the school district has purchased the textbook for use. Some textbooks list the Web site in their text with directions for accessing the electronic version. Otherwise, teachers can contact the school principal or district purchasing agent for more information. These textbooks come with special features that include hyperlinks to word definitions (many with speech), detailed descriptions of important persons or characters, online activities and critical-thinking questions, and other supports for readers. Some even include audio and Spanish language versions. Electronic textbooks provide support and enrichment for students with exceptional needs, including readers who are English language learners and/or gifted.

Many books that are no longer under copyright restrictions are available online electronically through various Internet databases (see Reference Desk and University of Virginia Library in the resources section of the Appendix). These books may be accessed and used freely by the general public. Most can be uploaded to a computer, saved in any word-processing program or as PDFs, and read with screen readers.

Additional electronic books may be found at Web sites dedicated to a specific author, such as Jane Austen or Herman Melville (see AT resources for information to access the above databases and author Web sites). Author Web sites often provide in-depth information about the author and their books. While some electronic books available online are bare-bones text copies of books, others offer hyperlinks to character sketches, graphic organizers of plots and subplots, maps, and photos. These hyperlinked texts give students support for learning and understanding complex plot lines, character motivation, and historical perspectives needed to fully enjoy and learn from literature.

ASSISTIVE TECHNOLOGY FOR MATHEMATICS

Students who may encounter barriers to learning and performing mathematical tasks include students with learning, cognitive, sensory, and physical disabilities—in other words, students with almost any disability may experience difficulty in mathematics classes. Mathematics requires the ability to read, comprehend the meaning of, and write numbers and symbols. Students who encounter difficulties with reading and writing may, although not in every case, have difficulties reading and comprehending word problems and complex formulas in mathematics. And since math symbols express numerical language concepts, language skills are very important to math achievement. Therefore, students who are not fluent Standard English users (such as students who are visually or hearing impaired and English language learners) may experience barriers to learning and using mathematics. Students with visual perception disorders may experience difficulties detecting the differences in shapes and forms, which would affect their ability to complete advanced math curriculum such as geometry. Students may have fine and gross motor skills that present handwriting and organizational difficulties in producing mathematical work on paper. Finally, students who experience many years of school failure may engage in behaviors associated with learned helplessness and math phobias, such as avoidance or disruptions.

Teacher attitude and seeming reluctance to allow AT in mathematics classes may have a negative impact on student's achievement in this content area. For example, Edyburn (2003) noted the reluctance of teachers to allow students with exceptional needs to use calculators for mathematics calculations. Teachers who are wary of using calculators reason that such aids undermine acquisition of the discipline required for learning basic facts, operations, and algorithms (Edyburn, 2003). Two additional reasons for disallowing calculator use are the general ban on these devices in mandated standardized assessments and the bias that only work that the student can do without assistance is acceptable (Edyburn, 2003). Until we are able to change the ban on and negative perception of calculator use for students with exceptional needs, AT in this curriculum area is likely to be underused.

Calculators of all types are the primary AT support recommended for use in mathematics classes. In addition to discussing a variety of calculators, we will share several additional ways to support student work in mathematics.

Text readers and word processors may be applied to work in the math class as they are in reading and writing. For example, if the student is using an audio source to read textbooks, she could continue to use the audio source for reading the math textbook (e.g., audio books or CDs; electronic text with a screen reader). If the student is using a word processor to complete written work, that software may be transferred to working in the math class. For example, the student whose hard-to-read or illegible handwriting hinders reading his answers might keyboard answers to problems or dictate problems and answers using speech-to-text software.

Calculators come in various forms. Handheld calculators are the most common currently available tools for supporting student work in mathematics. Many of the handheld calculators have a speech feature that vocalizes both input and output through speech synthesis. Others have special features that enable the user to select options to speak and simultaneously display numbers, functions, entire equations, and results. Calculators can include a wide variety of special keyboard and screen features, including big number buttons and large keypads or display screens that are suitable for young children and individuals with visual impairments and physical disabilities requiring the use of pointers.

A variety of calculators are available on the Internet and free to users. One example is the Web site Martindale's Calculators On-line Center, where over 20,000 calculators are available. Students in high school and college-level mathematics courses would find these particularly useful because the site has calculators for advanced mathematical functions, such as those found in advance math classes like calculus. Access to calculators is very relatively easy and inexpensive. Most office and computer stores as well as many Internet sites offer calculators for sale. In addition, on-screen calculators are routinely installed on computers, PDAs, and cell phones.

Summary

In this chapter we focused on AT that permits access to the curriculum taught in most classrooms. After defining AT, we discussed the SETT method for assessing students' skills and needs and the steps to be taken to select appropriate AT. We provided information about the school's responsibility to provide AT and also discussed how to obtain funding from third parties. Finally, we discussed a variety of specific AT applications for communication, writing, reading, and math that IEP teams should consider for diverse students with exceptional needs.

References

Alliance for Technology Access. (1996). *Computer resources for people with disabilities: A guide to exploring today's assistive technology*. Alameda, CA: Harper House.

Ashton, P. (2000). Assistive technology. *Journal of Special Education Technology, 15*(1), 57–58.

Behrmann, M. M. (1994). Assistive technology for students with mild disabilities: Details ways that assistive technology can be used in the classroom for students with mild disabilities. *Intervention in School and Clinic, 30*(2), 70–83.

Beigel, A. R. (2000). Assistive technology assessment: More than the device. *Intervention in School and Clinic, 35*(4), 237–243.

Blackhurst, A. E., & Edyburn, D. L. (2000). A brief history of special education technology. *Special Education Technology Practice, 2*(1), 21–35.

Bowe, F. G. (2000). *Universal Design in Education: Teaching nontraditional students*. Westport, CT: Bergin & Garvey.

Bryant, D. P., & Bryant, B. R. (2003). *Assistive technology for people with disabilities*. Boston: Allyn & Bacon.

Center on Disabilities at California State University, Northridge. (2002). *Training workbook: Assistive technology applications certificate program*. Northridge: Author.

Cook, A. M., & Hussey, S. M. (2002). *Assistive technologies: Principles and practice*. St. Louis: Mosby.

Council of State Administrators of Vocational Rehabilitation. *Assistive Technology Act of 2004 as passed by the Senate*. Retrieved on June 15, 2005, from http://www.rehabnetwork.org/assistive_tech_Act/atact04_pass_senate.htm

Erickson, K. (1998, March). *Right to technology from Medicaid*. Paper presented at the California State University, Northridge, 1998 Conference in Los Angeles, CA. Retrieved on June 15, 2005, from http://www.dinf.ne.jp/doc/english/Us_Eu/conf/csun_98/csun98_045.htm

Edyburn, D. L. (2003). Measuring assistive technology outcomes in mathematics. *Journal of Special Education Technology, 18*(4), 76–79.

Friend, M. (2005). *Special education: Contemporary perspectives for school professionals*. Boston: Pearson Education.

Hallahan, D., & Kauffman, J. (2003). *Exceptional learners: Introduction to special education* (9th ed). Boston: Allyn & Bacon.

Harden, B., & Rosenberg, G. (2001). Bringing technology to the classroom: Challenges and considerations in including assistive technology under IDEA. *The ASHA leader, 5*, 16.

Hutinger, P., Johanson, J., & Stoneburner, R. (1996). Assistive technology applications in educational program of children with multiple disabilities: A case study report on the state of the practice. *Journal of Special Education Technology, 13*(1), 16–35.

Institute for Matching Person and Technology. (2005). *Matching person and technology*. Retrieved June 26, 2005, from http://members.aol.com/IMPT97/mptdesc.html

King, T. W. (1999). *Assistive technology: Essential human factors*. Boston: Allyn & Bacon.

Long, T., Huang, L., Woodbridge, M., Woolverton, M., & Minkel, J. (2003). Integrating assistive technology into an outcome-driven model of service delivery. *Infants and Young Children, 16*(4), 272–283.

Male, M. (2003). *Technology for inclusion: Meeting the special needs of all students* (4th ed.). Boston: Allyn & Bacon.

Mandlawitz, M. (2006). *What every teacher should know about IDEA 2004*. Boston: Allyn & Bacon.

McGregor, G., & Pachuski, P., (1996). Assistive technology in schools: Are teachers ready, able, and supported? *Journal of Special Education Technology, 8*(1).

National Association of the Deaf. (n.d.). *Deaf against technology?* Retrieved on April 14, 2006, from http://www.nad.org/site/pp.asp?c=foINKQMBF&b=180439

National Information Center for Children and Youth with Disabilities. (1991). Related services for school-aged children with disabilities. *NCIHCY New Digest, 1*(2). Washington, DC: Author.

Roblyer, M. D. (2003). *Integrating educational technology into teaching* (3rd ed.). Upper Saddle River, NJ: Merrill/Pearson Education.

Sheldon, J., & Hager, J. (1997). The availability of assistive technology through Medicaid, public school special education programs and state vocational rehabilitation agencies. Tucson: AZ: Neighborhood Legal Services, Inc. Retrieved on June 30, 2005, from http://www.nls.org/atart.htm#a%20purchase%20of

Sheldon, J., & Hart, S. (2004). *Medicare funding of assistive technology*. Tucson, AZ: Neighborhood Legal Services, Inc., & Arizona Center for Disability Law. Retrieved on June 30, 2005, from http://www.nls.org/conf2004/medicare-funding.htm

Social Security Administration. (2001). *Benefits for children with disabilities*. Washington, DC: Author. An electronic booklet retrieved on June 16, 2005, from http://www.ssa.gov/pubs/10026.html

U. S. Census Bureau. (2009). *American fact finder*. Washington, DC: Author. Retrieved on September 5, 2009, from http://factfinder.census.gov/servlet/ACSSAFFFacts?_submenuId=factsheet_0&_sse=on

U. S. Department of Health and Human Services. (n.d.). *Medicaid information for your state*. Washington, DC: Author. Retrieved on June 16, 2005, from http://www.cms.hhs.gov/medicaid/

U. S. Department of Health and Human Services. (2004). *Your Medicare benefits—10-116*. Washington, DC: Author. Retrieved on June 16, 2005, from http://www.medicare.gov/Publications/Search/Results.asp?PubID=10116&Type=PubID&Language=English

Watts, E., O'Brian, M., & Wojcik, B. (2004). Four models of assistive technology consideration: How do they compare to recommended educational assessment practices? *Journal of Special Education Technology, 19*(1), 43–56.

Watson, V. (2005). *Word processing as an assistive technology tool for improving production of written work by students with disabilities*. Unpublished master's thesis, Winthrop University. Used with permission.

Zabala, J. S. (2002). Assistive technology assessment process. *Training workbook: Assistive technology applications certificate program* (p. 25). Northridge: Center on Disabilities at California State University.

Chapter 11

Written Literacy Requires Students to Think

After reading this chapter, you will be able to:

1. Discuss the prevalence, causes, and characteristics of writing problems

2. Describe the relationship between thinking (metacognitive) and written literacy

3. Describe the elements of effective writing instruction and assessment

4. Apply the LEARN strategy to identify and select effective methods and materials for remediating writing problems

PREVALENCE OF STUDENTS EXPERIENCING WRITING PROBLEMS

The National Assessment of Educational Progress (NEAP, 2007) findings, as described by *The Nation's Report Card*, suggest the writing skills of 8th- and 12th-grade students in most racial and ethnic groups improved in 2007 compared to earlier assessments in 2002 and 1998 (students in Grade 4 were not assessed in 2007). This is also true for student with disabilities.

The NAEP (2007) data for this population indicate an upward trend in scale scores since 1998, with average gains in writing scores for students with disabilities in the 8th and 12th grades outpacing those of students without disabilities from 2002 to 2007. Why do you think this is the case? What does this mean for classroom teachers?

While it is true that the NAEP (2007) data indicate that students with disabilities are showing improvement, they continue to score much lower than their peers without disabilities do over time. Data indicate that of the 12th-grade students with disabilities participating in the assessment, 33% scored at the basic level in 1998, 30% scored at basic in 2002, and 44% scored basic in 2007 (NAEP, 2007). During the same reporting period, students with disabilities scored at the proficient level at the alarmingly low rates of 1% in 1998, 3% in 2002, and 5% in 2007 (NAEP, 2007). To put the scores into perspective, students without disabilities during the same time period scored at the basic level 81%, 77%, and 85%, respectively, and at the proficient level 23%, 25%, and 26%, respectively.

Gains by minority students, male students, and students with disabilities seem to be narrowing previously existing achievement gaps. Nevertheless, despite these gains, overall student writing scores have remained relatively stagnant over time, with only modest increases being reported over time in either reading or writing (Applebee, Arthur, & Langer, 2006; Tachibana, 2008). The most recent NAEP (2007) writing scores data indicate 88% of all eighth graders and 82% of all high school seniors tested at the basic level on the assessment, with only a third of 8th graders and a fourth of 12th graders scoring at or above the proficient level, defined as competency over challenging subject matter. Visit the NationsReportCard.gov Web site to get a fuller understanding of the scope of the problem. I also encourage the reader to look at not only the national writing scores but those of your state as well.

Findings such as these are troubling and raise many questions. Among them, why do students continue to exhibit basic skills deficits across grade levels despite classroom instruction by highly qualified teachers? As it stands, the majority of our nation's seniors are at the basic writing level as they prepare to graduate and are only capable of demonstrating partial mastery of prerequisite knowledge and skills that are fundamental to producing proficient written work in their personal and professional lives. Are the students graduating from our schools academically and functionally illiterate? It is troubling to note that despite policy and programming changes aimed at improving student performance, employers continue to question the ability of our graduates to do so (Brady, 2003; Wolf & Hall, 2005). To solve this problem we must understand what is causing it and then seek a solution. As discussed earlier in this text, when a student is not learning there is a mismatch between students' abilities and needs and classroom demands.

CAUSES

Classroom Factors Contribute to Writing Problems

Despite advances in educational psychology, learning, and technology, how is it that students continue to perform poorly on writing achievement tests? Trends suggested by years of NAEP data (2002, 2003, 2005, and 2007) indicate one possible reason: There is not much time being spent on writing in classrooms. Nor are students being given writing for homework. NAEP (2002, 2007) data indicate two-thirds of students in Grade 8 were expected to spend only an hour or less on writing homework each week, and this number remains virtually unchanged today. In addition, NAEP data from 2002 and 2007 show that 11% of eighth graders reported they were never asked to write research reports on content they studied, and only 14% and 16%, respectively, reported that they had been asked to do so once. This may explain part of the problem in that extended writing is believed to develop the skills necessary to summarize and synthesize information, develop in-depth arguments, and in general promote the use of higher-order thinking skills necessary to become a proficient and advanced writer.

Applebee and Langer (2006) looked at trends across NAEP data and found strong patterns suggesting teachers' beliefs of what higher and lower performing students can achieve drove instructional decision making. Do you remember discussing the effects of teachers' beliefs on decision making in Chapter 6 on metacognition? Apply what you learned there here to help you better understand how these teachers' beliefs may have affected their actions and student outcomes.

Applebee and Langer (2006) also found that when they analyzed teachers' responses to questionnaires on how they teach writing that in addition to teachers' beliefs and practices there are external factors affecting the teaching of writing. In particular, time spent on teaching writing is in direct competition with standardized test preparation time. Applebee and Langer report that in some cases, the focus on high-stakes test may be shifting attention away from broad programs of writing instruction toward a much narrower focus on basic skills and how best to answer particular types of test questions.

As we know, instruction that focuses on basic skills is not an effective means of providing students with the necessary skills and abilities to become proficient writers. Teaching to the test, as has become popular in educational culture, often focuses on low-level cognitive skills such as recognition and recall, those skills needed only to read a sentence and circle or answer a factual question on a paper-and-pencil exam. However, as adults, the expectations of our daily lives and jobs require reading and writing skills beyond those with such a limited purpose. Adults in today's workforce must compose memos and write business reports, among other things, all of which require higher-order thinking. Yet, students are not being taught in many cases to read and write meaningfully. Writing taught via decontextualized *basic skills* lessons in which words and sentences are read in isolation without any authentic purpose or connection to previously learned knowledge do not engender these types of skills and knowledge. Granted, some students can and do learn to become proficient writers given these circumstances, but others do not. In particular, many students with learning and behavior disorders experience difficulty learning to write in a classroom environment that focuses on basic skills alone (e.g., Graham, Harris, & Macarthur, 2006).

INFORMATION PROCESSING, PHONOLOGICAL KNOWLEDGE, HIGHER-ORDER LINGUISTIC KNOWLEDGE, AND EXCEPTIONALITY CONTRIBUTE TO WRITING PROBLEMS

Information Processing

Writing problems may occur for a number of reasons, including information processing problems that affect the ability to develop or use higher-order linguistic knowledge and phonological knowledge related to reading. As you know, the brain functions as a storage and retrieval system whose success depends on its ability to manipulate information. In the case of language, the brain looks for patterns and consistencies, repetitions in visual input and auditory input (Kuhl, 2008). These experiences are recorded or mapped by the brain and used to make sense of what we hear and see.

The ability to discriminate between sounds in one's own language and those of other languages develops very early—in fact, babies within the first 6 months of life can differentiate between phonemes used in their language as opposed to those used in other languages (Kuhl, Conboy, Padden, Nelson, & Pruitt, 2005). It is believed that the ability to represent individual sounds, by binding them together, and storing them in a meaningful way makes it easier for the brain to perceive the phonological components of language (Tallal, 2008). These coded representations are thought to serve as the building blocks of language (Tallal, 2008).

Phonological Awareness

There is also a strong connection between reading and writing. Reading and writing are dependent on shared cognitive abilities, including phonological and memory systems. The key to learning to read and write is becoming aware that words can be broken down into smaller parts of speech called phonemes. Phonemes are a type of code used to build words for both oral and written language. Children who have trouble understanding the code are more likely to have trouble with written language. One early indicator of difficulty with this code can be trouble with word games. For example, children may have trouble understanding that the word *slate* can be decoded into the word *late* by removing the /s/ or that by replacing the /s/ with an /h/ the word becomes *hate* and conveys and entirely different meaning. Why might a student's inability to play word games signal a problem? Language, both oral and written, begins with understanding that sounds are used to form words. Sounds can be broken down and reformed into an almost infinite variety of words used to convey written and spoken meaning.

Higher-Order Linguistic Knowledge

Temporal processing deficits may explain why some children do not develop phonological awareness. When you think about it, our brains must pull together, coordinate, store, and then retrieve millions of bits of coded data rapidly and in an organized fashion if language use is to be efficient and effective. Researchers compared children who struggle with learning to talk with those who do not have difficulty learning to talk and found notable differences in the way they organized basic linguistic signals and complex auditory signals (Tallal, 2008). It is believed that children who struggle with language may do so due to temporal processing deficits that make tracking and integrating speech sounds difficult (Tallal, 2008). In essence, the brain must process large amounts of information to produce written or spoken language.

Children who have difficulty processing written and spoken language often experience problems with reading and writing in school. In addition to phonological processing deficits, the problems many students exhibit with the mechanics of writing, including spelling, handwriting, and composition, often result from verbal memory problems associated with oral language (e.g., August & Shanahan, 2006; Lennox & Siegel, 1996, 1998). Studies show that verbal working memory limitations can affect both quality and quantity of writing (e.g., Lennox & Siegel, 1996, 1998; Shanahan, 2006). For example, an overload of verbal working memory can lead to choppy writing, certain kinds of syntactic and semantic errors, and composition errors. Verbal working memory, oral language, and writing are closely related with children who have well-developed oral language doing better with writing than those who do not. In fact, research suggests that written language skill is reliant on the development of oral language.

Exceptionality

Writing well does not come easily to many people. It is a complex process with which many students, including those with learning and behavior disorders, experience difficulty (e.g., Graham et al., 2006; van den Bergh & Rijlaarsdam, 2001). Students may have difficulty with written language due to psychological processing disorders (learning disabilities), neurological problems (cerebral palsy, muscular dystrophy, and traumatic brain injury), communication (autism), intellectual (metal retardation), sensory (hearing loss), or emotional impairment (selective mutism) (American Speech-Language Association, 2008). The resultant language problems are described by a variety of terms, such as language delay and language disorder.

Students labeled as *language delayed* fail to acquire language abilities according to the usual development timetable. That is, these children's language is developing normally, in the right sequence, but at a slower rate. Children who have *language disorders*, on the other hand, are not developing language normally, which may include rate and sequence. These two terms are often used interchangeably (American Speech-Language Association, 2008).

CHARACTERISTICS OF STUDENTS EXPERIENCING WRITTEN EXPRESSION DIFFICULTY

Researchers have grouped writing problems into three broad categories: knowledge difficulties, skills difficulties, and motivation difficulties (Troia, 2002; Troia & Graham, 2003). Although students may experience writing difficulty for a number of different reasons, they will often share many of the same characteristics. Examples of student characteristics by category are as follows (Troia, 2002; Troia & Graham, 2003).

Knowledge Difficulties

- Less aware of what good writing is and how to produce it
- Limited understanding of genre-specific text structures (e.g., setting or plot elements in a narrative)
- Poor declarative, procedural, and conditional strategy knowledge (e.g., metacognitively unaware of the need to plan for writing, including goal setting, strategy use, monitoring, and modifying when it is most beneficial)
- Limited knowledge of relevant vocabulary
- Underdeveloped knowledge of word and sentence structure (e.g., phonology, morphology, and syntax)
- May have limited background knowledge on a given topic or experience difficulty accessing existing topic knowledge
- Unaware of the audience for whom they are writing or the intended function of their writing

Skill Difficulties

- Poor spelling, handwriting, and punctuation
- May be unaware of the need to reflect on or revise writing, and if they do revise they may focus on superficial aspects of writing (e.g., handwriting, spelling, and grammar)
- Limited self-regulatory ability may make is difficult to regulate thoughts, attention, and actions during the writing process

Motivation Difficulties

- Students may falsely attribute academic success to external and uncontrollable factors, such as task ease or teacher assistance.
- Students may falsely attribute a lack of academic success to limited intelligence, which they also believe is beyond their control.
- As a result, these students often give up easily, have low self-efficacy, experience learned helplessness, and are unmotivated due to repeated failure.

Learning to write is a complex process, involving the mental ability to combine multiple skills and knowledge of written and spoken language simultaneously in meaningful ways. Difficulty with the mental processes involved in the use of language, regardless of the cause, can and will affect written expression in a number of ways. To determine where students are experiencing barriers to learning, teachers can utilize a variety of assessment methods.

WRITTEN LANGUAGE ASSESSMENT

Overview

When assessing student performance, particularly those with special needs, there are legal and ethical mandates requiring educators to consider information from multiple sources and approaches. These are generally a combination of standardized or norm-referenced and curriculum-based instruments. Student achievement is typically measured relative to standards for literacy and written language set by professional organizations such as the Council for Exceptional Children (CEC) and the National Council of English Teachers (NCTE) as well as national, state, and local performance standards. An individual classroom teacher approach to assessment will, however, depend on the assessment goal, professional background, orientation, and of course abilities of the students.

When assessing written language, it is important to keep these principles in mind:

1. Collect assessment data over time from across a variety of contexts and a number of sources to increase validity.
2. Choose assessments that will measure those outcomes you wish to measure. Check to be sure the instructional goal and instrument design match.
3. Assessments and tasks must be age appropriate.
4. Perhaps most important, assessments should reflect classroom instruction if they are to be valid measures of student performance.

FORMAL TESTS OF WRITTEN EXPRESSION

Written language is by its very nature a complex process, and assessing it can be difficult. Educators use both informal and formal methods to obtain an accurate performance profile. Norm-referenced tests can provide a formal or standardized measure of written language skills that are a part of the school, state, or national standards. These tests compare student performance to other students in the school system or other more diverse populations. There are many standardized, norm-referenced test options available to educators. The choice of test depends on several factors, including the student's age and skill level, questions to be answered, and characteristics of the student. The following are some of the more widely used standardized assessments of written language.

The *Test of Written Expression* (TOWE; McGhee, Bryant, Larsen, & Rivera, 1995) is intended for use with students between the ages of 6 years, 6 months, and 14 years, 11 months. It uses two assessment methods to evaluate student's writing skills. The first method involves administering a series of 76 items that measure skills associated with writing. The second method requires students to respond to a prepared story starter and use it as a stimulus for writing an essay. The test is designed to assess student's strengths and weaknesses in areas such as spelling, vocabulary, grammar, syntax, punctuation, ideation, and sentence and story construction. The TOWE may be administered either individually or to groups of students and is reported to have good reliability and adequate validity (Taylor, 2006).

The *Test of Early Written Language*, 2nd edition (TEWL; Hresko, Herron, & Peak, 1996), is intended for use with children 3 years, 0 months, to 10 years, 11 months. The purpose of this test is to measure emergent or early writing ability. Two procedures measure writing skills including spelling, capitalization, punctuation, ideation, and sentence construction. In one, students are administered 14 items to measure general understanding of writing purposes, discrimination of verbal and nonverbal visual representational forms, and understanding of linguistic terms. In the second, students write a story from a prompt. These stories are scored for skills including ideation, vocabulary, mechanics, and spelling. The test, while valid and reliable for older students, is not recommended for children under the age of 4 (Taylor, 2006).

The *Test of Written Language*, 3rd edition (TOWL–3; Hammill & Larsen, 1996), measures contrived and spontaneous written language. The test is appropriate for students in Grades 2–12. It has eight subtests that assess contextual conventions, contextual language, story construction, vocabulary, spelling, style, logical sentences, and sentence combining. Three of the subtests measure skills including grammar, syntax, punctuation, and general composition. There are two forms of this test (A and B) to eliminate test/retest contamination between the pretest and post-test. Although this test is widely used and meets nationally recognized standards, Salvia and Yesseldyke (2007) suggested that it has limited usefulness because it lacks information concerning students with special needs.

The *Wide Range Achievement Test*, 4th edition (WRAT–4; Wilkinson & Robertson, 2006), is an individually administered test for students from 5 through 9.5 years. There are four subtests: word reading, spelling, math computation, and sentence comprehension. It is widely used as a screening test to diagnose learning disabilities in spelling (Pierangelo & Giuliani, 2006).

The *Woodcock–Johnson Tests of Achievement III* (WJ III; Woodcock, McGrew, & Mather, 2001) is a subset of *Woodcock–Johnson III*. Subtests include spelling, writing fluency, and sample writing, as well as letter–word identification, reading fluency, passage comprehension, calculation, math fluency, and applied problems. Due to the continuous-year norms of the WJ III, it is considered to be a valid and reliable source for identifying significant discrepancies in learning and guiding educational decision making (Venn, 2007).

The *Writing Process Test* (WPT; Warden & Hutchinson, 1992) is a direct measure of writing that requires students to plan, write, and revise an original composition. The WPT assesses both written product and process. The students analyze the product via a checklist and questions about their composition. The WPT gives the examiner insight into the student's metacognitive awareness of the writing process when planning recursive behaviors. The test is appropriate for students in Grades 2–12 and can be administered individually or in groups.

When determining how to assess written language, there a number of factors to consider, including the purpose of the assessment, the information needed, and how that information will be used. Standardized tests, for a number of reasons, do not generally generate the type of information that is useful for planning classroom instruction. For example, standardized tests often do not test what students are taught, often consider only one response correct, and do not allow room for students to generate answers based on their knowledge and experience (Cohen & Spenciner, 2007).

Standardized test data are, however, useful as a screening device. For example, they draw upon standardized test results to determine eligibility for special education services, measure student achievement against national norms for the purposes of establishing accountability, or determine students' admissions to institutions of higher education.

INFORMAL TESTS OF WRITTEN EXPRESSION

Formal assessments serve an important function: They allow school systems to compare the performance of large groups of students, monitor the effectiveness of programming, and make broad curricular decisions. Informal assessments differ from formal measures in that they help teachers identify student strengths and weaknesses, note particular skills that need attention, monitor student progress, and guide instructional planning, goal setting, materials selection (Venn, 2007). Moreover, informal assessments share a logical and intuitive connection with classroom instruction. They occur as a normal part of the educational process that emerges from everyday teaching and learning situations.

Teachers, for example, often utilize questioning and one-on-one interviews with students to provide them with a real-time error analysis of thought processes and strategy use. Portfolio assessment is another frequently utilized informal assessment method that offers a dynamic measure of student growth over time as opposed to the more static snapshot of ability provided by standardized assessment instruments. The advantages of the informal assessment methods are that they allow for immediate feedback and revision of teaching to accommodate learner needs and can also measure competence across a variety of cognitive levels, as defined by the revised version of Bloom's

Taxonomy of Educational Objectives (i.e., knowledge, comprehension, application, analysis, synthesis, and evaluating) (Anderson, & Krathwohl, 2001; Bloom, Englehart, Furst, Hill, & Krathwohl, 1956). The following is a list of competencies, verbs, and activities that can be used to construct assessments at each level.

- *Knowledge/Remembering Level.* At the knowledge level, the goal is to determine if the student can recall basic information and facts. Among the verbs used to construct assessment activities at this level are *define, duplicate, list, memorize, recall,* and *repeat.* To assess student ability at this level, have students write a paragraph in which they identify the main characters of a book.
- *Comprehension/Understanding Level.* At this level, the goal is to determine if the student can explain ideas or concepts. Among the verbs used to construct assessment activities at this level are *classify, describe, discuss, explain, report,* and *paraphrase.* To assess student ability at this level, have students write a report in which they describe relevant events from a field trip to the United Nations.
- *Application/Applying Level.* At this level, the goal is to determine if the student can use information in a new way. Among the verbs used to construct assessment activities at this level are *choose, demonstrate, dramatize, employ, illustrate, interpret, operate, schedule, sketch, solve,* and *use.* To assess student ability at this level, have students write a report in which they rewrite the story using the literary convention discussed in today's lesson.
- *Analysis/Analyzing Level.* At this level, the goal is to determine if the student can distinguish between relationships and different parts. Among the verbs used to construct assessment activities at this level are *appraise, compare, contrast, criticize, differentiate, discriminate, distinguish, examine, experiment, question,* and *test.* To assess student ability at this level, have students write a mock newspaper editorial in which they compare and contrast the presidency of Abraham Lincoln to that of any 20th- or 21st-century president.
- *Synthesis/Evaluating Level.* At this level, the goal is to determine if the student can make and justify a decision. Among the verbs used to construct assessment activities at this level are *appraise, argue, defend, judge, select, support, value,* and *evaluate.* To assess student ability at this level, have students write a journal entry in which you evaluate the effectiveness of the strategies they used to study for the last test.
- *Evaluating/Creating Level.* At this level, the goal is to determine if the student can create a new product or point of view. Among the verbs used to construct assessment activities at this level are *assemble, construct, create, design, develop,* and *formulate.* To assess student ability at this level, have students create a poem using the vocabulary words from the story.

These activities allow students to demonstrate a variety of skills and abilities within the dynamic context of instructional activities.

One of the most important features of informal assessment that differentiates it from standardized tests is the feedback component. Students' progress toward a given learning goal must be monitored and areas of strength or weakness assessed, so that instruction can be modified quickly to meet each student's individual needs. Remember, prompt feedback to students about their work increases the likelihood of producing meaningful changes in learning outcomes.

TABLE 11.1 Holistic Writing Rubric for Journaling Activity

Use this rubric to assess students' abilities to complete the journal activities assigned for a given lesson. Share this assessment with students prior to completing the journal-writing lesson so they will understand how they will be assessed. You can also use the rubric as a basis for discussion and feedback with each student. Each journal will be given one of three scores: E, A, or NA. The reader will write with these descriptors in mind.

Excellent	• Can easily complete process independently
	• Can pre-read and follow the writing prompts without assistance; has no more than three minor errors (mechanics, word choice, sentence structure)
	• Meets all requirements
Acceptable	• Requires some help to complete process
	• Can pre-read and follow the writing prompts with minimal assistance; has four to seven minor errors (mechanics, word choice, sentence structure)
	• Meets most requirements
Not Acceptable	• Must have extensive support to complete process
	• Does not follow writing prompts without extensive support
	• Has more than seven errors (mechanics, word choice, sentence structure)
	• Does not meet all requirements

Source: Spencer, S., & Evers, R. (2009). Unpublished course material. Center for Pedagogy, Winthrop University.

Rubrics like the one in Table 11.1 are excellent tools for grading activities such as journaling. This is an example of a holistic scoring rubric; however, they may take the form of either holistic scoring rubrics or analytical scoring rubrics. Both are useful for the analysis of students' written products or the writing processes itself (Brookhart, 1999). Holistic scoring rubrics provide a general overall impression of writing ability on one or two previously identified characteristics in a student's work. Each level describes the characteristics of a response that would receive the respective score. The disadvantage of this method is that it does not provide detailed information about specific areas of writing.

Informal assessments of student learning may also be scored using an analytic scoring rubric. This method offers an alternative to the holistic scoring rubric by providing some objectivity to evaluation of content. Teachers can choose from a general rating scale that will apply to most writing assignments, or they can design scoring scales that are specific to a given genre or text. For example, these rubrics might measure student performance as being experienced, capable, developing, emergent, pre-emergent, or experimental. Rubrics like these will allow teachers to pinpoint students' specific strengths and weaknesses and set clear performance goals.

INSTRUCTIONAL ASSESSMENT AND METHODOLOGICAL DECISION MAKING

Evaluating student work to improve learning is but one aspect of effective decision making. Teachers must also become skilled at analyzing their own expectations to determine the relationship between the setting demands of their classroom and student achievement. Standardized assessments seldom provide teachers with the type of information they need to determine where students are having difficulty with a given lesson. Misinterpretation of such data may in fact lead to a misidentification of the underlying academic problem, resulting in ineffective planning by the teacher.

While the importance of assessment data for guiding instructional decisions is clear theoretically, it is less clear to teachers from a practical standpoint how to apply this construct at the classroom level. A tool is needed that will assist teachers in determining where barriers to learning lie within their lessons before they teach them, one that can provide meaningful feedback and inform instructional planning in a timely manner. One such tool is the LEARNS strategy previously introduced in Chapter 7 on Universal Design for Learning (UDL). The LEARNS strategy for planning UDL lessons consists of six steps:

Step 1: Learning goal: Determine what content will be taught.

Step 2: Note teacher Expectations for lesson objective.

Step 3: Areas of strength and need for each student are noted.

Step 4: Review and determine barriers.

Step 5: Note accommodations needed.

Step 6: Specify individual accommodations needed for specific students.

The LEARNS strategy enables teachers to diagnose where problems lie within the curriculum. It facilitates educational planning by providing a metacognitive problem-solving framework from which to make informed instructional decisions. LEARNS will help teachers design their lessons with students' abilities in mind. Based on principles of Universal Design for Learning, LEARNS requires teachers to plan lessons recognizing that students have differing ability levels due to background knowledge, readiness, language, exceptionality, preferences in learning, inability to physically use instructional materials, or inability to effectively select and apply cognitive and metacognitive strategies.

Remember, lesson plans provided by textbooks or readily available materials from the Internet are general and can unwittingly create barriers to learning because they are not tailored to the unique needs of your students. The LEARNS strategy is a tool with which to design or revise lessons for the purpose of solving academic problems and removing barriers to learning based on students' unique needs.

Applying the LEARNS Strategy to Writing Assignments

Table 11.2 illustrates how a teacher might use the LEARNS strategy to design a writing lesson.

The following is a discussion of the LEARNS process.

Step 1: Identify a *learning goal* for the lesson you plan to teach. Learning goals typically support state or content area curriculum standards; therefore, what you are required to teach is unrelated to classroom demographics. What is the learning goal in the example?

Step 2: *Specify* expectations for the lesson. This step requires the teacher to conduct a task analysis of the writing lesson to determine how the students should

TABLE 11.2 LEARNS Strategy Lesson Plan Analysis

STEP 1: Learning goal	Students employ a wide range of strategies as they write and use different writing process elements appropriately to communicate with different audiences for a variety of purposes.	
Determine the learning goals based on state standards.	Students will develop and support a position on a particular book by writing a persuasive essay about their chosen title.	

STEP 2: Note teacher expectations	Teaching activity	Skills necessary to complete task or activity
What must students be able to do to complete learning tasks successfully or to achieve mastery of the content taught?	Students will examine issues of censorship as it relates to a videos, Internet, music, and books.	Understand the concept of censorship
	Students will read and evaluate books to determine biases.	• Must be able to read from book • Must be able to determine relevant features in the book that are controversial and why • Must be able to take notes
	Students must write a persuasive essay on a particular book in which they develop and support a position.	• Ability to plan, organize, sequence paper • Ability to write a grammatically correct essay • Ability to correctly identify main ideas and important details intended to persuade

STEP 3: Assess areas of strength/need	Area of need and name	Note specific ways in which these needs may manifest in a classroom and names of students to whom it applies
	Poor/advanced reading skills:	• Inability to pick out main ideas/important details • Trouble sounding out words; difficulty with word sounds, meanings, syntax • Slow oral reading rate • Difficulty connecting meaning of passages • Confuses the meaning of words
	Poor/advanced writing skills:	• Mental fatigue and frustration • Inconsistent legibility of writing due to letter formation, transposition problems • Many careless errors

(Continued)

TABLE 11.2 LEARNS Strategy Lesson Plan Analysis (*Continued*)

STEP 3: Assess areas of strength/need	Area of need and name	Note specific ways in which these needs may manifest in a classroom and names of students to whom it applies
		• Organizational problems lead to poorly planned reports and papers (lack transitions, poor sequencing)
		• Poor vocabulary, spelling, punctuation, grammar
		• Trouble generating ideas, awkward phrasing
		• Difficulty with writing tasks that require critical thinking
		• Write slowly, hard to form letters, lack of fluid cursive writing ability
	Poor/advanced prior knowledge:	• Inexperience with topic, subject, region, concept
		• Lacks academic or social readiness skill base
		• May have difficulty because has no prior exposure to the topic
	Attention problems:	• Difficulty getting started on assignments
		• Processes too little or too much information; can't distinguish between what is important and what isn't
		• Focuses too superficially or too deeply on information presented
		• Has difficulty connecting new information with information already known
	Poor/advance math skills:	• Has trouble ordering the steps used to solve a problem
		• Feels overloaded when faced with a worksheet full of math exercises
		• Not be able to copy problems correctly
		• May have difficulties reading the hands on an analog clock

TABLE 11.2 *(Continued)*

STEP 3: Assess areas of strength/need	Area of need and name	Note specific ways in which these needs may manifest in a classroom and names of students to whom it applies
		• May have difficulties interpreting and manipulating geometric configurations
		• May have difficulties appreciating changes in objects as they are moved in space
	Social/emotional skills deficits:	• Lack of or lowered levels of motivation due to learned helplessness or lack of interest
	Sensory or motor disability:	• Inability to see demonstrations, board, visual aids
		• May not understand concepts that require vision (i.e., colors, objects, patterns)
		• Inability to read print materials
		• Inability to move about the room freely or participate in activities that require physical movement
		• Inability to handle manipulatives

STEP 4: Review	Teaching activity skills	Note barriers to learning and names of students to whom it applies
Compare and contrast Step 2 and Step 3, and note major areas where any students will encounter barriers to learning if you do not make any accommodations.	Must be able to pick out relevant features of censorship and bias.	• Lack of background knowledge may make it difficult for some students to understand the concept of societal censorship and bias.
	• Must be able to read independently from book	• Lack of decoding ability may lead to slow reading rate.
	• Must be able to determine relevant features in the book that are controversial and why	• Confusion about the meaning of words may make it difficult for students to distinguish between relevant and irrelevant information.
	• Must have ability to plan, organize, sequence paper	• May miss important details and not know how to sequence their narrative

(Continued)

TABLE 11.2 LEARNS Strategy Lesson Plan Analysis (*Continued*)

STEP 4: Review	Teaching activity skills	Note barriers to learning and names of students to whom it applies
	• Must have ability to write a grammatical correct essay. • Must correctly identify main ideas and important details intended to persuade	• May have difficulty with vocabulary, spelling, and punctuation • May have trouble generating ideas • Difficulty with writing tasks that require critical thinking • May write slowly, hard to form letters, lack of fluid cursive writing ability

STEP 5: Note accommodations	Area of need and name	Accommodations and names of students to whom it applies
Determine methods, strategies, and materials that will meet students' needs.	Lack of decoding ability may lead to slow reading rate. Confusion about the meaning of words may make it difficult for students to distinguish between relevant and irrelevant information. • May miss important details and not know how to sequence their narrative • May have difficulty with vocabulary, spelling, and punctuation • May have trouble generating ideas • Difficulty with writing tasks that require critical thinking • May write slowly, hard to form letters, lack of fluid cursive writing ability	Allow the students to use books on tape or recorded materials. Provide students access to online dictionaries with pronunciation feature. • Graphic organizers or note-taking guides can also help students to distinguish between important and irrelevant information. • Provide students access to online dictionaries with pronunciation feature. Use the COPS strategy (see Table 11.5) for editing work. • Have students use the DEFENDS writing strategy (see Table 11.5) to organize thoughts, generate opinions, and produce a well-written persuasive paper. • Allow students to utilize computers to improve written product

STEP 6: Specify individual accommodations	Student names/unmet need	Accommodations
Identify students whose needs are not met by UDL	Miguel (ELL)	• Miguel does not read English well, so allow him to listen to

TABLE 11.2 (Continued)

STEP 6: Specify individual accommodations	Student names/unmet need	Accommodations
provisions. These students may represent an instructional subgroup.		materials in both his native language and English. Also provide written material in both his native language and English.
	Elsa (CP)	• Provide student with speech-to-text software such as Dragon Naturally Speaking to eliminate difficulty with writing.

Source: Spencer, S., & Evers, R. (2009). Unpublished course material. Center for Pedagogy, Winthrop University.

perform. Ask yourself, what will students need to do and what will they need to know to complete the learning tasks successfully? Begin by thinking about how you will sequence your instruction of the academic content covered in this lesson. Next, outline the instructional plan in the order in which it will be implemented. Note the instructional activities, student grouping, materials, technology, and/or resources, including the use of instructional aides, parents, or other adults in the room that you will use. Last, specify methods for monitoring and assessing student learning.

The example provided is that of a typical lesson from a grade-level textbook in which students are expected to examine issues related to censorship and bias in literature. They will produce a persuasive essay on the book of their choosing. Conduct an analysis of this task, remembering that each of the tasks in a given activity may present a barrier to any of the students in your classroom, depending on their special needs and abilities. Make a list of the specific skills and knowledge necessary to complete the assignment. Be sure to include any subskills related to the activities. This list could become extensive, so prioritize and rank in order of importance.

Step 3: Determine the *areas* of strength and need for each student. We suggest completing a demographic worksheet for your class at the beginning of each school year (see Table 11.3 for an example); it then serves as a reference for planning lessons throughout the year. Information you might collect includes gender, age, race/ethnicity, SES status, reading and math competency levels, and special needs, such as disability, ELL status, gifted/talented, and any other information that correlates highly with learning outcomes as discussed in Chapter 2 on learner characteristics. For example, secondary teachers may want to know how students preformed in prerequisite courses to be in the present class (i.e., how well did the student do in Algebra I if enrolled in an Algebra II class now?). Reading, writing, and spelling abilities, on the other hand, are not necessarily content or grade-level specific and may be relevant to many teachers. Collect additional data as needed.

TABLE 11.3 Student Demographic Sheet

ID #	First Name	Gender	Ethnicity	Race	SES/Lunch Status	Reading Level	Math Level	Exceptionality
1	Jose	M	American	Black	Regular	Low	Low	Visually Impaired
2	Tina	F	American	Caucasian	Regular	Average	Average	
3	Morris	M	American	Caucasian	Reduced	Average	Average	
4	Miguel	M	Hispanic	Mestizo	Regular	Low	Low	ELL
5	Elsa	F	Asian	Pacific Islander	Regular	High	High	Physical disability: Cerebral Palsy
6	Kisha	F	American	Black	Free	Low	Average	LD
7	Karl	M	American	Caucasian	Regular	Average	Average	
8	Daniel	M	English	Caucasian	Regular	High	Average	ADHD
9	Kendra	F	American	Black	Reduced	Average	Low	
10	Timothy	M	American	Caucasian	Free	Low	Average	
11	Gary	M	American	Caucasian	Regular	High	High	
12	Barbra	F	American	Caucasian	Reduced	High	High	
13	David	M	American	Black	Regular	Average	Average	
14	Betsy	F	American	Caucasian	Regular	Average	High	
15	Darnell	M	American	Mixed	Reduced	Low	Average	
16	Adam	M	American	Black	Free	Low	Low	
17	Martha	F	American	Caucasian	Regular	Average	Average	
18	Norton	M	American	Native Amer	Regular	Average	Average	
19	Wanda	F	Hispanic	Mestizo	Reduced	Average	Average	
20	Lori	F	American	Caucasian	Regular	Average	High	

Source: Spencer, S., & Evers, R. (2009). Unpublished course material. Center for Pedagogy, Winthrop University.

Teachers can get demographic information from a variety of sources, including IEPs, permanent records, and interviews. Once acquired, it then becomes necessary to organize the data for analysis. The authors suggest creating a spreadsheet for this purpose, which will assist with sorting information categorically. Sorting by categories makes it easier to identify factors and note patterns that might affect both individual and group performance.

The demographic data in Table 11.3 provide an example of such a table. Look at the hypothetical class represented by this table. Can you analyze the information? To assist you with the process, ask yourself the following:

- What are the unique learner characteristics associated with each category? For example, what definitional characteristics are associated with a learning disability or low SES?
- In general, which of these characteristics has a significant ability to influence learning?
- What are the types of learning problems that might be associated with each?

Once data analysis is complete, describe the patterns you find, noting how this information will guide specific instructional decisions. It may be necessary to revise your learning goal based on the results, which is what occurs in the next step of the process.

Step 4: *Review* and compare the required tasks (Step 2) with possible areas of need (Step 3) and determine potential barriers in the lesson. In the example, one of the tasks noted in Step 2 requires students to prepare a written essay on the censorship and bias. Barriers associated with this activity might include difficulty understanding concepts, identifying important details, or taking notes. These problems may be common to many students in the class, although they occur for different reasons. The ability to see barriers to learning in terms of what they share in common makes it easier to make accommodations. Once a teacher determines areas of mismatch between what a student needs and the demands of the lesson, accommodations can be chosen. Consider the elements of instruction listed in the example, such as instructional groupings, materials, methods, student tasks, and suggest possible barriers to learning in this lesson. There are many, and all may not be listed in the example.

Step 5: *Note* methods and materials that will remove barriers to learning. It is important to understand that there are many strategies and tools available to a teacher. That is not the issue. Knowing which tool to select requires expertise rather than guesswork. Look at the barriers listed in Step 5 and suggest other methods and materials that might effectively eliminate barriers to learning. You may choose from strategies in Table 11.4, where there are a variety of methods and strategies suggested for removing the barriers associated with note taking, spelling, vocabulary. In addition to these, there are many other options. One choice might be the James Madison University Learning Toolbox. It is an excellent online resource for teachers, parents, and students to see some of the many learning strategies available. Which would you choose, and why?

Step 6: *Specify* individualized instruction for students with special needs. Considering the accommodations specified in students' IEPs is a place to start, and then plan

TABLE 11.4 Writing Strategies

Strategy	Author	Steps to Implementation
WWW WHAT = 2 HOW = 2 (A story grammar strategy)	Graham, MacArthur, Schwartz, & Page-Voth (1992)	**W**ho is the main character, and who else is in the story? **W**hen does the story take place? **W**here does the story take place? **W**hat does the main character want to do? **W**hat do the other characters want to do? **W**hat happens when the main character tries to do it? What happens with the other characters? **H**ow does the story end? **H**ow does the main character feel? How do the other characters feel?
PLAN & WRITE (expository writing)	De La Paz (1997)	**P**ay attention to the prompt. **L**ist the main ideas. **A**dd supporting ideas. **N**umber your ideas. **W**ork from your plan to develop your thesis statement. **R**emember your goals. **I**nclude transition words. **T**ry to use different kinds of sentences. **U**se Exciting, interesting $100,000 words.
TREE (strategy for composing essays)	Graham & Harris (1989)	Note **t**opic sentence. Note **r**easons. **E**xamine reasons. Note **e**nding
STOP and LIST (strategies for writing a persuasive paper)	Troia & Graham (2002)	**S**uspend judgment, record ideas about each side of the topic. **T**ake a side. **O**rganize ideas into ideas you plan to use. **P**lan more as you write, remember to use the plan developed earlier. **L**ist ideas and sequence them.

for supports beyond those recommended in case they are insufficient to reach the students' learning goals. The hypothetical class depicted in Table 11.3 identifies two students with special needs that might require extra planning. They are Miguel and Elsa. The LEARNS strategy provides examples of additional supports for them. Can you suggest supplementary supports for the remaining students with exceptionalities (i.e., Kisha and Daniel)? Review the previous steps of LEARNS, reflect on what you know about the educational needs of these students, and anticipate where they might face academic barriers before making your choices.

All students will experience difficulty learning; by utilizing the principles of Universal Design, teachers build in the necessary supports sufficient to remove barriers to learning for most students when they design instruction. However, there will always be students for whom additional supports are necessary. Often these supports come in the form of programmatic lines of writing instruction. How will you decide which is most appropriate for your students?

EFFECTIVE WRITING INSTRUCTION

Historical Perspective

The traditional model of writing instruction in American schools until the 1960s was a product-oriented approach in which mechanics and grammar are emphasized over content and process. Product-oriented writing instruction gives limited attention or time to activities requiring sustained writing. Students are often expected to learn to write in isolation, with little taught about the processes or strategies involved in writing. Students are thought to be able to learn to write by reading the work of others and in so doing develop the capability to independently create similar compositions. There is often little feedback from teachers to guide the development of the skills and knowledge necessary to communicate effectively, because that is not the goal. In product-oriented models, the grade is the goal. This model of instruction fell out of favor in the 1960s but has remerged in recent years, given the focus on student outcomes and high-stakes testing. As evidenced earlier in this chapter (e.g., NAEP, 2005, 2007), national assessment data indicate that this approach to writing instruction is not proving effective.

In stark contrast to the product model, an alternative instructional model for teaching writing began to emerge in the 1960s, when researchers suggested a move toward a process-oriented, or whole-language approach. In the early years, this method of teaching writing did not involve any direct instruction; critics characterized it as an anything-goes approach that emphasized writing as a natural process. For example, teachers did not typically make specific assignments, activities were not based on specific objectives, and criteria for judging writing effectiveness were not taught. The three-stage model adopted by most involved a linear prewriting, writing, and rewriting format. It was considered unnecessary for students to receive a lot of feedback from teachers to guide their writing (Hillocks, 1984). It is not surprising that initially this approach had only minimal impact of the quality of student writing (Hillocks, 1984).

Despite early setbacks, the process model continued to evolve. Work by teachers in the San Francisco Bay Area in the 1970s led to methodological changes in the process model that were positively received. These teachers' ideas were based on the theory that the writing process could be improved by comparing how professional writers compose to how writing is taught in schools (Gray, 2000). Because of their initial efforts, a process model of writing has emerged over the past 40 plus years that combines elements of both the process and product approaches to writing instruction. Writing is no longer viewed as simply a linear process in which thinking about writing occur in a straight line, neatly resolved by the prewrite, write, rewrite format of teaching writing. Writing is the result of a mental recursive process in which the writer relies on metacognitive ability to self-regulate goal setting and guide the effective use of procedural strategies for monitoring and modifying output. Goldstein and Carr (1996) defined writing as a process requiring multiple decisions:

> "Process writing" refers to a broad range of strategies that include pre-writing activities, such as defining audience, using a variety or resources, planning the writing, as well as drafting and revising. These activities, collectively referred to as "process-oriented instruction," approach writing as problem solving (p. 1).

This approach to writing is philosophically and practically different from the product approach to writing in that composition has a social function and takes place within a meaningful literacy context. Students learn that the challenges associated with writing can be overcome with the right strategies. In this environment, students learn to take risks and collaborate with teachers and peers to produce work and evaluate it. Despite variations in how the steps of the process are taught, researchers who espouse this approach see writing as a complex problem-solving process requiring a mix of composition, mechanics, and self-regulatory skill.

Research indicates that students who apply the writing process methods tend to score higher on written products than those who do not (Dyson & Freedman, 2003). Perhaps that is why elements of the writing-process approach to teaching writing are currently mandated by many state and local school systems as the method of choice for instruction in K–12 classrooms (Patthey-Chavez, Matsumura, & Valdes, 2004). If this method is a better candidate for improving writing than the traditional method, why do NAEP (2007) writing scores remain stagnate? Cramer (2001) suggested poor implementation may be the reason.

If you will remember, earlier in this chapter NAEP (2002, 2007) data suggested that teachers are spending very little time on writing instruction. Applebee and Langer (2006) reported that in some cases, the focus on high-stakes test may be shifting attention away from broad programs of writing instruction toward a much narrower focus on basic skills and how best to answer particular types of test questions. Why are teachers doing this? Does the desire to raise test scores alone explain the phenomenon, or is it a philosophical belief that one approach is superior to the other? Research on best practices in the teaching of writing suggests there is no single approach to writing that is uniformly effective for all students (Graham & Harris, 1994, 1997). Fortunately, there are models for teaching writing available to teachers that combine effective elements of both approaches.

RESEARCH-BASED METHODS OF WRITING INSTRUCTION

Educational reform efforts have resulted in a number of innovative methods purported to increase students' writing performance. Over the years, there have been several respected reviews of the research on writing instruction (e.g., Graham & Perin, 2007; Langer & Applebee, 1987; Levy & Ransdell, 1995; MacArthur, Graham, & Fitzgerald, 2006; Smagorinsky, 2006). Perhaps one of the most powerful to date is that of Graham and Perin (2007). A meta-analysis of 142 scientific studies identifies 11 effective elements of writing instruction. Listed in order from most to least effective, they are as follows:

1. Teach writing strategies for planning, revising, and/or editing.
2. Teach rule-governed or intuitive strategies for summarizing text.
3. Teach students how to work collaboratively to plan, draft, revise, and edit their compositions.
4. State writing goals that are attainable and specific.
5. Utilize computers and word processors for writing assignments.
6. Teach students how to construct complex sentences by combining two or more basic sentences into one single sentence.
7. Teachers utilize prewriting activities designed to help generate or organize ideas.
8. Teachers employ the use of inquiry activities that require students to set goals and learn how to analyze concrete and observational data for the purpose of developing ideas and content.
9. Teaching instruction is interwoven into a number of writing activities that emphasize writing for real readers, self-reflective writing, and recursive writing.
10. Students learn to analyze good models of writing for the purpose of emulating them in their own writing.
11. Teachers teach students to view writing as a tool for learning content.

Individually, these elements do not constitute a full writing curriculum; however, when combined they can improve writing results for students, including those who are at risk due to limited English proficiency, low income, minority status, and those with disabilities (Graham & Perin, 2007). There are a number of models for teaching writing that incorporate these elements. Among the most widely adopted are the Self-Regulated Strategy Development (SRSD) model (Graham & Harris, 1994, 1997), the Strategic Instruction Model (SIM) (Deshler & Schumaker, 1988), the Early Literacy Project (ELP) (Englert et al., 1995; Englert & Mariage, 2003), and the Optimal Learning Environment (OLE) model developed by Ruiz (1995a, 1995b).

All of these models combine both the process and procedural approaches to writing as discussed earlier. These research-based approaches teach students a basic framework for planning, writing, and revising. They teach writing as a process of steps recursive in nature that provide guidelines by which to analyze material learned in the classroom for the purpose of writing personal narratives, persuasive essays, and in other genres. Each provides students with meaningful feedback that they can use to enhance self-regulatory ability. Together these components have proven successful in improving students' written work and have had a positive effect on students' self-efficacious beliefs regarding their ability to write.

Specific Methods

The Self-Regulated Strategy Development (SRSD) model (Graham & Harris, 1994, 1997; Harris & Graham, 2005), developed by Steve Graham and Karen Harris at the University of Maryland, can be used to teach spelling, reading, math, and writing. Writing, however, is perhaps the area for which it is best known. The SRSD model explicitly teaches combinations of mnemonic strategies to remind students of the steps in the writing process, prompting them to plan and reflect while composing. Strategies for writing simple opinion essays, stories, and narratives are among the family of writing strategies in the model, which facilitates planning, generating, framing, and revising text (see Table 11.4).

The SRSD model provides explicit instruction on writing, self-regulation, and content knowledge. Instruction is interactive, self-paced, and collaborative with feedback tailored to meet the needs and ablities of the individual student. There are six stages in SRSD instruction (Harris & Graham, 1992):

1. The class works together to develop and activate background knowledge.
2. The class discusses the strategy, including benefits and expectations.
3. The teacher models the strategy.
4. The students memorize the strategy.
5. The teacher and students practice using the strategy collaboratively. At this time, the teacher provides corrective feedback to promote self-regulation.
6. The students use the strategy independently while the teacher monitors and provides supportive feedback as needed.

These six instructional stages are taught along with four general strategies that promote self-regulation. The four are goal setting, self-instruction (e.g., talking-aloud), self-monitoring, and self-reinforcement. The SRSD technique directs students to utilize self-directed prompts that require them to (a) consider their audience and reasons for writing, (b) develop a plan for what they intend to say using strategies to generate or organize writing notes, (c) evaluate possible content by considering its impact on the reader, and (d) continue the process of content generation and planning during the act of writing. The fact that the self-regulatory component of the model is taught explicitly and not embedded in cognitive strategy instruction is what sets it apart from other programmatic lines of strategy instruction.

A large body of research that speaks to the effectiveness of the SRSD model has amassed over the years (e.g., Barry & Moore, 2004; Chalk, Hagan-Burke & Burke, 2005; Graham, 2006; Page-Voth & Graham, 1999; Troia & Graham, 2002). A meta-analysis of 18 research studies (Graham & Harris, 2003) found the SRSD model effective for improving the writing abililty of students with learning disabilities as well as low-, average-, and high-achieving students at both the elementary and middle school levels. In one study by De La Paz, Owen, Harris, and Graham (2000), students were taught the PLAN and WRITE expository writing strategies though the six stages cited above. Strategy use in this study proved more helpful than a rating scale and sample essay alone in preparing students for a state writing assessment. Similar results were noted by De La Paz (2001) for the PLAN and WRITE strategies when used with students who had learning disabilites and attention-deficit disorder. As with the previous study, students increased their use of plans for writing, increased essay length, and produced more quality content and better structured writing.

For additional information and an online interactive tutorial on SRSD, go to the Vanderbilt University IRIS Center home page (http://iris.peabody.vanderbilt.edu/pow/chalcycle.htm), select Resources, and then click on the Star Legacy Module labeled *Using Learning Strategies: Instruction to Enhance Learning*. The module labeled *Improving Writing Performance: A Stratgegy for Writing Expository Essays*, located under the heading Differentiated Instruction, also provides a tutorial on all stages of the model, along with activities and examples.

Since as early as 1988, the Strategic Instruction Model (SIM) of Deshler and Schumaker at the University of Kansas has sought to improve the academic and social outcomes of middle and high school students with learning disabilities. The scope of their research widened when later research indicated that many students, not just those with learning disabilities, were experiencing difficulty transitioning to upper grades. Their findings indicate that students' inabilities to learn academic content in some cases could be attributed to basic skills deficits. They also found that teachers did not as a rule address these deficiencies, focusing instead on teaching content (e.g., science, history, literature). It is not surprising, therefore, that many teachers were finding it difficult to teach subject matter.

The SIM framework for improving adolescent literacy is explained as existing along a continuum of literacy instruction (CLC) that provides increasing support to students at each of five levels (Deshler, Schumaker, & Woodruff, 2004). The *first level* is content enhancement. At this level, recognizing that mastery of content is critical for all students; teachers learn routines (e.g., lesson and unit organizers) for making the curriculum accessible to all students regardless of their literacy level.

At the *second level*, teachers are encouraged to routinely embed learning strategies instruction into all classes using large group instruction. At the *third level*, teachers are asked to provide students with more intensive and explicit strategy instruction as needed to support basic skills, such as decoding, word recognition, fluency, vocabulary, and comprehension. Beginning at the *fourth level* students who are lagging behind their peers receive intensive basic skills instruction. This may require collaboration with a literacy coach, special educator, or other professional. Last, the *fifth level* of instruction provides the most support. Students on this level receive individualized therapeutic interventions to help them learn the content. Instruction may take the form of strategic tutoring before, during, or after school.

In all, there are two basic types of interventions in the SIM framework. The first is a series of teacher-focused interventions directed at how teachers plan, adapt, and deliver content. Content-enhancement teaching routines, as specified in the first level of the CLC, guide planning and learning; direct exploration of text, topics, and details; how to teach concepts; and how to increase student performance. Content-enrichment routines are designed to help teachers reach an academically diverse group of students while maintaining the integrity of the content. They are appropriate for planning instruction in both general and special education settings. The second type of interventions in the SIM framework are student-focused interventions that provide students with strategies to learn content. As indicated by the CLC, strategies can either be taught independently or embedded into core content, depending on the level of support needed by the individual student. In all, there are over 30 learning strategies in SIM designed to improve students' skills and performance in the areas of reading, expressive writing, study skills and remembering, test taking, motivation, and interacting with others.

TEACHING LEARNING STRATEGIES

A strategy refers to a plan that specifies the sequence of actions needed to solve a given problem effectively (Ellis & Lenz, 1996, p. 24). Teaching learning strategies effectively involves following a multistep process:

1. Begin by *securing a commitment* to using learning strategies. To do this the teacher explains the benefits of learning strategies to the students. Due to faulty attributions,

many students do not realize that ineffective or inefficient strategy use underlies their academic difficulties.

2. *Determine where students are having difficulty* with the curriculum. Formal and informal assessment data discussed earlier in this chapter can be used for this purpose. Based on the analysis of the student's classroom performance, identify those areas that most need attention. It is helpful to prioritize problems according to the impact on learning.

3. *Select the learning strategy most appropriate for the job.* Table 11.5 provides examples of SIM learning strategies that researchers and teachers have used successfully to improve student writing performance.

4. *Provide a rationale* for why they should learn the strategy. Introduce the strategy to the students by reviewing previously mastered strategies and relate them to the new content to be learned. For example, "Yesterday, you learned how to use the five W's strategy. It helped you identify the characters, plot, and setting in the book *Moby-Dick*. Today, we will add another learning strategy. An attribute web is a strategy that will enable you to successfully complete the book report that is due Friday by helping you to identify important details in the story." This is a necessary step in securing participation and ensuring the information is retained in a meaningful way.

5. *Describe the strategy and model how to use it* by providing an example with which they are already familiar to limit processing demands. Model the strategy, checking off each step as you think aloud, talking the students through how you as an expert learner would use each of the steps in the strategy (e.g., "What do I do first?).

6. Provide opportunities for *guided practice.* As students work, the teacher provides feedback, prompts, and guidance. As they become more proficient, support is gradually faded.

7. During *independent practice*, the teacher continues to monitor student performance, conducts an error analysis when needed, and provides feedback and correction. The teacher can reteach or offer additional practice on any step of the strategy.

8. Last, *teach for generalization* by indicating how student success is directly related to using the correct strategy for the job. Point out where the strategy can be used in other academic situations with similar task demands. For example, an attribute web could also be helpful in writing book reports in both history and science class.

Although SIM has been taught with some success for years in schools nationally, it has failed to consistently ensure acquisition and generalization across settings (Spencer & Logan, 2005). You will remember from our discussions on metacognition in Chapter 6, that if there are to be any long-term benefits, cognitive strategies instruction depends at least in part on training at the metacognitive level as well as at the cognitive level (e.g., Flavell, 1979; Spencer & Logan, 2005). The lack of an explicitly taught metacognitive component, such as the one in the SRSD model, may be problematic. This component can, however, be added and/or supported by the use of metacognitive strategies (e.g., SODA).

The Early Literacy Project (ELP; Englert, Raphael, & Mariage, 1994 was a 4-year study that sought to improve the reading and writing literacy skills of young students

TABLE 11.5 Strategic Instruction Model Writing Strategies

Strategy	Author	Steps to Implementation
DEFENDS (strategy for writing positions)	Ellis & Lenz (1987)	**D**ecide on exact position. **E**xamine the reasons for the position. **F**orm a list of points that explain each reason. **E**xpose position in first sentence. **N**ote each reason and supporting points. **D**rive home the position in the last sentence. **S**earch for errors and correct.
PLEASE (strategy for writing a paragraph)	Welch (1992)	**P**ick a topic. **L**ist your ideas about the topic. **E**valuate your list. **A**ctivate the paragraph with a topic sentence. **S**upply supporting sentences. **E**nd with a concluding sentence, and **E**valuate your work.
COPS (error-monitoring strategy)	Schumaker, Nolan, & Deshler (1985)	**C**apitalization **O**verall appearance **P**unctuation **S**pelling
WRITER	Schumaker, Nolan, & Deshler (1985)	**W**rite on every other line, using PENS. **R**ead your paper for meaning. **I**nterrogate yourself, using COPS questions. **T**ake the paper to someone for help. **E**xecute a final copy. **R**eread your paper.

with mild impairments (e.g., learning disabilities, mental impairments, and emotional impairments). These students struggle with developing written literacy due to deficits in metacognitive knowledge and tend not to plan, monitor, or revise their written work (e.g., Englert et al., 1991; Graham & Harris, 2003; Williams, 2003). Difficulty generating ideas, words, and sentences serves to exacerbate their problems. It is no surprise these students' papers tend to be substantively different from those of their nondisabled peers in that they are shorter, poorly organized, and/or mechanically and grammatically challenged (Gersten & Baker, 2001; Graham, 2006).

ELP was among the first attempts to study the effects of a sociocultural learning theory curriculum on improving literacy outcome for this population. There are four principles underling the implementation and design of the ELP curriculum: (1) Literacy should be embedded within meaningful and authentic activities; (2) promote self-regulated learning; (3) instruction should be responsive to the needs, capabilities, and interests of the student; and (4) instruction should promote the social nature of learning by collaboratively constructing communities of learners (Englert & Mariage, 2005).

From within this framework, reading and writing skills are theorized as emerging from within the collaborative context of group meetings, employing a multitude of teaching methods to facilitate the development of literacy skills. The model included a variety of oral and written literacy activities, each serving a distinct purpose. Some of these activities include thematic units, choral reading, undisturbed silent reading, sharing chair, morning message, story response, journal writing, and author's center.

The ELP curriculum contains methods proven effective for teaching students with learning disabilities how to self-regulate the writing process. Using what Englert and colleagues (1988) call the POWER strategy, students have shown that they can learn to Plan, Organize, Write, Edit, and Revise their written work (Englert et al, 1988). The POWER strategy specifies hierarchical steps to follow when creating text. The planning stage prompts students to ask themselves, "What is my topic? Who am I writing for? And what do I already know about my topic?" The second step directs students to select and utilize pattern guides to help them organize their ideas. Patterns might include story guides for identifying the elements who, what, when, where, and why; compare/contrast guides for collecting information on a given topic; explanation guides for completing the writing process; and problem solution guides for identifying the problem, the cause of the problem, and the solution to the problem. The third step, writing, requires students to use information from the planning and organization steps to complete a first draft. Editing is the fourth step, and here students learn to self-evaluate and peer edit their drafts. Last, in the fifth step, revising, students incorporate edits and make changes or other improvements as they complete the writing assignment.

In 2004, Singer and Bashir altered POWER in an effort to help students with language learning disabilities who continued to struggle despite the support provided by the strategy. The revised strategy, EmPOWER, provides more linguistic structure by adding explicit step-by-step conversational prompts to replace the more abbreviated prompts of the original strategy. They also divided the plan step into two steps, Empower and mPLAN, in an effort to lessen the processing load and more clearly delineate the interdependent relationship of this component to the next. Their research suggests that these modifications can help to move students more effectively through the steps of the strategy, thus improving writing outcomes.

Englert and her colleagues are also interested in investigating the effects of varying support methodologies as means of improving the performance of low-achieving students. Their research (e.g., Englert, Manalo, & Zhao, 2004; Englert, Zhao, Dunsmore, Collins, & Wolbers, 2007; Englert, Wu, & Zhao, 2005) into the potential of Web-based programs to increase the writing performance of students with disabilities has yielded promising results. In a recent study (Englert, Zhao, Dunsmore,

Collins, & Wolbers, 2007), a control group and an experimental group of students were asked to plan and organize their ideas in order to write expository papers on topics of their choosing. Students in the experimental group used TELE-Web software that prompted them on how to frame their introductions based on their story maps, how to elaborate on paragraphs and details, and how to incorporate conclusions into the proper locations.

The students in the Web-based scaffolding condition produced lengthier pieces and received significantly higher ratings on traits associated with writing quality. However, the most significant improvement occurred in terms of the experimental students' abilities to produce topic sentences and to generate more topically coherent pieces overall. Their research suggests that a Web-based environment can be used successfully to scaffold aspects of the students' thinking processes and provide the necessary structure to write well, and it may in fact do so more effectively than a traditional paper-and-pencil format.

The Optimal Learning Environment (OLE) (Ruiz, 1995a, 1995b) program for English language learners (ELLs), bilingual students, and Spanish-speaking students shares much with the Early Literacy Project in that both models embrace sociocultural learning theory, a writing-as-a-process philosophy, and thematic units of instruction. In addition, each model advocates delivering instruction that is contextualized, meaningful, and purposeful to develop literacy skills. For Spanish-speaking students with learning disabilities, these instructional practices are proving to be particularly germane. Academic problems attributed to the typically decontextualized nature of the bilingual educational experience have led to low motivation and higher dropout rates among this population (CREDE, 2003; Ruiz, 1999).

The English immersion model, which is the most commonly used model of bilingual education in our nation's schools, does not provide students with native language learning opportunities. This is problematic, because without native language literacy learning, English can be more difficult. It seems the basic skills of the old language serve as a contextual bridge to the new language by making reading and writing meaningful and purposeful. Ruiz's OLE model recognizes this fundamental need, providing instruction and practice in the students' native language until the teacher feels they are ready for the transition to English.

The work of Ruiz and others has led to a set of five working principles for teaching Spanish-speaking and bilingual students with special needs how to write (e.g., Baca & Cervantes, 1998; Gallimore et. al., 1989; Graves, et al., 2000; Ruiz & Figueroa, 1995; Ruiz, Figueroa, Rueda, & Beaumont, 1992). These practices include the elements of both the ELP and OLE programs, as well as those of the most prestigious center for research in second language and literacy acquisition, the Center for Research on Education, Diversity, and Excellence (CREDE, 2003). The five principles are as follows:

Principle 1: Connect students' background knowledge and personal experiences with literacy lessons. Contextualize teaching and curriculum by tying instruction to home and community.

Principle 2: Foster the use of students' primary language in literacy lessons. Allow students to exercise a choice of language with text and during literacy events.

Principle 3: Create opportunities for students to meaningfully and authentically apply their developing oral language and literacy skills. Undoubtedly, basic literacy skills and subskills instruction, such as phonemic awareness, phonics, punctuation, grammar, and comprehension, are important components of any writing program. However, the research in second and foreign language education overwhelmingly establishes the link between meaning-driven, communicative instruction and second language and literacy development (CREDE, 2003; Ruiz, 1999). Language literacy development should be fostered through use and through purposive conversation between teacher and students, rather than relying solely on drills and decontextualized rules (CREDE, 2003).

Principle 4: Foster increased levels of interaction (oral language, reading, and writing) among students and teachers. Provide authentic reasons for students to collaborate on literacy and other academic tasks to improve ELL students' productive and receptive language skills (Gersten & Baker, 2003).

Principle 5: Engage students through dialogue, especially instructional conversation. ELL programs place a great deal of emphasis on developing communication competence. The OLE program utilizes interactive journaling for this purpose. This instructional strategy enacts the four principles of effective instruction, in that when writing in their interactive journals, students communicate with either teachers or peers on the topic of their choice and receive written responses to their journal entries. They are therefore able to bring their life experiences to the literacy event (Principle 1) to use the language of their choice (Principle 2), to exchange messages with real communicative intent with a real audience, and (Principle 3) to facilitate learning through collaborative dialogue with teacher and peers for authentic purposes (Principles 4 and 5).

In addition to the interactive journaling method, the OLE curriculum contains several strategies to facilitate the development of written literacy skills:

1. Writers workshop teaches writing as a process in the context of an authentic activity. Students learn that before producing each written product they must follow the steps of planning, writing a draft, and editing.
2. Patterned writing strategies have students read and copy key phrases.
3. Teachers provide wordless books, and students create the text.
4. Shared reading activities with predictable text lead to conversations with teachers and peers on literature from read-alouds.
5. Utilize "drop everything and read" time (DEAR) to encourage the development reading and writing literacy skills.

Summary

Students who struggle with writing share many of the same characteristics. Poor planning and revising of their work results in work that is poorly organized and shorter and typically contains irrelevant details and more mechanical errors and is weaker overall when compared to their more accomplished peers (Troia, 2005). These types of difficulties with written expression are attributable to an inability to execute and regulate the cognitive and metacognitive processes underlying writing (e.g., Graham, 2006; Graham & Harris

1997). Contrary to what many believe, simply having a plethora of writing strategies on hand is not as important as knowing when and how to use them. In short, the lack of regulatory ability can cause these students to experience more writing and motivational issues than do their peers (Pajares, 2003).

As noted, writing instruction for students with and without writing problems identify many of the same critical components of effective instruction and are congruent with the principles of effective instruction as noted in the bilingual education literature (e.g., Baker, Gersten, & Graham, 2003; Gersten & Baker, 2001; Gleason & Isaacson; 2001; Troia, 2005). While it is indeed necessary to identify research-validated instructional methods, it is but the first step. Sadly, research suggests that teachers implement few if any of them to help students who are struggling with basic writing skills (e.g., Graham & Harris, 2003). Do you know why? A review of Chapter 6 on metacognition will provide the answer to this vexing question.

References

American Speech-Language Association. (2008). *Speech and language disorders*. Retrieved September 7, 2008, from http://www.asha.org/public/speech/disorders/ChildSandL.htm

Anderson, L. W., & Krathwohl, J. (2001). *A taxonomy for learning, teaching, and assessing: A revision of Bloom's Taxonomy of educational objectives*. New York: Longman.

Applebee, A. N., & Langer, J. A. (2006). *The state of writing instruction in America's schools: What existing data tell us*. Albany: Center on English Learning & Achievement, State University of New York at Albany. Retrieved September 7, 2008, from http://www.albany.edu/aire/news/State%20of%20Writing%20Instruction.pdf

August, D., & Shanahan, T. (Eds.). (2006). *Developing literacy in second-language learners: Report of the National Literacy Panel on Language-Minority Children and Youth*. Mahwah, NJ: Lawrence Erlbaum Associates. Retrieved from http://www.cal.org/natl-lit-panel/reports/Executive_Summary.pdf

Baca, L., & Cervantes, H. (1998). *The bilingual special education interface* (3rd ed.). Upper Saddle River, NJ: Prentice Hall.

Baker, S., Gersten, R., & Graham, S. (2003). Teaching expressive writing to students with learning disabilities: Research-based applications and examples. *Journal of Learning Disabilities, 36*, 109–123.

Barry, L. M., & Moore, W. E. (2004). Students with specific learning disabilities can pass state competency exams: Systematic strategy instruction makes a difference. *Preventing School Failure, 48*(3), 10–15.

Bloom, B., Englehart, M., Furst, E., Hill, W., & Krathwohl, D. (1956). *Taxonomy of educational objectives: The classification of educational goals. Handbook I: Cognitive domain*. New York, Toronto: Longmans, Green.

Brady, R. C. (2003). *Can failing schools be fixed?* Washington, DC: Thomas B. Fordham Foundation. Retrieved September 3, 2005, from http://www.edexcellence.net/institute/publication/publication.cfm?id=2

Brookhart, S. M. (1999). The art and science of classroom assessment: The missing part of pedagogy. *ASHE-ERIC Higher Education Report, 27*(1). Washington, DC: The George Washington University, Graduate School of Education and Human Development.

Chalk, J. C., Hagan-Burke, S., & Burke, M. D. (2005). Self-regulated strategy development and the writing process for high school students with learning disabilities. *Learning Disability Quarterly, 28*, 75–87.

Cohen, L. G., & Spenciner, L. J. (2007). *Assessment of children and youth with special needs*. Boston: Allyn & Bacon.

Cramer, R. L. (2001). *Creative power: The nature and nurture of children's writing*. Boston: Addison-Wesley, Longman.

CREDE (Center for Research on Education, Diversity, and Excellence). (2003). Santa Cruz, California. Retrieved from www://crede.ucsc.edu

De La Paz, S. (1997). Strategy instruction in planning: Teaching students with learning and writing disabilities to compose narrative and expository essays. *Learning Disability Quarterly, 20,* 227–248.

De La Paz, S., Owen, B., Harris, K., & Graham, S. (2000). Riding Elvis's motorcycle: Using self-regulated strategy development to PLAN and WRITE for a state writing exam. *Learning Disabilities Research and Practice, 15*(2), 101–109.

De La Paz, S., & Graham, S. (2002). Explicitly teaching strategies, skills, and knowledge: Writing instruction in middle school classrooms. *Journal of Educational Psychology, 94,* 687–698.

Deshler, D. D., & Schumaker, J. B. (1988). An instructional model for teaching students how to learn. In J. L. Graden, J. E. Zins, & M. J. Curtis (Eds.), *Alternative educational delivery systems: Enhancing instructional options for all students* (pp. 391–411). Washington, DC: National Association of School Psychologists.

Deshler, D. D., Schumaker, J. B., & Woodruff, S. (2004). Improving literacy skills of at-risk adolescents. In D. Strickland & D. Alvermann (Eds.), *Bridging the literacy achievement gap, Grades 4–12.* New York: Teachers College Press.

Dyson, A. H., & Freedman, S. W. (1991). Writing. In J. Flood, J. Jensen, D. Lapp, & J. Squire (Eds.), *Handbook of research on teaching the English language arts* (pp. 754–775). New York: Macmillan.

Ellis, E. S., & Lenz, B. K. (1987). *Features of good learning strategies.* Retrieved November 6, 2008, from http://www.ldonline.org/ld_indepth/teaching_techniques/ellis_strategy features.html

Englert, C. S., Zhao, Y., Dunsmore, K., Collings, N. Y., Wolbers, K. (2007). Scaffolding the writing of students with disabilities through procedural facilitation: Using an Internet-based technology to improve performance. *Learning Disability Quarterly, 30,* 9–29.

Englert, C. S., Garmon, A., Mariage, T., Rozendal, M., Tarrant, K., & Urba, J. (1995). The early literacy project: Connecting across the literacy curriculum. *Learning Disabilities Quarterly, 18,* 253–277.

Englert, C. S., Manalo, M., & Zhao, Y. (2004). I can do it better on the computer: The effects of technology-enabled scaffolding on young writers' composition. *Journal of Special Education Technology, 19*(1), 5–21.

Englert, C. S., & Mariage, T. V. (2003). Shared understandings: Structuring the writing process through dialogue. In D. Carine & E. Kameenui (Eds.), *Higher order thinking* (pp. 107–136). Austin, TX: Pro-Ed.

Englert, C. S., & Mariage, T. V. (2005). The sociocultural model in special education interventions: Apprenticing students in higher order thinking. In H. L. Swanson, K.R. Harris, & S. Graham, (Eds.), *The handbook of learning disabilities* (pp. 450–467). New York: Guilford Press.

Englert, C., Raphael, T., Anderson, L., Anthony, H., Steven, D., & Fear, K. (1991). Making writing and self-talk visible: Cognitive strategy instruction writing in regular and special education classrooms. *American Educational Research Journal, 28,* 337–373.

Englert, C., Raphael, L., Fear, K., & Anderson, L. (1988). Students' metacognitive knowledge about how to write informational texts. *Learning Disability Quarterly, 11,* 18–46.

Englert, C. S., Raphael, T. E., & Mariage, T. V. (1994). Developing a school-based discourse for literacy learning: A principled search for understanding. *Learning Disability Quarterly, 17,* 2–32.

Englert, C. S., Wu, X., & Zhao, Y. (2005). Cognitive tools for writing: Scaffolding the performance of students through technology. *Learning Disabilities Research and Practice, 20,* 184–198.

Flavell, J. H. (1979). Metacognition and cognitive monitoring: A new area of cognitive–developmental inquiry. *American Psychologist, 34,* 906–911.

Gallimore, R., Tharp, R., & Rueda, R. (1989). *The social context of cognitive functioning in the lives of mildly handicapped persons.* London: Falmer Press.

Gersten, R., & Baker, S. (2001). Teaching expressive writing to students with learning disabilities: A meta-analysis. *Elementary School Journal, 101*(3), 251–272.

Gersten, R., & Baker, S. K. (2003). English-language learners with learning disabilities. In S. Graham (Ed.), *Handbook of learning disabilities* (pp. 94–109). New York: Guilford Press.

Gleason, M. M., & Isaacson, S. (2001). Using the new basals to teach the writing process:

Modification for students with learning problems. *Reading & Writing Quarterly, 17,* 75–92.

Goldstein, A., & Carr, P. G. (1996, April). *Can students benefit from process writing? NAEP facts, 1*(3). Washington, DC: National Center for Educational Statistics. Retrieved September 28, 2008, from http://nces.ed.gov/pubs96/web/96845.asp

Graham, S. (2006). Strategy instruction and the teaching of writing: A meta-analysis. In C. A. MacArthur, S. Graham, & J. Fitzgerald (Eds.), *Handbook of writing research* (pp. 187–207). New York: Guilford Press.

Graham, S. (2006). Writing. In P. A. Alexander & P. H. Winne (Eds.), *Handbook of educational psychology* (pp. 457–478). Mahwah, NJ: Lawrence Erlbaum Associates.

Graham, S., & Harris, K. R. (1989). Improving learning disabled students' skills at composing essays: Self-instructional strategy training. *Exceptional Children, 56,* 201–214.

Graham, S., & Harris, K. R. (1994). The effects of whole language on children's writing: A review of literature. *Educational Psychologist, 29,* 187–192.

Graham, S., & Harris, K. R. (1997). It can be taught, but it does not develop naturally: Myths and realities in writing instruction. *School Psychology Review, 26,* 414–424.

Graham, S., & Harris, K. R. (2003). Students with learning disabilities and the process of writing: A meta-analysis of SRSD studies. In H.L. Swanson, K. R. Harris, & S. Graham (Eds.), *Handbook of learning disabilities* (pp. 323–344). New York: Guilford Press.

Graham, S., Harris, K. R., & Macarthur, C. (2006). Explicitly teaching struggling writers: Strategies for mastering the writing process. *Intervention in School & Clinic, 41*(5), 290. Retrieved September 7, 2008, from Questia database: http://www.questia.com/PM.qst?a=o&d=5015045196

Graham, S., MacArthur, C., Schwartz, S., & Page-Voth, V. (1992). Improving the compositions of students with learning disabilities using a strategy involving product and process goal setting. *Exceptional Children, 58,* 322–334.

Graham, S., & Perin, D. (2007). *Writing next: Effective strategies to improve writing of adolescents in middle and high schools* (Carnegie Corporation Report). Washington, DC: Alliance for Excellent Education. Retrieved November 14, 2008, from http://www.all4ed.org/publications/WritingNext/WritingNext.pdf

Graves, A., Valles, E., & Prodor, C. (2000). The effects of optimal learning environment (OLE) vs. traditional instruction on compositions of bilingual students with learning disabilities. *Learning Disabilities Research & Practice, 15,* 1–9.

Gray, J. (2000). *Teachers at the center: A memoir of the early years of the National Writing Project.* Berkley, CA: National Writing Project. Retrieved September 27, 2008, from http://www.eric.ed.gov/ERICWebPortal/custom/portlets/recordDetails/detailmini.jsp?_nfpb=true&_&ERICExtSearch_SearchValue_0=ED461882&ERICExtSearch_SearchType_0=no&accno=ED461882

Hammill, D. D., & Larsen, S. C. (1996). *Test of written language* (3rd ed.). Austin, TX: Pro-Ed.

Harris, K. R., & Graham, S. (1992). Self-regulated strategy development: A part of the writing process. In M. Pressley, K. Harris, & J. Guthrie (Eds.), *Promoting academic competence and literacy in schools.* San Diego: Academic Press.

Harris, K. R., & Graham, S. (2005). *Writing better: Teaching writing processes and self-regulation to students with learning problems.* Baltimore: Paul H. Brookes.

Hooper, S., Wakely, M., de Kruif, R., & Schwartz, C. (2006). Aptitude-treatment interactions revisited: Effect of metacognitive intervention on subtypes of written expression in elementary school students. *Developmental Neuropsychology, 39,* 217–242.

Hillocks, G. (1984). What works in teaching composition: A meta-analysis of experimental treatment studies. *American Journal of Education, 93*(1), 133–170.

Hresko, W. P., Herron, S., & Peak, P. (1996). *Test of Early Writing,* second edition. Austin, TX: Pro-Ed.

Kuhl, P. K. (2008). Linking infant speech perception to language acquisition: Phonetic learning predicts language growth. In P. McCardle, J. Colombo, & L. Freund (Eds.), *Infant pathways to language: Methods, models, and research directions.* Mahwah, NJ: Lawrence Erlbaum Associates.

Kuhl, P. K., Conboy, B. T., Padden, D., Nelson, T., & Pruitt, J. (2005). Early speech perception and later language development: Implications for the "critical period." *Language Learning and Development*, 1, 237–264.

Lennox, C., & Siegel, L. S. (1996). The development of phonological rules and visual strategies in average and poor spellers. *Journal of Experimental Child Psychology*, 62, 60–83.

Lennox, C., & Siegel, L. S. (1998). Phonological and orthographic processes in good and poor spellers. In C. Hume & R. M. Joshi (Eds.), *Reading and spelling development and disorders* (pp. 395–404). Mahwah, NJ: Lawrence Erlbaum Associates. Retrieved on September 1, 2007, from Questia database: http://www.questia.com/PM.qst?a=o&d=113675485

Levy, C. M. & Ransdell, S. (1995). Is writing as difficult as it seems? *Memory & Cognition*, 23, 767–779.

MacArthur, C. A., Graham, S., & Fitzgerald, J. (Eds.). (2006). *Handbook of writing research*. New York: Guilford Press. Retrieved September 7, 2008, from Questia database: http://www.questia.com/PM.qst?a=o&d=113675485

McGhee, R., Bryant, B., Larsen, S., & Rivera, D. M. (1995). *Test of written expression*. Austin, TX: Pro-Ed.

National Assessment of Educational Progress. (2002, 2003, 2005, 2007). *The nation's report card: Writing 2007. National assessment of educational progress at grades 8 and 12*. Washington, DC: U.S. Department of Education, National Center for Education Statistics. Retrieved on September 1, 2008, from http://nces.ed.gov/nationsreportcard/pdf/main2007/2008468_1.pdf

Page-Voth, V., & Graham, S. (1999). Effects of goal setting and strategy use on the writing performance and self-efficacy of students with writing and learning problems. *Journal of Educational Psychology*, 91, 230–240.

Pajares, F. (2003). Self-efficacy beliefs, motivation, and achievement in writing: A review of the literature. *Reading and Writing Quarterly*, 19, 139–158.

Patthey-Chavez, G. G, Matsumura, L. C., & Valdes, R. (2004). Investigating the process approach to writing instruction in urban middle schools. *Journal of Adolescent and Adult Literacy*, 47(6), 642–476.

Pierangelo, R., & Giuliani, G. (2006). *The special educator's comprehensive guide to 301 diagnostic tests: Revised and expanded edition*. San Francisco: Jossey-Bass.

Ruiz, N. T., Figueroa, R. A., Rueda, R., & Beaumont, C. (1992). History and status of bilingual students in special education. In R. Padilla & A. Benavides (Eds.), *Critical perspectives in bilingual education* (pp. 349–380). Tempe, AZ: Bilingual Press.

Ruiz, N. T. (1995a). The social construction of ability and disability I: Profile types of Latino children identified as language learning disabled. *Journal of Learning Disabilities, 28*, 476–490.

Ruiz, N. T. (1995b). The social construction of ability and disability II: Optimal and at-risk lessons in a bilingual special education classroom. *Journal of Learning Disabilities, 28*, 491–502.

Ruiz, N. T., & Figueroa, R. A. (1995). Learning-handicapped classrooms with Latino students: The optimal learning environment (OLE) project. *Education and Urban Society, 27*, 463–483.

Ruiz, N. T. (1999). Effective literacy instruction for Latino students receiving special education services. *Bilingual Review*, 161–164. Retrieved November 23, 2008, from Questia database: http://www.questia.com/PM.qst?a=o&d=5001895873

Salvia, J., & Ysseldyke, J. E. (2007). *Assessment in special and inclusive education* (10th ed.). Boston: Houghton Mifflin.

Schumaker, J. D., Nolan, S. M. & Deshler, D. D. (1985). *The error monitoring strategy*. Lawrence: Center for Research on Learning, University of Kansas.

Singer, B. D., & Bashir, A. S. (2004). EmPOWER: A strategy for teaching students with language learning disabilities how to write expository text. In E. R. Silliman, R. Elaine, & L. C. Wilkinson (Eds.), *Language and literacy learning in schools* (pp. 239–272). New York: Guilford Press.

Spencer, S. S., & Logan, K. R. (2005). Improving students with learning disabilities ability to acquire and generalize a vocabulary learning strategy. *Learning Disabilities: A Multidisciplinary Journal, 13*, 87–94.

Tachibana, G. (2008). "Nation's Report Card" shows modest improvement in students' writing scores. Retrieved from http://www.nwp.org/cs/public/print/resource/2557

Tallal, P. (2008). *Neuroscience, phonology, and reading: The oral to written language continuum*. Retrieved October 9, 2008, from Rutgers University, Children of the Code Web site: http://www.childrenofthecode.org/interviews/tallal.htm

Taylor, R. (2006) *Assessment of exceptional students: Educational and psychological procedures*. Upper Saddle River, NJ: Allyn & Bacon/Pearson Education.

Troia, G. A., & Graham, S. (2002). The effectiveness of a highly explicit, teacher-directed strategy instruction routine: Changing the writing performance of students with learning disabilities. *Journal of Learning Disabilities*, 35, 290–305.

Troia, G. A. (2002). Teaching writing strategies to children with disabilities: Setting generalization as the goal. *Exceptionality*, 10, 249–269.

Troia, G. A. (2005). Responsiveness to intervention roles for speech language pathologists in the prevention and identification of learning disabilities. *Topics in Language Disorders*, 25(2), 106–119.

Van den Bergh, H., & Rijlaarsdam, G. (2001). Changes in cognitive activities during the writing process and relationships with text quality. *Educational Psychology*, 21(4), 373–385.

Venn, J. J. (2007) *Assessing students with special needs* (4th ed.). Upper Saddle River, NJ: Merrill/Pearson Education.

Warden, M. R., & Hutchinson, T. A. (1992). *Writing process test*. Chicago: Riverside.

Welch, M. (1992). The PLEASE strategy: A metacognitive learning strategy for improving the paragraph writing of students with mild learning disabilities. *Learning Disabilities Quarterly*, 15, 119–128.

Wilkinson, G. S., & Robinson, G. J. (2006). *Wide Range Achievement Test 4*. Richmond Hill, Onterio: Psycan Educational and Clinical Resources.

Williams, J. P. (2003). Teaching text structure to improve reading comprehension. In H. L. Swanson, K. R. Harris, & S. Graham (Eds.), *Handbook of learning disabilities* (pp. 293–305). New York: Guilford Press.

Wolf, M. A., & Hall, S. (July, 2005). Fighting the good fight. *T. H. E. Journal*, 32, 12. Retrieved September 3, 2008, from http://www.thejournal.com/magazine/vault/A5398.cfm

Woodcock, R. W., McGrew, K. S., & Mather, N. (2001). *Woodcock–Johnson III*. Allen, TX: DLM.

Facilitating Writing

From Chapter 13 of *Teaching Students Who Are Exceptional, Diverse, and At Risk in the General Education Classroom*, 5/e. Sharon Vaughn. Candace S. Bos. Jeanne Shay Schumm. Copyright © 2011 by Pearson Education. All rights reserved.

Facilitating Writing

Scott Cunningham/Merrill

FOCUS QUESTIONS

1. What are the current trends in writing curriculum and instruction and how do they align with your beliefs about writing instruction? How do your beliefs compare with belief statements published by the National Council of Teachers of English?

2. What are advantages of teaching writing as a process and how does this process promote effective writing instruction for all learners?

3. What strategies can you implement to establish an environment that promotes writing?

4. What strategies can you implement for conducting effective writing workshops?

5. What strategies can you implement for students who have difficulties writing stories?

6. What strategies can you implement for students who have difficulties with narrative writing?

7. What strategies can you implement for students who have difficulties with informational writing?

8. What strategies can you implement to help students who have difficulties with persuasive writing?

9. What strategies can you implement to help all students develop spelling skills?

10. What strategies can you implement to help all students develop handwriting skills?

INTERVIEW
MICHELLE LANGLOIS

Michelle Langlois is a special education teacher who has worked for 5 years at the elementary level as an "inclusion" teacher providing instructional support to teachers and specialized instruction to students with disabilities in kindergarten through third grade. During the past year she decided to tackle a new challenge and accepted a transfer to a middle school where she worked as a resource teacher with 18 students with disabilities. Michelle was very confident about her successes in teaching writing at the elementary school but was less confident after her first year teaching middle school.

Well I'm not sure who learned more this year, the students or me. I'm just kidding—I think—but it was a big learning experience for me. You see, when I taught elementary inclusion classes I worked cooperatively with a team of the kindergarten through third-grade teachers to establish writing centers that would give students experience in all of the elements of writing including composing, editing, rewriting, and publishing. We all agreed that students needed time to practice the craft of writing and to learn that good writers read and rewrite their work and then receive feedback from others including their classmates before revising and publishing. We didn't just let students develop writing independently but provided explicit instruction in those critical skills associated with effective writing including spelling, punctuation, and elements of

grammar. However, we all seemed to agree on the procedures and shared a common language for how we talked about writing and instruction to students.

I found that when I came to the middle school, many of the teachers were not accustomed to having the special education teacher be an active member of the team. I was hoping that I could extend many of the practices I used at the elementary level to establish and promote writing instruction across the content area using research-based instructional practices that would promote writing for all learners but especially for students with disabilities. For example, we know that when students identify the topic they are writing about and use a graphic organizer to help them include critical ideas, key words, and important parts of the writing piece (e.g., introduction, summary), students produce better writing. I was encouraging all of the middle-school teachers to work with me to identify common writing strategies we would all use—that way students could learn the new strategies and practice them across content areas. I was optimistic that I could then reinforce these instructional strategies by teaching and applying them in the resource room. I was not as successful at instituting these practices as I would like to have been though I am optimistic that many of the teachers I worked with last year had a positive experience and that we will start off this next year with these teachers eager to continue our work together.

Introduction

Like many teachers who have acquired knowledge about effective instructional practices and are eager to share them with other teachers, Michelle found that the process works best when the professional development includes open communication and careful planning. In this chapter, you will first read about current trends in writing curricula. The chapter continues with suggestions for helping all students succeed in composition of various genres, spelling, and handwriting.

Current Trends in Writing Curriculum and Instruction

Michelle realized that research-based writing practices can be applied at both the elementary and the secondary level and are especially helpful to students with disabilities who are included in general education classrooms. However, there are competing issues such as high-stakes assessment that influence writing curriculum. Current trends in writing curriculum and instruction include

- Movement toward standards-based writing instruction and research-based practices.
- Increased emphasis on assessment.
- Emphasis on balanced and effective writing instruction for all students.
- Implementation of writing practices that are based on research and represent standardized writing and spelling outcomes.

Standards-Based Writing Instruction and Research-Based Practices

Teachers such as Michelle realize that they need to consider the writing standards of the state in which they teach. Most frequently, state standards are based on standards recommended by professional organizations such as the International Reading Association and the National Council of Teachers of English (see Figure 13.1).

One way to ensure high-quality writing instruction is through the use of research-based practices. No Child Left Behind mandates "an emphasis on implementing education programs and practices that have been clearly demonstrated to be effective through rigorous scientific

FIGURE 13.1

International Reading Association/National Council of Teachers of English Standards

IRA/NCTE Standards for the English Language Arts

The 12 Standards

The vision guiding these standards is that all students must have the opportunities and resources to develop the language skills they need to pursue life's goals and to participate fully as informed, productive members of society. These standards assume that literacy growth begins before children enter school as they experience and experiment with literacy activities—reading and writing, and associating spoken words with their graphic representations. Recognizing this fact, these standards encourage the development of curriculum and instruction that make productive use of the emerging literacy abilities that children bring to school. Furthermore, the standards provide ample room for the innovation and creativity essential to teaching and learning. They are not prescriptions for particular curriculum or instruction.

1. Students read a wide range of print and nonprint texts to build an understanding of texts, of themselves, and of the cultures of the United States and the world; to acquire new information; to respond to the needs and demands of society and the workplace; and for personal fulfillment. Among these texts are fiction and nonfiction, classic and contemporary works.

2. Students read a wide range of literature from many periods in many genres to build an understanding of the many dimensions (e.g., philosophical, ethical, aesthetic) of human experience.

3. Students apply a wide range of strategies to comprehend, interpret, evaluate, and appreciate texts. They draw on their prior experience, their interactions with other readers and writers, their knowledge of word meaning and of other texts, their word identification strategies, and their understanding of textual features (e.g., sound–letter correspondence, sentence structure, context, graphics).

4. Students adjust their use of spoken, written, and visual language (e.g., conventions, style, vocabulary) to communicate effectively with a variety of audiences and for different purposes.

5. Students employ a wide range of strategies as they write and use different writing process elements appropriately to communicate with different audiences for a variety of purposes.

6. Students apply knowledge of language structure, language conventions (e.g., spelling and punctuation), media techniques, figurative language, and genre to create, critique, and discuss print and nonprint texts.

7. Students conduct research on issues and interests by generating ideas and questions, and by posing problems. They gather, evaluate, and synthesize data from a variety of sources (e.g., print and nonprint texts, artifacts, people) to communicate their discoveries in ways that suit their purpose and audience.

8. Students use a variety of technological and information resources (e.g., libraries, databases, computer networks, video) to gather and synthesize information and to create and communicate knowledge.

9. Students develop an understanding of and respect for diversity in language use, patterns, and dialects across cultures, ethnic groups, geographic regions, and social roles.

10. Students whose first language is not English make use of their first language to develop competency in the English language arts and to develop understanding of content across the curriculum.

11. Students participate as knowledgeable, reflective, creative, and critical members of a variety of literacy communities.

12. Students use spoken, written, and visual language to accomplish their own purposes (e.g., for learning, enjoyment, persuasion, and the exchange of information).

Source: National Council of Teachers of English and International Reading Association. (1998–2008). *Standards for the English language arts* (p. 3). Urbana, IL: Authors. Reprinted with permission.

Tips FOR TEACHERS 13.1

RESEARCH-BASED WRITING PRACTICES

- Teaching students writing strategies that include planning, revising, and editing their compositions. Many of the writing strategies discussed previously were developed to meet this recommendation.

- Helping students to combine sentences to achieve more complex sentence types and to summarize texts.

- Providing opportunities for students to work together in pairs and groups toward cooperative written products to facilitate quality of composition.

- Establishing goals for students' writing to improve outcomes.

- Giving students access to and instruction in word processing to facilitate writing.

- Assisting students in developing prewriting practices that help generate or organize ideas for writing.

- Using inquiry activities to analyze data related to writing reports.

- Using writing process approaches that provide extended time for writing and revision.

- Providing students with good models of writing to study and to compare with their own writing.

- Integrating writing as a tool to enhance content knowledge.

Source: Information from Graham, S. & Perrin, D. (2007). A meta-analysis of writing instruction for adolescent students. *Journal of Educational Psychology, 99,*445–476.

research" (U.S. Department of Education, 2004, p. 5). A growing body of knowledge exists that can ensure success in learning to write—even among students for whom learning to write is difficult, including students with learning disabilities (Graham & Perin, 2007) and English language learners (Graves, Valles, & Rueda, 2000). However, Baker, Gersten, and Graham (2003) emphasize the importance of teaching students strategies for composing text and for giving students specific feedback to help them improve their writing. Some of the research-based instructional practices for improving writing are provided in Tips for Teachers 13.1.

Emphasis on Assessment and Progress Monitoring

Many states now require high-stakes writing tests that potentially affect student promotion and graduation from high school. The emphasis on student outcomes has spawned greater emphasis on ongoing student progress monitoring and providing students with specific feedback about their performance. Although the debate about high-stakes tests will continue, the importance of learning to communicate in the written word using a variety of media and technologies remains. Students need feedback and monitoring to help them achieve success in written communication. Moreover, students with difficulties in writing need intensive and sustained interventions to improve their writing (e.g., Ferretti, Andrews-Weckerly, & Lewis, 2007). Figure 13.2 provides features of exemplary writing instruction.

Progress Monitoring and Writing

Why is it a good idea to monitor the progress of students with writing difficulties? When teachers monitor students' progress on critical elements regularly (at least every 2 weeks), students may make notable progress. Teachers record students' progress so that they, the students, and parents can see progress, such as the number of words written for younger children and developing a checklist of story elements and their quality for older students.

Teachers monitor students' progress by noting

- Whether students can complete the written project
- How proficient they are at each element of the writing process (e.g., planning, spelling, handwriting, composing)
- Whether they can apply the skills and knowledge to other contexts (e.g., at other times during the day)
- How they explain the process they are using

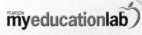
myeducationlab
Go to the Building Teaching Skills and Dispositions section of Topic 6: Assessment in the MyEducationLab for your course and complete the activity entitled *Assessing Students' Written Work.*

Go to **www.nwrel.org/edservices**, where you can read about writing assessment and instruction called 6 + 1 Trait Writing as well as other programs.

Features of Exemplary Writing Instruction

FIGURE 13.2

- A literate classroom environment where students' written work is prominently displayed, the room is packed with writing and reading material, and word lists adorn the walls.

- Daily writing with students working on a wide range of writing tasks for multiple audiences, including writing at home.

- Extensive efforts to make writing motivating by setting an exciting mood, creating a risk-free environment, allowing students to select their own writing topics or modify teacher assignments, developing assigned topics compatible with students' interests, reinforcing children's accomplishments, specifying the goal for each lesson, and promoting an "I can" attitude.

- Regular teacher–student conferences concerning the writing topic the student is currently working on, including the establishment of goals or criteria to guide the child's writing and revising efforts.

- A predictable writing routine where students are encouraged to think, reflect, and revise.

- Overt teacher modeling of the process of writing as well as positive attitudes toward writing.

- Cooperative arrangements where students help each other plan, draft, revise, edit, or publish their written work.

- Group or individual sharing where students present work in progress or completed papers to their peers for feedback.

- Instruction covering a broad range of skills, knowledge, [and] strategies, including phonological awareness, handwriting and spelling, writing conventions, sentence-level skills, text structure, functions of writing, and planning and revising.

- Follow-up instruction to ensure mastery of targeted writing skills, knowledge, and strategies.

- Integration of writing activities across the curriculum and the use of reading to support writing development.

- Frequent opportunities for students to self-regulate their behavior during writing, including working independently, arranging their own space, and seeking help from others.

- Teacher and student assessments of writing progress, strengths, and needs.

- Periodic conferences with parents and frequent communications with home about the writing program and students' progress as writers.

Source: Information from Graham, S., Harris, K.R. & Larsen, L. (2001). Prevention and intervention of writing difficulties for students with learning disabilities. *Learning disabilities research and practice, 16,* 74–84.

For example, as students write, teachers notice what strategies they use to compose text (e.g., outline, notes, keywords), reflect on the appropriateness of the task and teaching presentation, and keep written records to document student progress, such as notes, checklists, and samples of students' work. Monitoring students' progress in writing involves evaluating written products and observing the writing process. Teachers can observe students as they write and use conference times to assess and record their progress. By observing and examining writing processes and products, teachers can plan instruction to meet individual needs.

Many teachers keep anecdotal records by creating a record sheet to quickly document students' progress on writing projects. They include a summary of what they observe, the date, and context, and they list skills and writing strategies that need to be taught. Collections of students' written work help teachers, parents, and students to document growth and development as it occurs during the school year. Journals and writing folders also provide insight into writing growth. Teachers may periodically review and select representative pieces to show writing development and use progress monitoring as a means to establish writing goals for students.

Perhaps the most important activity is to determine how the teacher will measure writing progress for each student. For example, for young students, the teacher may monitor the number of words written, number of words spelled correctly, and use of capital letters and punctuation. As students mature in their writing, the teacher may decide to monitor the use of adjectives and vivid verbs, facility in editing and revising, and overall quality of the writing. It is important to focus on only one or two things at a time. After students demonstrate progress in the target areas, the teacher can add other elements of writing. This way, progress is recorded, and students are not overwhelmed by the number of writing conventions that they need to monitor.

Response to Intervention and Writing

Documenting students' response to writing instruction is a useful way of providing valuable information that would assist in determining whether they require special education or, for those students already receiving special education, whether they are making adequate progress in writing. How might response to intervention be used for students with writing difficulties? Students with extreme writing challenges should be provided extra time each day (20 minutes) and extra instruction to determine whether their writing improved. Teachers can maintain copies of students' writing to determine whether adequate progress in writing has occurred.

Writing Rubrics and Portfolios

Writing rubrics and portfolios can be used to structure assessment. These tools are helpful for both teachers and students in that they serve as a gauge of student progress.

Writing Rubrics. A writing rubric is a scoring guide that outlines expected performance on a written product. There are many variations of formats for rubrics (Arter & McTighe, 2000; Flynn & Flynn, 2004), but most include levels of performance from unacceptable to proficient. Rubrics can be developed by schools, district, or states based on required standards for writing. Textbook publishers are including more rubrics as supplemental material. A number of rubrics and "rubric generators" are available online. Teachers and students can construct rubrics as well (see examples in Figure 13.3). Often rubrics are accompanied by writing samples or exemplars that demonstrate different levels of performance.

Whatever the source, rubrics are best used to clarify what students are being expected to do and to provide a framework for self-, peer-, and teacher evaluation. Rubrics can also be used to give guided feedback that will direct students in reaching higher levels of performance. It is useful for parents to be informed about the number of levels in your rubric (the more levels the better) and the meaning of the categories in the rubric (e.g., what do you mean by "mechanical errors"), so that they can provide support to their youngster at home.

Writing Portfolios. You can use several types of writing portfolios in your classroom. Strickland, Galda, and Cullinan (2004) mention four types:

1. Showcase portfolios (featuring best work)
2. Documentation portfolios (includes artifacts over a period of time)
3. Process portfolios (evidence of development of a single piece from beginning to end)
4. Evaluation portfolios (used to determine grades based on a predetermined set of standards)

The type of portfolio you use will depend on your state and district requirements and on your own decision about how you want to track student progress and report to parents and administrators. Tips for Teachers 13.2 provides suggestions for implementing writing portfolios in your classroom.

FIGURE 13.3

Sample Rubric for Writing

	TIP TOP	PRETTY GOOD	GETTING THERE	KEEP WORKING
MEANING	Message clear, easy to follow	Message mostly clear and easy to follow	Message somewhat clear or easy to follow	Message not clear, hard to follow
PARAGRAPHS	Indented, has a main idea, and connects with paragraphs before and after	Mostly indented, has a main idea, and connects with paragraphs before and after	Mostly indented, has a main idea, or connects with paragraphs before and after	Not indented, has no main idea, and does not connect with paragraphs before and after
SENTENCES	Expresses complete thoughts and uses correct punctuation	Mostly expresses complete thoughts and uses correct punctuation	Mostly expresses complete thoughts or uses correct punctuation	Does not express complete thoughts nor use correct punctuation
WORDS	Spelling correct, capitalization correct, and uses a variety of words	Spelling mostly correct, capitalization mostly correct, and/or some use of a variety of words	Spelling needs correction, capitalization needs correction, or needs more use of a variety of words	Spelling needs correction, capitalization needs correction, and needs more use of a variety of words
NEATNESS	Easy to read and follows directions for format	Mostly easy to read and follows directions for format	Mostly easy to read or follows directions for format	Hard to read and does not follow directions for format

Source: Schumm, J.S. (2005). *How to help your child with homework* (p. 71). Copyright © 2005. Used with permission of Free Spirit Publishing, Inc., Minneapolis, MN; 1-866-703-7322; www.freespirit.com. All rights reserved.

Tips FOR TEACHERS 13.2

IMPLEMENTING WRITING PORTFOLIOS

- Introduce the portfolio. Describe the purpose for the portfolio, intended use and audience, type of artifacts to include, and examples.

- Introduce the rubric or scoring guide. Explain how the portfolio will be evaluated and by whom (e.g., teacher, parent, peer, self).

- Explain guidelines for inclusion of artifacts, including electronic artifacts.

- Outline logistical and ethical issues: how materials will be housed and maintained, appropriate times and procedures for working on the portfolio, and who has access to materials.

- Assist student in setting personal goals and planning artifacts/projects to meet those goals.

- Provide guided experiences for students to reflect on their work and to document those reflections.

Source: Adapted from Gredler, M. E. & Johnson, R. L. (2004). _Assessment in the literacy classroom._ Boston: Allyn & Bacon. Copyright © 2005 by Pearson Education. Adapted by permission of the publisher.

Teaching Writing as a Process

Think about some of your recent experiences as a writer. Perhaps you were writing a research paper for school. You might have been writing a letter or an email message to a friend. Maybe you were carefully crafting a letter of application for a job. Think about the process. To compose, you needed to do the following:

Go to **www.literacyconnections .com** for more ideas for teaching language arts, including sections on writing, to all students.

- Formulate your message in your head.
- Organize your ideas in a logical fashion.
- Think about the reader and how he or she might understand and react to the message.
- Choose words carefully to make the flow of language, or syntax, smooth.
- Select individual words to convey your meaning succinctly.
- Attend to your spelling, capitalization, and punctuation.
- Consider the appearance of the final product (the legibility of your handwriting, typing, or word processing).

As a teacher, you need to help your students write using this same process.

Writing as an Interactive Process

Writers use the sounds, grammar, and meaning of our language system to encode (or to put language into print) and to communicate a message to the reader. In writing, as in reading, students may have problems with any aspect of the language system—with using language interactively and with using it fluently. In addition, students may have problems with the physical act of writing. For example, Grant Ellsworth, a fifth grader with learning disabilities, loves to tell stories, especially about fishing with his father, but he is reluctant when asked to write them. Grant is a poor speller and for some reason cannot get the hang of capitalization and punctuation rules. In addition, his handwriting is illegible, and he hasn't learned to use a keyboard. Writing a single sentence takes Grant so long that he soon loses his story and its intended meaning. Even though Grant can tell stories in an entertaining way, he cannot get them on paper.

Effective teachers understand what research has demonstrated: Students need to know the mechanics of writing if they are going to communicate effectively with others. Earlier instruction in writing often focused too much on the mechanics and too little on conveying meaning. Today, some teachers may overemphasize a process approach to writing focusing too much on the meaning and too little on the mechanics. Successful teachers know that both are essential elements to successful writing and are best taught in an integrated fashion (National Council of Teachers of English [NCTE], 2004). For example, Mrs. Zakibe, Grant's teacher, knows that she must ensure that Grant and all her students understand the rules of language, including capitalization, punctuation, and spelling as well as the value of a well-organized story structure.

When teachers implement effective intervention approaches that use both the conventions of writing, such as capitalization, punctuation, and sentence structure, and strategies for improving written expression, such as planning and composing, the results are positive (Gersten & Baker, 2001). Effective writing instruction requires the following critical points (Fearn & Farnan, 2001):

- Attention to conventions does not disrupt the flow of writing but is part of the discipline of writing.
- Focus on the conventions of writing does not inhibit growth in writing but facilitates it.
- Even very young children can learn and perform simple conventions automatically.
- Students with disabilities need to spend about 20% of their instructional time in writing addressing the use and application of the conventions of writing.

Writing as a Strategic Process

Because writing is such a complex task, successful writers need a strategy or plan for communicating ideas clearly. It is important to have systematic procedures for being successful and productive at each stage of the authoring process. Students, especially those with learning and behavior problems, often have difficulty not only planning their writing but also monitoring and regulating themselves while they write. Since the 1980s, researchers have worked to develop ways to teach students to become strategic writers (Englert, Berry, & Dunsmore, 2001; Graham & Harris, 2006; Mason & Graham, 2008). Fortunately, research-based practices that can help students become more strategic writers are emerging in several areas, including learning the stages of the writing process, learning narrative and expository text structures, and getting systematic and specific feedback (Baker, Gersten, & Graham, 2003). Students may find a checklist like the one in Tips for Teachers 13.3 helpful for monitoring their own writing.

Courtesy of Julia Weaver

Should children be encouraged to write before they can read or spell? Why or why not?

Tips for Teachers 13.3

CHECKLIST THAT HELPS STUDENTS MONITOR THEIR WRITING

_____ I found a quiet place to work.
_____ I set up a schedule for when I would work on this paper.
_____ I read or listened to the teacher's directions carefully.
_____ I thought about who would read my paper.
_____ I thought about what I wanted my paper to accomplish.
_____ I started planning my paper before I actually started writing it.
_____ I tried to remember everything I already knew about the topic before I started to write.
_____ I got all the information I needed before starting to write.
_____ I organized my information before starting to write.
_____ I thought about the reader as I wrote.
_____ I thought about what I wanted to accomplish as I wrote.
_____ I continued to develop my plans as I wrote.
_____ I revised the first draft of my paper.
_____ I checked what I wrote to make sure that the reader would understand it.
_____ I checked to make sure that I accomplished my goals.
_____ I reread my paper before turning it in.
_____ I asked other students, the teacher, or my parents when I needed help.
_____ I rewarded myself when I finished my paper.

Source: Harris, K. R. & Graham, S. (1992). *Helping young writers master the craft: Strategy instruction and self-regulation in the writing process.* Boston: Brookline Books. Reprinted by permission.

Writing as a Process of Constructing Meaning

When writers compose, they need to keep potential readers in mind. Readers need to have background information and specific links (such as examples and definitions of new terms) to help them connect the new information with what they already know. In short, writers need to take responsibility for helping readers to construct meaning.

Students with writing difficulties might not understand the role of audience or potential readers or how to help readers construct meaning by providing background knowledge and using predictable story or informational writing structures. For example, Terry Macinello, a fifth grader, wrote a story about a recent trip but did not indicate where or why he went on his trip and gave only sketchy details of one event. In his narrative, which had no distinguishable beginning, middle, or end, he referred to family members without letting the reader know who they were. Terry doesn't realize that when he writes a story, it is for someone to read and that he needs to fill in some gaps so that readers can understand and enjoy his story.

The majority of students with disabilities benefit from effective instruction that assists them in progressing as writers. For example, in three year-long case studies, Zaragoza and Vaughn (1992) followed the progress of gifted, low-achieving, and learning disabled students over the course of the academic year. All three of the students benefited from participating in the writing process and from teacher's scaffolding of instruction. One student with learning disabilities was very hesitant about writing. He asked for constant teacher assistance and would not write unless a teacher worked closely with him. He wrote slowly and neatly, even on first drafts. His first piece of writing was untitled and incomplete. He was insecure about working with other students and never volunteered to share his writing. His piece, titled "Disneyworld," demonstrated an understanding that you can write down what you really think. He included his own dog in a Disneyworld theme ("Goofy is a dog I like to play with but Goofy is not better than my dog."). The other students loved this story, and asked him to read it again and again. Subsequently, he frequently volunteered to share his writing with the class. He had a flair for good endings and became the class expert on developing endings. For example, in "The Spooky Halloween," he ended with "Halloween is nothing to play with." "Freddy Is in My Room" ended with "Give it up."

Other students, like third grader Maya Bradley, get so wrapped up in basic writing skills (e.g., spelling, grammar, handwriting) that they lose track of the purpose of writing. When asked about good writing, Maya defines it as "when I am neat and get the words spelled right." Teachers often spend more time teaching basic skills to students who struggle (Graham, Harris, Fink-Chorzempa, & MacArthur, 2003). However, all students need to be taught the purpose of writing as a way to communicate a message. As the Tech Tips suggests, technology can provide support for students in communicating their message.

TechTips

WRITTEN EXPRESSION

Computer programs can help learners with written expression in many ways. The following software programs are particularly useful in helping students to master the writing process by giving them tools that help them compose with confidence.

Write:Outloud by Don Johnston Incorporated
▷ **www.donjohnston.com/products/write_outloud/index.html**
This program, for students in grades 3 through 12, is a talking word processor that allows students to hear letters, words, sentences, and paragraphs spoken as they type. Other speech features include speaking any selected text and changing voice and speed. Learners who can benefit from hearing what they have typed should have access to a talking word processor.

The Secret Writer's Society from SmartKids Software
▷ **www.smartkidssoftware.com/99v.htm**
This program is designed for students in grades 8 and up has levels (missions) of teaching topics such as capitalization, end punctuation, sentence writing, paragraph writing, planning and ordering sentences, and revision and editing. A final level guides the learner through the five-step writing process.

Draft: Builder by Don Johnston Incorporated
▷ **www.donjohnston.com/products/draft_builder/**
This word processing and writing program, designed for students in grades 3 though 8, helps students map and organize their written products. It also helps them to edit and revise their work.

Writing as a Student-Centered Process

The emphasis of a student-centered model of writing is on giving students ample opportunities to find personal meaning in what they write. Rather than being taught in isolation, as they are in more traditional models, skills are part of connected, meaningful experiences in communication. The work of Donald Graves (2003) has provided a major contribution to the understanding of writing as a student-centered activity. His observations of children as they write reveal that even young children go through an interactive authoring process of prewriting, composing (drafting), and postwriting (revising, editing, and publishing), providing educators with procedures for implementing this authoring process in the classroom and for helping students and teachers realize the importance of authorship and audience.

Charles Schwartz teaches eighth-grade language arts using a student-centered model. Charles integrates reading, writing, speaking, and listening activities in his language arts program. To document students' progress in writing, Charles uses writing samples, self- and peer evaluations, and teacher observation checklists. His classroom looks like a writers' workshop. Charles says that his role is to serve as a writing coach, providing not only encouragement but also direct skills instruction.

Although the student-centered model promotes creativity and student productivity, critics claim that teaching of skills is incidental, inconsistent, and not intensive enough for students who have problems learning to write. This chapter provides specific suggestions for making a student-centered model work for all students in your classroom by ensuring that the mechanics of writing are an essential feature of instruction.

Writing as a Socially Mediated Language-Learning Activity

To become more proficient writers, students must have social interactions with others to move forward (Vygotsky, 1978). Students who have experienced failure in learning to write may be reluctant to share their writing with teachers and peers because they are embarrassed about their lack of skill in writing mechanics. It is important, however, that students have the opportunity not only to share their writing but also to have that sharing focus on the intended meaning rather than on how many words are misspelled. It is also important for young writers to have time to talk with the teacher about composing strategies (Bereiter & Scardamalia, 1982; Mason & Graham, 2008). For students who are English language learners, interacting with teachers and peers during the process of writing builds language fluency (Peregoy & Boyle, 2005).

Strategies for Establishing an Environment That Promotes Writing

From what you have already read about current trends and effective writing instruction, you can imagine the importance of planning the environment in which writing is taught. Gina Terry, a general education teacher, and her teaching partner, Galia Pennecamp, a special education teacher, have created a classroom environment that encourages their fourth-grade students to write. Gina and Galia have learned that the classroom's physical and social environment both need to be considered when teachers establish a writing community.

Go to **http://www.read writethink.org/**, where you will find a wealth of resources for teaching writing.

Physical Environment

As they planned the physical arrangement of their classroom at the beginning of the year, Gina and Galia decided to create a writer's studio in their co-taught classroom. According to Graves (2003), the classroom setting should create a work atmosphere similar to that of a studio, which promotes independence and in which students can easily interact. Gina and Galia felt that structuring their classroom as a studio was especially important for students who had already experienced failure in writing. The message they wanted to convey from day one was "This is a place for writers, and all of us are writers. Enjoy!"

A publishing center is set up for making books. Writing materials and supplies are plentiful and readily available to students. At the beginning of the year, Gina and Galia explain guidelines for using materials in responsible ways. In addition to individual writing folders for ongoing writing projects, each student has an assessment portfolio that serves as a record of his or her progress in writing. Individual folders and portfolios are located in a permanent place in the classroom, ready for student or parent conferences. Gina and Galia wanted the room arranged so that students could work together or individually. They planned spaces for writing conferences of small groups of students, teacher and student, and student and student.

Gina and Galia also realized that many students with disabilities would benefit from having technology and tools readily available to facilitate their writing. For this reason, the following tools and technologies were available in their classroom:

- Computer
- Charts and markers
- Paper with raised lines, highlighted lines, etc.
- Adaptive grip for pencil or pen
- Word cards/word book/key words in a file
- Pocket dictionary
- Pocket thesaurus
- Electronic talking dictionary/thesaurus
- Voice recognition software
- Keyboard with easy access
- Adaptive devices for students with disabilities such as mouth stick/head pointer with alternate or standard keyboard
- Head mouse/head master with onscreen keyboard

Although not every classroom can be equipped with all of the tools that Gina and Galia were able to provide, there are still ways to establish an environment that is literature-rich and encourages writing.

Social Environment

Realizing that for students to write well, an environment of mutual trust and respect is essential, Gina and Galia posted the writing workshop's student guidelines (see Figure 13.4) in their classroom. The guidelines these teachers follow to establish a social environment for a productive writing community are presented in Tips for Teachers 13.4.

Tips for TEACHERS 13.4

ESTABLISHING A SOCIAL ENVIRONMENT FOR PRODUCTIVE WRITING

- *Have students write every day for at least 30 minutes.* Students need time to think, write, discuss, rewrite, confer, revise, talk, read, and write some more. Good writing takes time.

- *Encourage students to develop areas of expertise.* At first, students will write broadly about what they know. With encouragement, however, they can become class experts in a particular area, subject, or writing form. Take the time to help students discover their own writing "turf."

- *Model the writing process.* Write with students in the classroom. Using an overhead or easel, teachers may share how they compose.

- *Share writing.* Include in the writing time an opportunity for the whole class to meet to read their writing to others and to exchange comments and questions.

- *Read to the students.* Share and discuss books, poems, and other readings. Young authors can learn from the writing of others.

- *Expand the writing community outside the classroom.* Place books published by your students in the library so that other students can use them and so that students can share their writing with other classes. Encourage authors from other classrooms to visit and read their writing.

- *Develop students' capacity to evaluate their own work.* Students need to develop their own goals and document their progress toward them. By conferring with the teacher, they will learn methods for evaluating their own work.

- *Slow the pace.* Graves (1985) says, "Teachers need to slow down so kids can hurry up." When teachers ask questions, they need to be patient, giving students time to answer.

FIGURE
13.4

Writing Workshop

Writing Workshop

1. Write three first drafts.
2. Pick one draft to publish.
3. Self-edit your draft.
4. Have a friend edit your draft.
5. Take your draft to an adult to edit.
6. Publish your draft.

7. Read over your final copy and make corrections.
8. Give a friend your final copy to make corrections.
9. Give an adult your final copy to make corrections.
10. Put your final copy in a cover.
11. Share, help others, go back to step 1.

Our Rights

- ☺ We have the right to use the things in our classroom.
- ☺ We have the right to receive caring from our teachers.
- ☺ We have the right to be listened to by our teachers and friends.
- ☺ We have the right to call our families in cases of emergency.
- ☺ We have the right to be decision makers in our classroom.

Our Responsibilities

- ☺ We have the responsibility to encourage and be caring toward our friends and teachers.
- ☺ We have the responsibility to treat all things in our classroom carefully.
- ☺ We have the responsibility to participate in all activities and help our community to become strong and positive.
- ☺ We have the responsibility to help others to meet their responsibilities successfully.

Classroom Rules

- ☺ We try our best.
- ☺ We listen and look when others talk.
- ☺ We are kind and helpful to others.
- ☺ We help others remember the rules.

Rewards

- ☺ We feel proud.
- ☺ We have parties and free time.
- ☺ We call, tell, write our family.

Consequences

- ☹ We feel sad and disappointed.
- ☹ We lose parties and free time.
- ☹ We call, tell, write our family.

Source: Zaragoza, N. & Vaughn, S. (1995). *Writing workshop manual.* Unpublished manuscript.

Strategies for Conducting a Writing Workshop

If you were to visit Gina and Galia's classroom during their writing workshop, the first thing you would notice is the variety of activities. Some students would be working individually on a writing project; others would be working in small groups or pairs, generating ideas for a book or putting the final touches on a story. You would also observe that the teachers are busy. You might see Gina **conferencing** with a student. During conferencing Gina's goals are related to the individual student and would include asking the student to read part of his or her writing aloud, commenting on what particular aspects of the writing are successful, and asking questions that "teach" the student to revise and adjust for improved writing. These conferences typically end with joint decisions about what the student will do next to improve the writing.

In addition to conferencing, you might see Gina or Galia teaching a mini lesson on punctuation to a small group. You would discover that students often choose their own topics but also are expected to provide writing products that reflect a broad range of writing formats (e.g., letter to a pen pal, story biography, persuasive argument). Also, students often have two or three writing projects in progress at a time. Some students have even elected to co-author with a classmate. You would also note that amid all this activity, there is routine. Students seem to know exactly what to do and how to get help if they need it. See Activities for All Learners for writing activities that can include all learners.

Writing Activities for All Learners

INTERVIEW A CLASSMATE

Objective: To give students practice in developing and using questions as a means for obtaining more information for the piece they are writing

Grades: Adapted for all levels

Materials: Writing materials and a writing topic, a list of possible questions, a tape recorder (optional)

Teaching Procedures: Using the format of a radio or television interview, demonstrate and role-play "mock" interviews with sports, movie, music, and political celebrities. Give the students opportunities to play both roles.

1. Discuss what types of questions allow the interviewee to give elaborate responses (e.g., open questions), and what types of questions do not allow the interviewee to give a very expanded answer (e.g., closed questions). Practice asking open questions.

2. Use a piece that you are writing as an example, and discuss whom you might interview to obtain more information. For example, "In writing a piece about what it might be like to go to the New York World's Fair in 1964, I might interview my grandfather, who was there, to obtain more information."

3. Ask the students to select an appropriate person to interview for their writing piece and to write possible questions. In pairs, the students refine their questions for the actual interview. The students then conduct the interviews and later discuss how information from the interview assisted them in writing their piece.

FLASHWRITING

Objective: To improve writing fluency

Grades: Intermediate and above

Materials: Paper and pencil; timer

Teaching Procedures:

1. Give students 1 or 2 minutes to think of a topic.

2. Start the timer and give students 5 to 10 minutes to flashwrite about the topic.

3. The goal is to keep writing about the topic. If ideas don't come, just write, "I can't think of what to write," until an idea pops up.

4. At the end of the designated time, have pairs of students share their writing.

5. Have the pairs circle key ideas that might be worth developing during extended writing periods.

SENTENCE STRETCHING

Objective: To help students learn to elaborate simple sentences

Grades: Intermediate, middle school

Materials: Paper and pencil

Teaching Procedures:

1. On the board, write a simple sentence of two to four words—for example, "The king fell."

2. Have students expand the sentence by adding words and phrases.

3. If you choose, have students illustrate their expanded sentences and share with the class.

UP IN THE AIR FOR A TOPIC

Objective: To provide support to students with problems with topic selection

Grades: Primary and intermediate

Materials: Poster with suggestions for topic selection; paper and pencil

Teaching Procedures:

1. During writing workshop, discuss topic selection and ask students what they do when they are "stuck" for a topic.

2. Present the following suggestions on a poster:
   Check your folder and reread your idea list.
   Ask a friend to help you brainstorm ideas.
   Listen to others' ideas.
   Write about what you know: your experiences.
   Write a make-believe story.
   Write about a special interest or hobby.
   Write about how to do something.
   Think about how you got your last idea.

3. Model or solicit examples for each suggestion, add students' other suggestions, and post the chart in the room for students to consult whenever they are "stuck" for a topic.

What is involved in the writing process?

- In **prewriting**, a writer collects information about a topic by observing, remembering, interviewing, and reading.
- In **composing** (or **drafting**), the author attempts to get ideas on paper in the form of a draft. The drafting process tells the author what he or she knows or does not know.
- In **postwriting**, the author revises, edits, and publishes the work.
  - During **revising**, the focus is on meaning; points are explored further, ideas are elaborated, and further connections are made.
  - When the author is satisfied with the content, **editing** takes place as the author reviews the piece line by line to determine whether each word is necessary. Punctuation, spelling, and other mechanical processes are checked.
  - The final element is **publishing.** If the author considers the piece a good one, it is published.

FINDING THE TOPIC BY USING THE GOLDILOCKS RULE ⑤

Objective: To help students brainstorm for expository writing topics

Grades: Intermediate and above

Materials: Timer, paper, and pencil

Teaching Procedures:

1. Describe the "Goldilocks procedure."
   Brainstorm as many ideas as possible in 5 minutes.
   Write down all ideas. Don't stop to read or judge them.
   Stop when timer goes off.
   Organize ideas into categories with the Goldilocks Rule:
   Too broad
   Too narrow
   Just right
   Choose a topic from the Just Right category.

2. Model the use of the Goldilocks procedure.

3. Try out the procedure as a whole-class activity.

4. Have students try out the procedure independently and then share their topics in small groups.

Source: Schumm, J. S., & Radencich, M. (1992). School power. Minneapolis: Free Spirit Publishing.

TELL IT AGAIN ⑥

Objective: To help students learn story elements

Grades: Primary, intermediate

Materials: Paper, pencil, crayons, markers

Teaching Procedures: Story retellings are a good way to determine which elements of a story are familiar (and unfamiliar) to your students. To help students "Tell It Again," follow these steps:

1. Provide a story for your students. It might be a story you read, a story they read independently or with a partner, or a story they hear on TV or on a video.

2. Decide on a retelling format. Students can retell the story by drawing pictures of major events (making a wordless picture book), rewriting and illustrating the story, dramatizing the story, or orally retelling the story to you or to a friend.

3. Keep tabs on the story elements your students include in their retellings. If a story element (such as setting, character or plot) is missing, provide instruction (either individually, in small groups, or with the class as a whole) about one element at a time. Monitor that element in subsequent retelling assignments.

THE RAFT TECHNIQUE ⑦

Objective: To help students learn to vary their writing with respect to writer's role, audience, format, and topic

Grades: Intermediate and above

Materials: Paper and pencil

Teaching Procedures: The RAFT technique was developed by Santa (1988) to help secondary students write in the content areas. RAFT provides a framework for thinking about how to write for different purposes by varying the writer's role, audience, format, and topic. Here's how to teach it:

1. Explain the components of RAFT:
   Role of the writer. Who are you? A professor? A volcano? An ancient Egyptian?
   Audience. Who will be your reader? A friend? A famous athlete? A lawyer?
   Format. What form will your writing take? A brochure? A letter? A newspaper article?
   Topic. What topic have you chosen? Hazards of smoking? Need for gun control? How cheese is made?

2. Write R–A–F–T on the board or on a transparency. Brainstorm with students about possible roles, audiences, formats, and topics. Following is an example:
   R—Role = a liver
   A—Audience = alcoholic
   F—Format = script for TV commercial
   T—Topic = the ill effects of drinking

3. Have students work in cooperative groups to generate other RAFT ideas.

4. Have students work independently to complete a RAFT assignment.

Making Adaptations for Struggling Writers: Teachers' Practices

How do teachers adapt writing instruction for struggling writers? Graham, Harris, Fink-Chorzempa, and MacArthur (2003) surveyed 153 primary-grade teachers to learn more about the adaptations they make. Twenty percent of the teachers reported that they made no adaptations at all; 24% made only one or two adaptations. The majority of adaptations involved additional instruction in basic writing skills. With respect to the writing process, additional instruction in the planning and revising stages was most common. In general, teachers reported that they spent more time reteaching, conferencing, and encouraging struggling writers. Graham and colleagues emphasized the importance of getting young writers off to a good start and the complexities they face in achieving a command of writing.

Students with writing problems differ in the degree to which components of the writing process are difficult for them (Scott & Vitale, 2003). Many students with writing problems experience significant difficulty in editing and writing final copy because they have difficulty with mechanics. These students often produce well-developed stories that are hard to read because of the mechanical errors. Other students with writing problems have difficulty organizing during the composing stage and need to rethink the sequencing during revision. There is considerable agreement that students use the writing process best when they are taught explicitly how to use each of the elements (e.g., prewriting, revising, conferencing) (Baker, Gersten, & Graham, 2003; Thompkins, 2008).

Prewriting: Getting Started

"What should I write about?" As a teacher, it's easy to say, "Write about what you did during your summer vacation," but the key to engaging students as writers is to have them select topics. Saying to students "Just write about anything" isn't enough. The following section shows how to help students approach topic selection.

Selecting Topics.   Deciding what you say to students to help them generate a list of topics they either know about or want to learn about varies somewhat by grade level. It is critical to each grade level that teachers provide students with some time to generate their own topics of interest in addition to writing about topics generated by the teacher.

For example, with elementary students, you might say, "You know lots of things about yourself, about your family, and about your friends. You have hobbies and activities that you like to do. You have stories about things that have happened to you and to people you know. You have lots of things to share with others. I want you to make a list of things you would like to share with others through writing. Do not put them in any specific order—just write them down as you think of them. You will not have to write on all of these topics. The purpose of this exercise is to think of as many topics as you can. I will give you about 10 minutes. Begin."

For older students, teachers might want to talk about the different genres of writing, including personal biography, persuasion, sarcasm, humor, narrative story, and reporting, as a means to facilitate topic generation. You might say, "Identify two to four of the genres you might like to use for your writing. Then under each genre, identify two to four topics you would like to write about."

One way to model brainstorming for a topic is to use an LCD or overhead projector. Write a list of things you do very well—in which you're an expert. Then select one item from the list to write about. Have your students develop their own "expert list" and add it to their writing folder (Thompkins, 2008). Model the process by writing as many topics as you can think of during the assigned time. When time is up, tell the students to pick a partner and share their topics. They may add any new topics they think of at this time. Then share your list with the entire group and comment on topics you are looking forward to writing about. Ask for volunteers to read their topic lists to the entire group. Have students select the three topics they are most interested in writing about and place their topic lists in their writing folders as a resource for future writing. Finally, ask students to select one of their top three topics and begin writing.

Teachers may want to hold students accountable for writing in multiple genres. For example, you might say, "During this 6-week period, I need you to submit a completed composition in each of the following areas: story, opinion, and expository factual report on a topic of interest."

Problems in Topic Selection.   Maintaining a supply of writing topics is difficult for some students. When students tell you stories, ask them whether the story generates a topic they might want to write about. When students read or you read to them, ask whether the reading has given them ideas for their own writing. If they were going to write the end of the story, how would they do it? If they were going to continue this story, what would happen? If they were going to add characters to the story, what types of characters would they add? Would they change the setting?

Some students want to repeat the same topic or theme, especially students with writing problems, who may find security in such repetition. Before suggesting that students change topics, check whether their stories are changing in other ways (through development of vocabulary, concept, story, or character). Students may be learning a great deal about writing, even though the topic is the same.

Planning.   Prewriting entails developing a plan for writing. Planning for writing includes the following three steps:

1. *Identify the intended audience.* To make a writing project meaningful, the writer must identify the audience. Who will be the reader? The audience might be family, friends, business people, politicians, teachers, potential employers—or oneself.
2. *State a purpose for writing.* The purpose for writing may be to inform, entertain, or persuade. An example of a purpose statement might be: "I am writing this story about my imaginary pet shark, Gums, to entertain my friends."
3. *Decide on a format.* Before writing begins, it's good to have a general idea of how the piece will be structured. Although the structure may change during drafting and revision, writers should have an initial road map at the prewriting stage.

Some students are limited in text-organization skills because they have difficulty categorizing ideas related to a specific topic, providing advance organizers for the topic, and relating and extending ideas about the topic (Mason & Graham, 2008; Tomlinson, 2008). As you teach the thinking process that goes into a piece of writing, you can model your own thinking as you move from topic selection to planning for audience, purpose, and format to drafting. During whole-class sharing time, you can also encourage students to describe how they generated topics and planned for their own writing.

Katelyn Metzger/Merrill

What are the stages of the writing process? What are some effective strategies for teaching each stage to students?

Composing

The purpose of the composing stage is to develop an initial draft that will be refined later. Some teachers call this a *sloppy copy*. Many students with learning and behavior problems think of a topic and, without much planning, begin writing. Composing is also difficult for students who lack fluency in the mechanics of writing or in the physical act of writing (Scott & Vitale, 2003). During composing, you should assume the role of coach and encourage students to concentrate on getting their ideas on paper.

Revising and Editing

The purpose of revision is to make certain that the meaning is clear and that the message can be understood by others. *Editing* focuses mainly on mechanics, such as proofreading. After the students and teacher are happy with the content, it is time to finalize the correction of spelling, capitalization, punctuation, and language.

During editing, students circle words whose spelling they are not sure of, put boxes where they are unsure of punctuation, and underline sentences in which they feel the language may not be correct. Students are not expected to correct all errors, but are expected to correct known errors. Revising and editing are difficult tasks for all writers, especially beginning writers and students for whom writing is difficult. Getting the entire message down on paper the first time is difficult enough; making changes so that the piece is at its best and can be understood by others is a most formidable task.

Revising, which means attending to meaning and making adjustments to a written document, is an ongoing process. Through modeling and feedback, students will learn that they may need to revise once, twice, or more until their intended meaning is expressed clearly and completely. Most students with learning and behavior problems have difficulty revising their work (Scott & Vitale, 2003). Teachers often find it best initially to let students move to publication without much revision and then gradually show them the benefits of revision and editing. Explicit teaching of the differences between revising and editing and structured formats for this aspect of composition is necessary (Bradley, 2001; Saddler, 2004).

Adolescents with disabilities can learn procedures such as *compare, diagnose,* and *operate* to assist them during the revision process (De La Paz, Swanson, & Graham, 1998; Wong, Butler,

Tips FOR Teachers 13.5

TEACHING STUDENTS TO COMPARE, DIAGNOSE, AND OPERATE

1. Compare and diagnose. Read your writing and consider the following:

   - Does it ignore the obvious point against my idea?

   - Does it have too few ideas?

   - Part of the essay doesn't belong with the rest.

   - Part of the essay is not in the right order.

2. Tactic operations.

   - Rewrite.

   - Delete.

   - Add.

   - Move.

3. Compare. Reread the paper and highlight problems.

4. Diagnose and operate.

   - This doesn't sound right.

   - This isn't what I intended to say.

   - This is an incomplete idea.

   - This part is not clear_____.

   - The problem is.

   The following suggestions to help students remove the mechanical barriers from their writing:

   - Have students dictate their story to improve the flow of their writing.

   - Provide students with a list of key words and difficult-to-spell words to assist with writing and editing.

   - Promote peer collaboration in editing.

Source: Information from Isaacson, S. & Gleason, M. M. (1997). Mechanical obstacles to writing: What can teachers do to help students with learning problems? *Learning Disabilities Research and Practice, 12*(3), 188–194.

Ficzere, & Kuperis, 1997). When teachers model, demonstrate, and provide feedback using the procedure described in Tips for Teachers 13.5, students' revisions and writing improve.

In addition to revising and editing their own work, students can serve as editors for the work of their peers. **Peer editing** can work several ways. One way is to have students edit their own work first and then ask a friend to edit it. Another way is to establish a class editor who is responsible for reading the material and finding mechanical errors. The role of class editor can rotate so that every student has an opportunity to serve in that capacity.

It is important that students not be too critical while revising and editing one another's work. You can communicate that the purpose of revising and editing is to support the author in developing a finished piece. You can also model acceptable ways to give feedback.

Publishing

Not all student writing is published; often only one in five or six pieces is published. **Publishing** means preparing a piece so that others can read it. Publication is often in the form of books with cardboard bindings decorated with contact paper or scraps of wallpaper. Books can include a picture of the author, a description of the author, and a list of books published by the author. Young children writing short pieces may publish every 2 weeks; older students who spend more time composing and revising publish less frequently.

Publishing is a way to confirm a student's hard work and share the piece with others. Publishing is also a way to involve others in school and at home with the students' writing. It is important for all students to publish, not just the best authors.

Sharing

Sharing work with others is important during all stages of the writing process. The author's chair (Graves & Hansen, 1983) is a formal opportunity to share writing. When Romain, a student who recently moved from Haiti to the United States, signed up for author's chair early in the school year, Galia and Gina were surprised. Romain, the most reluctant writer in their class, was also extremely self-conscious about not being able to spell. During author's chair, Romain sat on a special stool in a circle of peers and read his letter to an imaginary pen pal in Haiti. He described life in Miami and ended with a wish: "I hope that you are happy and have enough food to eat." It turned out that most of Romain's story wasn't written at all—he held a paper in front of him and made up the letter as he spoke. But because Romain got a positive response from his audience about how well he communicated his ideas, he was encouraged to become a writer. The author's chair experience was his launching point. Using author's chair can be facilitated by having the student present the writing on a computer and then projecting it on an LCD so that all of the students can view the work at the same time (Labbo, 2004).

Teachers often need to set rules for students' behavior when a classmate is sharing work in the author's chair. Such rules might include raising one's hand, asking a question, making a positive comment, and giving feedback when asked. A simple but powerful framework within which students can give one another feedback about their writing is called **TAG** (Zaragoza, 1987):

Tell what you like.
Ask questions.
Give suggestions.

After an author has read his or her writing, the author leads the class in a TAG session, asking class members the three questions "What did you like?," "Do you have any questions?," and "Do you have any suggestions?" Three or four responses are usually allowed for each question. TAG sessions give authors valuable feedback about their writing as well as a chance to lead a class discussion.

Conferencing. The heart of the writing workshop—the student–teacher writing conference—is ongoing. The student comes to the writing conference prepared to read his or her piece, to describe problem areas, and to respond to questions. Students know that the teacher will listen and respond and that they will be asked challenging questions about their work. Questions should be carefully selected, with enough time allotted for the student to respond. Even though you may see many problems with the piece of writing, try to focus on only one or two specific areas. Some key points about conferencing with students are presented in Tips for Teachers 13.6.

Tips for TEACHERS 13.6

GUIDELINES FOR CONDUCTING A WRITING CONFERENCE

Big Principles of a Writing Conference

- *Follow the student's lead during the conference.* Avoid imposing your ideas about the topic or the way you would write the story.

- *Listen to and accept what the student says.* When you talk more than the writer does during conferences, you are being too directive.

- *Ask questions that teach.* Ask students questions that help them understand what needs to be revised and what steps to take next with their writing.

- *Make conferences frequent and brief.* Although conferences can range from 30 seconds to 10 minutes, most last 2 to 3 minutes.

- *Listen to what students have written and tell them what you hear.* Learning to listen to what they are communicating from the perspective of a reader is essential for students to learn to make effective revisions.

Suggestions to Compliment Writing

- I like the way your paper began in this way . . .

- I like the part where . . .

- I like the way you explained . . .

- I like the order you used in your paper because . . .

- I like the details you used to describe . . .

- I like the way you used dialogue to make your story sound real. In particular, this section . . .

- I like the action and the descriptive words you used in your writing, such as . . .

- I like the facts you used, such as . . .

- I like the way the paper ended because . . .

- I like the mood of your writing because it made me feel . . .

Questions and Suggestions to Improve Writing

- I got confused in the part about . . .

- Could you add an example to the _____ part about . . .

- Could you add more to this part because . . .

- Do you think your order would make more sense if you . . .

- Do you think you could leave this part out because . . .

- Could you use a different word for _____ because . . .

- Is this _____ paragraph on one topic?

- Could you write a beginning sentence to "grab" your readers?

- What happens in the end?

- Can you think of another word for "said"?

Teaching Writing Skills.   A frequently asked question is, "When do I teach skills?" This question is especially important for teachers whose students have poor writing skills to begin with. Prolific writing without help from a teacher will not lead to improvement (Graham & Perin, 2007).

Skills lessons can be taught to the class as a whole and then in small groups composed of students who need additional knowledge and practice with a specified skill. Skills lessons, or mini lessons, should be brief (15–20 minutes), and the topics for these lessons should be based on the students' needs. Ideas for topics can come from your observations of student writing, requests for help, and data from writing conferences.

After teaching a skill and providing ample opportunities to practice it, help students to generalize and apply the skill in their daily writing. As Graham (1992) recommended for students with writing problems, skills are best taught in the context of "real" writing and have the most impact when they bring the greatest rewards in writing improvement.

Strategies for Teaching Narrative Writing

In the elementary grades and in middle school, students typically practice narrative writing (writing stories). For many students, story writing is not a problem. Through hearing and reading stories, they have learned the basic elements of a story and can incorporate them into their own storytelling and writing. Students with writing problems may be aware of story elements but may not incorporate them into their writing in a systematic way unless they are provided instructional support (Graham & Harris, 2006; Montague & Graves, 1993). Students with writing problems may also exhibit the following problems when they compose stories:

- Lack of organization
- Lack of unity and coherence
- Lack of character development
- Incomplete use of story elements

Story webbing and direct instruction on the development of story elements are effective ways to address these difficulties.

Using Story Webs to Plan

Story webs, or *maps,* were originally developed as visual displays to help students understand the structure of the stories they read. Stories are composed of predictable elements and have a characteristic narrative structure or story grammar. Elements of stories include the setting, characters, a problem statement, the goal, the event sequence or episodes, and the resolution or ending. Using story webs such as the one shown in Figure 13.5, students can trace these elements when they read, plan, or write a story.

You can conduct mini lessons on webbing with your whole class or just with students who need help with story planning. To introduce the story web, first talk about its components and model its use in planning a story. You might want to have students work together in small, mixed-ability groups to plan a group story.

Instruction in Story Development

As previously stated, some students might include a story element, such as a main character, in their stories but fail to develop the element fully. Graves and Hauge (1993) developed the cue sheet shown in Figure 13.6 to help students improve their story writing.

Strategies for Teaching Expository Writing

Expository writing, or informational writing, once reserved for middle and upper grades, is now being included in the curriculum for even very young students. Expository writing poses particular problems for students with writing problems who may be unaware of the purpose of informational writing (Englert et al., 1988; Mason & Graham, 2008). Graham and Harris (1989b) reported that the informational writing of students with learning disabilities often contains irrelevant information and inappropriate conclusions.

An Example of a Story Web

FIGURE
13.5

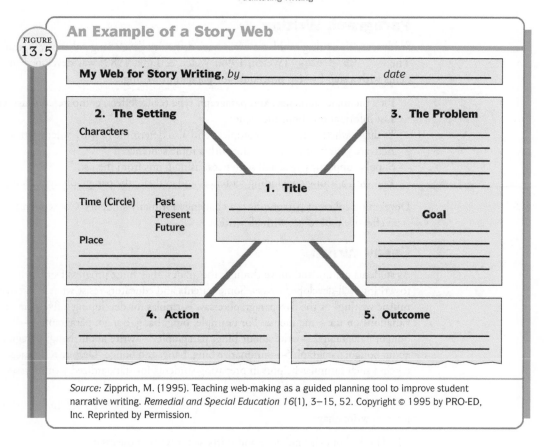

My Web for Story Writing, *by* _____ *date* _____

2. The Setting

Characters
_____
_____
_____

Time (Circle) Past
  Present
  Future

Place
_____
_____

1. Title
_____
_____

3. The Problem
_____
_____
_____

Goal
_____
_____

4. Action
_____
_____

5. Outcome
_____
_____

Source: Zipprich, M. (1995). Teaching web-making as a guided planning tool to improve student narrative writing. *Remedial and Special Education 16*(1), 3–15, 52. Copyright © 1995 by PRO-ED, Inc. Reprinted by Permission.

Story Check

FIGURE
13.6

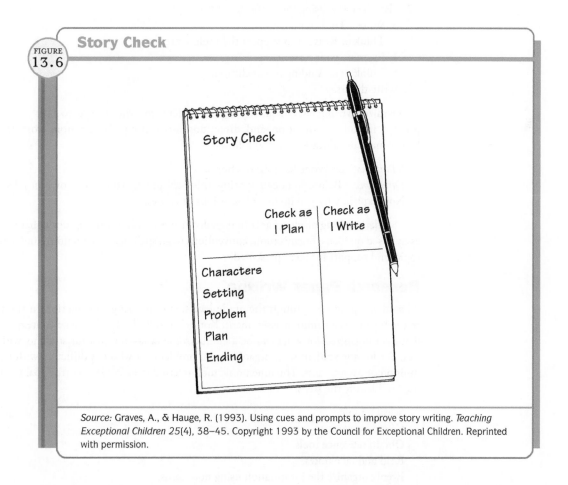

Story Check

	Check as I Plan	Check as I Write
Characters		
Setting		
Problem		
Plan		
Ending		

Source: Graves, A., & Hauge, R. (1993). Using cues and prompts to improve story writing. *Teaching Exceptional Children 25*(4), 38–45. Copyright 1993 by the Council for Exceptional Children. Reprinted with permission.

Paragraph Writing

Students with writing problems often have difficulty developing coherent, logical paragraphs. The **PLEASE strategy** (Welch, 1992; Welch & Link, 1989) was developed to provide students with a step-by-step procedure for paragraph writing:

Pick the topic, audience, and paragraph type (cause/effect, compare/contrast, etc.).
List information about the topic.
Evaluate whether the list is complete and also determine how to order items in the list.
Activate your writing by starting with a topic sentence.
Supply supporting or detail sentences, using items from the list.
End with a strong concluding sentence, and evaluate the paragraph by revising and editing.

Developing coherent paragraphs is a challenge for many students. Consequently, this strategy is an effective tool to use with all writers.

Essay Writing

As students mature and move through the grades, they must progress from writing paragraphs to writing well-developed essays. Some parents and educators resist what is referred to as "formulaic writing" or the five-paragraph essay. Formulas for developing a five-paragraph essay are variations on the same theme. For example, bing, bang, bongo: paragraph 1—list bing, bang, bongo; paragraph 2—write about bing; paragraph 3—write about bang; paragraph 4—write about bongo; paragraph 5—summarize bing, bang, and bongo. Despite resistance, many teachers find such formulas helpful in preparing students for standardized writing tests, particularly for students who need scaffolding and structure.

Graham and Harris (1989a, 1989b) developed a three-step strategy for helping students learn to write essays:

1. Think about the audience and purpose for writing the essay.
2. Plan the essay, using the **TREE method**:
   - Write a **T**opic sentence.
   - Think of **R**easons to support the topic sentence.
   - **E**xamine your reasons.
   - Think of an **E**nding or conclusion.
3. Write the essay.

Standardized writing tests frequently require students to write an essay to a **prompt**. A writing prompt includes a situation and directions for writing. An example from the Florida Department of Education (2005) follows:

Situation: Everyone has jobs or chores.
Directions: Before you begin writing, think about why you do one of your jobs or chores. Now explain why you do one of your jobs or chores.

Student writing products are often graded using a holistic scoring rubric that evaluates the essay based on focus, organization, conventions (e.g., spelling, punctuation), understanding of topic, and support for ideas presented.

Research Paper Writing

As students progress through the grade levels, summarizing information in the form of a research paper is a common assignment. Korinek and Bulls (1996) offer a strategy to help students get organized for what can be a cumbersome task—not just for students with disabilities, but for any student with organizational problems or who has difficulty with long-range, multiphase assignments. The mnemonic tool, referred to as **SCORE A** (the goal for a grade) is used to identify the steps:

Select a topic.
Create categories.
Obtain reference tools.
Read and take notes.
Evenly organize the information using note cards.
Apply writing process steps (i.e., prewriting, drafting, etc.).

Once students are able to master this process, they are more likely to succeed in producing a well-thought-out paper. This success will then contribute to future successes.

Strategies for Teaching Persuasive Writing

Many state assessments include persuasive writing components. Writing persuasive essays can be incorporated into content areas such as science and social studies. **Persuasive writing** is a format in which the writer provides evidence in order to convince or persuade the reader of his or her position or opinion. Writing persuasive essays involves planning and critical thinking. Whereas most students have difficulty with persuasive writing, many students with LD have even more problems (De La Paz, 2001). To help all students compose well-developed and supported persuasive pieces, De La Paz and Graham (1997) developed and researched the **STOP and DARE strategy**. Here are the steps:

1. *Suspend judgment.* First, ask students to suspend their own judgment about the topic, keep an open mind, and write a list of pros and cons about the topic.
2. *Take a side.* Next, ask students to decide which side they believe in and can build the best argument.
3. *Organize ideas.* Tell students to reflect on their pro/con sheet and identify the strongest points they can make to support their point of view. Have students identify points from the opposite side that they want to refute.
4. *Plan more as you write.* As students refine and reorganize their essays, ask them to keep the components of DARE in mind (see the STOP and DARE cue card in Figure 13.7).

FIGURE 13.7

STOP and DARE Cue Cards

Step 1

Suspend judgment
Did I list ideas for both sides? If not, do this now.

Suspend judgment
Can I think of anything else? Try to write more.

Suspend judgment
Another point I haven't considered is . . .
Think of possible arguments.

Step 2

Take a side
Place a "+" at the top of one box to show the side you will take in your essay.

Step 3

Organize ideas
Put a star next to ideas you want to use.
Choose at least _____ ideas to use.

Organize ideas
Did I star ideas on both sides?
Choose at least _____ arguments that you can dispute.

Organize ideas
Number your ideas in the order you will use.

Step 4

Plan more as you write
Remember to use all four essay parts:
Develop your topic sentence.
Add supporting ideas.
Reject possible arguments.
End with a conclusion.

Source: Information from De La Paz, S. (2001). STOP and DARE: A persuasive writing strategy, *Intervention in school and clinic, 36.* 237. Copyright 2001 by PRO-ED, Inc.

For additional strategies that will help students understand and practice persuasive writing, find examples of persuasive writing for them to consider. There are examples all around in our everyday lives, including advertisements, commercials, letters to the editor, campaign speeches, and movie or book reviews (Medina, 2006).

Strategies for Helping All Students Acquire Spelling Skills

Even in the age of computers with spell-check programs, learning how to spell is important. If a writer is bogged down with the spelling of even commonly used words, progress in writing is stymied. Many students with reading and other disabilities are poor spellers. Spelling, like reading, involves phonological awareness (see Figure 13.8).

Spelling instruction is important for all students, but the students in your class are likely to differ in terms of their stages of development, the types of errors they make, and what they need to learn in spelling to become more fluent writers. What instructional methods can you use to teach all your students to spell?

Traditional Spelling Instruction

Mary Jacobs uses a traditional spelling instruction model in her third-grade class. All students in the class have the same third-grade spelling book. Each lesson in the speller focuses on a particular pattern (e.g., long vowels, short vowels, vowel plus *r*, prefixes). On Monday, Mary gives a spelling pretest on the 15 new words, and for homework students write (five times) each word they missed. On Tuesday and Wednesday nights, students are assigned exercises in the spelling book. On Thursday night, they write one sentence for each word on the list.

PEARSON
myeducationlab

Go to the Assignments and Activities section of Topic 10: Content Area Teaching in the MyEducationLab for your course and complete the activity entitled *Direct Instruction: Spelling Lessons.*

FIGURE 13.8

Characteristics of Learners in Five Stages of Development

Stage 1: Precommunicative Spelling

• Uses scribbles, letter-like forms, letters, and sometimes numbers to represent a message.

• May write from left to right, right to left, top to bottom, or randomly on the page.

• Shows no understanding of phoneme–grapheme correspondences.

• May repeat a few letters again and again or use most of the letters of the alphabet.

• Frequently mixes upper- and lowercase letters but shows a preference for uppercase letters.

Stage 2: Semiphonetic Spelling

• Becomes aware of the alphabetic principle that letters are used to represent sounds.

• Uses abbreviated one-, two-, or three-letter spelling to represent an entire word.

• Uses letter–name strategy to spell words (e.g., U for you).

Stage 3: Phonetic Spelling

• Represents all essential sound features of a word in spelling.

• Develops particular spellings for long and short vowels, plural and past tense markers, and other aspects of spelling.

• Chooses letters on the basis of sound, without regard for English letter sequences or other conventions.

Stage 4: Transitional Spelling

• Adheres to basic conventions of English orthography.

• Begins to use morphological and visual information in addition to phonetic information.

• May include all appropriate letters in a word but reverse some of them.

• Uses alternate spellings for the same sound in different words, but only partially understands the conditions governing their use.

• Uses a high percentage of correctly spelled words.

Stage 5: Correct Spelling

• Applies the basic rules of the English orthographic system.

• Extends knowledge of word structure, including the spelling of affixes, contractions, compound words, and homonyms.

• Demonstrates growing accuracy in using silent consonants and doubling consonants before adding suffixes.

• Recognizes when a word doesn't "look right" and can consider alternate spellings for the same sound.

• Learns irregular spelling patterns.

• Learns consonant and vowel alternations, and other morphological structures.

• Knows how to spell a large number of words.

Source: Gentry, J. R. (1982). An analysis for developmental spelling in GYNS at WRK. *The Reading Teacher, 36,* 192–200. Copyright by the International Reading Association.

On Friday during class, Mary gives students a spelling test on the 15 words. Some teachers vary this traditional pattern by selecting words from the basal reader or from the current science or social studies unit.

Spelling Instruction for Students with Learning Difficulties and Disabilities

How appropriate is the traditional approach for classrooms that include students of different academic levels? Many students who are good spellers know all the words at the beginning of the week and so have no real challenge. For students with learning difficulties, 15 words may be too many to learn, feedback about their errors may be ineffective, and the amount of practice may be insufficient. In addition, traditional spelling instruction does not teach for transfer to new situations. Students often learn words from their spelling list and get 100% on the test, but misspell those same words in their compositions.

A review of spelling interventions (Gordon, Vaughn, & Schumm, 1993; Wanzek, Vaughn, Wexler, Swanson, Edmonds & Kim 2006) indicated that spelling practices that provide students with spelling strategies or systematic study and word practice methods yield the highest rates of spelling improvement. Findings from the studies can be grouped into seven areas of instructional practice:

Go to **www.edbydesign.com**, then under the section on Learning Resource, you will find practical resources for spelling and writing.

1. *A weekly list of words.* Students perform better in spelling when they have a list of words each week that are related (e.g., same spelling patterns or thematically related), when they are required to demonstrate proficiency, and when they realize that spelling these words correctly in their writing is expected.

2. *Error imitation and modeling.* Students with learning disabilities need to compare each incorrectly spelled word with the correct spelling. The teacher copies the incorrect spelling and then writes the word correctly, calling attention to features in the word that will help students remember the correct spelling.

3. *Unit size.* Students with learning disabilities tend to become overloaded and have difficulty when they have to study several words at once. These students can learn to spell if the unit size of their assigned list is reduced to three words a day and if effective instruction is offered for those three words.

4. *Modality.* When studying words, students with learning disabilities learned equally by (a) writing the words, (b) arranging and tracing letter shapes or tiles, and (c) typing the words at a computer. Most students preferred to practice their spelling words at a computer.

5. *Computer-assisted instruction.* Computer-assisted instruction (CAI) has been shown to be effective in improving the spelling skills of students with learning disabilities. CAI software programs for spelling improvement often emphasize awareness of word structure and spelling strategies and make use of time delay, voice simulation, and sound effects.

6. *Peer tutoring.* A teacher's individual help is preferable, but structured peer tutoring can be a viable alternative. Burks (2004) and Keller (2002) have adapted classwide peer tutoring to structure peer support for learning to spell.

7. *Study techniques.* Study techniques provide a format and a standard procedure that help students with learning disabilities organize their study of spelling. Wheatley (2005) advocates strategic spelling rather than rote memorization of words. Figure 13.9 is a flow chart that can be used with intermediate grade and secondary students to help them become more strategic spellers.

Meredith Millan is a third-grade teacher whose three students with learning disabilities require that they receive specialized instruction. Meredith and the special education teacher have agreed that Meredith will assign students their weekly spelling words. Meredith has worked hard to integrate spelling instruction into her ongoing writing program. She likes the idea of having weekly spelling tests but knows that the range of student spelling levels in her class is too broad for all students to benefit from having the same words and the same number of words to learn. The following sections describe the way Meredith has structured her spelling program.

Selecting Words. Meredith teaches spelling words that correspond with the phonics rules she is teaching in reading. For example, if she is teaching students the VCe rule (vowel, consonant, long e as in "time") by which the first vowel says its name, as part of word study she

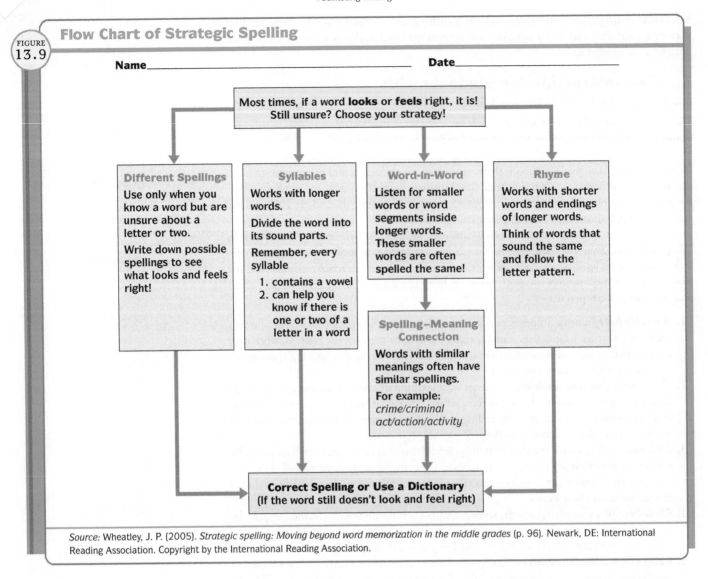

FIGURE 13.9

Flow Chart of Strategic Spelling

Name_____ Date_____

Most times, if a word **looks** or **feels** right, it is!
Still unsure? Choose your strategy!

Different Spellings

Use only when you know a word but are unsure about a letter or two.

Write down possible spellings to see what looks and feels right!

Syllables

Works with longer words.

Divide the word into its sound parts.

Remember, every syllable

1. contains a vowel
2. can help you know if there is one or two of a letter in a word

Word-in-Word

Listen for smaller words or word segments inside longer words. These smaller words are often spelled the same!

Spelling–Meaning Connection

Words with similar meanings often have similar spellings.

For example:
*crime/criminal
act/action/activity*

Rhyme

Works with shorter words and endings of longer words.

Think of words that sound the same and follow the letter pattern.

Correct Spelling or Use a Dictionary
(If the word still doesn't look and feel right)

Source: Wheatley, J. P. (2005). *Strategic spelling: Moving beyond word memorization in the middle grades* (p. 96). Newark, DE: International Reading Association. Copyright by the International Reading Association.

also uses VCe word types for her spelling list. This allows her to connect reading and spelling rules and capitalize on the patterns of language (Carreker, 1999; Moats, 2000). This procedure can be used for older students as well. If students are progressing beyond rule-based instruction in reading, then spelling words can be selected from their writing errors or from key words needed in their social studies and science instruction.

Each student in Meredith's class keeps a spelling log, which is a running list of words. At the beginning of the week, students select words from the log for the Friday spelling test and write the words on their homework sheet. Meredith and each student agree in advance on the number of words. Some students have 5 or 6 words, others as many as 20. Meredith also assigns all students 2 to 3 words from the thematic unit they are studying at the time. Words that students misspell are taken from the edited drafts of their compositions. During a writing conference, Meredith not only discusses the words a student should add to his or her spelling log, but also asks, "Are there other words you really would like to learn to spell?" and adds them to the log.

Providing Instruction and Practice.   Meredith provides spelling instruction and practice in four ways: through mini lessons, student pairs, parental involvement, and collaboration with the special education teacher. Each week Meredith provides mini lessons on spelling patterns. For example, she noticed that about 20 students were using *-ing* words in their writing and spelling them incorrectly. Meredith met with this group for 2 weeks, gave them mini lessons on adding *-ing,* and included *-ing* words on their spelling tests.

Early in the school year, Meredith figured out that 10 of her students needed more practice preparing for spelling tests. She decided to have these students work in pairs. The pairs meet for 15 minutes three times a week, usually while other students are composing during writing workshop. Meredith involves parents in the spelling program in two ways. First, at the beginning of the year, she writes parents a letter about the spelling program and ways in which parents can help their child study for spelling tests. Second, she invites parents to add one or two words to the spelling list each week. Parents observe their children's writing at home and can pick up on important misspellings.

Two of the students with learning disabilities, Kara and Mitchell, need additional help learning their words. In collaboration with Meredith, the special education teacher helps Kara and Mitchell learn and maintain new words by using individualized approaches to word study including ensuring that students know the phonics patterns in the words and use practices for writing, checking, correcting, and rewriting spelling words until they are written correctly and automatically.

Monitoring Student Progress.   There are basically three ways to assess student spelling: dictation, error detection or proofreading tasks, and examination of student spelling in their composition products (Hallahan, Lloyd, Kauffman, Weiss, & Martinez, 2005). Meredith includes a spelling rubric she uses in writing workshop (see Figure 13.10). She includes both dictation and error detection formats as part of her weekly spelling tests.

All students take their Friday spelling test during the same class period. Because it is not possible to give 36 students individual spelling dictation tests based on the words in their spelling logs, Meredith pairs the students so they can test each other. Students follow these strict guidelines during the test period:

- You can talk only to your partner and only about the test.
- You cannot give or receive information about how to spell words.
- You must take your test in ink—no erasing allowed.

FIGURE 13.10

Spelling Rubric

Name: _____   Date: _____

Spelling Rubric

Title of Writing Assignment: _____   Spelling Strategy Used: _____

CRITERIA	5	4	3	2	1
Circles all misspelled words	Student found and circled all misspelled words.	Student circled 75%–99% of misspelled words.	Student circled 50%–74% of misspelled words.	Student circled 25%–49% of misspelled words.	Student circled 1%–24% of misspelled words.
Accurately corrects all circled misspelled words	Student accurately corrected all circled misspelled words.	Student accurately corrected 75%–99% of circled misspelled words.	Student accurately corrected 50%–74% of circled misspelled words.	Student accurately corrected 25%–49% of circled misspelled words.	Student accurately corrected 1%–24% of circled misspelled words.
Always uses sounding-out, spell checker, dictionary, or similar words to spell words without help	Student always used one of the taught spelling strategies to spell words correctly on his or her own.	Student almost always used one of the taught spelling strategies to spell words correctly on his or her own.	Student sometimes used one of the taught spelling strategies to spell words correctly on his or her own.	Student always used one of the taught spelling strategies to spell words correctly with some help from an adult.	Student sometimes used one of the taught spelling strategies to spell words correctly with some help from an adult.
Spells all words correctly in writing	Student correctly spelled all the words in his or her writing.	Student correctly spelled 75%–99% of the words in his or her writing.	Student correctly spelled 50%–74% of the words in his or her writing.	Student correctly spelled 25%–49% of the words in his or her writing.	Student correctly spelled 1%–24% of the words in his or her writing.
Grade	/20 points	% =	Letter grade =		

Source: Loeffler, K.A. (2005). No more Friday spelling tests? An alternative spelling assessment for students with learning disabilities. *Teaching Exceptional Children, 37,* 24. Copyright 2005 by the Council for Exceptional Children. Reprinted with permission.

Meredith monitors the test process, collects and grades papers, and adds words missed to next week's spelling list.

Each week Meredith also gives an error detection test with words representing phonics patterns she taught that week as well as review patterns. The test consists of 20 word pairs. Each word pair consists of a correctly and incorrectly spelled word. Students are directed to circle the correct spelling.

Principles of Effective Spelling Instruction

The following sections describe principles of effective spelling instruction that Meredith observes. Any approach that is used with students who have spelling problems should include these principles.

Teaching Spelling Patterns.   Learning to spell can be facilitated by understanding the patterns of our language. That is why early phonics instruction and later instruction in multisyllable words helps students become better spellers. Thus, students benefit when they are taught common word patterns such as base words, prefixes, suffixes, consonants, consonant blends, digraphs, and vowel sound–symbol associations.

Teaching in Small Units.   Teach students with spelling problems three words a day rather than four or five. In one study, students with learning disabilities who were assigned three words a day performed better than a control group of students with learning disabilities who were assigned four or five words (Bryant, Drabin, & Gettinger, 1981).

Providing Sufficient Practice and Feedback.   Give students opportunities to practice words each day, with feedback. Many teachers do this by having students work with spelling partners who ask them words and provide immediate feedback. Another procedure for self-correction and practice is presented in the 60-Second Lesson.

Selecting Appropriate Words.   The most important strategy for teaching spelling is to make sure that students know how to read the word and already know its meaning. Selection of spelling words should be based on students' existing vocabularies.

Maintaining Previously Learned Words.   For students to be able to remember how to spell words, you must frequently assign (for review) words they have already learned, along with new words. Previously learned words must be reviewed frequently to be maintained.

Teaching for Transfer of Learning.   After spelling words have been mastered, provide opportunities for students to see and use the words in different contexts.

Motivating Students to Spell Correctly.   Using games and activities, selecting meaningful words, and providing examples of the use and need for correct spelling are strategies that help motivate students and give them a positive attitude about spelling (Graham & Miller, 1979).

60 Second LESSON
PROCEDURE OF SELF-CORRECTION AND PRACTICE

To help students learn how to correct misspellings, try the following procedure:

1. Fold a paper into five columns, and write the correctly spelled words in the first column.

2. The student studies one word, folds the column back, and writes the word in the second column. The student then checks his or her spelling against the correctly spelled word in column 1.

3. After folding columns 1 and 2 back, the student writes the word in the third column. When the word is spelled correctly three times, the student moves on to the next word. The student continues until each word is spelled correctly from memory three times in a row.

Including Dictionary Training. Dictionary training (which includes alphabetizing, identifying target words, and locating the correct definition when several are provided) should be developed as part of the spelling program. Some teachers may decide to use computers to assist with this instruction.

Strategies for Helping All Students Develop Handwriting and Keyboarding Skills

Before computers, legible handwriting was a must. Even though children grow up using computers, learning how to write legibly is still important for students who are physically able. For most students, learning how to write legibly and fluently is a key to success in school. Indeed, many states have writing examinations that require students to write manually rather than using a computer.

Traditional Handwriting Instruction

In traditional handwriting instruction in the United States, students learn **manuscript writing** (printing) in the early grades and move to **cursive writing** (script) in the later grades (second or third, depending on the district). Clare Whiting, a third-grade teacher, teaches handwriting as a whole-class activity. To plan her lessons, she uses a commercial handwriting program that includes individual student booklets and extra worksheets to serve as models. Clare begins the school year by reviewing manuscript writing and then introduces the cursive alphabet after the first grading period. Clare assigns grades on the basis of her judgment of the legibility of students' handwriting.

What strategies work with students who have difficulty learning to spell? How can you help students who have difficulty with handwriting?

Critics of traditional handwriting instruction say that spending valuable class time on developing legible handwriting is not time well spent, and that time could be better spent teaching students to keyboard. Some educators maintain that handwriting should be taught during composition rather than whole-class instruction. Others argue against teaching two handwriting systems, some arguing for manuscript and others for cursive (see Figure 13.11). Frose (1981) proposed that both systems be maintained and that students be allowed to decide individually which form is most comfortable for them. The controversy over manuscript and cursive handwriting adds to the problems of students who have difficulties learning to write.

There are some advantages to learning early and well to print since it corresponds more obviously with the print students read (Spear-Swerling, 2006). In general, manuscript should be taught early on and maintained. Students who can make the transition to cursive should have the opportunity to do so.

FIGURE 13.11

Manuscript versus Cursive

Manuscript

1. It more closely resembles print and facilitates learning to read.

2. It is easier for young children to learn.

3. It is more legible than cursive.

4. Many students write manuscript at the same rate as cursive and this rate can be significantly influenced through direct instruction.

5. It is better for students with learning disabilities to learn one writing process well than to attempt to learn two.

Cursive

1. Many students want to learn to write cursive.

2. Many students write cursive faster.

3. Many adults object to students using manuscript beyond the primary grades.

Students with Difficulty in Handwriting

Students with dysgraphia have severe problems learning to write. Hamstra-Bletz and Blote (1993) define dysgraphia as follows:

> *Dysgraphia* is a written-language disorder that concerns the mechanical writing skill. It manifests itself in poor writing performance in children of at least average intelligence who do not have a distinct neurological disability and/or an overt perceptual–motor handicap. Furthermore, dysgraphia is regarded as a disability that can or cannot occur in the presence of other disabilities, like dyslexia or dyscalculia. (p. 690)

Poor handwriting, whether of students with dysgraphia or others, can include any of the following characteristics (Weintraub & Graham, 1998):

- Poor letter formation
- Letters that are too large, too small, or inconsistent in size
- Incorrect use of capital and lowercase letters
- Letters that are crowded and cramped
- Inconsistent spacing between letters
- Incorrect alignment (letters do not rest on a base line)
- Incorrect or inconsistent slant of cursive letters
- Lack of fluency in writing

With direct instruction and regular practice, most of these problems can be handled and corrected. There are six letters that account for 48% of the errors students make when forming letters: *q, j, z, u, n,* and *k* (Graham, Berninger, & Weintraub, 1998). It may be useful to spend more time teaching these letters and ensuring that students know how to connect them to other letters without changing their formation.

Principles of Effective Handwriting Instruction

It is important to address handwriting problems for several reasons. For one thing, they are associated with reduced interest in writing and thus influence written expression. Also, students with handwriting difficulties spell worse than those without handwriting problems even when spelling interventions are provided (Berninger et al., 1998). See Tips for Teachers 13.7 for some helpful strategies for teaching effective handwriting.

To teach handwriting, you must focus on two major components—legibility and fluency—both of which can be improved when students have correct posture, pencil grip, and paper position.

- ***Posture.*** Lower back touches the back of the chair and feet rest on the floor. The torso leans forward slightly in a straight line. Both forearms rest on the desk, with elbows slightly extended.

Tips FOR TEACHERS 13.7

INSTRUCTIONAL PRINCIPLES FOR EFFECTIVE HANDWRITING

- Use direct instruction.
- Use individualized instruction.
- Use a variety of techniques and methods, matching the students' individual needs.
- Teach handwriting frequently (several times a week).
- Teach brief handwriting lessons within the context of students' writing.

- Teach handwriting skills separately and then encourage students to use them.
- Have students evaluate their own handwriting and, when appropriate, the handwriting of others.
- Present your handwriting as a model for the students to follow.
- Teach handwriting not as only a visual task or only a motor task, but as both.

Source: Information from Hagins, R. A. (1983). Write right or left: A practical approach to handwriting. *Journal of Learning Disabilities, 16,* 266–271.

- *Pencil grip.* The pencil is held lightly between the thumb and first two fingers, about one inch above the point. The first finger rests on top of the pencil. The end of the pencil points toward the shoulder.
- *Paper position.* For manuscript writing, the paper is held straight in front of the writer, and the nonwriting hand holds the paper in place. For cursive writing, the paper is slanted counterclockwise for a right-hander and clockwise for a left-hander.

Monitoring Student Progress.   At the beginning and end of the school year, have students copy a short poem to get a sample of their handwriting and to indicate progress—you will be amazed at what you see. Hallahan and colleagues (2005) recommend using student writing samples on a variety of tasks to assess their legibility and fluency: freewriting, dictation, near-point copying, and far-point copying (see Table 13.1).

Legibility.   Legibility is the most important goal of handwriting, and incorrect letter formation is the most frequent obstacle to reaching that goal. A survey of primary teachers indicated that their students displayed the following handwriting problems: overall neatness (76%), spacing between words (66%), letter size (59%), letter formation (57%), alignment of letters (54%), and reversals (52%) (Graham et al., 2008).

Teaching letter formation includes

- Identifying the critical features of the shapes of letters by comparing and contrasting them.
- Using physical prompts such as guiding the student's hand.
- Providing paper and materials that have the letters faded or with dots so that students have a model for tracing the letters.

TABLE 13.1

Guidelines for Assessing Handwriting

	PURPOSE	DIRECTIONS	ACCURACY STANDARD	SPEED STANDARD
FREEWRITING	To provide a baseline for evaluating other tasks and for assessing programs	Identify the letters (i.e., alphabet) or words (e.g., names and familiar words) that the student can write readily. Direct the student to write the identified materials repeatedly, as quickly as possible.	95–100%	60 characters per minute (cpm); 100 cpm, better
DICTATION	To evaluate a student's production of writing when she or he does not know what will come next	Decide whether to test individual letters, words, or phrases. Identify items you are sure the student can write without requiring much thinking (i.e., "known" items); you can use the same item several times in a test. Direct the student to write items as you say them. Watch closely, and, as the student finishes an item, say the next one.	90–100%	70% of standard for freewriting
NEAR-POINT COPYING	To evaluate a student's production of writing when she or he copies from materials on the desk	1. Familiar: Select highly familiar material for the student to copy. 2. Unfamiliar: Select material the student has not previously seen but that is at about the same difficulty level as in the familiar condition. Compare the performances to estimate the contribution of familiarity.	95–100%	75–80% of standard for freewriting
FAR-POINT COPYING	To evaluate a student's production of writing when she or he copies from a distant source (e.g., the chalkboard)	1. Familiar: Select highly familiar material for the student to copy. 2. Unfamiliar: Select material the student has not previously seen but that is at about the same difficulty level as in the familiar condition. Compare the performances to estimate the contribution of familiarity.	90–100%	75–80% of standard for freewriting

Source: Adapted from Hallahan, D. P., Lloyd, J. W., Kauffman, J. M., Weiss, M. P., & Martinez, E. A. (2005). *Learning disabilities: Foundations, characteristics, and effective teaching* (p. 412). Boston: Allyn & Bacon. Copyright © 2005 by Pearson Education. Reprinted by permission of the publisher.

■ Giving students specific reinforcement for letters or parts of letters that are formed correctly and then giving specific feedback and correction for letters or parts of letters that need to be rewritten.

Hanover (1983) provided a system for teaching cursive writing based on the similarities of letters or letter families. Because students learn letters in groups with similar strokes, learning to write letters is easier. The position of the pencil when you start the letter and some of the significant "loops" or "shapes" used to form the letter allows you to teach letters with common shapes together. It makes sense that some letters can be taught in more than one family. Letter families in the **Hanover method** (Hanover, 1983) are shown here in the order recommended for teaching them:

e family:	*e, l, h, f, k*
hump-shaped family:	*n, m, s, y*
c family:	*c, a, d, o, q, g*
hump family:	*n, m, v, y, x*
back-tail family:	*f, q*
front-tail family:	*g, p, y, z*

One of the most effective ways to develop legibility is to provide a **moving model**. Modeling how to form letters and words is more helpful to students than simply having them copy letters and words (Wright & Wright, 1980). To provide a moving model, sit next to the student. As you form a letter or word, talk the student through the motions you are making. If the child writes with a different hand from you, have another child, a volunteer, or another teacher who writes with that hand provide the model. If you decide to have whole-class handwriting lessons, first provide a model by using the chalkboard or overhead projector; then circulate around the room, providing an individual moving model for students who seem to need the extra support.

Fluency.   After students begin to master basic letter forms and their writing becomes more legible, the next goal is to learn to write quickly and with ease. Tom Reynolds helps students in his class improve their fluency through timed writings and journal writing.

Tom has three students in his fifth-grade class who have improved the legibility of their writing considerably during the school year but who still need to learn to write more quickly. He decided to group the three students together for timed writings. (In a timed writing, students copy a 50-word passage and record the number of minutes the process takes.) When the group met for the first time, Tom showed them how to conduct a timed writing and keep records. For each student, he set up a folder with a collection of passages and a chart for recording progress. During this first meeting, Tom also explained that the idea is to work toward personal improvement, not to compete, and he talked about ways in which they could encourage one another. In time, the students could see that each was becoming a more fluent writer.

The daily 15-minute journal-writing activity Tom plans for all his students is a good way to enhance fluency. Because students know that their journals will not be graded for spelling or handwriting, they take risks and write more. Tom encourages students to evaluate their own journal writing and makes certain that students with fluency problems evaluate how much they write.

At the beginning of the year, Tom talked with the first-grade teacher, Helen Byers, and they decided to initiate a dialog journal activity (Atwell, 1984; Bode, 1989; Gambrell, 1985). A **dialog journal** is an ongoing written conversation between two students (or, in some cases, between a student and an adult). Each of Tom's fifth graders was paired with one of Helen's first graders. Once a week, the fifth graders visit the first-grade class and tell or read aloud a story to their first-grade partners. Then the pairs spend some time writing in a dialog journal.

Principles of Effective Keyboarding Instruction

Using the computer is frequently recommended as an adaptation for students who have difficulty with handwriting and spelling (Lerner, 2006). Learning to keyboard or type is essential for school success. Grade 4 is typically recommended for formal keyboarding instruction (see Table 13.2). Many software programs are available for teaching keyboarding skills. Such programs can monitor

TABLE 13.2

Keyboarding Curriculum

	TOPIC	TIME FRAME	SKILL LEVEL ALPHABETIC COPY
Grade 1 or 2	Home keys	3–4 hours	Don't measure
Grade 2 or 3	1. Alphabetic keys and commonly used punctuation marks 2. Spelling words and other short activities	30–35 hours	20 wam*
Grade 4 or 5	1. Review alphabetic keys and introduce numbers and commonly used symbols. 2. Incorporate in language arts.	25 hours	30 wam
Grade 6 or 7 or 8	Review skills. Use skills in all language arts. Use for personal use, reports, essays, letters, etc.	min. of 1 semester—190 hrs 1 yr if preparing for vocational skill	40 wam
Grades 9–10	Introduction to business skills (word processing, database, spreadsheets, etc.)	1 semester	40–50 wam
Grades 11–12	Advanced business skills (word processing, database, spreadsheets, etc.)	1–2 semesters	50 +

Note: Students can use word processing programs and microcomputers at any grade level where equipment is available.

*Words a minute—a standard word is five strokes, spaces, etc.

Source: Bartholome, L. W. (2003). Typewriting/keyboarding instruction in elementary schools. Retrieved June 10, 2005, from www.usoe.k12.ut.us/ate/keyboarding/Articles/Bartholome.

student progress and give feedback about accuracy. However, they may be lacking in that students' fingering cannot be monitored directly. Direct instruction with feedback and sufficient time for practice are necessary. Although students may exhibit some frustration using word processing to compose, when keyboarding fluency develops the frustration often fades (Cotton, 2001).

Summary

- Current trends in writing curriculum and instruction include (a) movement toward standards-based writing instruction and research-based practices, (b) increased emphasis on assessment, and (c) emphasis on balanced and effective writing instruction for all students.

- Writing is a complex process with many areas of potential difficulty for students. In addition to needing extra time for writing, students who have difficulty need direct instruction in composing, spelling, and handwriting. As a process, writing (like reading) is (a) interactive, (b) strategic, (c) constructed by meaning, (d) student centered, and (e) socially mediated.

- The elements of the authoring process include prewriting, composing, revising, editing, and publishing.

- Skills lessons can be taught in conjunction with students' ongoing writing using flexible grouping practices. The topics of skills lessons can be based on observations of student writing, requests for help, and data collected from writing conferences.

- Writing portfolios and writing rubrics can be used to assess student compositions and as guides for self-, peer-, and teacher assessment.

- Although students with writing problems may be aware of the elements of a story, they do not necessarily incorporate these elements into their writing. Students need direct instruction in narrative writing.

- Students need instruction in expository writing, including typical informational writing patterns and strategic planning for composing informational text.

- Spelling is an important tool for writers. Effective instruction for students with spelling problems includes teaching spelling patterns, teaching in small units, providing feedback and practice, selecting appropriate words, and maintaining previously learned words.

- Because handwriting is still necessary for success in school, students need specific instruction in how to write legibly and fluently. Handwriting assessment should include assessment of freewriting, dictation, near-point copying, and far-point copying.

Think and Apply

1. Now that you have read this chapter, reread the interview with Michelle Langlois. What strategies does she use to plan a writing program that meets state standards and encourages student appreciation for the writing process?

2. Think about your own experience in developing your writing skills. What instructional methods and procedures were most helpful? Least helpful? Develop a personal writing portfolio to share with your students. In your portfolio include samples of your own writing from different phases of the authoring process. If possible, include some samples of your writing (and perhaps pictures of yourself) as a child. The portfolio will demonstrate to your students that you are a writer and will illustrate your own progress as a writer.

3. Plan the following activities: story writing, informational writing, spelling, and handwriting mini lessons. Then, make a list of all the tools and technologies you might use to make accommodations and adaptations for students with disabilities who have difficulties writing.

PEARSON myeducationlab

Now go to Topic 6: Assessment; Topic 8: Instructional Practices and Learning Strategies; and Topic 10: Content Area Teaching in the MyEducationLab (www.myeducationlab.com) for your course where you can:

- Find learning outcomes for these topics along with the national standards that connect to these outcomes.

- Complete Assignments and Activities that can help you more deeply understand the chapter content.

- Examine challenging situations and cases presented in the IRIS Center Resources.

- Apply and practice your understanding of the core teaching skills identified in the chapter with Building Teaching Skills and Dispositions learning units.

ndex